Black Liberation
and the American Dream

Black Liberation and the American Dream

The Struggle for Racial and Economic Justice

Analysis, Strategy, Readings

Second Edition

Edited by Paul Le Blanc

Haymarket Books
Chicago, Illinois

Original published in 2003 by Humanity Books

This edition published in 2017 by
Haymarket Books
P.O. Box 180165
Chicago, IL 60618
www.haymarketbooks.org

ISBN: 978-1-60846-785-3

Trade distribution:
In the US, Consortium Book Sales and Distribution, www.cbsd.com
In Canada, Publishers Group Canada, www.pgcbooks.ca
In the UK, Turnaround Publisher Services, www.turnaround-uk.com
All other countries, Ingram Publisher Services International,
IPS_Intlsales@ingramcontent.com

This book was published with the generous support of Lannan Foundation
and Wallace Action Fund.

Cover design by Ragina Johnson.

Printed in Canada by union labor.

Library of Congress Cataloging-in-Publication data is available.

10 9 8 7 6 5 4 3 2 1

CONTENTS

PREFACE TO THE 2017 EDITION

I am pleased that Haymarket Books has found this volume from 2003 worth making available in a new edition. Much of what I offered here—particularly the notion of interconnections between racial justice and economic justice—has been further developed in the volume I coauthored ten years later with Michael Yates, *A Freedom Budget for All Americans: Recapturing the Promise of the Civil Rights Movement in the Struggle for Economic Justice Today* (New York: Monthly Review Press, 2013). Perspectives offered in both books, however, were added to and enriched by experience over the past few years, particularly in the Black Lives Matter struggle. It seems to me that life experience—and especially *struggles* against oppression in all its forms—have at least as much to teach as the contents of books. One of the virtues of this volume, however, is the fact that it makes available the thoughts and experiences of many amazing people who have been engaged in the liberation struggle for more than a century, and there is much to learn from them.

Regarding the portions of this book that I wrote, I feel keenly that it might have been a better book if I'd had an opportunity to engage with certain other books before 2003. These include: August H. Nimtz, Jr., *Marx, Tocqueville, and Race in America: The "Absolute" Democracy" or "Defiled Republic"* (Lanham, MD: Lexington Books, 2003); Karen E. Fields and Barbara J. Fields, *Racecraft: The Soul of Inequality in the United States* (London and New York: Verso Books, 2012); Michelle Alexander, *The New Jim Crow: Mass Incarceration in the Age of Colorblindness*, revised edition (New York: New Press, 2012); Göran Hugo Olsson, *The Black Power Mixtape 1967–1975* (Chicago: Haymarket Books, 2014); John H. Bracey, Jr., Sonia Sanchez, and James Smethurst, eds., *SOS—Calling All Black People: A Black Arts Movement*

Reader (Amherst: University of Massachusetts Press, 2014); two by David R. Roediger, *How Race Survived U.S. History: From Settlement and Slavery to the Obama Phenomenon* (London and New York: Verso Books, 2010) and *Seizing Freedom: Slave Emancipation and Liberty for All* (London and New York: Verso Books, 2015); and Keeanga-Yamahtta Taylor, *From #BlackLivesMatter to Black Liberation* (Chicago: Haymarket Books, 2016). The list is hardly complete.

Built into the very structure of this book is the conviction that we must actively engage in, learn from, and advance the struggle to overcome the racism that has permeated the history of our country, which has resulted in so much damage to humanity in our own society and beyond, and which has done so much to prevent the realization of the better world that we dream about. If at least some of what is in these pages can help people be more effective in that collective effort, then the republication of this volume will have been worthwhile.

Paul Le Blanc
April 2017

PREFACE

This volume was developed as part of two specific antiracist projects. The Thomas Merton Center, a longtime peace and justice center in Pittsburgh, had launched, at the end of the 1990s, campaigns to advance racial and economic justice in Pittsburgh. I volunteered to develop a manual designed to guide some of its work. A couple of years later I helped to develop an antiracism class series for a socialist organization called Solidarity, drawing together a set of readings that would help advance discussion among its members and supporters. In each case, what I was doing was seen as a work in progress, which we intended to revise and refine on the basis of new insights and experiences. This book can best be seen and utilized in that spirit.

Especially important for us as we make our way in the twenty-first century is a renewed and deepened commitment to help confront and overcome racism. In Pittsburgh, as in some other U.S. cities, the racial divide is primarily that between blacks and whites, and this set the focus for the "manual" that is presented here in revised form. That was a limitation of *Black Liberation and the American Dream*, but also a reflection of its very practical purpose. In addition to that, however, I would make the following point: there has been no deeper nor longer-lasting form of racism in the United States than that directed against African Americans. It has been central to the American experience, throughout the country, from the 1600s down to the present day. It is the most difficult form of racism to eradicate, and its persistence contributes to the racism experienced by other racial and ethnic groups in our country. American racism can neither be understood nor overcome without a focus on antiblack racism.

The fact remains that this *is* a significant limitation of the present volume. Racism cannot be fully understood or overcome without dealing with seeing how it has impacted on Native American (Indian) peoples, various groupings of Asian Americans, Mexican Americans and Puerto Ricans, and others. Some of the works cited in the bibliography are relevant to this understanding—particularly the invaluable work by Ronald Takaki.

In creating the components of this book, I have given emphasis to the profound link between the quest for *racial justice* and the quest for *economic justice*. It is my conviction that neither can be realized without the other. Another consideration was the belief that effective action in the present and future must be grounded in an understanding of the past. Special attention has been given to the history of racism and of the efforts to overcome it.

The quotations and the readings in this volume seek to introduce a wide array of voices—especially but not exclusively from African Americans—to the readers. There is a range of views to be found in these pages—some of them provocative, but perhaps useful for those wrestling with difficult questions.

I would like to conclude with several acknowledgments. Significant contributions to my experience and thought have been provided by two central leaders in the projects mentioned earlier, Rev. Thomas Smith of Monumental Baptist Church, who at the time chaired the executive board of the Thomas Merton Center, and Theresa El-Amin of the Southern Anti-Racism Network (SARN), who initially headed Solidarity's Anti-Racism Commission. Two comrades from Africa have also, over the years, contributed much to my consciousness—Dennis Brutus (South African poet sometimes based at the University of Pittsburgh) and Mike Matambanadzo (professor of history at Slippery Rock University). The long-ago opportunity to work as a teaching assistant with Dr. Larry Glasco in his African American history course was quite important, as was the extended opportunity to work with and learn from ethnographer Dr. Carol McAllister, both of these admirable colleagues also being associated with the University of Pittsburgh. And the late George Breitman also taught me essential lessons about race, racism, and much else. Elizabeth Waclawski, the History Department's capable secretary at LaRoche College, provided generous assistance in retyping most of the "readings" section of this book, and the department chair, Professor Edward T. Brett, provided much encouragement and support. My editors at Humanity Books, Ann O'Hear and Peggy Deemer, were essential in overseeing—with admirable commitment and professionalism—the wondrous transformation of manuscript to book.

1.

REACHING FOR THE AMERICAN DREAM

Confronting racism, understanding it, overcoming it. We must do this if the United States of America is to survive. It is essential not only for African Americans and other "people of color," but for each and every one of us. This is a central struggle that increasing numbers of us must engage in if we are to have any hope of realizing the American dream.

"If we are to implement the American dream, we must continue to engage in creative protest in order to break down all of those barriers that make it impossible for the dream to be realized," Martin Luther King Jr. commented in 1961. He emphasized: "We must move on with determination and zeal to break down the unjust systems we find in our society, so that it will be possible to realize the American dream." In saying such things, Dr. King was not simply speaking to African Americans. He was speaking to everyone in the United States.

Implementing the "American dream" is something that almost all of us long for. For many of us this longing is embedded in things we were taught in our early childhood. It is also embedded in the early history of our country.

The ideals that inspire many of us are related to what seems to be unique about the United States of America. As Abraham Lincoln put it in his Gettysburg Address, we are a nation conceived in liberty and dedicated to the proposition that all of us are created equal. Lincoln was paraphrasing the point made by Thomas Jefferson in the Declaration of Independence: it is a self-evident truth that each and every one of us is endowed by our Creator with certain basic human rights, among which are life, liberty, and the pursuit of happiness. The Declaration of 1776 held that this leads to the notion that governments are legit-

13

imate only if they have the consent of the governed, and that it is right to challenge and even overthrow governments that fail to protect our basic human rights. Lincoln explained the logic of this as favoring *rule by the people*—a government of the people, by the people, and for the people. Ours was the first modern nation established on these principles.

Yet from the beginning such ideals were in conflict with stubborn realities. From the beginning, another distinguishing characteristic of our country was its *diversity*—different kinds of people, sometimes competing against each other. A more powerful group sought to advance itself at the expense of those less powerful. Those who were on the winning side of such conflicts usually persuaded themselves that they were "better" (religiously, racially, morally, or whatever) or even more human than those who were being oppressed or (as in the case of many Indians) annihilated. A distinguishing characteristic of our nation's history involves the determined struggles, and sometimes violent conflicts, through which more and more sectors of our diverse population sought to secure those equal rights that the Declaration of Independence had promised.

This struggle for inclusion is reflected in the different sectors of the population who secured the right to vote:

- in the 1820s, white males who were not property owners, by various state laws;
- in the late 1860s, black men, by constitutional amendment;
- in 1920, women, by constitutional amendment;
- in the 1960s, black women and men in the South, through the Voting Rights Act;
- in 1971, those from eighteen to twenty-one years of age, by constitutional amendment.

The way such human rights are won was shrewdly emphasized by the ex-slave Frederick Douglass: "If there is no struggle, there is no progress. Those who profess to favor freedom and yet deprecate agitation are men who want crops without plowing up the ground, they want rain without thunder and lightning. They want the ocean without the awful roar of its many waters. . . . Power concedes nothing without a demand. It never did and it never will" (Douglass 1975, 437).

Various layers of our country's laboring majority (whether free workers or slaves) have had to confront wealthy property-owning elites. Women have had to confront those seeing them as unworthy of full citizenship. Religious minorities have had to confront self-righteous majorities. Immigrants and ethnic minorities have had to confront those who refused to see them as "real Americans." All of this has been necessary for those wishing to be included in the promise of "liberty and justice for all."

And while this promise has yet to be fully realized for every American, enough progress was made through the struggles of our diverse people so that many waves of immigrants and immigrants' children saw truth in the poetic words that the poet Emma Lazarus attributed to Lady Liberty in New York Harbor:

> Give me your tired, your poor,
> Your huddled masses yearning to breathe free,
> The wretched refuse of your teeming shore,
> Send these, the homeless, tempest-tossed to me,
> I lift my lamp beside the golden door!

Many of us were taught as children to believe in and support the notion that all of us in this land have the right to "breathe free" and—if we are prepared to engage in honest labor—not to be homeless or wretched or poor. We have been taught to believe that each and every one of us has this right, regardless of race or ethnicity, religion or creed—just as we have been taught to honor the Golden Rule: Do unto others as you would have them do unto you.

There is also the quip of Benjamin Franklin to his fellow signers of the Declaration of Independence: "If we don't hang together, we most assuredly will hang separately." Translated into the realities of our own time: If we don't stick together and stick up for each other, if we don't join together to defend the rights of each and every one of us to a decent life, if we don't unify for the American dream—then more and more of us will find it harder to breathe free, to lead a decent life, to survive with dignity, to survive at all.

We face the growth of many forms of inequality, not only racial inequality, but widespread economic inequality. For the past two decades, a strong trend has been for wealthy and powerful minorities to implement "lean and mean" policies for the rest of us. The result has been declining incomes and living standards, declining quality of life for a majority, unemployment for many, deteriorating working conditions for many more, and increases in corruption and crime weighing on all of us. Many of us in these deteriorating situations feel anger and fear and take things out on each other—sometimes in the same family or neighborhood. But often the target becomes another racial or ethnic group.

In order to realize the American dream, we have to be more successful in pushing things in the opposite direction. For moral and ethical reasons, and also for very practical reasons, it is vital to confront, understand, and overcome racism. The future of each and every one of us, and the future of our children, depends on how successful we are.

2.

CONFRONTING RACISM
IN SOCIETY . . .
AND IN OURSELVES

"Racism" has to do with realities that exist in society. It also has to do with what is in our own minds. Let's start with our minds, then look at society, then look at the interplay between the two.

Even before looking at racism, it will be helpful to look at the quirkiness of our own minds.

MENTAL TRICKS AND QUIRKS

Regardless of race, creed, or color, human beings are complicated creatures. We often kid ourselves and others. If we are alert to some of the ways we do that, we'll be less apt to fool ourselves and others (or to be fooled by others). Such "foolishness" is usually not cold-blooded deception but simply part of being human. By accepting our own (and others') humanity—limitations and all—it will be easier to make sense of racism.

"I Know Everything"

Sometimes we make mistakes, we do something wrong, we don't understand something—and we kid ourselves. We tell ourselves that we didn't make a mistake; we tell ourselves that we really did understand something. We pretend that we know more than we really know. If someone challenges us, we might get defensive. We might get insulted. We might get angry. But for those of us who are lucky, we finally admit to ourselves that we are not perfect, and that there were (and are) some things we didn't or don't really know. (The unlucky ones delude themselves that they are perfect, which makes it harder for them to learn things.)

Connecting the Dots—Even without the Dots

Also, in our thinking we often try to "connect the dots"—to take fragments of the truth (it is unlikely that anyone knows "the whole truth" about everything) and try to connect them together in a way with which we can make sense of reality. Sometimes we do pretty well in gaining at least a rough understanding of certain realities this way. But sometimes we lack any information about something important and can only make more or less wild guesses. In some cases we've been given misinformation that we assume to be true, or we have only partial information that will give us a false understanding if we try to generalize from it. Sometimes—even with no information, misinformation, or partial information—we still try to "connect the dots," with the result that we end up with a badly distorted picture of reality.

We Don't Always Know What's in Our Minds

One problem is that although a person's mind contains some things that he or she is conscious of, it also includes things that he or she is *not* always conscious of. Maybe there's a fear or a desire that I have repressed (I don't want it to be there, so I don't think of it consciously, but it's still there influencing how I think). Maybe there's some unexamined assumption—something that I assume is true but don't really know and don't even think about—that affects my conscious thought. Maybe there's some half-forgotten or completely forgotten experience lingering in the unconscious part of my mind that affects how I think about something in my conscious mind.

"I'm Better Than That Other Person"

There's another trick that we sometimes pull on ourselves. We have a tendency to be very dismissive of things that we don't understand or of people who are very different from ourselves. The way that we do things, the way that we have been taught to do things, the way that most people around us do things, are naturally seen as the "normal" way of doing things. These are the ways we function as human beings. But people who do such things differently, because they come from different cultures and have learned different customs, are often dismissed as strange, rude, abnormal, less civilized, less human. Related to this, sometimes (even with friends, relatives, neighbors, or acquaintances who are not significantly different from us) we compare ourselves with others in order to see what's "wrong" with them, which makes us feel superior. Putting down another person is a way of affirming ourselves, of feeling better about ourselves.

RACIAL PREJUDICE

It is possible to see that each of these human quirks can contribute to racial prejudice. As we'll see in a moment, this does not simply mean white prejudice toward blacks. But that *is* one form it can take. It is worth considering how this might be played out by outlining a possible checklist of factors that could dovetail with the psychological quirks outlined above.

- A white person has grown up in a white neighborhood where there are all kinds of characterizations, caricatures, and jokes that put down African Americans. Such things may also be common in one's family—though sometimes not.
- In part this all is rooted in experience going back several generations, when one's great-great-grandparents emphasized their "whiteness" as part of a survival strategy to rise at least somewhat above their immigrant or "lower-class" status. In such a situation, living or working next to blacks might have been perceived as degrading—and the ability to exclude blacks might be seen as part of one's elevated status.
- Another experience might have involved deep bitterness over blacks being used as scabs to break the strike involving one's great-grandfather (since being used as scabs was often the only way African Americans could secure better-paying jobs).
- There is also the fact that throughout the nineteenth century and for most of the twentieth century viciously distorted images of African Americans were predominant in mainstream ("white") culture. It was common to portray black people as clowns and fools, oversexed young women and obese "mammies," irresponsible or brutish men.
- It is likely that some sense of fear (of violence, of sex, etc.), perhaps related to bigoted allegations of black "savagery," would exist somewhere in one's mind. There might also be a more conscious fear that African Americans seeking gains in employment, education, housing, and so on might lead to a decline in one's own situation.
- Encounters with African Americans on the part of other friends and family might have involved a sense of how different they seemed compared to what one was familiar with. Also, at least an occasional negative—in some cases even violent—experience with certain African Americans, espe-

cially if it was not fully understood, could be overgeneralized into a negative image of all African Americans.

Such factors as these can contribute to the development and persistence of racial prejudice toward blacks by whites. Novelist James Baldwin has perceptively described such whites as being "still trapped in a history which they do not understand; and until they understand it, they cannot be released from it." Various historical pressures generated a felt need to view blacks as inferior to whites. The sense of identity of such whites, their very sense of "the order of nature," is threatened if African Americans refuse to remain in an inferior position. "Any upheaval in the universe is terrifying because it so profoundly attacks one's sense of one's own reality. Well, the black man has functioned in the white man's world as a fixed star, as an immovable pillar: and as he moves out of his place, heaven and earth are shaken to their foundations" (Baldwin 1964, 19–20). As a consequence, sometimes efforts to overcome racial prejudice initially lead to an increase of racial animosity among whites.

Of course prejudice and animosity can go both ways. Consider the observations of Prof. Henry Louis Gates Jr.:

> Perhaps you didn't know that Liz Claiborne appeared on *Oprah* not long ago and said she didn't design her clothes for black women—that their hips were too wide. Perhaps you didn't know that the soft drink Tropical Fantasy is manufactured by the Ku Klux Klan and contains a special ingredient designed to sterilize black men. (A warning flyer distributed in Harlem a few years ago claimed that these findings were vouchsafed on the television program *20/20*.) Perhaps you didn't know that the Ku Klux Klan has a similar arrangement with Church's Fried Chicken—or is it Popeye's?
>
> Perhaps you didn't know these things, but a good many black Americans think they do, and will discuss them with the same intentness they bring to the "shadowy figure" in a Brentwood driveway (allegedly proving O. J. Simpson's innocence). Never mind that Liz Claiborne has never appeared on *Oprah*, that the beleaguered Brooklyn company that makes Tropical Fantasy has gone as far as to make available an FDA assay of its ingredients, and that those fried chicken franchises pose a threat mainly to black folks' arteries. The folklorist Patricia A. Turner, who had collected dozens of such tales in an invaluable 1993 study of rumor in African American culture, *I Heard It through the Grapevine*, points out the patterns to be found here: that these stories encode pregnant anxieties, that they take root under particular conditions and play particular social roles, that the currency of rumor flourishes where "official" news has proved untrustworthy. (Gates 1997, 105–106)

Gates goes on to note that some of this "paranoid" thinking has been powerfully encouraged by the genuinely "paranoid" realities of antiblack racism. Thus it has been documented that Los Angeles policeman Mark Fuhrman, centrally involved in the Simpson case, indeed "hated interracial couples, fantasized about making a bonfire of black bodies, and boasted of planting evidence." He reminds us of "the federal government's forty-year study of how untreated syphilis affects black men." He quotes an anonymous letter sent by the FBI to Martin Luther King Jr. in a 1964 effort to manipulate the civil rights leader into committing suicide over extramarital incidents: "There is but one way out for you. You better take it before your filthy, abnormal, fraudulent self is bared to the nation." (Of course King, his wife, and his followers stood up to this vicious intimidation and continued the struggle.)

As Gates's comments indicate, race prejudice of blacks toward whites has different sources and dynamics than antiblack prejudice among whites. In the late 1930s, Afro-Caribbean historian and cultural critic C. L. R. James, after an extensive tour of black America, commented that "the awakening political consciousness of the Negro not unnaturally takes the form of independent action uncontrolled by whites," with a demand—since they had been subordinated to whites for so many years—for "their own organizations under their own leaders." James also made an interesting argument that antiblack feelings are not "just the same" as antiwhite feelings. Antiblack sentiment among whites is an expression of racial domination, he noted, whereas antiwhite sentiment among blacks involves a desire to end such domination, reflecting "the natural excess of the desire for equality" (James 1994, 5). The fact remains, however, that racial bias goes both ways between white and black people in America.

But this is not the only way that these human dynamics work. For example, it is possible for whites who consider themselves "antiracist" to develop self-righteous attitudes toward other whites that involve the same kind of psychological quirks we have been examining. In his book *Dismantling Racism*, Rev. Joseph Barndt offers the following reflection:

> At one time, because of a we/they mentality, I thought it was possible to separate white Americans into two camps: the righteous and the racist. I, of course, was a member of the righteous camp. I assumed that the occupants of each camp were there by choice. I believed that my friends and I had wisely chosen to be nonracists, and those in the other camp had chosen to be racists. Now I know differently. . . . I never wanted to be a racist. I still don't. For a long time, I even thought I wasn't, but now I know I am. . . . All of us who are white are part of and inseparable from a society that continually and systematically subordinates people of color. Whether or not we are intentional bigots, we are all locked inside a system of structured racism. As American citizens, every white person supports, benefits from, and is unable to be separated from white racism. (Barndt 1991, 43–44)

In the next chapter, "Understanding Race and Racism," we will need to evaluate more closely this notion that there is "a system of structured racism" in the United States that we are all part of. But Reverend Barndt's confession that he very much wanted to see himself as superior to other whites—when in fact he wasn't—demonstrates yet again how the mental quirks discussed earlier can kick in as complicated human creatures try to come to grips with the complicated realities of race in America.

In an extensive survey of various social reform movements in the United States (the abolitionist, populist, progressive, women's rights, labor, and socialist movements), Robert L. Allen noted that at least major sections of each of them "(with certain limited exceptions) have either advocated, capitulated before, or otherwise failed to oppose racism at one or more critical junctures in their history . . . even when the reforms they sought to institute appeared to demand forthright opposition to racism." Especially prevalent were "paternalistic attitudes that merely confirmed, rather than challenged, the prevailing racial ideology of white society." Even in the best of circumstances, "white reformers, themselves largely unaffected by racism, generally fail to perceive its full ramifications and subtleties. This is why militant blacks and other nonwhites, who can't escape racial oppression, have so often taken the lead in promoting and consolidating opposition to racism" (Allen 1975, 261, 295).

In the early 1960s James Baldwin identified one form of racist paternalism among well-meaning whites who consciously oppose racism but find it difficult "to divest themselves of the notion that they are in possession of some intrinsic value that black people need, or want." He explained that

> this assumption—which, for example, makes the solution to the Negro problem depend on the speed with which Negroes accept and adopt white standards—is revealed in all kinds of striking ways, from Bobby Kennedy's assurance that a Negro can become president in forty years to the unfortunate tone of warm congratulation with which so many liberals address their Negro equals. It is the Negro, of course, who is presumed to have become equal—an achievement that not only proves the comforting fact that perseverance has no color but also overwhelmingly corroborates the white man's sense of his own value. (Baldwin 1964, 27)

It is possible to say that all people in the United States—blacks and whites and all others—are affected by and damaged by racism. It distorts each person's sense of self. It poisons our relations with each other and poisons our communities. It divides us and diverts our attention away from larger social crises that threaten all of us. We cannot afford to feel superior toward one another. It is not helpful for whites to delude themselves with the notion that their "whiteness" makes them superior human beings. Nor is it helpful for small handfuls of self-righteous whites to make moralistic speeches pointing out to other whites how guilty they should feel about being white. "Dealing with our racism does not mean allowing ourselves to become puppets controlled by our guilt-strings," Reverend Barndt argues. "The alternative to racism is freedom, not another kind of slavery. Too many people never get beyond the question of guilt" (Barndt 1991, 44).

It is normal to feel guilty, frightened, resentful, angry, and more as we confront the realities of racism in our society, in each other, and in ourselves. But if we want to *understand* racism, we need to go beyond guilt, fear, and anger in order to make good use of our critical minds.

AN EXAMPLE OF RACISM

At this point, it may be helpful to examine the views of an articulate racist. Not all racists are the same, nor do they all have the same ideas about race and racism. Many people whose thinking is influenced by racist ideas have not thought through all the implications of those ideas. There are some who have, and who have developed elaborate belief systems and analyses whose central focus is racism. One of the most famous of these was Adolf Hitler, whose book *Mein Kampf* is a racist classic. The racial ideologist we will examine here, however, is an American, quite critical of "Hitler's racial excesses"—just as he is critical of slavery, which he describes as "abominable to the body and the spirit." An examination of his theorizing helps shed light on the logic of racism.

Wilmot Robertson's *The Dispossessed Majority*, published in the 1970s, "hammers home the theme that America has changed for the worse . . . because its once-dominant population group, the Americans of northern European descent—the Majority—has been reduced to second-class citizenship." Robertson indicates that he is not ashamed to be a racist. He embraces "the definition of racism as a belief in the race idea," or even better, "the overt or covert expression of the concept of race at one or more levels of human activity." His initial explanation of "the race idea" is "the belief that every man belongs to a distinct human breed," although he adds that "the concept of race leans . . . heavily on the *awareness* of blood relationship as it does on the *fact* of blood relationship." He tells us that "to the racial historian, race is the being and the becoming of organized humanity. As race has been the controlling factor of much of the human past, so will it assume even greater importance in the future." He sees race as "the highest manifestation of the team spirit," which "may be nature's way of organizing men for the accomplishment of the unaccomplishable."

Robertson goes on to survey the ideas of various race theorists. He gives special emphasis to the work of anthropologist Carlton Coon, who defined "the five living races of mankind" as Caucasoid, Mongoloid, Australoid, Capoid, and Congoid (the last being blacks, deemed by Coon and Robertson to be the last of the races to evolve into human beings). But Robertson also goes on (utilizing another anthropologist of a bygone era, E. A. Hooton) to divide the Caucasoids into racial categories—in his words "nine separate racial divisions for the white population of the United States," with different physical traits and different points of origin in Europe. He sees those white groups connected to Anglo-Saxon stock of northern Europe as constituting "the American Majority [which] comprises the Nordic, Alpine, Nordic-Alpine, and Nordic-Mediterranean elements of the population, as distinguished from the darker Mediterranean and colored elements."

The proliferation of other racial types—the Irish, eastern and southern Europeans, Jews, blacks, Hispanics, Asians—created an avalanche of "minority participation in politics and in every other sector of American life" to the extent that "the Majority is no longer the racial Establishment in the United States." Now "Western man as derived from northern European (principally Anglo-Saxon) antecedents and as modified by the frontier and other peculiarly American environmental conditions—is being effaced by other racial and cultural imprints." Negative cultural influences emanating from "the new Negro cultural celebrities" are especially troubling to Robertson: "white women are fair game for rape; white males have serious sexual deficiencies; looting, arson, mayhem, murder, insurrection, and massacre are often worthy and understandable goals." Obviously, "the zeal for racial leveling" unleashes a dynamic in which "equality edges toward superequality and superequality laps over into superiority" on the part of non-Majority elements.

Robertson favors a particular notion of "democracy," as a political form appropriate to the once-dominant American stock of northern European origins, with a pragmatic concern for moderation and property rights as the basis of liberty. He contrasts what he sees as wrongheaded passages in the Declaration of Independence, complaining that Thomas Jefferson "must assume responsibility for loading American democracy with the ambiguity and cant which have pursued it down to the present day," with the radical notion that "all men are created equal and endowed by their Creator with certain unalienable rights."

This opened the door, in fact, to "greater racial friction," and also to a fatal evolution of democratic thought: "Political democracy orders members of different population groups to vote together, legislate together, and rule together. Economic democracy makes it necessary for them to work together. Social democracy, however, exponentially enlarges the area of contact by forcing the most diverse elements to live together." Helping to advance this degradation are pro-equality liberals of northern European stock who split the ranks of the Majority, working in tandem with Jews and the Catholic Church, to forge a liberal-minority coalition.

Of all the minorities undermining the Majority, Robertson is most concerned about "the Negro minority, the largest and most violent minority," which has "grounded" the American spirit and "is threatening to mutilate it beyond all recognition." The civil rights movement led by "white liberals and minority members" began by converging on the South "both to contain and spread the violence which greeted the Supreme Court's school desegregation decision (1954)," but "the wind had been sown and the whirlwind was reaped" when antiwhite hatred was unleashed in the black ghetto riots in northern cities during 1964–1968. He goes on to express some sympathy for the wisdom of those African Americans favoring black separatism: "Instead of trying to be equals of whites, Negroes should try to be better Negroes. Instead of playing the white man's game with dice that heredity has loaded against them, they should develop their own special talents in their own special ways. Negro frustrations . . . will only vanish when American Negroes lead a black rather than a white life."

All of the racial equality crusades threaten to lead "the way back to the primeval ooze and the plasma—the way of devolution." Robertson insists that "the race best suited to shoulder the main weight of the evolutionary burden would appear to be the northern European," which "has managed to soar a little higher above the animal kingdom than the other divisions of mankind." The Majority must reject its dispossession and move forward:

> To put northern Europeans back on the evolutionary track—to rekindle the northern European efflorescence—is a project of monumental complexity. Of all the northern European peoples, only a rehabilitated American Majority, mindful of the history it has made and is about to make, would have the strength and the resources to bring about a northern European ingathering—not merely a political and economic ingathering cemented by treaties and trade agreements or by the common nationality and citizenship which might come in time, but an ingathering of race consciousness, the most lasting and tenacious of all social binding forces.

The more or less politely worded perspective offered by Robertson is consistent with the outlook of a variety of white racist groups that sometimes utilize less polite wording in their practical agitation. Researchers such as Michael Novick have documented a thick undergrowth of shared ideological influences and organizational interconnections among such groups as the Ku Klux Klan, the National Association for the Advancement of White People, the White Aryan Resistance, the Populist Party, the Liberty Lobby, the Christian Patriots Defense League, the American White Separatists, and others. Some of these influences and connections extend into certain law-enforcement agencies. This has been true of the Los Angeles Police Department, for example, according to findings of a 1991 independent commission of inquiry headed by the soon-to-be U.S. secretary of state Warren Christopher.

Sometimes organizational links to racist groups may be absent, but racist ideology still plays a key role. A dramatic example was the Federal Bureau of Investigation under J. Edgar Hoover, which was notorious for employing no African Americans as FBI agents and for spying on all major black leaders. A number of historians have documented that Hoover was "a formidable enemy of the civil rights movement," who believed "that sit-ins, bus boycotts, and public protests were unjustified, illegal, and the work of communist terrorists," and that he felt an "incredible antipathy" toward Martin Luther King Jr. and wanted "to use the vast resources of the FBI to discredit King and 'remove King from the national picture.'" Hoover undoubtedly did not see himself as a racist, and at times he sought to nurture a positive relationship with those civil rights figures whom he considered more "responsible" and moderate. But his underlying racial attitudes are suggested in a 1956 presentation made to President Dwight D. Eisenhower's cabinet, in which he accused early civil rights activists of seeking to foment "racial hatred" in the South through stirring up white fears of "racial intermarriages" and "mixed education." His years-long campaign to detect and circulate rumors about the "Communist influences" within King's inner circle suggest the view, expressed in 1965 by right-wing journalist Alan Stang, that "the 'civil rights movement' is for the most part a Communist operation" and that "there is a real problem between the races in this country today, and that it has been caused almost entirely by the Communists to help them capture the country" (O'Reilly and Gallen 1994, 14–15, 25; Garrow 1988, 381–82; Cook 1984, 174; Theoharis and Cox 1988, 358; Stang 1965, 213).

Another version of this approach was advanced by Nathaniel Weyl's *The Negro in American Civilization* (1960). Himself an ex-leftist and erstwhile liberal, Weyl scoffed at "bohemian and left-wing groups who viewed the Negro as a symbol of class exploitation and wished to give him heroic stature." The evidence, he argued, demonstrates "the failure of the Negroes to create any sort of civilization." Instead, as a group they demonstrate an "amorphous and irresponsible sexuality," and a " general affinity for impulsive major crimes of violence," with an "absence of guilt sense and deficiency of ego continuity." Weyl believed he had documented that "the mental differences between Negroes and Caucasians are probably innate and biological in origin." While "a large element in the colored population would seem to be mentally submarginal," however, Weyl argued that opportunities for advancement should be provided for that fraction of the whole that consists of "the intelligent and capable Negro," who should be "permitted to step aside from the problems of his ethnic group as a whole and demand that he be treated solely on the basis of his own individual merit."*

---

*A more rigorous articulation of the Weyl perspective was produced during the 1980s by J. Phillippe Rushton (unlike Weyl, an academically trained professor of psychology), whose work is presented in the controversial volume *Race, Evolution, and Behavior*. Harvard research professor

Weyl's book was embraced in right-wing circles. "Weyl's statistics are breathtaking and, in the opinion of this writer, formidable," enthused political scientist Willmoore Kendall, a senior editor of the influential conservative weekly *National Review*. "Could it be we shall never do justice to the Negroes in our midst, nor the Negroes to themselves, save as we all recognize that as a group they may have a lesser capacity than the rest of us for civilizational achievement?" (Kendall 1985, 216). This was an essential element in many conservatives' opposition to the civil rights movement. *National Review* founder and editor in chief William F. Buckley stated the position bluntly:

> The central question that emerges . . . is whether the white community in the South is entitled to take such measures as are necessary to prevail, politically and culturally, in areas in which it does not predominate numerically. The sobering answer is *Yes*—the white community is so entitled because, for the time being, it is the advanced race. . . . The question, as far as the white community is concerned, is whether the claims of civilization supersede those of universal suffrage. . . . *National Review* believes that the South's premises [that is, the premises of the South's white supremacists] are correct.

While this general approach of establishing a racial hierarchy of intelligence and civilization has been scientifically discredited—as documented in such studies as Stephen Jay Gould's *The Mismeasure of Man* and Dean Keith Simonton's *Origins of Genius*—it certainly played a profound role in the social and political history of the United States throughout the twentieth century. Although its intellectual power faded even among some of the conservatives (such as Buckley) who had once embraced it, the fact remains that the effects and persistent influence of the "weird science" of racism continue to be felt.

IMPLICATIONS OF RACISM AND ANTIRACISM

The implications of a consistent racist worldview for the majority of Americans (who do not derive from "Anglo-Saxon stock") is rather grim—as it is for those "northern Europeans" whose notions of what democracy is about and what constitutes a good society are more inclusive than what we have just reviewed.

Richard Lewontin suggests Rushton "botched the job rather badly" by advancing sloppy data to claim "that Africans are duller but sexier than Europeans and Asians because evolution in a tropic clime endowed them with smaller brains and larger genitalia." In such studies as these—that employ "categories as inclusive as Mongoloid, Caucasoid, and Negroid (which necessarily include representatives who have occupied a tremendous diversity of habitats)," in the words of Dean Keith Simonton—critics have noted that there is a tendency to cut, merge, and bend the data to confirm the "correct" prejudice.

A consistent application of racist ideology—that of Robertson no less than any other—would destroy our society and our lives as we know them. Compared to the brutal ideology of Hitler or to the more polite ideology of Robertson, the fragments and glimmerings of racist thinking on the part of most people who entertain such notions seem benign. But taken together, they can add up to a force that is not benign, with a potential for destructiveness that could ultimately engulf many of these same people.

The questionable politics is, not surprisingly, based on outdated "science" of dubious quality. "Developments in late-twentieth-century science reveal a growing repudiation of the idea of biologically distinct races as anthropologists and human biologists are providing us with new ways of understanding human biophysical variation," writes anthropologist Audrey Smedley in a recent study of *Race in North America*, which offers a comprehensive survey and analysis of racial theorizing. "Given the increasing power and role of science in revealing the 'objective' world, and guiding our thoughts about it, this may represent the early and tentative first step of a major social transformation, the beginning of the end of the racial worldview in the United States and perhaps elsewhere."

What Robertson and many other "race theorists" have done is what mental health specialist Dr. William Ryan has called *blaming the victim*, which he defines as "justifying inequality by finding defects in the victims of inequality." Ryan suggests, however, that many theorists who reject racism have also fallen into a "blame the victim" trap. Often such people have written and talked about a "culture of poverty" or an alleged "cultural deprivation" of African Americans that results in their suffering from poor health, poor housing, and so on. Yet he observes that this turns the reality upside down. Regarding housing, he comments: "No, slum tenants don't ruin good housing. The buildings are worn out and used up first, then the slum is ready for the poor and the black to move in." Regarding the health of the poor: "The facts are plain: their health is bad. The cause is plain: health costs money, and they don't have money. The rationalization that the poor suffer from bad health because of their ignorance of health matters, their culture, or their class-linked disinterest in health is simply one more version of Blaming the Victim" (Ryan 1976, xiii, 170, 182). More recently, however, a version of the biological-genetic "deficiencies" argument has surfaced in intellectual and political circles that would not accept Wilmot Robertson's *Dispossessed Majority* perspective.

A very different type of book than Roberston's was produced in 1994 by Richard Herrnstein and Charles Murray, *The Bell Curve: Intelligence and Class Structure in American Life*, which nonetheless goes some distance in the same direction. The authors—aware of the increasingly doubtful scientific value of the "biological essentialism" associated with the concept of race—appear to reject the "racial idea" so important to Robertson. They prefer to substitute the term "ethnic groups" for the term "races," but they go on to assert: "Some ethnic groups nevertheless differ genetically for sure, otherwise they would not have differing skin colors or hair textures or muscle mass. They also differ intellectually on average." The authors proclaim: "A substantial difference in cognitive ability distributions separates whites from blacks, and a smaller one separates East Asians from whites. These differences play out in public and private life."

The book's theme, in the terse summary of hostile critic Adolph Reed Jr., is "that people with power and privilege really are superior and that everyone else is defective." More relevant to the question of racism is the complaint of conservative critic Eugene Genovese: "Herrnstein and Murray begin by rejecting 'race' as a category that will not withstand scientific analysis. . . . They then go on for more than 800 pages to explore the ramifications of the category they have rejected. . . . They insist that blacks, considered not individually but as a group, have lower intelligence than whites." As Russell Jacoby and Naomi Glauberman comment, the *Bell Curve* authors hold that "the ills of welfare, poverty, and an underclass are less matters of justice than of biology" (Jacoby and Glauberman 1995, ix–x, 263, 334).

Genovese implies, and others have documented, that the scientific validity of such notions is dubious. (A rich collection of material—including Genovese's essay—is available in the collection edited by Jacoby and Glauberman, *The Bell Curve Debate: History, Documents, Opinions*.) But some have suggested that it is politics rather than science that may be at the bottom of the positive response to *Bell Curve* ideas among many college-educated whites who no longer have confidence in the vision of a multicultural democracy that animated Martin Luther King:

> Let us be dissatisfied until integration is not seen as a problem but as an opportunity to participate in the beauty of diversity. Let us be dissatisfied until men and women, however black they may be, will be judged on the basis of the content of their character and not on the basis of the color of their skin. . . . Let us be dissatisfied until justice will roll down like waters and righteousness like a mighty stream. . . . And men will recognize that out of one blood God made all men to dwell upon the face of the earth. (King 1986, 251)

3.

UNDERSTANDING RACISM

It is sometimes necessary to define basic terms in order to think clearly about larger problems. It would be helpful to understand what is meant by "race" before we come to grips with the meaning of racism. One logical place to turn is an encyclopedia, which should provide a clear and thorough introduction to such a term. If we look at the *Encyclopedia Britannica* or any other major encyclopedia, however, we will find that the answer to our question is not entirely clear, and if we compare what the different encyclopedias have to say, we may find that things are even more complicated.

WHAT IS RACE?

Race is a concept developed after the 1400s, in large measure to set up hierarchies of "superior" and "inferior" peoples in an age of European expansion and global conquest. It has had an impact on the consciousness and practices of different sectors of the U.S. population. Often used as a synonym for what are now labeled *ethnic groups* (which we will discuss shortly), race was even more commonly utilized to create a category of "whiteness." This category was used by people of European origin to claim certain rights and benefits that set them above those with African, Asian, or native American "Indian" origins.

Scientifically, race can be defined as a biological grouping within the human species, classified according to specific genetically inherited differences such as skin pigmentation, hair texture and color, body proportions, and the like. Many scientists prefer the defining characteristics of race to be restricted to more precisely measurable differences in blood type, amino acid excretions, and enzyme deficiencies. Yet such races are in a continual state of flux, with genes constantly flowing from one gene pool to another.

Since all racial groups currently existing are, consequently, quite mixed, there is significant variation in racial classification systems. Some scientists have identified three races: Mongoloid, Caucasoid, and Negroid. Others refer to five racial groups, yet others to more than thirty, and still others to over two hundred. Other scientists have questioned the value of racial categories altogether. Much use of the term "race" is biologically and scientifically meaningless, being an ideological construction, at best loosely related to scientific notions, utilized to explain or justify differences, conflicts, and inequalities that are actually rooted in cultural and socioeconomic developments.

What places someone in a specific race is often illogical. There are dark-skinned "whites" with darker complexions than light-skinned "blacks." The child of a black mother and a white father is considered black, yet the child of a white mother and a black father is also considered black. Nonetheless, race has a genuine social meaning, since most people consider themselves (and are considered by others) to be in one or another distinct race, and this is deeply rooted in the historical experience and consciousness of those living in the United States.

In some ways, African Americans (as opposed, for example, to those with Negroid genetic characteristics who reside in Africa) are best considered as an *ethnic group*. An ethnic group is a group of people at least partly set off from others because of an identification with a distinctive regional or national origin, and who share at least some elements of a common cultural background. There have been many such groups in the United States, who identify as Irish American, Polish American, Italian American, African American, Chinese American, Mexican American, and so forth. Sometimes ethnic groups have been termed "races" and have been subjected to racist bigotry. Some have concluded that while "ethnicity" may have some scientific validity, race is simply a myth or illusion that should be dispensed with.

Yet perceptive sociologists Michael Omi and Howard Winant—while insisting that race cannot be reduced to some biological "essence" and noting that it has more to do with "complex meanings constantly being transformed"—have warned against efforts to somehow dispose of the concept:

> In the U.S., race is present in every institution, every relationship, every individual. This is the case not only for the way society is organized—spatially, culturally, in terms of stratification, etc.—but also for our perceptions and understandings of personal experience. Thus as we watch the videotape of Rodney King being beaten, compare real estate prices in different neighborhoods, select a radio channel to enjoy while we drive to work, size up a potential client, cus-

tomer, neighbor, or teacher, stand in line at the unemployment office, or carry out a thousand other normal tasks, we are compelled to think racially, to use racial categories and meaning systems into which we have been socialized. Despite exhortations both sincere and hypocritical, it is not possible or even desirable to be "color-blind." (Omi and Winant 1994, 158–59)

So today, more than ever, opposing racism requires that we notice race, not ignore it, that we afford it the recognition it deserves and the subtlety it embodies. By noticing race we can begin to challenge racism, with its ever-more-absurd reduction of human experience to an essence attributed to all without regard for historical or social context. By noticing race we can challenge the state, the institutions of civil society, and ourselves as individuals to combat the legacy of inequality and injustice inherited from the past. By noticing race we can develop the political insight and mobilization necessary to make the United States a more racially just and egalitarian society.

RACISM . . .
AND WHAT IT DOES TO MANY OF ITS VICTIMS

In their study *Racial Formation in the United States: From the 1960s to the 1990s*, Omi and Winant have pointed out that "whites tend to locate racism in color consciousness and find its absence color-blindness," whereas nonwhites often tend to "see racism as a system of power, and correspondingly argue that blacks, for example, cannot be racist because they lack power." They note that "there is nothing inherently white about racism," but that the focus on the question of *power* is not misplaced. They argue that something is racist if, and only if, it creates or reproduces structures of domination based on essentialist categories of race." By "essentialism" they mean a belief that one group of people is inherently and unchangeably—biologically—different (and by implication superior or inferior) in regard to another. This combined with structures of domination constitutes racism.

More simply, racism is often described as negative attitudes, practices, and policies directed at people because of their race or ethnic background. Some people who study racism make a distinction between *race prejudice* (which they identify as having distorted opinions about people of other races) and *racism* (which they define as race prejudice plus power). As Reverend Barndt puts it: "Racial prejudice is transformed into racism when one racial group becomes so powerful and dominant that it is able to control another group and enforce the controlling group's biases."

Not everyone uses such labels in the same way—but the important thing is the reality being described. It is worth giving additional thought to what this reality involves. We will attempt to do that here by beginning to develop an analysis of racism in the United States, with a focus on blacks and whites. Whether or not you are entirely comfortable with what follows, it's important to use all of your thoughtfulness and critical thinking to wrestle with the issues that are raised.

Most white Americans do not want to be racist. Regardless of the personal intentions of whites, however, every white person benefits in certain ways from being white in our society. This means that—in certain ways—every white American benefits from racism.

Some might object that this is not true, that such things as "affirmative action" (or what's left of affirmative action) give advantages to people of color in certain employment and school admissions situations. Those who defend affirmative action respond that this only helps to correct the racial imbalances that had been created by previous years of overtly racist discrimination against African Americans and other people of color. In any case, affirmative action has only been a reality in certain specific situations—not always carried out to begin with, and currently being eroded and dismantled in many places. (And even up to the 1990s, as sociologist Andrew Hacker points out, "the number of whites who have suffered due to affirmative action is relatively small.")

In a majority of situations, on the other hand, it is a liability *not* to be white. Those who are white are more apt to receive benefits and privileges (whether they want them or not) because they are white. They are treated better in many, many places. They are much less likely to have their race thrown up in their faces in everyday situations. They are more apt to have greater educational and employment opportunities. They are more likely to have access to decent housing. They are even more likely to live longer. Here are some representative statistics.

Income, Wealth, Poverty

For three decades, black males have averaged only a little more than half the income of white males (median incomes for each being roughly $12,000 per year as opposed to roughly $20,000 per year); the yearly median income gap between black and white *families* has been about $15,000. According to a 1998 report for the National Urban League by Melvin Oliver and Thomas Shapiro, for every dollar earned by a white household, black households earn only 62 cents. They go on to note that if one compares wealth, far deeper inequalities emerge: "Whites possess nearly twelve times as much median net worth (all assets minus liabilities) as blacks—$43,800 versus $3,700." For three decades, 30 percent of blacks and 10 percent of whites have lived in poverty. About 15 percent of all white children live in poverty, as opposed to over 44 percent of all black children.

Employment

Sociologist Andrew Hacker notes that "for as long as records have been kept, white America has ensured that the unemployment imposed on blacks will be approximately double that imposed on whites" (Hacker 1992, 102). Even among college graduates, blacks are more than two times as likely as whites to be unemployed. In 1996, a 5.4 percent unemployment rate translated into a 10.8 percent rate among blacks. According to William Julius Wilson, "The levels of inner-city joblessness reached during the first half of the 1990s were unprecedented," especially when factoring in with official unemployment those discouraged unemployed workers no longer searching for jobs. For example, "in 1990 only one in three adults held a job in the ghetto poverty areas of Chicago," with similar figures emerging from a survey of one hundred cities (Wilson, in National Urban League 1998, 89).

Education

While about 82 percent of black youth (as opposed to 89 percent of white youth) tend to graduate from high school, more than 63 percent of school-aged black youth still attend segregated schools. (Some of the highest percentages of such segregation are in northern states.) White students taking the Scholastic Aptitude Tests (SAT) average scores about two hundred points higher than black students. About 25 percent of white youth attend four or more years of college, as opposed to about 12 percent of black youth. Inner-city schools are one-third less likely than suburban schools to have computer and Internet facilities.

Housing

In 1976, a report of the Department of Housing and Urban Development found that "the housing of blacks is more than twice as often physically flawed as is the housing of the total population. And to live in adequate accommodations, a black household must spend a larger proportion of its income on housing than the average householder needs to." Nearly 10 percent of all housing, but 21 percent of black housing, was found to be flawed in terms of heating, plumbing, kitchen equipment, electrical fixtures, maintenance, sewage, and toilet access. Since this report, the situation has further deteriorated. Also worth noting is the continuing high rate of segregation in the early 1990s: 78 percent of blacks in northern cities and 67 percent of blacks in southern cities (and 86 percent of suburban whites) live in segregated neighborhoods.

Life Expectancy

In 1990, the average life expectancy among whites was seventy-six years and among blacks was seventy years. The tuberculosis death rate is four times as high among blacks as whites. Among blacks 22 per 100,000 (as opposed to 17 per 100,000 for whites) die of diabetes. Blacks are twice as likely as whites to die from hypertension.

Infant Mortality

In 1990, infant mortality rates were more than double in the black community: 8.1 per thousand among whites, 16.5 per thousand among blacks.

In a report written for the National Urban League, Dr. David H. Swinton, dean of the Business School at Jackson State University, commented: "This 1991 report unfortunately has much the same findings as in previous reports. The economic state of African Americans continues to be unhealthy. Their income rates are too low, their poverty rates are too high, and both remain very unequal. . . . The consistency of these results for the last decade leads to one inescapable conclusion. *The disadvantaged status of the African American population is a permanent feature of the American economy.* The permanence of this disadvantaged status implies that it is perpetuated by the normal operations of the American economy."

Seven years later, in a 1998 report for the National Urban League, William Julius Wilson noted that job prospects of predominantly African American inner-city workers "have diminished not only because of decreasing relative demand for low-skilled labor in the U.S. economy, the suburbanization of jobs, and the social deterioration of ghetto neighborhoods, but also because of negative employer attitudes." Wilson made another important point:

> In 1950, a substantial portion of the urban black population was poor but they were working. Urban poverty was quite extensive but people had jobs. However, as we entered the 1990s, most adults in many inner-city neighborhoods were not working a typical week. . . . The disappearance of work has had devastating effects not only on individuals and families, but on the social life of neighborhoods as well.

Economic developments in the United States have also been impacting very negatively on a growing number of whites—an extremely important point that we will return to later. (For that matter, the number of whites living in poverty is greater than the number of blacks: of those on welfare, 48 percent are white and 27 percent are black.) But the statistics consistently show that a much higher percentage of African Americans face greater economic difficulties than whites. Nor do whites generally face the realities described by Dr. C. Eric Lincoln:

> The power that shaped life in the black ghetto was not, of course, black power. It does not originate in the ghetto. It is power from the outside. It is alien power, with many faces. It is the nonresident merchants who come into the ghetto with the sun in the morning and who leave with the sun in the evening, taking with them the day's toll for their visitation. It is also the vexatious blue presence— that alien anonymous, contemptuous phalanx known as "the law" but more often than not considered an army of occupation pursuing its own private system of spoils. It is the ubiquitous presence of alien school teachers, case workers, process servers, rent collectors, repossessors, bailiffs, political hustlers, and assorted functionaries and racketeers whose economic stakes in the black ghetto require their temporary and grudging presence imposed upon a community they detest and which detests them. (Lincoln 1984, 10–11)

There are other aspects of the racial reality that afflict blacks but not whites. Some of these are described by Dr. Andrew Hacker:

> Except when you are in your own neighborhood, you always feel you are on display. On many occasions, you find you are the only person of your race present. You may be the only black student in a college classroom, the only black on a jury, the sole black at a corporate meeting, the only one at a social gathering. With luck, there may be one or two others. You feel every eye is on you, and you are not clear what posture to present. You realize that your presence makes whites uncomfortable; most of them probably wish you were not there at all. But since you are, they want to see you smile, so they can believe that you are being treated well. Not only is an upbeat air expected, but you must never show exasperation or anger, let alone anything that could look like a chip on you shoulder. Not everyone can keep such tight control. You don't find it surprising that so many black athletes and entertainers seek relief from those tensions. (Hacker 1992, 39)

Hacker, a white sociologist, adds perhaps self-critically: "You and your people have been studied and scrutinized and dissected, caricatured, and pitied or deplored, as no other group ever has. You see yourself reduced to data in research, statistics in reports. Each year, the nation asks how many of your teenagers have become pregnant, how many of your young men are in prison. Not only are you continually on view; you are always on trial."

According to a 1990 survey of the University of Chicago's National Opinion Research Center, insult is added to injury: "Fifty-three percent of nonblacks believe that African Americans are less intelligent than whites; 51 percent believe they are less patriotic; 56 percent believe they are more violence-prone; 62 percent believe they are more likely to 'prefer living off welfare' and less likely to 'prefer to be self-supporting'" (Terkel 1993, v).

A final point needs to be emphasized, however. *A majority of whites are also victims of antiblack prejudice and racist policies.* Derrick Bell's thorough summary is worth quoting at length:

> Throughout history, politicians have used blacks as scapegoats for failed economic or political policies. Before the Civil War, rich slaveowners persuaded the white working class to stand with them against the danger of slave revolts—even though the existence of slavery condemned white workers to a life of economic privation. After the Civil War, poor whites fought social reforms and settled for segregation rather than see formerly enslaved blacks get ahead. Most labor unions preferred to allow plant owners to break strikes with black scab labor than allow blacks to join their ranks. The "them against us" racial ploy—always a potent force in economic bad times—is working again: today whites—as disadvantaged by high-status entrance requirements as blacks, fight to end affirmative action policies that, by eliminating class-based entrance requirements and requiring widespread advertising of jobs, have likely helped far more whites than blacks. And in the 1990s, as through much of the 1980s, millions of Americans—white as well as black—face steadily worsening conditions: unemployment, inaccessible health care, inadequate housing, mediocre education, and pollution of the environment. The gap in national incomes is approaching a crisis as those in the top fifth now earn more than their counterparts in the bottom four fifths combined. . . . Whites are rallied on the basis of racial pride and patriotism to accept their often lowly lot in life, and encouraged to vent their frustration by opposing any serious advancement by blacks. (Bell 1992, 8–9)

INDIVIDUAL RACISM AND INSTITUTIONAL RACISM

It should be clear, in the discussion of racism offered in chapter 2, that there are different forms of racism. As individuals, whites are certainly responsible for their attitudes and personal actions, but it would be wrong to hold them personally responsible for excessively high black infant mortality rates, poverty rates, and so on. Many who analyze racism distinguish between *individual racism* and *institutional racism*.

Individual Racism

Individual Racism, or personal racism, is complicated—as we have already noted—and it can take different forms. Some analysts make a distinction between *race prejudice* (bigoted opinions about another race) and *racism* (prejudice plus power, or prejudice resulting in actions). But the borderline between thoughts and actions is sometimes fairly hazy. Another way to go, in looking at individual racism, is to divide it into *conscious racism* and *unconscious racism* (each of which can also contain subcategories):

Conscious Racism involves a conscious belief that, for example, whites are superior to blacks. There are different possibilities as to how this gets played out. One conscious racist might join a white supremacist organization devoted to "keeping blacks in their place" through circulating racist propaganda and utilizing force and violence. Another conscious racist might oppose using force and violence but make antiblack jokes and openly favor racial segregation. One might be opposed to such jokes and segregation—but studiously exclude any contact with African Americans. Yet another might favor some measure of "fair treatment" for and polite contact with blacks but emphatically not favor interracial socializing, dating, sexual relations, and marriage between blacks and whites.

Unconscious Racism involves a conscious rejection of the belief that whites are superior to blacks; but—at the very least—it also involves unresolved issues regarding black-white relations at an unconscious level. One white person may feel that black people have the right not to be treated differently from whites in any way, but have mixed feelings about interracial relations between men and women. Another may believe that there's "no difference" between blacks and whites and yet not feel comfortable in the company of blacks (partly because, in fact, there *are* differences). One may be nervously aloof. Another, anxiously overcompensating, may seek to be overly chummy and familiar while in the company of blacks. Someone else may simply be insensitive to the actual situation of African American individuals and of African Americans in society.

We can see that individual racism involves a spectrum of possibilities. One can evolve from one position to another. Under some circumstances we may become more racist, while under other circumstances we can become less racist.

But there is also a point made by black psychologist Kenneth Clark many years ago: "In contemporary society, no one, Negro or white, can be totally without prejudice. No one should expect purity of himself or others." Given the deep-rooted impact of racism on our history and culture, and its pervasiveness throughout society, it is unlikely that any one of us—whether black or white or pink or yellow or brown—can be entirely and forever free of the distorting influence of racism in some portion or another of our conscious or unconscious mind. If we are aware of this, we can be better able to deal with the racism that we might find within ourselves, and also less self-righteous as we interact with others on this difficult issue.

Institutional Racism

Institutional Racism is also complex and multifaceted. It powerfully reinforces individual racism (although it should also be obvious that it receives important reinforcement from individual racism). There are two subdivisions that analysts have sometimes utilized in discussing this—making use of the Latin words *de jure* (by law) and *de facto* (in fact). Joseph Barndt has usefully tagged these, respectively, as "direct institutional racism" and "indirect institutional racism."

Direct Institutional Racism has been the most blatant and obvious form of racism. From 1789 until the Civil War of 1861–65, racism—in the form of compromises between the northern and southern "Founding Fathers" over the institution of slavery—was written into the Constitution of the United States. There were plenty of laws buttressing slavery as well. At the conclusion of the Civil War, at the beginning of the Reconstruction era, there were important amendments to the Constitution that moved toward the dismantling of racism by law: the Thirteenth Amendment, which eliminated slavery, the Fourteenth Amendment, which guaranteed civil rights to every person in every state, and the Fifteenth Amendment, which removed the color bar from the right to vote.

After the 1877 abandonment of Reconstruction, however, there was a steady accumulation throughout the southern states of racist segregation laws (called "Jim Crow" laws, after a racist caricature from the old-time minstrel shows). These laws were upheld by the 1896 *Plessy* v. *Ferguson* decision of the U.S. Supreme Court, which said that such laws were not a violation of the Fourteenth Amendment because they provided "separate but equal" facilities for blacks and whites. In his 1944 classic *An American Dilemma*, Gunnar Myrdal described aspects of this reality in the decade before it was at last effectively challenged. Myrdal was struck by two things. First, political realities in the South were designed to prevent blacks from having any voice in government. Second, in regard to social realities "sexual segregation is the most pervasive form of segregation, and the concern about 'race purity' is, in a sense, basic." This ranged from bans on interracial marriage to taboos against simple flirtations (which could put a black man "in danger of his life"). Myrdal elaborated on various other aspects of the Jim Crow system:

> Every Southern state and most Border states have structures of state laws and municipal regulations which prohibit Negroes from using the same schools, libraries, parks, playgrounds, railroad cars, railroad stations, sections of streetcars and buses, hotels, restaurants, and other facilities as do the whites. In the South there are, in addition, a number of sanctions as well as etiquette. Officials frequently take it upon themselves to force Negroes into a certain action when they have no authority to do so. The inability of Negroes to get justice in the courts extends the powers of the police in the use of physical force. Beating and other forms of physical violence may be perpetuated by almost any white man without much fear of legal reprisal. Equally important sanctions are the organized threat and the risk of Negroes getting the reputation of being "bad" or "uppity," which makes precarious all future relations with whites. The Negro's

reliance on the tolerance of the white community for his economic livelihood and physical security makes these threats especially potent. (Myrdal 1962, 628)

In 1954, however, the Supreme Court reversed itself in the *Brown v. Board of Education* decision, which concluded that historically segregated facilities had proved to be unequal. The South's segregation laws became the target of the civil rights movement of the 1950s and 1960s (discussed in chapter 4), which brought about the adoption and implementation of federal Civil Rights Acts that eliminated de jure racism.

Indirect Institutional Racism has proved to be far more resilient. One thing it involves is segregation not based on laws but on privately (and often secretly) made decisions within predominantly white institutions. It can also involve policies, practices, structures, and dynamics that *even without conscious intentions* of decision makers maintain and reinforce the subordinate situation of African Americans in society. French author Daniel Guerin, who familiarized himself with U.S. realities in the 1940s, noted that "segregation, public and legal in the South, is hypocritical and private in the North." He offered these observations:

> In the very heart of New York stretches an immense ghetto, the largest in the world—Harlem. I lived for a time on the dividing line between the white and Negro worlds. Nothing could have been more instructive. West 96th Street is one of the main crosstown streets, and a number of blocks are inhabited by well-to-do white families. The highest rent apartment buildings have canvas awnings to protect the ladies from the weather as they get out of their cars, and uniformed doormen to meet them at the entrance. Two blocks away we are already in the Negro quarter. Large families are squeezed into tiny apartments with the most rudimentary furnishings. The streets are dirty and swarm with ragged children. The whites seem to be completely unaware of this disinherited world that displays its sores just a few steps away from their comfortable and respectable dwellings. One day I took my daughter to visit a Negro family on 98th Street. Despite their poverty, they were a family of dignity and distinction; but so great was the contrast with the world we had just come from that the child could not believe her eyes. (Guerin 1956, 66–67)

One of the most notorious forms of de facto racism has been in the real estate industry. Particularly in the 1940s, in the wake of a massive black migration to northern and western industrial areas, various cities saw a combination of city councils, real estate boards, and banks make far-reaching decisions to restrict African Americans to inner-city areas that were beginning to deteriorate. As part of this strategy, an especially vicious tactic (known as "blockbusting") was developed. The real estate companies would spread rumors, in order to generate both economic and racial fears among white home owners, about a "black invasion" that would allegedly cause a decline in real estate values. This enabled the companies to buy up multiple blocks of city housing (at a good price, of course) that could be rented to blacks for inflated rents. Then "better" housing areas, often in suburban areas, would be made available to the whites—with blacks being openly excluded.

When such practices were deemed to be illegal by the courts in the 1950s, other ways were found to get the same results. As Rev. Joseph Barndt has explained, "There are ingenious schemes and systems of 'steering' customers toward or away from locations that have been primarily designated for one particular racial group. Likewise, banks that once gave or refused mortgages to anyone they chose, or designated by fiat the composition of entire communities, have created such strategies as 'redlining' to achieve the same results" (Barndt 1991, 88–89).

Some manifestations of this "indirect" approach require the utilization of conscious racism, while others do not. Andrew Hacker indicates some of the other forms this variant of institutional racism can take:

> The institutions can be colleges and churches, or business firms or governmental bureaus. The Federal Bureau of Investigation and the Los Angeles Police Department, for example, have long had reputations for antipathy toward blacks and other minorities. But not all organizations are so blatant in their biases. Most develop more subtle cultures of their own, which their members usually internalize, often without pause or reflection. Of course, organizational cultures take many forms. But in the United States an overarching feature is that they tend to be inherently "white."
>
> This is not to say that churches and colleges and corporations actually proclaim a racial preference. All will assert that they welcome parishioners and students and employees of every color, and they hope to increase that diversity. Executives at firms like General Motors and General Electric would be shocked if told that they headed racist firms, as would administrators at Cornell or Columbia. Indeed, the issue barely arises in the minds of their members. (Hacker 1992, 22)

It is not always clear to what extent such racial discrimination is conscious and to what extent it is unintentional. "Employers who, not so long ago, could accept and reject persons of color according to their personal racist views," observes Reverend Barndt, "have learned to use other criteria to disqualify and exclude unwanted persons. . . . Like moles that respond to threats by burrowing deeper into the ground, people who engage in such practices develop increasingly subtle and sophisticated methods of deception" (Barndt 1991, 89). Law professor and social analyst Derrick Bell points out additional complications in such de facto racism:

Modern discrimination is, moreover, not practiced indiscriminately. Whites, ready and willing to applaud, even idolize, black athletes and entertainers, refuse to hire, or balk at working with, blacks. Whites who number individual blacks among their closest friends approve, or do not oppose, practices that bar selling or renting homes or apartments in their neighborhoods to blacks they don't know. Employers, not wanting "too many of them," are willing to hire one or two black people, but will reject those who apply later. Most hotels and restaurants who offer black patrons courteous—even deferential—treatment, uniformly reject black job applicants, except for the most menial jobs. (Bell 1992, 6)

We can see that this indirect form of institutional racism has a viciousness all its own. In some cases it involves conscious racism that is openly expressed, but in other cases it involves conscious racism that is kept hidden while being openly denied. In yet other cases it may involve the self-deception of unconscious racism. And in some cases it may involve neither conscious nor unconscious racism, but instead the working of blind economic forces that combine with the effects of past racist developments, which nonetheless reinforce and deepen black-white inequality. Taken together, all of this can breed debilitating suspicions, tensions, self-doubt, frustrations, guilt, and rage among blacks and whites.

Confronting racism, understanding racism—these we have begun to do. But how is one to overcome racism? One of the most useful ways to approach this task is with an understanding that it is a process that has been going on for some time. In order to maximize our own efforts, we must see how they will connect with what has gone on before.

4.

THE HISTORY OF
RACISM AND ANTIRACISM

The modern civil rights movement could be said to have lasted from the early 1950s to the late 1960s. It effectively challenged the Jim Crow system, leading a successful assault on the system of racial segregation in the South, eliminating what we have described as direct institutional racism. In doing so, it also did much to bring unconscious racism to consciousness, helping many whites overcome aspects of both forms of individual racism. Yet the goals and perspectives of its most far-sighted leaders—such as Martin Luther King Jr.—went significantly beyond this accomplishment.

Civil rights leaders recognized that economics is at the center of racism in our own time, just as it was central to the origins of racism. Economics involves the activities and relationships people enter into, and the resources they use, to get the things they need and the things they want. Different kinds of economies work differently. The rise of racism is linked with relatively recent economic developments. In order to overcome racism, it is certainly necessary to address certain psychological dynamics and engage with moral and ethical issues. But it is also necessary to come to grips with the underlying economic developments that have created specific conditions and experiences that influence people's psychologies and ethical choices.

In this chapter we will review the economic developments that created and sustained racism, and also touch on some of the earlier efforts to resist racism. In the following chapter we will seek an understanding of the accomplishments and limitations of the modern civil rights movement.

DEVELOPMENT OF ANTIBLACK RACISM IN THE UNITED STATES

In his massive study *Caste, Class, and Race*, Prof. Oliver C. Cox surveyed ancient and medieval Europe and discovered—despite many invasions, much oppression, widespread slavery, and bloody crusades—that racial prejudice, interracial laws, or anything akin to modern racial conceptions were more or less absent from most of human history. In his more recent study *The Mismeasure of Man*, naturalist Stephen Jay Gould has concurred that the biological determinism at the heart of racist ideology—the notion that certain groups of people "are constructed of intrinsically inferior material"—has only developed over the past three centuries, a period that scholars label modern history. "Racism is a creation of our own time," as anthropologist Ruth Benedict once put it.

With the rise of the European nation-states and the global spread of the market economy from the fifteenth through the eighteenth centuries, the African slave trade became big business as well as an essential source of labor for the lucrative plantation economies of the Americas. These developments were accompanied by the creation of allegedly scientific racial classifications and rationalizations that stressed the "inferiority" of "backward races" in parts of the world being conquered and dominated by the new European powers. Or as Richard Wright put it:

> Buttressed by their belief that their God had entrusted the earth into their keeping, drunk with power and possibility, waxing rich through trade and merchant marines at their disposal, their countries filled with human debris anxious for any new adventures, psychologically armed with new facts, white Western Christian civilization during the fourteenth, fifteenth, sixteenth, and seventeenth centuries, with a long, slow bloody explosion, hurled itself upon the sprawling masses of colored humanity in Asia and Africa [and also in the Americas]. (Wright 1964, 57–58)

The wave of democratic revolutions—of which the 1776 Declaration of Independence was one of the greatest documents—seemed to contradict such racism. But the development of the Industrial Revolution in the late eighteenth and early nineteenth centuries gave a powerful push to new waves of racist theorizing. Such stuff seemed more compelling due to the global spread of the industrial capitalist powers seeking markets, raw materials, and investment opportunities at the expense of the "colored" peoples of the world. And in the United States itself, the southern plantation economies based on slave labor found powerful encouragement thanks to the voracious appetite for cotton of the new textile industries in England (and soon in New England). Racist stereotypes of African Americans, and widespread propaganda about their inferiority and their "happiness" under slavery, began to permeate U.S. cultural life. (Similar racial bigotry toward Indians, Mexicans, and Asian immigrants also became part of the consciousness of many Americans of European origin.)

Considerable bigotry was also lavished upon the many immigrants drawn from Europe to the opportunities provided by industrializing the American republic. But as one immigrant group after another sought to be accepted into their adopted homeland, there was a powerful temptation to emphasize one's "whiteness" in order to secure more of the benefits to which true Americans should be entitled. And this reinforced the racist oppression of African Americans.

The needs of the industrializing North based on a free-labor system increasingly diverged from the needs of the agricultural South based on a slave-labor system. The consequent economic and political stresses finally exploded into a bloody Civil War (1861–1865). While President Abraham Lincoln was reluctant to offend white public opinion by making slavery a central issue of the conflict, he soon concluded that in fact it *was* a central issue, and that the abolition of slavery was essential to the success of the Northern war effort. The growing understanding of this, and the vital role that African Americans came to play in the defeat of the slave South, did much to challenge and push back (though by no means eradicate) institutional and individual racism.

In the Reconstruction era (1866–1877), some northern politicians were committed to reunifying the country in a manner that would both (1) secure full rights for African-Americans (the Thirteenth, Fourteenth, and Fifteenth Amendments to the Constitution were part of that) and at the same time (2) facilitate the more thoroughgoing industrial development of the United States (which had been blocked by the Southern plantation owners until the Civil War). In the South the newly formed antiblack terrorist organization the Ku Klux Klan, as well as racist laws passed by the various southern states, were utilized to keep blacks "in their place" in a status of semislavery. Northern troops were used to put a stop to that, and to allow ex-slaves and poor whites to form new state governments that would be more democratic. It was expected that this new bloc of voters would support the North's industrialization program. This they did, as well as adopting various social reforms beneficial to the South's lower classes.

But one key economic plan that probably would have destroyed much of the economic basis of racism in the South was blocked by the most powerful northern political and business interests. The proposal would have taken the big plantations away from the rich southerners and provided forty-acre farms to all ex-slaves and loyal whites—breaking the economic power of the racist elite, ensuring economic independence for a majority of blacks and whites in the region, and providing a strong basis for interracial unity among the South's laboring elements. This was seen by most northern leaders as an unacceptable violation of property rights. It was therefore easier for the southern elite to mobilize poor whites into Ku Klux Klan-type organizations to attack the black-supported state governments, and also to participate in election campaigns designed to reestablish "white power" governments throughout the region. Also, some representatives of the southern racist elite made it clear that they would go along with the industrial policies favored by northern leaders. By 1877 a compromise was worked out-with northern troops withdrawn from the South, and racist state governments established through fraud and extreme violence.

Many blacks resisted violations of their Constitutional and human rights, but in 1896 the U.S. Supreme Court articulated the doctrine of "separate but equal." This gave legal cover to the consolidation of the Jim Crow system—thoroughgoing racist segregation and systematic elimination of black voting rights. A majority of blacks in the South were also forced into becoming tenant farmers or sharecroppers-working intensively on the land (raising cotton, tobacco, and other cash crops) in impoverished conditions, completely under the economic domination of white landowners and businessmen. Blacks in the North—though enjoying somewhat more freedom and economic opportunity- also found themselves facing racial prejudice and discrimination. But they generally were not subjected to the same violence (beatings, rapes, and over a hundred lynchings each year) and threat s of violence used to "keep them in their place" in much of the South.

World War I (1914–1918) brought a dramatic change, especially when the United States became involved in 1917. The booming war production combined with the wartime cut-off of European immigrants, plus many northern factory workers were going into the army. (After the war Congress passed bigoted legislation that continued to restrict those coming from eastern and southern Europe.) The resulting labor shortage caused northern employers to encourage black migration from the rural South to the urban North—thus generating the great northward migration of African Americans. This migration continued for decades after the war's end.

As we have seen, city governments plotted with real estate companies and banks to force these new arrivals into inner-city ghettoes. Many immigrant workers—already stressing their "whiteness"—found themselves competing for employment with African Americans. In many instances employers would play off different racial an d ethnic groups against each other to keep wages down and the labor force disunited and therefore more easily controlled. In many cases, labor unions—made up of white workers anxious to maintain their own "superior" status—also discriminated against African Americans. In 1919, after the war, black communities in such industrial cities as St. Louis and Chicago became the targets of race riots initiated by bigoted whites.

During the 1920s a revitalized Ku Klux Klan (KKK) spread throughout much of the country, North and South, with four million members. The revival was encouraged by D. W. Griffith's racist film *Birth of a Nation* (1915), based on

Thomas Dixon's best-selling novel *The Clansman*, which glorified the post–Civil War Klan with such justifications as this: "For a thick-lipped, flat-nosed, spindle-shanked negro, exuding his nauseating animal odor, to shout derision over the hearths and homes of white men and women is an atrocity too monstrous for belief. . . . The issue, sir, is Civilization! . . . whether society is worth saving from barbarism." Just as the novel and film were embraced by President Woodrow Wilson, so was the new KKK embraced initially by many prominent politicians, including President Warren G. Harding. An emboldened Klan went on to utilize terror, cross-burnings, and violence against a variety of enemies—immigrants from southern and eastern Europe, Catholics, Jews, labor unions, and the like—but a primary purpose was to keep African Americans "in their place." Discredited by scandals and negative publicity in the late 1920s, the KKK's diminished numbers were predominantly restricted to the South by 1930.

The Great Depression of the 1930s caused such massive unemployment, poverty, and insecurity among so many whites that—although in some cases racial antagonisms were intensified—a growing number of whites became open to making common cause with blacks in the struggles of the unemployed. As times improved slightly, the struggles to organize industrial workers into the relatively democratic unions of the Congress of Industrial Organizations (CIO) also fostered black-white solidarity. But for the most part, institutional racism remained very much intact throughout the country.

And yet additional economic shifts would soon help generate immense changes. The decline of certain sectors of southern agriculture combined with the development of mechanization in much of southern farming to dislodge increasing numbers of African Americans from their traditional places in the economy. In 1940, 80 percent of the nation's blacks still lived in the South. But the war-time industrial production generated by World War II (1939–1945), and the later period of Cold War prosperity, created such economic opportunities for African Americans that more than three million migrated to central cities of the North between 1940 and 1960. Between 1890 and 1970 the percentage of African Americans living in urban areas increased from 20 percent to 80 percent. The world that had enabled southern racists to maintain the Jim Crow system, the controls that had been possible and the balance of forces that had existed for so long, were now dramatically eroded. This development created one major component in what would be a profound shift in race relations.

Another factor helping to alter the American racial scene was the role of the United States in world affairs, and the consequent pressures of U.S. foreign policy. In the early 1940s the U.S. government claimed to be leading a "people's war" for democracy and against Hitler's racism. This placed pressures on the government to begin overcoming at least some of the most blatant aspects of racism at home. Such pressures increased with the end of the war, as a wave of anticolonial revolutions in Asia and Africa began creating important new nations of colored peoples who themselves had suffered under various forms of individual and institutionalized racism. The Cold War—during which the capitalist Free World was in competition with the Communist bloc for the "hearts and minds" of masses of (mostly nonwhite) people throughout the world—made it imperative that the U.S. government find ways to project itself as a force against the persistence of racism in its own land.

These domestic and global realities set the stage for the rise of the civil rights movement that was able to bring about a dramatic shift in the structures of racism in the United States. The achievements of the civil rights movement, however, were not able to secure racism's elimination. Yet if we hope to move more effectively toward its elimination, we should look more closely at the often desperate, often magnificent struggles waged to achieve racial justice in the past—in the civil rights period, but also in the previous years. We will find important insights to help guide us in the future.

AFRICAN AMERICAN FREEDOM STRUGGLES

Sometimes the victims of racism are seen passively, as powerless victims. But this is certainly not the case for the African and African American peoples subjected to the various forms of racism we have been examining here. They drew on all of the considerable power that they had—in their rich cultures, in their bodies, in their minds, in their spirits, in their relationships with each other—in order to survive and, as much as possible, to triumph over their circumstances.

African American freedom struggles took many forms during the slavery era. Among the most dramatic were the slave conspiracies and revolts led by such people as Gabriel Prosser (1800), Denmark Vesey (1822), Nat Turner (1831), and Joseph Cinquez on the slaveship *Amistad* (1841). A more common form of resistance involved running away—sometimes to Indian territories (such as among the Seminoles in Florida, where an African-Indian alliance fought off the whites for many years). The Underground Railroad—a network of escape routes and hiding places maintained by free blacks and sympathetic whites—helped about 100,000 people escape from slavery to the northern states or Canada.

Some became leading activists in the movement that worked for the abolition of slavery.

A majority of enslaved blacks—unable to rise up in open rebellion or find the means to escape—developed other forms of resistance. For some, "tricksterism" was employed to outsmart and cheat or steal from those who oppressed them—much of which was glorified in slave folk tales about Br'er Rabbit.

Related to this strategy were faked ignorance and laziness, inefficient working methods, and "accidentally" breaking tools.

Forms of psychological survival and self-affirmation were sometimes reflected in music, dance, and other artistic activity, as well as storytelling and magic—all of which often provided a sense of community among enslaved African Americans and also channels for the covert passing on of aspects of African culture that were generally forbidden by the white slave owners.

The passionate engagement with Christianity on the part of many slaves was another means through which one's self-worth might be affirmed—with additional opportunities for reshaping and revitalizing this "white man's religion" with African cultural patterns that very much made it a source of personal strength and community among the oppressed.

With the outbreak of the Civil War, increasing numbers of slaves and free blacks found ways to play an active role in fighting against the slave system—especially at the beginning of 1863 when the Emancipation Proclamation was issued and the recruitment of black troops was initiated. About 185,000 African Americans were part of the Union army, and they suffered 37,638 casualties. More than this, the Southern economy, dependent on slave labor, was fatally undermined as increasing numbers escaped to Union lines and many more "slowed down," worked inefficiently, and in some cases refused to work at all—constituting in the view of some historians a sort of "general strike" of slave labor.

During the Reconstruction era, innumerable heroes and heroines struggled to bring themselves and their brothers, sisters, and children up from slavery, seeking to build a new South and a new nation in which democracy and equality would exist more thoroughly than ever before. And when Reconstruction was betrayed, many paid with their lives, and many more continued the struggle to hold on to some of the gains. Some black activists involved themselves in alliances with whites through trade unions, the populist movement of embattled poor farmers, and other struggles for radical reform. In some cases the same activists played leadership roles in struggles more specifically for African American rights.

The urban and northward migrations were also part of the struggle for a better life. For many, careful decisions had to be made about when to fight back and when to bide one's time, and when to choose less direct forms of resistance and self-affirmation. For some, the contribution to the forward movement of their people might take the form of excelling in one or another profession, in entertainment or sports, in the arts and sciences, and so on. In some cases, one's contribution to the freedom struggle might involve laboring to advance education for one's self and for others, building a church, keeping together a family, and nurturing children.

It would be a serious mistake to see the freedom struggles we have sketched here as being on the margins of the historical mainstream. Pioneering historians such as C. L. R. James noted in the 1930s that "the Negro's revolutionary history is rich, inspiring, and unknown," but also that they played a central—often a decisive—role in the modern world as the tidal waves of democratic revolutions and Industrial Revolution washed away the old order in the eighteenth and nineteenth centuries. Far from being outside the mainstream of world history, and far from being simply the passive victims of white oppression or beneficiaries of white generosity, they powerfully helped to shape the United States and the world.

Several years later W. E. B. Du Bois similarly emphasized "how critical a part Africa has played in human history, past and present, and how impossible it is to forget this and rightly explain the present plight of mankind." And in the 1960s Benjamin Quarles commented that "if, strictly speaking, there is no such thing as Negro history, it is because his past has become so interwoven into the whole fabric of our civilization." He added that "the Negro's role in the United States throws light upon some of the major trends in the history of the Western world since Columbus." Their experience was, in the words of John Hope Franklin, "an integral part of the struggle for freedom." Each of these historians—and others—have produced impressive scholarship that amply demonstrates the truth of such generalizations.

The achievements and limitations of the modern civil rights movement in the United States in the 1950s and 1960s are central to developing an understanding of the recent history of the United States, and to comprehending whether our future will turn out to be the American dream or the American nightmare. In preparing to turn our attention to that movement, it may be helpful to take note of several prominent black activists from earlier times.

TWELVE LIVES

Consider the poetry in prose of W. E. B. Du Bois's *Souls of Black Folk*:

Before the Pilgrims landed we were here. Here we have brought our three gifts and mingled them with yours: a gift of story and song—soft, stirring melody in an ill-harmonized and unmelodious land; the gift of sweat and brawn to beat back the wilderness, conquer the soil, and lay the foundations of this vast economic empire two hundred years earlier than your weak hands could have done it; the third, a gift of the Spirit. Around us the history of the land has centered for thrice a hundred years; out of the nation's heart we have called all that was best to throttle and subdue all that was worst; fire and blood, prayer and sacrifice, have billowed over this people, and they have found peace only in the altars of the God of the Right. Nor has our gift of the Spirit been merely passive. Actively we have woven ourselves with the very warp and woof of this nation—we have fought their battles, shared their sorrow, mingled our blood with theirs, and generation after generation have pleaded with a headstrong, careless people to despise not Justice, Mercy, and Truth, lest the nation be smitten with a curse. Our song, our toil, our cheer, and warning have been given to this nation in blood-brotherhood. Is not this work and striving? Would America have been America without her Negro people?

In a way, it greatly distorts our understanding of freedom struggles to focus on a few individuals—because they were influenced and made relevant by their connections with hundreds and thousands of lesser-known and unknown people whose interwoven lives made up the struggles for survival and liberation that we have so briefly sketched here, and who were yet again connected with the energies and aspirations of millions more.

At least some initial insights and a sense of orientation can be drawn, however, from a brief look at several key individuals: Frederick Douglass and Martin Delany, Harriet Tubman and Sojourner Truth, Ida B. Wells-Barnett, Booker T. Washington and Marcus Garvey, W. E. B. Du Bois and A. Philip Randolph, Paul Robeson and Bayard Rustin, and Ella Baker. In these lives we can detect the regenerative themes that help to define the survival and upward striving of a people.

Frederick Douglass and Martin Delany

Frederick Douglass (1817–1895) and Martin Delany (1812–1885) were two of the most important figures in the movement to end slavery. During the Civil War, Douglass played a central role in recruiting African Americans into the Union Army, in which Delany himself became an officer (rising to the rank of major). After the Civil War both men were politically active—Douglass a significant figure in the Republican Party (and for a time U.S. ambassador to Haiti), Delany active in Reconstruction politics in South Carolina. But it was in the pre–Civil War period that both men made their greatest contributions.

Douglass was an escaped slave who—while still in bondage during his childhood—had illegally learned to read. Delany, on the other hand, was born free of ex-slave parents; able to attend Harvard University Medical School (he was not able to stay when the white students objected), he became a physician. Douglass's escape from slavery and immense talents led, however, to his becoming the foremost African American leader in the movement to end slavery. He was a brilliant lecturer and writer. His brilliant insights into the social dynamics and psychology of slavery and racism, contained in each of his three biographical works, constitute an enduring contribution to U.S. culture.

More than this, Douglass was animated by a principled radicalism, a powerful militancy, and a shrewd understanding of practical political realities which was different, and in some ways more effective, than that of his white mentor

William Lloyd Garrison. This plus the determination to publish his own abolitionist newspaper the *North Star* (rather than subordinate himself to Garrison's
periodical the *Liberator*) led to a break that established Douglass as an independent force in the abolitionist movement.

Where Delany differed from Douglass was over the question of racial integration, of which Douglass was an unswerving partisan. Delany, on the other
hand, pioneered in the development of black nationalism. During the pre–Civil
War period, despairing of blacks ever finding justice and equal rights in a white-
dominated United States, Delany advocated black emigration back to Africa for
the purpose of founding an independent black-controlled state.

Sojourner Truth and Harriet Tubman

Sojourner Truth (1797–1883) and Harriet Tubman (1820–1913) were the best-
known African American women in the antislavery movement—"big-souled,
God-intoxicated women," as Lerone Bennett once called them. Truth (who had
abandoned her slave name Isabella after she was freed by the New York Emancipation Act of 1827) became an itinerant preacher with "mystical gifts" and
magnificent oratory skills as well. Her talents were employed in various reform
struggles—the most important of these being in the abolitionist movement and
the women's rights movement (for which her speech "Ain't I a Woman?" has left
an indelible imprint in American culture). She also aided blacks who had escaped
from slavery to find employment, places to live, and educational opportunities.

Tubman, who had escaped from slavery when she was twenty-eight years
old, played an important role as a "conductor" on the Underground Railroad,
making twenty trips to the South in order to help more than three hundred slaves
find their way to freedom. She explained: "I had reasoned this out in my mind:
there were one or two things I had a *right* to, liberty or death; if I could not have
the one, I would have the other, for no man should take me alive; I should fight
for my liberty as long as my strength lasted, and when the time came for me to
go, the Lord would let them take me."

Both women did what they could to support the Union army during the Civil
War, Tubman serving as a nurse, soldier, spy, and scout. After the war both did
what they could—each in her own way—to improve the human condition,
though each labored in impoverished circumstances.

Ida B. Wells-Barnett

Ida B. Wells-Barnett (1864–1931) spent almost all of her life in freedom, and
most of it fighting for human rights. As a teacher in Memphis, Tennessee, she
exposed the corrupt and unequal mismanagement of funds in the city's segregated school system—and, naturally, lost her job. She also fought in the courts—

with some initial success but ultimate failure—against racial discrimination in the public transportation system.

Wells-Barnett became best known as a journalist and public speaker who crusaded against the widespread lynching of African Americans that blighted the South. According to her research, approximately ten thousand people had been lynched between 1878 and 1898. Especially provocative was her devastating exposure of the sexual politics underlying much white racism—which defended "the honor of white womanhood" from the alleged threat posed by black men (denying the fact that some white women sought sexual contact with black men), while at the same time covertly encouraging white male molestation of black women.

Driven out of the South with extreme violence and threats of death, she made her home in Chicago, where she became a central figure in the establishment of the black women's club movement and the leading organizer among African Americans for women's right to vote. Always engaged in the struggle for racial justice, she was a founding member of the National Association for the Advancement of Colored People.

Booker T. Washington and Marcus Garvey

Booker T. Washington (1856–1915) and Marcus Garvey (1887–1940) both rejected the notion that African Americans should struggle for equal rights in the United States. Washington rose from slavery to become an influential and effective black educator, in 1881 becoming the founder and first president of Tuskegee Institute, devoted to the development of black teachers as well as agricultural and vocational education. He also helped to establish the National Negro Business League to encourage the development of black-owned business—seeing "black capitalism," in addition to working with white-owned big businesses willing to employ black labor, as the way to advance the economic well-being of the African American community. This—not struggles for political equality or racial integration within the context of a white-dominated United States—would provide solutions to the problems faced by African Americans, he insisted. The 1896 Supreme Court affirmation of "separate but equal" did nothing to undermine the perspective that Washington articulated. Whites should be reassured that blacks would have no desire to end their status of racial separation. At the same time, in the space secured through such accommodation, blacks must rely on themselves to improve their own condition.

Jamaican-born Marcus Garvey strongly agreed with much of Washington's separatist message as, in 1916, he established the Universal Negro Improvement Association (UNIA) with an attractive newspaper, the *Negro World*. But he gave the message a global vision and radical black nationalist twist. Washington had sought to assure both white racists and wealthy white philanthropists who gave massive financial contributions to his black self-improvement projects that the black community would not seek to make an issue of racial injustice or in any other way to "rock the boat." Garvey, on the other hand, insisted on rocking the boat by aggressively publicizing racial injustices toward blacks throughout the United States and the world, by aggressively proclaiming the equality of the black race with all others, by insisting on black control of all aspects of African American life (including, as was the case with Washington, the establishment of an extensive "black capitalism"), and by boldly advancing a "Back to Africa" movement. In doing this, he built a large urban movement that generated tremendous enthusiasm and attracted the support of many of thousands of African Americans throughout the country.

Whereas Washington had been seen as a respectable moderate, Garvey was seen as a dangerous radical. Washington cultivated important contacts with the wealthy and the powerful in the white elite, and his "separate but equal" and "black self-improvement" accommodation to the U.S. power structure—despite growing criticisms from more militant black activists—helped him become (with massive white economic aid) the most powerful African American in the United States. Garvey, on the other hand, did not shy away from fierce controversies, nor did he exercise Washington's caution in financial matters. This made it possible for the U.S. government to unfairly target him on charges of fraud, which resulted in prison in 1925 and deportation in 1927.

Yet Washington and Garvey, each in his own way, secured substantial support among masses of black Americans who saw "black self-reliance" as a practical and necessary goal. Their influence can be felt down to our own time.

W. E. B. Du Bois and A. Philip Randolph

W. E. B. Du Bois (1868–1963) and A. Philip Randolph (1889–1979) shared much in common and yet were also profoundly different. In sharp contrast to Washington and Garvey, both Du Bois and Randolph favored an orientation of overcoming racism by struggling for equal rights in the United States. Yet their distinctive approaches to this task were shaped by their own early development. Du Bois had the opportunity to pursue higher education at Fisk University, Harvard University, and the University of Berlin. This naturally put him in touch with well-to-do and influential circles. Randolph, on the other hand, was a more modestly educated intellectual and Socialist Party member who published a radical magazine, the *Messenger*, that had significant impact among black activists.

Du Bois in his earlier years focused his attention on developing a "talented tenth" among African Americans—a highly educated elite that could raise the standards of and provide capable leadership for the African American masses. In contrast, Randolph focused on the need for those masses to raise themselves, especially by black workers forming strong trade unions, and also working to eliminate racism in the labor movement, so that black and white workers could join together in the struggle for a better future. While both men considered themselves socialists (that is, favoring social ownership and democratic control of the economy), Randolph never shared Du Bois's positive assessment of the Soviet Union under the Stalin and Khruschev regimes. In his later years Randolph was sometimes criticized for going too far in compromises with trade union officials and Democratic Party officeholders, whereas Du Bois became so alienated from the American scene that he renounced his U.S. citizenship and assumed residence in Ghana. Yet in the decades leading up to the emergence of the modern civil rights movement, both men had a profound impact that left a strong imprint on that movement.

As a central founder and early leader of the National Association for the Advancement of Colored People (NAACP), and as editor of its influential monthly magazine, *Crisis*, Du Bois focused on carrying out research and educational work, aggressive court campaigns to challenge segregation, and persistent public relations efforts to challenge racism in the country's political and cultural life. As a central founder and leader of the Brotherhood of Sleeping Car Porters, Randolph sought to raise the material conditions of black workers, also educating within the ranks of the American Federation of Labor on the wisdom of overcoming racism, and seeking to build coalitions that would effectively pressure for black rights and economic justice for all.

In 1941 Randolph built an effective March on Washington movement to protest racial discrimination in the armed forces and war industries—forcing President Roosevelt (as a condition for calling off the march) to sign an Executive Order banning discrimination in war industries, government training programs, and government industries. In 1948 Randolph led a successful effort to force the end of racial segregation in the armed forces. In the same period, Du Bois played a significant role in efforts for world peace (for example, he was a consultant on the 1945 founding meeting of the United Nations) and the increasingly important Pan-African movement (he was elected president in 1945 of the Fifth Pan-African Congress which met in England). Given their importance for what would emerge in the 1950s and 1960s, it may be worth considering the comments of two of their close associates.

Paul Robeson and Bayard Rustin

Paul Robeson (1898–1976), a cultural activist who saw Du Bois as a mentor, gives a vivid sense of some of the man's qualities:

> He wrote clearly, constructively, and militantly on the complex problems of the American scene, on the Negro question, on Africa, and on world affairs. He called

upon the American people, and particularly upon the whole labor movement, to understand the need for unity in the struggle of the working masses, including the Negro, for a decent standard of living. . . . He insisted upon first-class citizenship for all Americans, upon full equality of opportunity, dignity, legal rights for us all. And he directed universal interest and attention to our Negro history and our rich African ancestry, to give us solid background for our struggle. . . . Dr. Du Bois was a distinguished historian as well as a social scientist. We often talked about the wealth and beauty of our folk heritage, particularly about Negro music which he loved and found deeply moving. He often stressed the importance of this special contribution to American culture. (Clark et al. 1970, 34–35)

Bayard Rustin (1910–1987), a social activist who was one of Randolph's closest aides, gives a vivid sense of some of the man's qualities:

A. Philip Randolph . . . has maintained a total vision of the goal of freedom for his people and of the means for achieving it. From his earliest beginnings as a follower of Eugene V. Debs and a colleague of Norman Thomas [Socialist Party leaders], he has understood that social and political freedom must be rooted in economic freedom, and all his subsequent actions have sprung from this basic premise. . . . While he has felt that Negro salvation is an internal process of struggle and self-affirmation, he has recognized the political necessity of forming alliances with men of other races and the moral necessity of comprehending the black movement as part of a general effort to expand human freedom. Finally, as a result of his deep faith in democracy, he has realized that social change does not depend upon the decisions of the few, but on direct political action through the mobilization of masses of individuals to gain economic and social justice. (Rustin 1971, 261)

What Robeson and Rustin say about their mentors also contains elements of self-description. Robeson—whose father was a runaway slave who became a respected minister—was a Princeton University graduate (Phi Beta Kappa) who rose to international fame as a singer and actor. While living in London from 1927 to 1939, he connected with the Pan-African and socialist movements. "The fact that Robeson viewed the Soviet Union and the world communist movement as reliable allies of the colonial liberation movements," his son later recalled, "led him to form a close alliance with Communists despite his private misgivings about the Stalinist purges of 1936–1938 and his disagreement with the Communist Left's exaggerated emphasis on class priorities over 'nationalist' priorities in the Third World." Immensely popular and influential during the late 1930s and the 1940s among many blacks and whites in the United States, he effectively challenged racism and connected the ideas of racial and economic justice—but found himself marginalized and blacklisted in the atmosphere of Cold War anti-Communism that became dominant by the early 1950s.

Rustin, the son of West Indian immigrants, had also been drawn to the Communist movement, but broke from it in the early 1940s, working with the radical pacifist Fellowship of Reconciliation and War Resisters League, as well as with A. Philip Randolph. In 1947 he helped to organize the first "Freedom Ride" to challenge racial segregation on interstate buses traveling in the South. In 1955 he became a key aide to Rev. Martin Luther King Jr. during the Montgomery bus boycott. He played a key role in the organization of the Southern Christian Leadership Conference (SCLC), which was the organization through which King worked for the rest of his life. Attacked for his former Communist ties and his homosexuality, Rustin was temporarily sidelined in the civil rights movement, but then became the central organizer (under Randolph) of the historic 1963 civil rights march for "jobs and freedom" in Washington, D.C. While his politics increasingly adapted to Cold War anti-Communism, Rustin's outlook remained socialist, and—like Robeson—he persistently linked the struggles for racial and economic justice.

Ella Baker

While influenced by the radical currents of the 1930s that had impacted on Robeson and Rustin, Ella Baker (1903–1986) was never aligned with the Communist or Socialist Parties. Her grandparents were freed slaves who—along with other plantation laborers—were able to assume ownership of and establish a farming community on the land they had worked before emancipation. A graduate of North Carolina's Shaw University and the left-wing Brookwood Labor College, she traveled throughout the South during the 1940s as an NAACP field secretary, and later was NAACP branch president in New York City. Baker worked with Bayard Rustin, Martin Luther King Jr., and others to organize the SCLC, serving as its first executive director. A strong woman in a period that was not hospitable to strong women, and a champion of radical decentralization, in 1960 she shifted away from SCLC in order to facilitate the creation of the Student Nonviolent Coordinating Committee (SNCC). As SNCC's "godmother" she insisted on the importance of serious organizational practices and grassroots democracy, also encouraging socialist perspectives that enabled many civil rights activists to deepen their analysis of the need for fundamental changes to overcome racism. In 1964 Baker was a coordinator of the Mississippi Freedom Democratic Party, which challenged that state's white racist "regular" Democratic Party, and in later years she shifted her efforts to working through the interracial Southern Conference Educational Fund. "In order for us as poor and oppressed people to become a part of a society that is meaningful, the system under which we now exist has to be radically changed," she insisted. "I use the term radical in its original meaning—getting down to and understanding the root cause. It means facing a system that does not lend itself to your needs and devising means by which you change that system."

Baker expressed a conception of leadership and "followership" that has relevance for those discussed in this section of the present book (and also for readers of this book):

> In order to see where we are going, we not only must remember where we've been, but we must understand where we have been. This calls for a great deal of analytical thinking and evaluation of methods that have been used. We have to begin to think in terms of where do we really want to go and how we can get there.
>
> Finally, I think it is also to be said that it is not a job that is going to be done by all the people simultaneously. Some will have to be in cadres, the advanced cadres, and some will have to come later. But one of the guiding principles has to be that we cannot lead a struggle that involves masses of people without getting the people to understand what their potentials are, what their strengths are. (Grant 1998, 230–31)

5.

OVERCOMING RACISM

In this chapter we will seek an understanding of ways in which racism was overcome in the United States. As we have already seen in earlier chapters, however, it was *not* overcome in a number of important ways. We will then turn our attention to the views of Malcolm X and Martin Luther King Jr. on how this fact can be understood and what that means for "where we go from here."

ACHIEVEMENTS AND LIMITATIONS OF THE MODERN CIVIL RIGHTS MOVEMENT

The 1954 U.S. Supreme Court decision that racial segregation is a violation of the Constitution is often cited as inaugurating the modern civil rights movement. But important as this was, much more was involved than simply that.

Ferment

There were important shifts taking place in the United States that made possible the rise of this movement. Economic changes in the southern agricultural and northern industrial scenes altered black geographical, employment, and income realities. An increasing number of African Americans had migrated to urban and northern areas, found themselves in a politically freer atmosphere, and gained access to somewhat improved economic conditions. This gave greater strength to black organizations, and it also created a potential voting base in the North that could create greater pressure on elected officials than was possible in the "Jim Crow" South.

The experience of World War II—ostensibly a "people's war" against Hitlerite racism, in defense of democratic values that would embrace all of humanity—generated among some African Americans a commitment to the notion of a "double-V" effort: victory over Nazi racism overseas, victory over racism here at home. This was enhanced by the gains for blacks secured by A. Philip Randolph's March on Washington movement as the United States prepared to enter the war. "This war undeniably belongs to the Negro as well as the white man," wrote Roi Ottley in a 1943 study of life and thought in contemporary black America. "To this extent, it may be called a 'People's War'—for in spite of selfish interests a new world is a-coming with the sweep and fury of the Resurrection." Sentiment for liberation from racist oppression was sent soaring after the war by the proliferating anticolonial revolutions that swept through Asia and Africa, bringing into being an increasing number of newly independent nations of colored peoples.

The development of the U.S. Cold War confrontation against Communism, and the need to project a good image among the newly independent nations, had also created powerful pressures on the U.S. government. Indeed, in 1951 William L. Patterson, Paul Robeson, Howard Fast, and others from the Civil Rights Congress (initiated and led by members of the U.S. Communist Party) launched a dramatic campaign around a petition to the United Nations, with over two hundred pages of documentation, asserting that "the oppressed Negro citizens of the United States, segregated, discriminated against, and long the target of violence, suffer from genocide as the result of consistent, conscious, unified policies of every branch of government." Many in the circles of power were concluding that changes had to be made if the country's reputation was not to be damaged in the world's new political atmosphere.

While the modern civil rights movement emerged from the 1954 Supreme Court decision, some of the forces that would help lead it had come into being earlier. Not only was there an accumulation of experience (partly summarized above), but there were also some of the key organizations—particularly the NAACP (formed in 1909), the National Urban League (formed in 1919), the Brotherhood of Sleeping Car Porters (formed in 1925), and the Congress on Racial Equality (CORE, formed in 1942 by a religious-pacifist organization, the Fellowship of Reconciliation, led by A. J. Muste). The leaders of these organizations were prominent in the struggles of the future: Roy Wilkins of the NAACP, Whitney Young of the Urban League, A. Philip Randolph of the Brotherhood of Sleeping Car Porters, and James Farmer of CORE.

Other groups and institutions had also been playing a role that would prepare the way for the immense changes, and would help provide activists and resources for the new struggles. Some (although hardly all) churches, especially within African American communities, were forces for racial justice.* So were some (although hardly all) unions, especially among those affiliated with the Congress of Industrial Organizations (CIO), which advanced a vision of black-white unity in the struggle for economic and social justice. In the words of NAACP lawyer (later U.S. Supreme Court justice) Thurgood Marshall, "The CIO has become a Bill of Rights for Negro labor in America." There were also left-wing groups that drew a minority of whites and blacks together to oppose racism, in the North and the South, as part of a broader struggle for fundamental social change: the Socialist Party and Communist Party, revolutionary socialist followers of Leon Trotsky, and others unaffiliated with any specific group but favoring the replacement of capitalism with socialism. For a time there was a broadly liberal and antiracist Southern Conference on Human Welfare, later a much smaller and more radical Southern Conference Educational Fund. In the 1930s the Highlander Folk School was established in Tennessee by left-wing labor activists who increasingly—in the 1940s and 1950s—focused on antiracist efforts. Highlander provided education and training, resources for early civil rights activists, plus opportunities for political reflection and long-range strategizing. One of its staff members, Septima Clark, eloquently explained the importance of such an institution for social change:

> Highlander had always believed in people and the people trusted its judgment and accepted its leadership. It was accepted by Negroes and whites of all religious faiths because it had always accepted them and made them feel at home. The staff at Highlander knew that the great need of the South was to develop more people to take leadership and responsibility for the causes in which they believed. It set out on a program designed to bring out leadership qualities in people from all walks of life. (West and Mooney 1993, 223)

Especially important in the early period was the NAACP. Despite its relative moderation, it was a vital force in helping to sustain local branches of heroic activists in the 1940s and 1950s, which would provide the organizational basis

---

*Howard Thurman, in his 1949 work *Jesus and the Disinherited* (which influenced Martin Luther King Jr. and many other African American Christians), explains: "The basic fact is that Christianity as it was born in the mind of this Jewish thinker appears as a technique of survival for the oppressed," adding: "The striking similarity between the social position of Jesus in Palestine and that of the vast majority of American Negroes is obvious to anyone who long tarries over the facts." That Christianity "became, through the intervening years, a religion of the powerful and the dominant, used sometimes as an instrument of oppression, must not tempt us into believing that it was thus in the mind and life of Jesus," Thurman insists. "His message focused on the urgency of a radical change in the inner attitude of the people. He recognized fully that out of the heart are the issues of life and that no external force, however great and overwhelming, can at long last destroy a people if it does not first win the victory of the spirit against them. . . . The disinherited will know for themselves that there is a Spirit at work in life and in the hearts of men which is committed to overcoming the world."

for much of what was to come. More than this, its legal staff brilliantly utilized the courts to challenge various manifestations of institutionalized racism.

The Movement Emerges

It was through the legal battles of the NAACP that racial segregation in public education was finally declared a violation of the Fourteenth Amendment of the U.S. Constitution in the 1954 Supreme Court decision *Brown* v. *Board of Education*. This did not end racial segregation, but it opened the way for effective legal and social protest struggles which finally dismantled the Jim Crow system— although this took many years, immense effort, and a number of lives.

In 1955, a local NAACP activist named Rosa Parks was arrested in Montgomery, Alabama, for refusing to obey a segregation law requiring her to give up her bus seat to a white man. E. D. Nixon, a local leader of the Brotherhood of Sleeping Car Porters and the NAACP, helped to organize a coalition to boycott the buses, but the most famous figure to emerge from this victorious struggle was Rev. Martin Luther King Jr. (Parks, Nixon, and King all had contact with Highlander Folk School.) In 1956 King and others formed another key organization, the Southern Christian Leadership Conference (SCLC). In addition to a large number of African American ministers, a number of women—such as longtime NAACP activist Ella Baker and Highlander's Septima Clark—played important roles in making this an effective organization. Influenced by the independence movement in India led by Mohandas Gandhi, King and others advanced the tactic of nonviolent direct action to challenge unjust laws, designed to minimize violence, to help win public support, and to pressure the U.S. government to compel the Southern state and local governments to stop violating the Fourteenth Amendment.

Other challenges were pushed forward against institutionalized racism in the South, for example in Little Rock, Arkansas—where in 1957 violent white mobs sought to prevent court-ordered desegregation, and U.S. troops were brought in to protect the nine black schoolchildren who were integrating a previously all-white high school. In reaction to such developments, Ku Klux Klan activities (in some cases coordinated with local "law enforcement" efforts) plus more "respectable" White Citizens Councils proliferated throughout the South.

By 1960 a new organization came into being, started by black college students (soon joined by some white students as well) who organized lunch counter sit-ins to desegregate eating facilities, first in Greensboro, North Carolina, and then elsewhere. The new group was called the Student Nonviolent Coordinating Committee (SNCC). But the other groups also continued to mount antisegregation efforts. SCLC waged desegregation campaigns in Albany, Georgia, and elsewhere—then launched an important campaign in Montgomery, Alabama. In 1962 CORE, largely a northern organization, initiated "Freedom Rides" (modeled on similar efforts of twenty years earlier) which involved integrated black and white civil rights activists boarding Greyhound buses destined for the South, where they would maintain desegregated seating arrangements on the buses and also desegregate bus station facilities. In some cases they met with beatings and bus-burnings.

Ella Baker tried to explain the difference she found between the more moderate older groups and the more radical newer ones. "The NAACP, Urban League, etc., do not change society, they want to get in," she noted, whereas for a group like SNCC "it's a combination of concern with the black [equal rights] goal for itself and, beyond that, with [changing] the whole society, because this is the acid test of whether the outs can get in and share in equality and worth." She added: "By worth, I mean creativity, a contribution to society" (West and Mooney 1993, 198).

Nonetheless, despite their differences, the working coalition of civil rights organizations gave immense strength to the efforts to challenge and dismantle the Jim Crow system. And the civil rights tide was irreversible. Beatings, burnings, bombings, police assaults, massive jailings, and the murder of a number of civil rights activists proved incapable of preventing the advance of the movement— which increasingly turned its attention also to securing voting rights for African Americans in the South.

In 1963, A. Philip Randolph was able to use his prestige within the black community and civil rights movement to engineer a national "March on Washington for Jobs and Freedom." It was sponsored by a coalition of the major civil rights organizations with some major labor and religious groups, drawing more than 250,000 participants. The emphasis on "*jobs* and freedom" highlighted Randolph's conviction that racial justice and a broader economic justice are necessarily interconnected. It was here that the famous "I Have a Dream" speech was delivered by Martin Luther King Jr.

The Strategic Vision

King and Randolph shared a strategic vision of how racism is to be overcome, and the achievements and tragedy of the modern civil rights movement cannot be understood unless we consider that vision. They had a profound grasp of all forms of racism: individual (both conscious and unconscious) as well as institutional (both the legal form predominant in the South and the de facto form predominant in the North). They recognized that it made sense to focus the antiracist struggle where racism was most vulnerable (given the new national and world situation after World War II)—against the Southern Jim Crow system. If the struggle was both militant and nonviolent, it would be possible to win victories and at the same time to help increasing numbers of whites to push back within and among themselves various forms of conscious and unconscious racism.

One aspect of the erosion of unconscious racism among whites involved their moving beyond the conception of their own "whiteness" and in many cases realizing the oppression experienced by their own ethnic group. "There were people who came South to work in the movement who were not black," recalled Bernice Johnson Reagon. "Most of them were white when they came. Before it was over, that category broke up—you know, some of them were Jewish, not simply white, and some others even changed their names. Say if it was Mary when they came South, by the time they were finished it was Maria, right?" She emphasized: "It's called finding yourself. At some point, you cannot be fighting oppression and be oppressed yourself and not feel it" (Anderson and Hill Collins 1995, 546).

Other divisions no less capable of splintering the privileged category of "whiteness" involve the existence of socioeconomic classes—the dividing line between the very rich and everybody else, between the blue-collar and white-collar working-class majority and the elite of business owners and executives above them who seek to control and profit from their labor. The majority of blacks and whites happened to be part of this majority class. But such shifts in identity consciousness among whites—involving a further erosion of racism— would have the possibility of coming to the fore only when the civil rights move-ment transcended the focus on legal segregation in the South.

And at a certain point, Randolph and King believed, it *would* become nec-essary to challenge the de facto form of institutionalized racism prevalent in the North. This could only be done effectively by attacking its underlying economic roots, which in turn could only be done effectively by developing a broader pro-gram for economic justice. While such a program would be initiated by blacks, it would be powerfully relevant to a majority of whites. The resulting interracial coalition for economic justice would have the dual function of eliminating the roots of institutional racism and creating an atmosphere of idealism and common struggle that would help to further push back various forms of individual (con-scious and unconscious) racism. This orientation was advanced at a conference held just after the 1963 March on Washington, reported by the perceptive inde-pendent journalist I. F. Stone:

On that dismal rainy morning-after, in a dark union hall in the Negro section [of Washington, D.C.], I heard A. Philip Randolph speak with an eloquence and a humanity few can achieve. When he spoke of the abolitionists, and of the heroes of the Reconstruction, it was with a filial piety and an immediacy that made them live again. One felt the presence of a great American. He reminded the black nationalists gently that "we must not forget that the civil rights revolution was begun by white people as well as black at a time when the winds of hate were sweeping the country." He reminded the moderates that political equality was not enough. "The white sharecroppers of the South," he pointed out, "have full civil rights but live in bleakest poverty." One began to understand what was meant by a march for "*jobs* and freedom." For most Negroes, civil rights alone will only be the right to join the underprivileged whites. "We must liberate not only ourselves," Mr. Randolph said, "but our white brothers and sisters."

The direction in which full emancipation lies was indicated when Mr. Randolph spoke of the need to extend the public sector of the economy. His brilliant assistant on the March, Bayard Rustin, urged an economic Master Plan to deal with the technological unemployment that weighs so heavily on the Negro and threatens to create a permanently depressed class of whites and blacks living previously on the edges of an otherwise affluent society. It was clear from the discussion that neither tax cuts nor public works nor job training (for what jobs?) would solve the problem while automation with giant steps made so many workers obsolete. The civil rights movement, Mr. Rustin said, could not get beyond a certain level unless it merged into a broader plan of social change. (Stone 1968, 123–24)

The importance of such an approach was highlighted in an analysis, *The Economics of Equality*, elaborated by Tom Kahn within the framework articulated by Randolph and Rustin. He pointed out that racism was being sustained by a combination of two factors: "the weight of centuries of past discrimination combining with portentous economic forces that are themselves color-blind." What was most decisive were the economic forces. In a sense, according to Kahn's analysis, the northward migration of African Americans from World War I up to the 1960s constituted the last great wave of "immigration" into the industrial North. The earlier immigrant waves from Europe had been absorbed into the U.S. economy during a period of industrial development. But economic changes were now resulting in the closing off of such possibilities for African Americans.

In the period of 1940 to 1953 blacks had made genuine economic gains and had begun to close the gap between blacks and whites (for example, the unemployment gap between the two dropped from 25 percent to 13 percent). But technological innovations and other shifts in the economy were leading to a gradual erosion of the relatively well paying unskilled and semiskilled jobs that had provided substantial employment and income for much of the working class in earlier times. Thus, while in the relatively prosperous postwar period, the unemployment rate among blacks was about 60 percent higher than the white rate, since 1954 it had become at least 200 percent higher. In the absence of the "radical programs for the abolition of poverty and unemployment," Kahn warned, "persistent economic inequalities will undermine the drive toward legal and social equality."

In 1966 Randolph issued *A "Freedom Budget" for All Americans*, endorsed by over two hundred prominent civil rights, labor, and social activists and academic figures. He described the Freedom Budget as being dedicated "to the full goals of the 1963 March." One of its strongest supporters was Martin Luther

King Jr., who insisted that "the ultimate answer to the Negroes' economic dilemma will be found in a massive federal program for all the poor along the lines of A. Philip Randolph's Freedom Budget, a kind of Marshall Plan for the disadvantaged." Randolph himself elaborated on the Freedom Budget's specifics (involving a ten-year federal expenditure of $180 billion) and its meaning:

> The "Freedom Budget" spells out a specific and factual course of action, step by step, to start in early 1967 toward the practical liquidation of poverty in the United States by 1975. The programs urged in the "Freedom Budget" attack *all* of the major causes of poverty—unemployment and underemployment; substandard pay, inadequate social insurance and welfare payments to those who cannot or should not be employed; bad housing; deficiencies in health services, education, and training; and fiscal and monetary policies which tend to redistribute income regressively rather than progressively. The "Freedom Budget" leaves no room for discrimination in any form, because its programs are addressed to *all* who need more opportunity and improved incomes and living standards—not just to some of them. (Randolph 1966)

Randolph explained that such programs "are essential to the Negro and other minority groups striving for dignity and economic security in our society," but that "the abolition of poverty (almost three-quarters of whose victims are white) can be accomplished only through action which embraces the totality of the victims of poverty, neglect, and injustice." He added that "in the process everyone will benefit, for poverty is not an isolated circumstance affecting only those entrapped by it. It reflects—and affects—the performance of our national economy, our rate of economic growth, our ability to produce and consume, the condition of our cities, the levels of our social services and needs, the very quality of our lives." In Randolph's opinion the success of this effort would depend on "a mighty coalition among the civil rights and labor movements, liberal and religious forces, students and intellectuals—the coalition expressed in the historic 1963 March on Washington for Jobs and Justice."

The realization that such a course was necessary to achieve the goals of the civil rights movement propelled Martin Luther King and the Southern Christian Leadership Conference to begin focusing more sharply on economic struggles in the last year of King's life, such as the Poor People's Campaign and union organizing efforts of the striking sanitation workers in Memphis, Tennessee.

Victory and Crisis

The wisdom of this approach was highlighted by the achievements of the civil rights movement, which made clear the *limits* of those achievements. In 1964 a coalition of major civil rights organizations, spearheaded by SNCC, launched a massive and truly heroic Freedom Summer project in Mississippi. Young black and white activists, many of them volunteers from the North, flooded into the state to help carry out educational work and voter registration, and to help organize a powerful challenge to the white segregationist Democratic Party there, in the form of the Mississippi Freedom Democratic Party. In 1965 SCLC had also mobilized national protests in Selma, Alabama. In both cases, racist violence was met by nonviolent antiracist persistence and tremendous national (and international) attention. Such pressure helped to generate a succession of Civil Rights Acts (1964, 1965, and 1968) and the Voting Rights Act (1965), legally eliminating the Jim Crow system. Poet and civil rights veteran June Jordan gives a vivid sense of what the civil rights movement had been about:

> Repeatedly, we marched and we sang and we kneeled and we prayed and we sat down at coffee shop counters and we rode Greyhound buses and we attempted to use public bathrooms or we tried to stop our thirst by drinking a little cold water from public water fountains. And we did all of this at the risk of our multitudinous black lives because we believed, absolutely, we believed in something almost holy. . . . We did not believe that we could alter the ideological bent of those ever devising new systems for the degradation of the weak and the poor. But we believed that our fierce and our massive and our nonviolent rebellions against racist tyranny would lead to a changing of the laws of this country. We believed in the law. . . . Our route to redemption was the law. . . . (Jordan 1985, 99)

The massive nonviolent struggle in communities throughout the South in the 1960s was often met by violence. Many civil rights activists faced arrests, beatings, and threats to livelihood and life itself. Some lost their lives. But many thousands of heroines and heroes persisted and moved forward in actions and campaigns described by Anne Braden, Taylor Branch, Clayborne Carson, and others. And finally, through all the struggle and sacrifice and rising expectation, the laws were changed and the Jim Crow system dismantled.

Yet, the racially oppressed condition of African Americans continued. The growing frustrations of the growing and relatively impoverished African American populations in urban areas created a volatile situation. One or another incident during the "long, hot summers" of 1963 through 1968 could often spark violent confrontations and riots in one or another (actually several, then many) of the black ghetto areas throughout the nation.

In 1967 President Lyndon Johnson appointed a National Advisory Commission on Civil Disorders, which in the following year issued a massive, fact-filled report on the causes of the riots. The commission found "twelve deeply held grievances," felt at different levels of intensity, which contributed to the uprisings. These are worth listing because they were relevant well before 1967, and continued to be relevant for the rest of the twentieth century.

First Level of Intensity
1. Police practices
2. Unemployment and underemployment
3. Inadequate housing

Second Level of Intensity
4. Inadequate education
5. Poor recreation facilities and programs
6. Ineffectiveness of the political structure and grievance mechanisms

Third Level of Intensity
7. Disrespectful white attitudes
8. Discriminatory administration of justice
9. Inadequacy of federal programs
10. Inadequacy of municipal services
11. Discriminatory consumer and credit practices
12. Inadequate welfare programs

Surveying the deteriorating condition of the African American inner-city communities, the commission saw these as generating deep frustrations among blacks whose expectations had been raised by the civil rights movement. Out of this came both the specific grievances listed above and the violent protests (the riots) against those grievances. But the analysis of the commission went further. Comparing the deteriorating condition of black communities to the relatively better condition of white communities, which had been created in large measure through an exodus of whites from the inner-city (largely to avoid living with blacks), the commission concluded: "Our nation is moving toward two societies, one black and one white—separate and unequal."

Significantly, a 1966 effort by King and SCLC to challenge de facto racism in northern housing, designed to remove such barriers between black and white communities, led to only a hollow victory. An application of the nonviolent tactic of "creative tension" to help overcome the deep-rooted patterns of segregation in housing in Chicago powerfully revealed the racial fear and hatred in that area's white neighborhoods. Violent mobs of whites turned out to confront and attack the interracial demonstrations. Also revealed, however, was a combination of thinly veiled bigotry and manipulative skill on the part of the Democratic machine that ran the city. A "victory"—in the form of promises that were not kept—resulted in no significant change.

Militancy and Decline

A growing number of African Americans—including civil rights activists—were beginning to find persuasive the dynamic message of Malcolm X, a militant black nationalist and Muslim who had been assassinated in 1965. In his famous speech "The Ballot or the Bullet," he explained:

> All of us have suffered here, in this country, political oppression at the hands of the white man, economic exploitation at the hands of the white man, and social degradation at the hands of the white man. Now speaking like this doesn't mean that we're anti-white, but it does mean we're anti-exploitation, we're anti-degradation, we're anti-oppression. And if the white man doesn't want us to be anti-him, let him stop oppressing and exploiting and degrading us. . . .
>
> If we don't do something real soon, I think you'll have to agree that we're going to be forced to use the ballot or the bullet. It's one or the other in 1964. It isn't that time is running out—time has run out! . . . I'm not a Democrat, I'm not a Republican, and I don't even consider myself an American. If you and I were Americans, there'd be no problem. . . . No, I'm not an American. I'm one of the 22 million black people who are the victims of Americanism. One of the 22 million black people who are victims of democracy, nothing but disguised hypocrisy. . . . I'm speaking as a victim of this American system. And I see America through the eyes of the victim. I don't see any American dream; I see an American nightmare. . . .
>
> We're behind where we were in 1954. There's more segregation now than there was in 1954. There's more racial animosity, more racial hatred, more racial violence today in 1964, than there was in 1954. Where is the progress? . . . This government has failed the Negro. This so-called democracy has failed the Negro. And all these white liberals have definitely failed the Negro. . . . To those of us whose philosophy is black nationalism, the only way you can get involved in the civil rights movement is give it a new interpretation. . . . And these handkerchief-heads who have been dillydallying and pussyfooting and compromising—we don't intend to let them pussyfoot and dillydally and compromise any longer. . . .
>
> African Americans—that's what we are—Africans who are in America. You're nothing but Africans. . . . The political philosophy of black nationalism means that the black man should control the politics and the politicians in his community; no more [than that]. . . . The economic philosophy of black nationalism is pure and simple. It only means that we should control the economy of our community. . . . Why should the economy of our community be in the hands of the white man?. . . . The social philosophy of black nationalism only means that we have to get together and remove the evils, the vices, the alcoholism, drug addiction, and other evils that are destroying the moral fiber of our community.

Such views became prevalent within SNCC beginning in 1966 in the form of the "black power" orientation. Many sectors of the black freedom movement shifted

from the seemingly discredited "civil rights" label to a more radical "black liberation" label. The new urban-based Black Panther Party's call for "armed self-
defense" gained support among many young activists. Some of the Black
Panthers' more thoughtful members sought to build a revolutionary nationalist
alternative that would learn from and move beyond previous efforts. But as the
militant black lawyer Conrad Lynn later commented, some Panthers' "foolhardy
courage" resulted in provocative statements and actions that made it seem "almost
as if they were prepared to commit suicide." A glorification of violence and a
descent into destructive internal dynamics opened the group to victimization by
the authorities and a disintegration of morale, which soon destroyed it. SNCC also
passed out of existence. Other currents were more successful in applying radical
insights to durable efforts for social justice (for example, among black auto
workers and others drawn to such groups as the Revolutionary League of Black
Workers, and among some of the activists involved in the National Black Political
Convention, which drew over three thousand people in 1972). Yet this black liberation movement did not succeed where the civil rights movement had failed.

And failure was certainly what the civil rights effort experienced in the years
following 1966. There had been some hopes that a breakthrough toward economic
justice might be made with the federal government's War on Poverty, launched in
1964 with over $947 million. Yet the funds were channeled through an elaborate
bureaucracy—the Office of Economic Opportunity—which served to neutralize
many activists by giving them high-paying jobs while deflecting serious efforts to
attack the roots of poverty and racism. Another outcome, August Meier and Elliott
Rudwick observed, was that "the antipoverty program unintentionally served to
increase the frustration and discontent among the black poor by further escalating
their expectations but failing to deliver anything substantial." This contributed to
escalating "civil disorders" and intensifying racial tensions.

The Freedom Budget, on the other hand, proved far too radical for most of
the politicians in whom Randolph and King had placed their hopes. Randolph's
strategic perspective involved the assumption that a Democratic-controlled Congress and White House could be induced to embrace and implement the Freedom
Budget. But his top aide Bayard Rustin (according to biographer Jervis
Anderson) found that

> the Freedom Budget "didn't sell"—not under the Lyndon Johnson presidency
> and surely not under that of his conservative successor, Richard Nixon. Johnson
> was preoccupied with the war in Vietnam. And Nixon had made his position
> clear while running for the White House in 1968: "The demand for a Freedom
> Budget, amounting to billions of dollars for the poor, is not the road to bring
> people out of poverty into the sunshine of self-respect and human dignity."
> (Anderson 1997, 289–90)

Ironically, the year before the Freedom Budget was put forward, Rustin had identified the moderate orientation that would render it "unrealistic":

> During the first New York school boycott, the *New York Times* editorialized that Negro demands, while abstractly just, would necessitate massive reforms, the funds for which could not realistically be anticipated; therefore the just demands were also foolish demands and would only antagonize white people. Moderates of this stripe are often correct in perceiving the difficulty or impossibility of racial progress in the context as fixed. . . . They apparently see nothing strange in the fact that in the last twenty-five years we have spent nearly a trillion dollars fighting or preparing for wars, yet throw up our hands before the need for over-hauling our schools, clearing the slums, and really abolishing poverty. My quarrel with these moderates is that they do not even envision radical change; their admonitions of moderation are, for all practical purposes, admonitions to the Negro to adjust to the status quo, and are therefore immoral. (Rustin 1971, 116)

Obviously, the rejection of the Freedom Budget was bipartisan. A fatal flaw in their strategy was the inability of Randolph and Rustin to break with a two-party politics that was tied to the capitalist system and would not accept their radicalism. An aging and defeated Randolph commented acidly that "this system is a market economy in which investment and production are determined more by the anticipation of profits than by the desire to achieve social justice."

The Price of Failure

King, who had broken with the mainstream of the Democratic Party through his opposition to the Vietnam War, was uncertain as to the way forward. "The decade of 1955 to 1965, with its obstructive elements, misled us. Everyone underestimated the amount of rage Negroes were suppressing, and the amount of bigotry the white majority was disguising." He conceded that "the movement for social change has entered a time of temptation to despair, because it is clear now how deep and how systematic are the evils it confronts." He argued that "we must formulate a program, and we must fashion the new tactics which do not count on government good will, but instead compel unwilling authorities to yield to the mandates of justice."

Just before his assassination, King was still grappling with the dilemma of how to rebuild an effective movement as the old one was splintering, in part over the Vietnam War. Some portions were hurtling into an ultraradical direction that would prove to be politically ineffective. Others (including Randolph and Rustin, in spite of themselves) were drawing back from the struggle in order to maintain a positive relationship with the Democratic Party leadership. King's hopes were with the Poor People's Campaign: "The dispossessed of this nation—the poor, both white and Negro—live in a cruelly unjust society. They must organize a rev-olution against that injustice, not against the lives of the persons who are their fellow citizens, but against the structures through which the society is refusing to take means which have been called for, and which are at hand, to lift the load of poverty." But time ran out for him in 1968, when he was cut down by an assassin's bullet. In reaction, riots erupted in 125 cities.

In the years that followed, African Americans and the country as a whole paid a high price over the defeat of the economic justice orientation underlying the Freedom Budget and the Poor People's Campaign. The civil rights movement slowly disintegrated—conducting various campaigns without the strong sense of purpose and morale that had characterized it in earlier years. Some black activists burned themselves out in unsuccessful confrontations. Others were able to grad-uate from protest to finding career security in one or another profession, in many cases seeking to be of service to their people, but also doing better as part of an enlarged "black middle class" than would be possible for the great majority of African Americans. A growing number sought to advance their fortunes, and the fortunes of African Americans, through successful political careers. In some cities, in fact, the notion of "black power" was translated into growing represen-tation on city councils and in some cases the election of black mayors, repeating a pattern of earlier ethnic groups. The resulting dilemma was discussed by econ-omists Raymond Franklin and Solomon Resnik in 1973:

> The city that blacks will inherit if they achieve control is very different from that inhabited by other immigrant groups. The city that blacks may inherit is one des-perately lacking financial resources; while it may present them with the appear-ance of power, the actual power they will have to change things may be less than anticipated. One facet of this relates to the changing surface of the metropolitan area, for example, the movement of the white middle and upper classes to new suburban communities, the flight of industry (along with job opportunities) from the central cities, and the deterioration of the city's public facilities.

Franklin and Resnik described what would become distinguishing character-istics of the growing urban crisis in much of the United States, which would be part and parcel of the economic and social decline of black America. The situa-tion of the majority of African Americans continued to decline, as Randolph and King had warned, and as Malcolm X had predicted.

In a 1976 preface to his updated classic *Blaming the Victim*, William Ryan indicated that the problems were actually impacting on the great majority of Americans:

> Since 1970, I have enlarged my vision of who the "victims" in American society really are. I had been focusing primarily on the plight of the poor and of blacks.

In fact, everyone who depends for the sustenance of himself and his family on salary and wages, and who does not have a separate source of income through some substantial ownership of wealth, is a potential victim in America. He is vulnerable to the disaster of catastrophic illness in a private enterprise medical care system; he is vulnerable to the deliberate manipulation of inflation and unemployment; he is vulnerable to the burden of grossly unfair taxes; he is vulnerable to the endemic pollution of air and food and to the unattended hazards of the factory and the highway that will likely kill him before his time; he is vulnerable to the greed of the great oil companies and food corporations.

The victims in American society are not simply the 10 percent of us who are black, the 15 percent or so who are officially below the "poverty line." The majority of us who are nonblack and, officially at least, nonpoor, are also victims. At least two-thirds, perhaps three-fourths of us are relatively poor compared to the standards of the top 10 or 5 percent, and relatively vulnerable. Others own America, we're just the workers, whether we realize it or not.

The deterioration accelerated in the 1980s and was not reversed in the 1990s. "For nearly two decades," in the words of Cornel West, "we witnessed a decline in the real wages of most Americans, and a new racial divide in the minds and streets of fellow citizens, a massive transfer of wealth from working people to the well-to-do, and an increase in drugs and guns (along with fear and violence) in American life." West added that "many conservative Republicans played the old racial card to remain in office and most liberal Democrats lacked the courage to tell the truth about the new levels of decline and decay engulfing us" (West 1994, 157–58).

WHERE DO WE GO FROM HERE?

From our survey of the history of racism and antiracist struggles in the United States, it may be possible to approach with some realism the question of "where we go from here" in the effort to overcome racism.

It is unlikely that racism can be "dismantled" easily—and some have suggested that it cannot be dismantled at all. Derrick Bell is not the only thoughtful commentator to suggest that "black people will never gain full equality in this country. . . . We must acknowledge it, not as a sign of submission, but as an ultimate act of defiance." He adds: "Only in this way can we prevent ourselves from being dragged down by society's racial hostility. Beyond survival lies the potential to perceive more clearly both a reason and a further means for struggle" (Bell 1992, 12).

Others don't accept this pessimism. "We must keep moving," exhorts Vincent Harding, "to engage at every level in the continuing struggle which seeks to turn 'the whole future of America' toward the last best movements of our brother,

Martin, and then to burst beyond. . . . Let Martin Luther King Jr. be our guide to the Twenty-first Century. Then, holding the children and keeping faith with our own best possibilities, let us move forward" (Harding 1997, 114, 137).

Understanding the Insights of Malcolm X

Given the experience of the past forty years, it seems to be a valid question whether the future will bring us to the American dream or the American night-mare. The two great betrayals which African Americans have endured—the betrayal of the Reconstruction promises in the 1870s and the betrayal of the civil rights promises a century later—pose the question of whether the black nation-alist orientation that runs from Martin Delany to Marcus Garvey to Malcolm X is not the most realistic path for black liberation.

Malcolm X was the foremost spokesman of the Nation of Islam (NOI, also known as the Black Muslims) until his 1964 break with NOI leader Elijah Muhammed. The NOI had a powerful impact among African Americans in the 1960s, and has had a resurgence in the 1980s and 1990s under current leader Louis Farrakhan. But it has been primarily a religious organization. Historically the NOI has sought to improve the condition of African Americans not by changing the larger white-dominated society but by condemning and separating from it. The development of black nationalism by Malcolm X as an overtly polit-ical perspective was one of the causes of his break from the NOI.*

Many whites have found it difficult to understand the insights of black nationalism that Malcolm X articulated. But they have become commonplace even among many African Americans who don't necessarily consider themselves "black nationalist." And they must become part of any serious framework for understanding and dealing with the problem of race in the United States.

"Malcolm X was the first great black spokesperson who looked ferocious white racism in the eye, didn't blink, and lived long enough to tell America the truth about this glaring hypocrisy in a bold and defiant manner," according to Cornel West, who also comments that "he did not live long enough to forge his own distinctive ideas and ways of channeling black rage in constructive channels to change American society." James Cone makes a similar point:

---

*In recent years Louis Farrakhan has led the NOI in the direction of more direct political engagement, especially through initiating and organizing the 1995 Million Man March, one of the most impressive political actions of the decade, hailed even by many who dissent from Farrakhan's antiwhite rhetoric and sometime anti-Semitism. And yet Farrakhan's own speech at the gathering focused more on spiritual than political themes, and there was no effort to make the event into an effective force for black rights. The U.S. Congress was on the verge of making various leislative deci-sions detrimental to African Americans, but as Rev. Jesse Jackson later complained, the Million Man March had "essentially a religious theme—atonement—disconnected from public policy."

What most people did not like about Malcolm was actually his strength: speaking the truth about the black condition in America in clear, forceful, and uncomplicated language. He was not tactful because he believed that "diplomacy fools people." "It's better to be frank," he said, "then you know how each other thinks." But whites, as well as many blacks, did not like Malcolm's frankness. It merely made it easy for most of them to dismiss him as a fanatic or an extremist. Malcolm did not mind the labels that people put on him as long as he knew he was telling the truth. When accused of being an extremist, he shot back: "Yes, I'm an extremist. The black race in North America is in extremely bad condition. You show me a black man who is not an extremist and I'll show you one who needs psychiatric attention!" (Cone 1995, 118–19)

While this quality remained constant throughout his political career, Patricia Hill Collins comments that "Malcolm X's definition of race and his perceptions of the connections among race, color, and political consciousness changed." She describes his earlier thinking as involving "biologically essentialist definitions of race" that projected darker complexions among blacks as superior to lighter complexions, that viewed blacks as inherently superior to whites, and that viewed racism as "a political, economic, and social system [that] rests on the foundation of a biological definition of race." His black nationalist philosophy was affected by this, and it was also affected by the fact that his views changed: "Relinquishing this biological essentialism in the last year of his life opened the doors for a greatly reformulated black nationalism, one encompassing different notions of black political consciousness and the types of political coalitions that blacks might forge with other groups." (Wood 1992, 61). This comes through in the Basic Unity Program of the Organization for Afro-American Unity (OAAU) which he established shortly before his death:

We Afro-Americans feel receptive toward all people of goodwill. We are not opposed to multi-ethnic associations in any walk of life. In fact, we have had experiences which enable us to understand how unfortunate it is that human beings have been set apart or aside from each other because of characteristics known as "racial" characteristics.

However, Afro-Americans did not create the prejudiced background and atmosphere in which we live. And we must face the facts. A "racial" society does exist in stark reality, and not with equality for black people; so we who are nonwhite must meet the problems inherited from centuries of inequalities and deal with the present situations as rationally as we are able.

The exclusive ethnic quality of our unity is necessary for self-preservation. We say this because: Our experiences backed up by history show that African culture and Afro-American culture will not be respectably expressed nor be secure in its survival if we remain the divided, and therefore helpless, victims of an oppressive society.

We appreciate the fact that when the people involved have real equality and justice, ethnic intermingling can be beneficial to all. We must denounce, however, all people who are lacking in justice in their dealings with other people, whether the injustices proceed from power, class, or "race." We must be unified in order to be protected from abuse or misuse. (Breitman 1968, 119)

In seeking to understand what is essential to black nationalism, George Breitman once suggested: "It is the tendency for black people in the United States to unite as a group, as a people, into a movement of their own to fight for freedom, justice, and equality. Animated by the desire of an oppressed minority to decide its own destiny, this tendency holds that black people must control their own movement and the political, economic, and social institutions of the black community. Its characteristic attributes include racial pride, group consciousness, hatred of white supremacy, a striving for independence from white control, and identification with black and nonwhite oppressed groups in other parts of the world" (Breitman 1968, 55–56).

Patricia Hill Collins has added: "The importance of being able to distinguish worthwhile political coalitions from dangerous ones becomes increasingly important to an African American community in today's complex multiethnic, multinational political economy." This concern for coalitions—particularly relevant for matters raised in the next section of this chapter—implies a synthesis of the orientations represented by Malcolm X and Martin Luther King. At the same time, if the distinctive perspective represented by Malcolm X is not to be diluted out of existence, potential coalition partners would need to recognize the following points:

1. African Americans are an oppressed people (or national group, or ethnic group), who must define themselves as they seek to survive and overcome their oppression. They must resist being defined by members of the group that has oppressed them (even by well-meaning members of that group).
2. African Americans must control their own organizations, their own struggles, their own institutions, their own communities. It is not acceptable for members of the group that has oppressed them (even well-meaning members of that group) to determine their goals, activities, and future.
3. In short, African Americans have the right to self-determination—to determine their own future independently of the white society in which they have been oppressed.

Adolph Reed Jr. has commented that "Malcolm made his reputation by attacking entrenched elites and challenging their attempts to constrain popular action and the vox populi [voice of the people]. Now he is canonized as an icon, an instrument of an agenda that is just the opposite of popular mobilization" (Wood 1992, 232). But those who respect what he was must reject this effort to make him "safe," and those who are serious in the struggle to overcome racism must hold fast to his most basic insights.

Advancing the Vision of Martin Luther King Jr.

Whichever way one sees it, the struggle against racism will not yield an easy victory. Nor will any substantial pushing back of racism come simply through the generous application of goodwill. Moralistic appeals are not enough. "Negroes must convince the majority, who are white, that continued oppression of the Negro minority hurts the white majority too," Kenneth Clark warned in 1965, a notion that had long been grasped by such figures as Randolph and King. The implications of this are important for building an interracial majority for racial and economic justice along the lines of *The "Freedom Budget" for All Americans*.

Yet Clark also expressed the somewhat more problematical view that "the value of ethical appeals is to be found only when they can be harnessed to more concrete appeals such as economic, political, or other power advantages to be derived *from those with the power to facilitate or inhibit change*." It is necessary to stress, as Clark does, the importance of turning moral sentiments into a moral force that can be mobilized in support *of specific and winnable demands*. But there is an additional point that seems to be implicit in Clark's reasoning: certain government officials, political officeholders, and powerful business leaders must see that changes for social justice will be in their interest. This suggests a reliance on figures and forces within the upper levels of the political and economic power structure. This is, in fact, an aspect of the civil rights victories that were won in the 1950s and 1960s.

There are two potential problems that make this "implicit" point problematical:

1. Gains won through an understanding between a black protest movement and a white power structure potentially leave out the majority of whites who are not in the power structure, and this can generate a "white backlash" of those not included (as it did), which can be pulled into a racist counteroffensive and mobilized as an effective pressure in opposition to the gains secured by the protest movement.

2. There may be some changes which are necessary for the elimination of racism that a decisive sector of government officials and business leaders will oppose because those changes fundamentally threaten their power and privileges, so that yesterday's tacit allies become today's sophisticated opponents (who may be willing to "buy off" protest leaders, and

even to offer limited reforms beneficial to a few, but not to eliminate those aspects of institutional racism that keep the majority in an oppressed condition).

This was the dilemma that ultimately faced Martin Luther King. It is worth considering at length his reflections on the situation in his final speech to the Southern Christian Leadership Conference, "Where Do We Go from Here," that he offered in 1967:

> I want to say to you as I move to my conclusion, as we talk about "Where do we go from here," that we honestly face the fact that the movement must address itself to the question of restructuring the whole of American society. There are forty million poor people here. And one day we must ask the question, "Why are there forty million poor people in America?" And when you begin to ask that question, you are raising questions about the economic system, about a broader distribution of wealth. When you ask that question, you begin to question the capitalistic economy. And I'm simply saying that more and more we've got to begin to ask questions about the whole society. . . .
>
> Now when I say question the whole society, it means ultimately coming to see that the problem of racism, the problem of economic exploitation, and the problem of war are all tied together. These are the triple evils that are interrelated.
>
> If you will let me be a preacher for just a little bit—One night, a juror came to Jesus and he wanted to know what he could do to be saved. Jesus didn't get bogged down in the kind of isolated approach of what he shouldn't do. Jesus didn't say, "Now Nicodemus, you must stop lying." He didn't say, "Nicodemus, you must stop cheating if you are doing that." He didn't say, "Nicodemus, you must stop committing adultery." He didn't say, "Nicodemus, now you must stop drinking liquor if you are doing that excessively." He said something altogether different, because Jesus realized something basic—that if a man will lie, he will steal. And if a man will steal, he will kill. So instead of just getting bogged down in one thing, Jesus looked at him and said, "Nicodemus, you must be born again."
>
> He said, in other words, "Your whole structure must be changed." A nation that will keep people in slavery for 244 years will "thingify" them—make them things. Therefore they will exploit them, and poor people generally, economically. And a nation that will exploit economically will have to have foreign investments and everything else, and will have to use its military might to protect them. All of these problems are tied together. What I am saying today is that we must go from this convention and say, "America, you must be born again!"

What King offers here is the key insight that racism cannot be overcome if it is abstracted from the larger set of interconnected problems facing society as a whole. The problem with this is that it necessarily calls for radical solutions that the existing power structure will not be willing to consider. What King was trying to do, in the final year of his life, was to begin organizing a massive inter-racial movement that would be capable of creating a new balance of power. "The dispossessed of this nation—the poor, both white and Negro—live in a cruelly unjust society," King argued. "They must organize a revolution against that injustice, not against the lives of the persons who are their fellow citizens, but against the structures through which society is refusing to take means which have been called for, and which are at hand, to lift the load of poverty."*

In supporting the Freedom Budget and initiating the Poor People's Cam-paign, King was targeting the economic structures that are responsible for the persistence of institutional racism oppressing African Americans but which at the same time oppress a majority of whites. Such an interracial struggle for eco-nomic justice would help to push back the various forms of conscious and uncon-scious individual racism, just as the earlier civil rights movement had done.

The civil rights movement certainly involved moral appeals, but its victories were not won through abstract moralizing. Its strategy was related to historic possibilities that had evolved in the course of the twentieth century, and its prac-tical organizing was related to actual dynamics developing in society. This is vitally important as we look at the political, economic, and cultural develop-ments that have taken place since the 1960s.

The cultural developments are quite important. If we consider what has now become common in the mass media, public life, and popular culture of the United States, there seems to be a more widely shared sense today than in the 1960s that ours is a multiracial and multicultural society. The influx of additional ethnic groups from Asian and Latin American origins also contributes to many Ameri-cans seeing ours as a land of diversity and variety. The fact that Martin Luther King's birthday is a national holiday—while critical questions can be raised about how widely or deeply King's message is understood or accepted—is not without significance. As we have already seen, this hardly means that racism has been eliminated, but certain aspects of it have been pushed back somewhat, increasing the base of support in our country for the goal of racial justice.

There are other developments, no less important, that are far more grim. It is striking that some of the same economic developments identified in Tom Kahn's 1964 study *The Economics of Equality* have advanced dramatically. His primary point was that the majority of African Americans were part of an eco-nomic class that had been able to make important gains through employment in an industrial economy but that "the position of this class is deteriorating because

---

*In his meticulous biography, David Garrow documents that King believed capitalism would be unable to bring about economic justice, and that the revolution against injustice would have to involve establishing, as King put it, "some form of socialism"—meaning a socially owned and dem-ocratically controlled economy in which resources are utilized to provide for the basic human needs and the possibility for free development of each person.

of technological developments which are revolutionizing the structure of the labor force." Because they were the last major wave to come to the nation's industrial centers in a period when this change was beginning, African Americans were its first victims. But what was seen as a "black problem" in the 1960s became a dramatic problem for a growing number of white workers by the 1980s. Of course, something like the Freedom Budget would have counteracted this. For that matter, something like the Freedom Budget would do much to overcome the problem today.

Economist William Tabb commented in 1970 that "the questions blacks have raised concerning how society's resources should be distributed, the rights of all citizens to quality housing, jobs, and education—these are questions of profound importance to whites as well as blacks." Tabb noted that "there is a natural alliance of those excluded from the bounty of society—the blacks and other minorities, and the overtaxed white who has before him a life of continuous, boring, dreary, and alienating labor." He also expressed the opinion that "at present, white worker racism stands in the way of the emergence of this alliance. The task is to find ways of breaking down this racism."

In a pathbreaking study of the U.S. working class written in 1974, Andrew Levison* demonstrated that the notion of racism being stronger among white workers than among upper-class whites is a myth. Racism certainly exists, and few white workers "can relate to the liberal intellectual's focus on issues like improving welfare benefits or seeking to understand the black criminal." On the other hand, research indicates that racist attitudes are simply *not* stronger among white workers, many of whom "genuinely accept the demands for simple justice being made by black workers." As white workers "see a common working-class issue, they respond 'tolerantly.' But when the issue poses the needs of blacks as a whole against all whites, workers often become incensed at being lumped together with the affluent and seeing their problems ignored."

Levison quoted one of Martin Luther King's last statements about the civil rights movement: "It has developed into more than a quest for simple equality. It is a challenge to a system that has created miracles of production, to create justice." Noting that "the years since then have shown in many ways that the same statement applies to all workers, black and white," Levison suggested that this has been "the central challenge of every revolt and every progressive struggle of this century," and that a coming-together of a resurgent civil rights movement and revitalized labor movement could be "the beginning of a new stage in the ongoing struggle for a better world."

It is arguable that such black-white working-class unity has become a greater possibility under the impact of recent economic developments. Not only have a

---

*This is the son of a top advisor to Martin Luther King named Stanley Levison, whose left-wing background had made him a special target of King opponents such as FBI chief J. Edgar Hoover.

growing number of whites been pushed into poverty and unemployment, but even among a high percentage of those who are more fortunate, their "middle-class" income has been dramatically eroded, with deteriorating working conditions as well. An increasing number of white workers have come to realize that their plight is similar to that of their black coworkers. Commenting that in 1997 "the U.S. economy appeared to be in a permanent crisis," New York University's professor of history and Africana studies Robin D. G. Kelley elaborated:

> Actually, it was the working class that experienced the crisis, not the wealthy. For the past sixteen years, at least, we have witnessed a greater concentration of wealth while the living conditions of working people deteriorate—textbook laissez-faire capitalism, to be sure. Certainly the Reagan/Bush revolution ushered in a new era of corporate wealth and callous disregard for the poor. Income inequality is staggering: the richest 1 percent of the American families have nearly as much wealth as the bottom 95 percent; between 1980 and 1993, salaries for American CEOs increased by 514 percent while workers' wages rose by 68 percent—well behind inflation. In 1992 the average CEO earned 157 times what the average factory worker earned. And as a result of changes in the tax laws, average workers are paying more to the government while CEOs and their companies are paying less. Sweatshops and slave labor conditions that accompany them are on the rise again. Corporate profits are reaching record highs, while "downsizing" and capital flight have left millions unemployed. Between 1979 and 1992 the Fortune 500 companies' total labor force dropped from 16.2 million worldwide to 11.8 million. Yet in 1993, these companies reaped profits of $62.6 billion. (Kelley 1997, 7–8)

Also quite significant is the changing face of the U.S. labor movement. Although it was predominantly white when the civil rights movement began (60 percent white as opposed to today's 49 percent), now a very much increased percentage of unionized workers is African American and Hispanic—a fact reflected in that movement's leadership bodies. What all of this means is that historical developments have caught up with the vision of Martin Luther King Jr. in the last year of his life—and in some ways may be about to surpass it. Today more than in 1968, there is potentially a stronger base among the working-class white majority and within the labor movement for the interracial movement dedicated to economic and racial justice.

But it may be the case that the blending of movements, issues, and struggles will be even more complex. Audre Lourde commented in 1980 that "as a forty-nine-year-old Black lesbian feminist socialist mother of two, including one boy, and a member of an interracial couple, I usually find myself a part of some group defined as other, deviant, inferior, or just plain wrong." In the spirit of Randolph and King, she reflected that "in a society where the good is defined in terms of profit rather than in terms of human need, there must always be some group of people who, through systematized oppression, can be made to feel surplus, to occupy the place of the dehumanized inferior." Implying the need for a coalition of forces to overcome this situation, she concluded: "Within this society, that group is made up of Black and Third World people, working-class people, older people, and women" (Anderson and Collins 1995, 532).

Regardless of specific details, the realization of Martin Luther King's vision may lie in the direction sketched by Robin Kelley: "The hope and future of America lie with the very multicolored working class that for so long has been seen as the problem rather than the solution. The new 'wretched of the earth' are building the labor movement, reinventing the civil rights movement, and reconfiguring scholarship in ways that radically challenge the status quo" (Kelley 1997, 12–13).

But one must move beyond hopeful generalizations. What is necessary for those serious about overcoming the intertwined evils of racial and economic injustice is the development of specific, local projects, strategies, and tactics that are grounded in an understanding of historical realities, previous struggles, and present possibilities. Such efforts must provide modest but meaningful victories that can be the basis for more substantial efforts. At the same time, it will be necessary for such localized efforts increasingly to be connected on a national scale—because as Dr. King pointed out many years ago, the goals of racial and economic justice cannot be realized, ultimately, until "America is born again."

6.

PRACTICAL STEPS

It is not enough to try to understand things. When one is looking at injustice, one must strive to change things for the better. There are things that need to be changed, and they can only be changed if people who care actually organize themselves to bring about such change. The present chapter is necessarily a work in progress. It is impossible—certainly at the present time—to offer a detailed blueprint of what to do. Rather, one can only offer:

- a few suggestions, flowing from hard-won insights of past struggles;
- an indication of a general approach, flowing from material presented above; and
- some practical checklists and lists of resources to aid those engaging in this effort.

What follows will be an initial and only partial discussion. It will need to be evaluated and elaborated, criticized and revised, reviewed and reformulated on the basis of the actual, practical experience of those engaged in the work of struggling for racial and economic justice.

INITIAL REFLECTIONS

We have noted that the struggle against racism is individual as well as institutional. One begins on the personal level. Often those who are white are blind to the privileges that the color of their skin frequently gives them, because it is part of everyday reality and seems "normal." To question it seems odd—to speak of it as an aspect of racism can even seem insulting and threatening. What seems "normal" for people of all races is something that has been shaped by the history that we have been examining. But history is an ongoing process made by each and all of us, and we have seen that it is possible to shift what is "normal" to something less oppressive and more inclusive. Racism is, as we have seen, a complex reality. It touches all of us, and this makes it necessary to be self-aware and self-critical as we seek to deal with and transcend aspects of racism within ourselves and in each of us.

Generally, if we find ourselves slipping into self-righteousness and moralistic preaching at others, this is an indication that it is *we* who have a problem—with our own ability to communicate, our own anxieties, our own egos, our own feelings, or whatever. There is a need to reach for self-respect and mutual respect for each person as a basis for dealing with problems of individual (conscious and unconscious) racism. It is necessary to be able to respect and respond to people's passions and emotions, and to be in touch with our own feelings, but it is also necessary to continue using our critical and analytical minds as we seek to understand and to push back racism.

To overcome individual racism, it is necessary to deal with institutional racism. Beyond a fairly limited extent, individual action cannot overcome the problems of institutional racism. We have seen, also, that a serious concern over racial justice naturally leads to a serious concern over economic justice. In both cases, collective action—increasing numbers of individuals working together to bring about a desired change—is necessary to alter institutional realities. This requires the development of organizations dedicated to such a purpose. The following suggestions focus on this task.

It is necessary for African Americans to develop their own organizations and for antiracist whites to concentrate on reaching out to other whites. But it is not possible to move forward unless, at the same time, groups with a multiracial and multicultural composition come into being. In working for racial and economic justice, sometimes an all-black organization is necessary—but generally an all-white group is problematical.

Obviously, it is never a good idea to reinvent the wheel. A number of organizations are already dealing with the issues of racial and economic justice. It will be important to develop a list—both locally and nationally—of what these organizations are, what they hope to accomplish, what their activities are, and so on. It would seem that what these organizations are doing has not been sufficient to solve the problems we are dealing with. But it will be possible and valuable to connect with those groups that seem to be going in the right direction. (Depending on the group and the circumstances, sometimes it might make sense to join them. Sometimes it will make sense to utilize their resources and help build some of their activities, or to work in coalition with them).

It can be assumed, however, that it will also make sense to develop a new grouping or coalition that can concentrate, very practically and locally, on addressing the problems of racial and economic justice. In that case, there is a need for those who will be working together to be more or less "on the same page." It is neither necessary nor possible nor desirable for everyone to agree with each other on everything—but the identification and development of common assumptions and a shared orientation will make it possible for the group to be more effective.

It is especially important to include people in collective activity on a local level. This can help people learn how to function politically and organizationally, developing their own minds and creative abilities. Such an approach encourages those involved to grow as people who will be able to help bring about meaningful social change. The organization must seek ways that enable people to function together democratically—the group deciding on and doing things together— while at the same time allowing for individual initiatives. Learning how to work together for common goals is incredibly important but fraught with difficulties.

Arrogance is all too often an occupational hazard in this type of situation— some of us who know something often think that we know more than we really know. This makes it hard to work together and hard to learn from each other. It also makes it harder to learn from other people outside the group, and harder to learn from reality itself. In order to teach, we have to learn from our would-be "students." In order to communicate, we need to listen. To help a group develop, we have to be willing to let others help us develop. At the same time, an excessive amount of modesty can also be a barrier. If we know something, we need to share it. If we think something, we shouldn't be afraid to say it (even if we are disagreeing with someone else). If we don't understand what people are saying, we should try to get them to explain themselves. The group will tend to function more effectively if:

- each person in a group strives for a dynamic balance of modesty and self-confidence;
- each strives for a dynamic balance of having opinions and being open to other opinions; and
- those in the group strive for a dynamic balance of being thoughtful leaders and thoughtful followers.

The purpose of the kind of group we are discussing should not simply be to provide opportunities for talk and social interactions, although both of these things are positive and necessary. But they should also have the purpose of engaging in activity that will help to bring about desired changes. Often, members of a group will lose sight of this fact or will only see it in a very abstract way.

If a group has a series of discussions without these resulting in the development and implementation of a plan of action, then something is wrong. If a group jumps from one "worthwhile" activity to another and then another—without there being any clear connection between the activities, and without there being a clear forward motion toward the alleged goals of the organization—then something is wrong. Instead there should be a progression from one activity to another that then helps to achieve a specific goal that can be the basis for future actions leading to the realization of more specific goals. This accumulation of interrelated accomplishments should be designed to advance an overarching plan to bring about actual changes that will increase racial and economic justice. At the same time, it should be designed to build a social or political movement capable of advancing the struggle still further.

In order to be effective in developing such a group, it is important for there to be a general approach for social change that the group is attempting to implement.

A GENERAL APPROACH

No general approach to racism represents the Absolute Truth. Any orientation that claims to do this, or that contains elements that cannot be questioned or criticized, is seriously deficient. At the same time, there can be no coherent antiracist activity without a definite approach to guide such activity. We can learn through doing—learning more deeply the practical meaning of a particular approach and also learning the limitations of that approach. Practical activity will help us to strengthen the approach, and when necessary to revise it.

The Crossroads Ministry, an interfaith ministry for racial justice that provides education and training to dismantle racism, has identified what it calls four organizing tasks for dismantling racism: (1) claiming an antiracist institutional identity; (2) dismantling institutional racism; (3) building antiracist multicultural diversity; and 4) shaping/reshaping antiracist cultural identity. The orientation developed by the Crossroads Ministry calls for a number of steps, including:

a) to analyze, understand, and dismantle racism in its three manifested forms: individual racism, institutional racism, and cultural racism;

b) to work for institutional change, recognizing that individual prejudice reduction and cross-cultural relations are important but not sufficient for long-term and effective change; and

c) to build antiracist multicultural diversity within institutions in ways that develop mutual trust, share power, equalize benefits, and provide positive results for all.

Such an approach is in harmony with that developed in this book. Half a dozen points summarize the approach that emerges from our review of the antiracist struggles in U.S. history.

Antiracist Work Must Be at Two Levels: Individual and Institutional

It has been argued in previous chapters that racism involves individual and institutional dimensions. Pushing back racism in one dimension is linked to pushing back racism in the other. Psychology is linked to sociology and economics—addressing the question of racism in the one is most effectively accomplished by *at the same time* addressing racism in the other. The economic underpinnings of institutional racism must be exposed in order to begin undermining the social conditions that help breed the psychology of racism. At the same time, the psychology of racism (conscious and unconscious) must also be pushed back in order to facilitate the struggle for social and economic justice.

An Oppressed People Has the Right to Self-Determination

There is an absolute need for the existence of multiracial organizations and struggles to overcome racism—but it is also absolutely necessary to respect the right to self-determination of a people (such as African Americans) oppressed on the basis of race. This would mean that all-white or predominantly white organizations must respect and consult with African American organizations, and never presume to speak on behalf of, or in the "best interests" of, the black community. It also means recognizing that there are differences within the black community, and diverse organizations and currents within that community, and that it is not the place of well-meaning whites to decide which of the different perspectives or groups is the "true voice" of the black community. It means respecting the notion that the future of the black community should be determined by the people of that community. And it means seriously seeking to work with African American organizations in struggles for racial and economic justice, and as much as possible to shift the racial balance in predominantly white organizations so that they become, instead, genuinely multiracial.

A Class Approach Is a Key to Success

It is necessary to develop greater awareness of the connections between the questions of race and economics through education, and then increasingly to translate this awareness into practical activity. This necessarily involves dealing with the question of socioeconomic class. The great majority of blacks and whites are part of a large and diverse working class (about 80 percent of the population) that is oppressed by the economic structures and dynamics perpetuating institutional racism. There has been considerable confusion over how to understand such a term as "working class." It can be said to include individuals and families at middle-income and low-income levels, dependent on a paycheck for the white-collar or blue-collar labor someone does for an employer, and also those who are unemployed or retired from such employment. Programs and policies that will eliminate the economic basis of institutional racism will at the same time, in very practical and direct ways, advance the interests of the working class as a whole.

A Multicultural Approach Is a Key to Success

A recognition and valuing of, and serious education around, the rich multiethnic history of the United States helps to erode the racist conception of "whiteness," and it helps to nurture a sense of common experience as well as a valuing of difference among the majority of our people, regardless of racial categories. While the category of "African American" can be seen as racial, it is also an ethnic category. There has developed a definite African American subculture, just as there are Italian American, Polish American, Chinese American, Mexican American, Native American ("Indian"), Appalachian, and Jewish American subcultures. One can refer to an overarching "American culture" which in many ways is shaped and revitalized by these various subcultures, and within which elements of racism also persist. In contrast to this, anything that could be labeled "*white culture*" is necessarily an artificial concoction generated by neo-Nazi and other racist currents. Combined with a working-class approach, a multicultural approach has the potential for creating an antiracist majority.

A Combination of Self-Interest and Moral Force Is Necessary

The veteran community organizer Saul Alinsky once wrote: "To many the synonym for self-interest is selfishness. The word is associated with a repugnant conglomeration of vices such as narrowness, self-seeking, and self-centeredness, everything that is opposite to the virtues of altruism and selflessness. This common definition is contrary, of course, to our everyday experiences, as well as to the observations of all great students of politics and life" (Alinsky 1972, 53). Kim Bobo, Jackie Kendall, and Steve Max of the Midwest Academy, a noted organizing center, offer an interesting elaboration:

> Self-interest is one of the most important and misunderstood concepts in direct action organizing. Basically, what it comes down to is this: Unless you really are a member of the clergy, in whom people have voluntarily placed the

authority to tell them what they morally ought to do, then preaching at them is not the best way to motivate them. What motivates people is their self-interest, not as the organizer interprets it, but as they actually express it to those who listen carefully.

Self-interest is sometimes thought of in the most narrow sense: people want more "stuff," and will organize to get it (often to get it away from someone else). But self-interest is actually a much broader concept. People will fight to end their own oppression when they recognize it, and when there is a clear solution. People are also motivated across generational lines to do things that will help their children or their grandchildren. Self-interest, then, applies to what makes people feel good, as well as to what materially benefits them. Helping others, being active in the community, being useful, doing something important, or doing what is morally right, are all forms of self-interest motivation. Self-interest can be very long range, as in working for peace or the environment.

More broadly still, many people feel a need to take on the responsibilities of citizenship and to play a role in shaping public affairs. People want interaction with the larger community and often enjoy working collectively for the common good. Self-interest generalized is often class interest or community interest. (Bobo, Kendall, and Max 1991, 6–7)

The organizers add that different forms of self-interest motivate different people—but it is clear that genuine self-interest can be compatible with the highest morality. The experience of the civil rights movement, and of other effective movements for social change, have shown that moralistic exhortations and admonitions in the abstract have little impact on most people, but moral appeals can have a powerful impact when sensitively interwoven with some explicitly expressed aspects of self-interest.

Genuine self-interest is inseparable from the notion of justice. It is an essential element in any coherent moral perspective. This is indicated by the powerful commentary of Rabbi Hillel: "If I am not for myself, who will be for me? If I am for myself alone, what am I? If not now, when?"

There is much to be said for "bearing moral witness" in the face of injustice and "Speaking Truth to Power" when there is nothing else that can be done. But the goal should be, when possible, to build a force for Truth that can alter the balance of power so that our social and political reality becomes more consistent with a genuinely moral order. "There is nothing wrong with power if power is used correctly," as Martin Luther King put it. "Now, we've got to get this thing right. What is needed is a realization that power without love is reckless and abusive, and love without power is sentimental and anemic. Power at its best is love implementing the demands of justice, and justice at its best is power correcting everything that stands against love."

Win Real Victories and Build the Power of the Movement

Martin Luther King Jr.'s comments on power have an importance and clarity that make them worth reflecting on:

> Another basic challenge is to discover how to organize our strength in terms of economic and political power. . . . The plantation and the ghetto were created by those who had power, both to confine those who had no power and to perpetuate their powerlessness. The problem of transforming the ghetto, therefore, is a problem of power—confrontation of the forces of power defending change and the forces of power dedicated to the preserving of the status quo. Now power properly understood is nothing but the ability to achieve purpose. It is the strength required to bring about social, political, and economic change. Walter Reuther defined power one day. He said, "Power is the ability of a labor union like the UAW [United Auto Workers] to make the most powerful corporation in the world, General Motors, say, 'Yes' when it wants to say 'No.' That's power."

There is much that is packed into, and implied by, what King says here. It will be useful to construct a list of what is involved.

- There is a need to focus sufficient organized force around an issue to win real victories (which implies: strong organizations; unity in struggle for a specific goal; energetic outreach efforts to educate, agitate, organize, and mobilize; and building inclusive coalitions).
- Real victories are capable of giving people a sense of their own power.
- Every victory helps create the basis for more victories.
- Real victories alter the relations of power or the balance of power.
- Victories involve a new balance or compromise between oppressor and oppressed (which means an ability to find a *balance* between accommodating to and remaining independent of those who hold institutional power).
- The eventual victory will be to eliminate structures that oppress people (locally, regionally, nationally, globally).

"Change comes from power, and power comes from organization," Saul Alinsky once wrote. "In order to act, people must get together." This brings us to the next item on which we must focus our attention.

CHECKLISTS AND RESOURCES

At this point, it may be helpful to focus on more "nitty-gritty" practical things that can help advance the implementation of the general approach toward racial and economic justice presented here. There are different kinds of checklists that help move our thinking and activity forward as we seek to bring about meaningful social change.

The discussion by Bobo, Kendall, and Max on the art of planning and facilitating a meeting, in their valuable book *Organizing for Social Change*, is packed with a number of checklists, including the following guidelines for meeting facilitation: (1) start the meeting promptly (within ten or fifteen minutes of the publicized starting time); (2) welcome everyone; (3) introduce people; (4) review the agenda; (5) explain the meeting rules; (6) encourage participation; (7) stick to the agenda; (8) avoid detailed decision making (details can be worked out by subcommittees); (9) move to action; (10) seek commitments; (11) bring closure to discussions; (12) respect everyone's rights; (13) be flexible; (14) summarize the meeting results and follow-up; (15) thank people; (16) close the meeting on or before the ending time.

In considering such a list, we can see how it is designed to move the meeting forward in a way that can make it an effective tool for decision making and organization building. Some of us with extensive activist experience have attended far too many meetings that were badly in need of the orientation such a list would have provided! Or consider this list of "do's and don'ts" that they offer on how to participate in a meeting:

Do

Personally welcome new people
Actively listen to others
Support the facilitator in moving the agenda
Recommend ways to resolve differences
Participate in discussions
Encourage new people to speak and volunteer
Help set up and clean up the room
Be positive and upbeat throughout the meeting
Tell a joke or add a light comment to ease the tension in a difficult discussion.

Don't

Dominate the discussion
Bring up tangents
Dwell on past problems
Insist that people support your ideas. (Bobo, Kendall, and Max 1991, 98–101)

Of course, the function of an organization dedicated to racial and economic justice is not just to have well-run and relatively pleasant meetings. There are checklists, as well, designed to facilitate actual struggles for social change. For example, in his "Letter from a Birmingham Jail," Martin Luther King offered this list: "In any nonviolent campaign there are four basic steps: (1) collection of the facts, to determine whether injustices are alive, (2) negotiation [with those who hold power, to determine the possibility of removing the injustices], (3) self-purification [in order to build up the numbers and the inner-strength of activists through training sessions], and (4) direct action [involving demonstrations, rallies, boycotts, nonviolent civil disobedience, etc.]" (King 1986, 290).

Another example is Saul Alinsky's list of tactical rules (Alinsky 1972, 126–30), which suggest a dynamic orientation adding up to a strategic approach designed to challenge powerful institutions and force concessions from them:

(1) Power is not only what you have but what the enemy thinks you have.
(2) Never go outside the experience of your people.
(3) Wherever possible, go outside the experience of the enemy.
(4) Make the enemy live up to their own book of rules.
(5) Ridicule is man's most potent weapon.
(6) A good tactic is one that your people enjoy.
(7) A tactic that drags on too long becomes a drag.
(8) Keep the pressure on.
(9) The threat is usually more terrifying than the thing itself.
(10) The major premise for tactics is the development of operations that will maintain a constant pressure upon the opposition.
(11) If you push a negative hard enough and deep enough it will break through into its counterside—which means that, with enough thought and attention, your movement's limitations or disadvantages can be transformed into strengths.
(12) The price of a successful attack is a constructive alternative—which means that you will suffer ultimate defeat if you engage in a protest campaign without a practical plan for a policy that can be implemented if those you are protesting against actually give in.
(13) Pick the target, freeze it, personalize it, polarize it—which means that complex and powerful institutions will (if they are permitted to) evade, deny, or shift responsibility, so that careful and often dramatic measures must be taken to prevent this possibility.

Bobo, Kendall, and Max offer a more succinct discussion. They make a distinction between problems, issues or reforms, strategies, and tactics. For them a *problem* is a broad area of concern, such as racism. A *reform* (they use the term "issue") is a solution or partial solution to a problem. A *strategy* is an overall plan of activities (involving short-term goals, intermediate goals, and long-term goals) designed to win a reform. *Tactics* are steps designed to help in carrying out the strategy. They go on to list criteria for a good tactic: (1) it is focused on the primary or secondary target of the campaign (and therefore is directly relevant to what you are trying to accomplish); (2) it puts power behind a specific demand (mobilizing people not simply around an abstract issue but around a specific— therefore winnable—demand); (3) it meets your organizational goal as well as your reform goal (helping to build the organization that advances the reform struggle); (4) it is outside the experience of the target; (5) it is within the experience of your own members and they are comfortable with it.

In discussing strategy, Martin Oppenheimer and George Lakey have urged the development of another type of list, categorizing groups and individuals in a community along the following lines:

1. Active associates and friends in the cause.
2. Support, but not active participation. Financial help.
3. Moral support, some individuals giving money.
4. Neutral—organization divided evenly.
5. Hostile, but not active . . . wait and see.
6. Actively hostile.

They comment: "Your primary job is (a) to decide which of the above is your target group in a particular campaign; your secondary task is (b) to move everybody one step up. Each of the groups will require a somewhat different approach" (Oppenheimer and Lakey 1965, 20).

In fact, any activity designed to help bring about meaningful change must be carefully thought through and organized. To engage in the struggle for social change is to embark on a journey that will be filled with a rich accumulation of lists.

There will also be the need for a rich accumulation of resources to help advance the cause of racial and economic justice. These are the kinds of things that you can utilize for your own personal enlightenment but also that you can refer others to, or even use as the basis for group discussions or educationals. Only a few items can be mentioned here.

Some basic reading will be important to absorb information and perspectives for the kind of work outlined here. Most of the titles listed in the "Sources" are valuable, but if one were to prioritize, one might urge people to read the material in *A Testament of Hope*, by Martin Luther King Jr. Much additional food for thought, especially on connections among different sectors of the population that are oppressed, can be found in *Race, Class, and Gender*, the anthology edited by Margaret Anderson and Patricia Hill Collins, a fine collection of essays and excerpts. A very readable history of African Americans is Lerone Bennett's *Before the Mayflower*. Joanne Grant's collection of documents and readings,

Black Protest, is also a good starting place. A beautifully written, fascinating, and thoughtful multicultural history of the United States, Ronald Takaki's *A Different Mirror*, is a powerful tool for understanding our society's past, present, and future. A radical analysis with much information and many provocative opinions is Howard Zinn's *A People's History of the United States*. The National Urban League provides invaluable yearly surveys in *The State of Black America*. And a practical workbook for activists is *Organizing for Social Change* by Kim Bobo, Jackie Kendall, and Steve Max.

Also of immense value are videos, which are often available at public or university libraries (or can be ordered by them), or which may be owned by and available from one or another peace and justice institution such as the Thomas Merton Center. "Roots of Resistance: The Underground Railroad" is a very well done documentary on slavery and antislavery struggles. Ruby Dee and Ossie Davis (with the support of Bill Moyers) offer a survey of twentieth-century antiracist struggles, *The Second American Revolution*. A devastating examination of antiblack racism in mainstream U.S. culture can be found in *Ethnic Notions*. The series *Eyes on the Prize* provides a detailed and moving examination of the modern civil rights movement. Two of the most important figures in shaping that movement are the focus of biographical documentaries: *A. Philip Randolph*, and either the relatively short *The Legacy of Martin Luther King Jr.* or the Academy Award–winning full-length documentary *From Montgomery to Memphis*. The powerful story of Freedom Summer and the Mississippi Freedom Democratic Party in 1964 is presented in *Freedom on My Mind*. The intersection of racial and economic justice is at the heart of *By the River I Stand*, dealing with the 1968 Memphis sanitation workers' strike during which King was assassinated. Two documentaries focusing on issues of economic justice are *Controlling Interest* and *Global Assembly Line*.

Publications dealing, in different ways, with racial justice and economic justice include:

America@Work (official publication of the AFL-CIO)
American Legacy (Celebrating African American History and Culture)
Crisis (official publication of the NAACP)
Dollars and Sense
Ebony
Labor Notes
Left Business Observer
National Catholic Reporter
Progressive
Sojourners
Teaching Tolerance
Z

The following Web sites on the Internet are also worth looking at:

American Federation of Labor–Congress of Industrial Organizations (AFL-CIO): www.aflcio.org

Center on Budget and Policy Priorities: www.cbpp.org

Children's Defense Fund: www.childrensdefense.org

Crossroads Ministry home.pacbell.net/rodgvml/Crossroads.html

HateWatch: www.hatewatch.org

Martin Luther King Jr. Center for Nonviolent Social Change: www.thekingcenter.com

National Association for the Advancement of Colored People (NAACP): www.naacp.org

National Urban League: www.nul.org

Southern Poverty Law Center: www.splcenter.org

Thomas Merton Center: www.realpittsburgh.com/community/groups/TMC

W. E. B. Du Bois Institute for African-American Research: web-dubois.fas.harvard.edu

The most important resource, however, consists of people who will contribute to, and at the same time be educated and trained by, sustained efforts to challenge and overcome racial and economic oppression. The blending of their dreams adds up to the American dream, and it is only through the blending of their energies that we will be able to come closer to making the American dream a reality. "There is always a moment in any kind of struggle when one feels in full bloom.

Vivid. Alive. One might be blown to bits in such a moment and still be at peace," Alice Walker recently wrote, referring to Martin Luther King Jr., Mohandas Gandhi, Sojourner Truth, and Harriet Tubman. She went on to say:

> To be such a person or to witness anyone at this moment of transcendence is to know that what is human is linked, by a daring compassion, to what is divine. During my years of being close to people engaged in changing the world I have seen fear turn into courage. Sorrow into joy. Funerals into celebrations. Because whatever the consequences, people standing side by side, have expressed who they really are, and that ultimately they believe in the love of the world and each other enough *to be that*—which is the foundation of activism.
>
> It has become a common feeling, I believe, as we have watched our heroes falling over the years, that our own small stone of activism, which might not seem to measure up to the rugged boulders of heroism we have so admired, is a paltry offering toward the building of an edifice of hope. Many who believe this choose to withhold their offerings out of shame.
>
> This is the tragedy of our world.
>
> For we can do nothing toward changing our course on the planet, a destructive one, without rousing ourselves, individual by individual, and bringing our small, imperfect stones to the pile. (Walker 1997, xxiii)

The imperfect stones become a monument to the future, a wall against injustice, a bridge to a better world. Hopefully this modest book will contribute to such a building process.

SOURCES

What follows is a list of sources that have been consulted in the development of this book. Some of these sources are excellent for the general reader; some are for those who are more scholarly minded. Most are stimulating and generally valuable; some offer views that I find highly questionable at best.

Alexander, Amy, ed. *The Farrakhan Factor: African-American Writers on Leadership, Nationhood, and Minister Louis Farrakhan.* New York: Grove Press, 1998.

Alinsky, Saul. *Rules for Radicals: A Pragmatic Primer for Realistic Radicals.* New York: Vintage Books, 1972.

Allen, Robert L. *Black Awakening in Capitalist America, An Analytic History.* Garden City, N.Y.: Anchor Books, 1970.

———. *Reluctant Reformers: Racism and Social Reform Movements in the United States.* Garden City, N.Y.: Anchor Books, 1975.

Anderson, Jervis. *A. Philip Randolph, A Biographical Portrait.* New York: Harcourt Brace Jovanovich, 1973.

———. *Bayard Rustin: The Troubles I've Seen, A Biography.* New York: HarperCollins, 1997.

Anderson, Margaret, and Patricia Hill Collins, eds. *Race, Class and Gender,* 2d ed. Belmont, Calif.: Wadsworth Publishing Co., 1995.

Aptheker, Herbert, ed. *A Documentary History of the Negro People in the United States,* 7 vols. New York: Citadel Press, 1989–94.

Arthur, John, and Amy Shapiro, eds. *Color, Class, Identity: The New Politics of Race.* Boulder, Colo.: Westview Press, 1996.

Baldwin, James. *The Fire Next Time.* New York: Dell, 1964.

Banks, William M. *Black Intellectuals: Race and Responsibility in American Life.* New York: W. W. Norton, 1996.

Baraka, Amiri. *The LeRoi Jones/Amiri Baraka Reader.* Edited by William J. Harris. New York: Thunder's Mouth Press, 1999.

Barndt, Joseph. *Dismantling Racism: The Continuing Challenge to White America.* Minneapolis: Ausburg, 1991.

Bell, Derrick. *Faces at the Bottom of the Well, The Permanence of Racism.* New York: Basic Books, 1992.

Benedict, Ruth. *Race: Science and Politics.* New York: Viking Press, 1959.

Bennett, Lerone, Jr. *Before the Mayflower: A History of Black America.* 6th rev. ed. New York: Penguin Books, 1993.

Bobo, Kim, Jackie Kendall, and Steve Max. *Organizing for Social Change: A Manual For Activists in the 1990s.* Arlington, Va.: Seven Locks Press, 1991.

Braden, Anne. *The Southern Freedom Movement in Perspective*, special issue of *Monthly Review*, July–August 1965.

Branch, Taylor. *Parting the Waters: America in the King Years 1954–63.* New York: Simon and Schuster, 1989.

———. *Pillar of Fire: America in the King Years 1963–65.* New York: Simon and Schuster, 1998.

Breitman, George. *Anti-Negro Prejudice: When It Began, When It Will End.* New York: Pioneer Publishers, 1960.

———. *The Last Year of Malcolm X: The Evolution of a Revolutionary.* New York: Schocken Books, 1968.

Buckley, William F., Jr., ed. *American Conservative Thought in the Twentieth Century.* Indianapolis, Ind.: Bobbs-Merrill, 1970.

Buhle, Mari Jo, Paul Buhle, and Dan Georgakas, eds. *Encyclopedia of the American Left.* New York: Oxford University Press, 1998.

Carson, Clayborne. *In Struggle: SNCC and the Black Awakening of the 1960s.* Cambridge: Harvard University Press, 1981.

Carson, Clayborne, David J. Garrow, Gerald Gill, Vincent Harding, and Darlene Clark Hine, eds. *The Eyes on the Prize Civil Rights Reader: Documents, Speeches, and Firsthand Accounts from the Black Freedom Struggle, 1954–1990.* New York: Penguin, 1991.

Chideya, Farai. *Don't Believe the Hype: Fighting Cultural Misinformation about African-Americans.* New York: Plume/Penguin, 1995.

Civil Rights Congress. *We Charge Genocide: The Crime of the Government against the Negro People, A Petition to the United Nations.* New York: Civil Rights Congress, 1951.

Clark, Kenneth. *Dark Ghetto, Dilemmas of Social Power.* New York: Harper & Row, 1967.

Clarke, John Henrik. *Africans at the Crossroads: Notes for an African World Revolution.* Trenton, N.J.: African World Press, 1991.

Clarke, John Henrik, Esther Jackson, Ernest Kaiser, and J. H. O'Dell, eds. *Black Titan, W. E. B. Du Bois.* Boston: Beacon Press, 1970.

Cleaver, Kathleen and George Katsiaficas, eds. *Liberation, Imagination, and the Black*

Panther Party: A New Look at the Panthers and Their Legacy. New York: Routledge, 2001.

Cone, James H. *Martin and Malcolm and America, A Dream or a Nightmare*. Maryknoll, N.Y.: Orbis Books, 1995.

Cook, Blanche Wiesen. *The Declassified Eisenhower*. New York: Penguin, 1984.

Cox, Oliver C. *Caste, Class and Race: A Study in Social Dynamics*. New York: Monthly Review Press, 1970.

Cruse, Harold. *The Crisis of the Negro Intellectual*. New York: William Morrow, 1967.

Curry, George E., ed. *The Affirmative Action Debate*. Reading, Mass.: Addison-Wesley, 1997.

Delany, Martin. *The Condition, Elevation, Emigration and Destiny of The Colored People of the United States*. 1852. Reprint, New York: Arno Press and the *New York Times*, 1969.

Dent, Gina, ed. *Black Popular Culture, A Project by Michele Wallace*. Seattle: Bay Press, 1992.

Douglass, Frederick. *The Life and Times of Frederick Douglass*. Secaucus, N.J.: Citadel Press, 1983.

————. *The Life and Writings of Frederick Douglass*. 5 vols. Edited by Philip S. Foner. New York: International Press, 1975.

D'Souza, Dinesh. *The End of Racism: Principles for a Multiracial Society*. New York: Free Press, 1995.

Duberman, Martin Bauml. *Paul Robeson*. New York: Alfred A. Knopf, 1989.

W. E. B. Du Bois. *The Autobiography of W. E. B. Du Bois*. New York: International Publishers, 1968.

————. *Black Reconstruction in America 1860–1880*. 1936. Reprint, New York: Atheneum, 1985.

————. *The Souls of Black Folk*. Greenwich, Conn.: Fawcett Publications, 1967.

————. *The World and Africa*. New York: International Publishers, 1990.

Feagin, Joe R. *Racist America: Roots, Current Realities, and Future Reparations*. New York: Routledge, 2001.

Ferman, Louis A., Joyce L. Kornbluh, and J. A. Miller, eds. *Negroes and Jobs*. Ann Arbor: University of Michigan Press, 1968.

Foner, Philip S., ed. *The Black Panthers Speak*. New York: De Capo Press, 1995.

Foner, Philip S., and Ronald L. Lewis, eds. *Black Workers: A Documentary History from Colonial Times to the Present*. Philadelphia, Pa.: Temple University Press, 1989.

Franklin, John Hope. *From Slavery to Freedom, A History of Negro Americans*. 3d ed. New York: Vintage Books, 1969.

Franklin, Raymond S., and Solomon Resnik. *The Political Economy of Racism*. New York: Holt, Rinehart and Winston, 1973.

Fredrickson, George M. *Racism: A Short History*. Princeton: Princeton University Press, 2002.

Garrow, David J. *Bearing the Cross, Martin Luther King Jr. and the Southern Christian Leadership Conference*. New York: Vintage Books, 1988.

Gates, Henry Louis, Jr. *Thirteen Ways of Looking at a Black Man*. New York: Vintage 1997.

Georgakas, Dan, and Marvin Survin. *Detroit: I Do Mind Dying, A Study in Urban Revolution*. New York: St. Martin's, 1975.

Geschwender, James A. *Class, Race, and Worker Insurgency: The League of Revolutionary Black Workers*. New York: Cambridge University Press, 1977.

Goldfield, Michael. *The Color of Politics: Race and the Mainsprings of American Politics*. New York: New Press, 1997.

Gould, Stephen Jay. *The Mismeasure of Man*. New York: W. W. Norton, 1981.

Grant, Joanne, ed. *Black Protest, 350 Years of History, Documents, and Analyses*. 2d ed. New York: Fawcett Columbine, 1996.

————. *Ella Baker, Freedom Bound*. New York: John Wiley and Sons, 1998.

Guerin, Daniel. *Negroes on the March, A Frenchman's Report on the American Negro Struggle*. New York: George L. Weissman, 1956.

Hacker, Andrew. *Two Nations: Black and White, Separate, Hostile, Unequal*. New York: Ballantine Books, 1992.

Harding, Vincent. *Hope and History: Why We Must Share the Story of the Movement*. Maryknoll, N.Y.: Orbis Books, 1990.

————. *Martin Luther King, The Inconvenient Hero*. Maryknoll, N.Y.: Orbis Books, 1997.

Harrington, Michael. *The New American Poverty*. New York: Holt, Rinehart and Winston, 1984.

Herrnstein, Richard J., and Charles Murray. *The Bell Curve: Intelligence and Class Structure in American Life*. New York: Free Press, 1994.

Higham, John. *Strangers in the Land: Patterns of Nativism, 1860–1925*. New York: Atheneum, 1971.

Hill, Patricia Liggins, Bernard W. Bell, Trudier Harris, William J. Harris, R. Baxter Miller, Sondra A. O'Neale, and Horace Porter, eds. *Call and Response: The Riverside Anthology of the African American Literary Tradition*. Boston: Houghton Mifflin, 1998.

Jacobson, Julius, ed. *The Negro and the American Labor Movement*. Garden City, N.Y.: Anchor Books, 1968.

Jacoby, Russell, and Naomi Glauberman, eds. *The Bell Curve Debate: History, Documents, Opinions*. New York: Random House, 1995.

James, C. L. R. *C. L. R. James and Revolutionary Marxism, Selected Writings of C. L. R. James 1939–1949*. Edited by Scott McLemee and Paul LeBlanc. Amherst, N.Y.: Humanity Books, 1994.

Jordan, June. *On Call, Political Essays*. Boston: South End Press, 1985.

Judis, John B. *William F. Buckley Jr., Patron Saint of the Conservatives*. New York: Simon and Schuster, 1988.

Kahn, Tom. *The Economics of Equality*. New York: League for Industrial Democracy, 1964.

Kelley, Robin D. G. *Yo' Mama's Disfunktional: Fighting the Culture Wars in Urban America*. Boston: Beacon Press, 1997.

Kendall, Willmoore. *The Conservative Affirmation in America*. Chicago: Regnery Gateway, 1985.

King, Martin Luther, Jr. *A Testament of Hope: The Essential Writings and Speeches of*

Martin Luther King Jr. Edited by James M. Washington. San Francisco: Harper-Collins, 1986.

Kirk, Russell. *The Conservative Mind.* Chicago: Gateway, Henry Regnery, 1960.

————, ed. *The Portable Conservative Reader.* New York: Penguin Books, 1982.

Kottak, Conrad Phillip, and Kathryn A. Kozaitis. *On Being Different: Diversity and Multiculturalism in the North American Mainstream.* Boston: McGraw-Hill, 1999.

Lazaraus, Emma. *Emma Lazarus, Selections from Her Poetry and Prose.* Edited by Morris U. Schappes. New York: Emma Lazarus Federation of Jewish Women's Clubs, 1982.

Le Blanc, Paul. *A Short History of the U.S. Working Class.* Amherst, N.Y.: Humanity Books, 1999.

Leiman, Melvin M. *The Political Economy of Racism, A History.* London: Pluto Press, 1993.

Levine, Lawrence W. *Black Culture and Black Consciousness, Afro-American Folk Thought from Slavery to Freedom.* New York: Oxford University Press, 1978.

Levison, Andrew. *The Working Class Majority.* New York: Coward, McCann and Geoghagen, 1974.

Lawrence, Charles R., III, and Mari J. Matsuda, eds. *We Won't Go Back: Making the Case for Affirmative Action.* Boston: Houghton Mifflin, 1997.

Lewontin, Richard. "The Inferiority Complex." In *It Ain't Necessarily So: The Dream of the Human Genome and Other Illusions,* 2d ed. New York: New York Review of Books, 2001.

Lincoln, C. Eric. *Race, Religion and the Continuing American Dilemma.* New York: Hill and Wang, 1984.

Lynn, Conrad. *There Is a Fountain: The Autobiography of a Civil Rights Lawyer.* Westport, Conn.: Lawrence Hill and Co., 1979.

Malcolm X. *Malcolm X Speaks.* Edited by George Breitman. New York: Grove Press, 1966.

Marable, Manning. *The Crisis of Color and Democracy: Essays on Race, Class and Power.* Monroe, Maine: Common Courage Press, 1992.

————. *How Capitalism Underdeveloped Black America.* Boston: South End Press, 1983.

Meier, August, and Elliott Rudwick. *From Plantation to Ghetto.* 3d ed. New York: Hill and Wang, 1976.

Meier, August, and Elliot Rudwick, eds. *The Making of Black America.* 2 vols. New York: Atheneum, 1974.

Merton, Thomas. *A Thomas Merton Reader.* Rev. ed. Edited by Thomas P. McDonnell. Garden City, N.Y.: Image Books, 1974.

Myrdal, Gunnar. *An American Dilemma: The Negro Problem and Modern Democracy.* 2 vols. New York: Harper and Row, 1962.

National Urban League. *The State of Black America 1991.* New York: National Urban League, 1991.

————. *The State of Black America 1998.* New York: National Urban League, 1998.

Nash, George H. *The Conservative Movement in America Since 1945.* New York: Basic Books, 1979.

Nieman, Donald G. *Promises to Keep: African-Americans and the Constitutional Order, 1776 to the Present.* New York: Oxford University Press, 1991.

Novick, Michael. *White Lies, White Power: The Fight against White Supremacy and Reactionary Violence.* Monroe, Maine: Common Courage Press, 1995.

Oates, Stephen B. *Let the Trumpet Sound, The Life of Martin Luther King Jr.* New York: New American Library, 1985.

Omi, Michael, and Howard Winant. *Racial Formation in the United States, from the 1960s to the 1990s.* New York: Routledge, 1994.

Oppenheimer, Martin, and George Lakey. *A Manual for Direct Action, Strategy and Tactics for Civil Rights and All Other Nonviolent Protest Movements.* Chicago: Quadrangle Books, 1965.

O'Reilly, Kevin, and David Gallen, eds. *Black Americans: The FBI Files.* New York: Carroll and Graf, 1994.

Ottley, Roi. *'New World A-Coming,' Inside Black America.* Boston: Houghton Mifflin, 1943.

Patterson, William L. *The Man Who Cried Genocide, An Autobiography.* New York: International Publishers, 1971.

Pearson, Hugh. *The Shadow of the Panther: Huey Newton and the Price of Black Power in America.* Reading, Mass.: Perseus Books, 1994.

Pinkney, Alphonso. *The Myth of Black Progress.* New York: Cambridge University Press, 1990.

Ploski, Harry A., and James Williams, eds. *The Negro Almanac, A Reference Work on the Afro-American.* 4th ed. New York: John Wiley and Sons, 1983.

Quarles, Benjamin. *The Negro in the Making of America.* New York: Colliers Books, 1968.

Randolph, A. Philip, et al. *A "Freedom Budget" for All Americans.* New York: A. Philip Randolph Institute, 1966.

Record, Wilson. *Race and Radicalism: The NAACP and the Communist Party.* Ithaca, N.Y.: Cornell University Press, 1964.

Reed, Adolph, Jr. *Class Notes: Posing as Politics and Other Thoughts on the American Scene.* New York: New Press, 2000.

Report of the National Advisory Commission on Civil Disorders. New York: Bantam Books, 1968.

Robertson, Wilmot. *The Dispossessed Majority.* Cape Canaveral, Fla.: Howard Allen, 1976.

Roediger, David R. *The Wages of Whiteness, Race and the Making of the American Working Class.* London: Verso, 1991.

Rushton, J. Phillippe. *Race, Evolution, and Behavior: A Life History.* New Brunswick, N.J.: Transaction Publishers, 1995.

Rustin, Bayard. *Down the Line: The Collected Writings of Bayard Rustin.* Chicago: Quadrangle Books, 1971.

Ryan, William. *Blaming the Victim.* Rev., upd. ed. New York: Vintage Books, 1976.

Schuyler, George S. *Black and Conservative.* New Rochelle, N.Y.: Arlington House, 1966.

Simonton, Dean Keith. *Origins of Genius: Darwinian Perspectives on Creativity.* New York: Oxford University Press, 1999.

Sitkoff, Harvard. *The Struggle For Black Equality, 1954–1980.* New York: Hill and Wang, 1981.

Smedley, Audrey. *Race in North America, Origin and Evolution of a Worldview.* Boulder, Colo.: Westview Press, 1993.

Solomon, Mark. *The Cry Was Unity: Communists and African Americans, 1917–1936.* Jackson: University of Mississippi Press, 1998.

Sowell, Thomas. *The Economics and Politics of Race.* New York: William Morrow, 1983.

Stang, Alan. *It's Very Simple: The True Story of Civil Rights.* Boston: Western Islands Press, 1965.

Steinberg, Stephen. *The Ethnic Myth: Race, Ethnicity, and Class in America.* Boston: Beacon Press, 1982.

Stone, I. F. *In a Time of Torment.* New York: Vintage Books, 1968.

Tabb, William K. *The Political Economy of the Ghetto.* New York: W. W. Norton, 1970.

Takaki, Ronald. *A Different Mirror, A History of Multicultural America.* Boston: Little, Brown and Co., 1993.

————, ed. *From Different Shores: Perspectives on Race and Ethnicity in America.* New York: Oxford University Press, 1987.

————, ed. *A Larger Memory: A History of Our Diversity, With Voices.* Boston: Little, Brown and Co., 1998.

Terkel, Studs. *Race: How Blacks and Whites Think and Feel about the American Obsession.* New York: Anchor Books, 1993.

Theoharris, Athan G., and John Stuart Cox. *The Boss: J. Edgar Hoover and the Great American Inquisition.* Philadelphia: Temple University Press, 1988.

Thurman, Howard. *Jesus and the Disinherited.* Boston: Beacon Press, 1996.

Turner, Patricia A. *I Heard It through the Grapevine: Rumor in African American Culture.* Berkeley: University of California Press, 1993.

Wade, Wyn Craig. *The Fiery Cross: The Ku Klux Klan in America.* New York: Simon and Schuster, 1987.

Walker, Alice. *Anything We Love Can Be Saved, A Writer's Activism.* New York: Random House, 1997.

Wells-Barnett, Ida B. *On Lynchings: Southern Horrors; A Red Record; Mob Rule in New Orleans.* Salem, N.H.: Ayer Company, 1990.

West, Cornel. *Race Matters.* New York: Vintage Books, 1994.

West, Thomas R., and James W. Mooney, eds. *To Redeem a Nation: A History and Anthology of the Civil Rights Movement.* St. James, N.Y.: Brandywine Press, 1993.

Weyl, Nathaniel. *The Negro in American Civilization.* Washington, D.C.: Public Affairs Press, 1960.

Wigginton, Eliot, ed. *Refuse to Stand Silently By: An Oral History of Grass Roots Social Activism in America, 1921–1964.* New York: Anchor Books, 1992.

Wilson, William Julius. *The Declining Significance of Race: Blacks and Changing American Institutions.* 2d ed. Chicago: University of Chicago Press, 1980.

————. *The Truly Disadvantaged.* Chicago: University of Chicago Press, 1987.

————. *When Work Disappears, The World of the New Urban Poor.* New York: Vintage Books, 1997.

Wood, Joe, ed. *Malcolm X: In Our Own Image.* New York: St. Martin's, 1992.

Woodward, C. Van. *The Strange Career of Jim Crow*. 3d rev. ed. New York: Oxford University Press, 1975.

Wright, Richard. *White Man, Listen!* Garden City, N.Y.: Anchor Books, 1964.

Zinn, Howard. *A People's History of the United States*. New York: Harper and Row, 1980.

READINGS

INTRODUCTION

The selections offered in this portion of *Black Liberation and the American Dream* add up to a rich array of ideas, insights, and experience—with diverse and sometimes divergent reflections consistent with the complex and contradictory reality of race, racism, and antiracist struggle. While the contributions here are overwhelmingly from African Americans, a handful of others are also drawn into this important discussion.

Section I provides a sampling from a dozen of the great pioneers of black liberation, stretching over a period of more than a century. Section II focuses our attention on essential elements of the civil rights and black liberation movement of the twentieth century. Section III explores analytical, strategic, and organizational contributions of the Left—involving interpenetrations between the black liberation struggle with Communist, Socialist, Trotskyist, and other currents. Section IV draws our attention to the broader and more profound intersections of race, ethnicity, class, and gender.

There are limitations to this volume and to its selection of readings. Among the most obvious is the restrictive focus on racism as it relates to the African American experience. This is related to a perception of the author/editor that this variant of racism has run deeper and more persistently in the history of the United States than other variants. Consequently, in my view, black liberation is central to the elimination of racism in our culture and the achievement of economic justice for all. On the other hand, black liberation cannot be achieved without understanding and struggling to overcome other forms of racism in our culture. In certain ways the African American focus is helpful—in other ways it

109

is not. Obviously, not everything can be accomplished with a single book (although Ronald Takaki's very fine *A Different Mirror: A Multicultural History of the United States* in many ways comes close).

While there is hardly uniformity in the perspectives presented here, there are definitely a number of recurring themes. One is that the oppression of African Americans historically requires that the principle of self-determination guide the struggle for black liberation: it is a struggle whose direction, goals, strategy, tactics, and leadership must be provided by African Americans. Another issue that keeps surfacing involves the sometimes divergent and sometimes interpenetrating goals of achieving equal rights in the larger U.S. society and of establishing one or another degree of separation from that society to allow for one or another form of black control of the black community. (Sometimes this has been tagged as a difference between perspectives of *racial integration* and *black nationalism*.)

Other recurring themes involve the interconnection of antiracist struggles and other liberation struggles. This includes, but is not restricted to, struggles of other racially oppressed groups, of other ethnic minorities, of women, and of the diverse working-class majority that makes up at least 80 percent of the U.S. population. Intimately related to this is the theme reflected in the very title of this book. The realization of "the American dream" has meant, for most people in this country, each giving the best of their abilities in order to achieve human dignity, including freedom from fear and want, freedom of belief and expression, and the freedom to shape one's own future. The achievement of the American dream requires the achievement of black liberation, just as the achievement of racial justice and economic justice are inseparable.

I.

PIONEERS IN THE STRUGGLE FOR AFRICAN AMERICAN LIBERATION

The people highlighted here are the twelve whose biographies and contributions were touched on in chapter 4. Frederick Douglass's views from 1857, 1864, and 1883 shed light on important perspectives of black freedom fighters in the abolitionist movement against slavery, in the Civil War, and in the bitterly disappointing post–Civil War period after the abandonment of Reconstruction. An excerpt from Martin Delaney's 1852 classic book on black oppression and struggle advances what would become some of the classic themes of black nationalism. Two other activists in the antislavery struggle were Sojourner Truth and Harriet Tubman. Truth's speeches, providing a powerful defense of women's rights from a black perspective, were written down by others at feminist conventions. Tubman was not literate. She was a black liberation warrior in the Underground Railroad and in the Civil War, not a speech maker. Only a few of her precious words are available here.

Ida B. Wells-Barnett was not only an outspoken foe of lynching, but also a penetrating analyst of white racism, and she discussed tactics that would be found in the thought of later black radicals, from economic boycotts to armed self-defense. Quite different are the moderate "racial cooperation" nostrums of Booker T. Washington, who nonetheless gave powerful voice to the conviction that striving for education and employment represent a superior path to "unmanly cowering and stooping." W. E. B. Du Bois—certainly no foe of education and employment for black Americans—rejected Washington's moderation when he (as a leader of the Niagara Movement that culminated in the forming of the NAACP) issued an uncompromising call for an end to all forms of racial discrimination and oppression.

Although there were sharp differences between the perspective of Washington on the one hand and that of Wells-Barnett and the young Du Bois on the other, each of them appears to be seeking the improvement of the African-American condition within the existing framework of U.S. society. Sharp challenges were raised to this shared conceptual framework. One of the sharpest was that of Marcus Garvey, who—advancing the perspective of black nationalism—articulated the notion of a global "empire" of African peoples as the touchstone of African American identity. From a different standpoint, A. Philip Randolph emphasized a socialist orientation: black liberation could be achieved through economic justice being advanced by the black working class, in eventual alliance with white workers.

Ultimately, it was W. E. B. Du Bois who—in his own way—synthesized these perspectives in a Pan Africanism and a distinctive interpretation of Communism that was embraced and given eloquent articulation by Paul Robeson, to which Bayard Rustin's reflection of Randolph's socialist variant of civil rights stands as an alternative. Echoes of each can be heard in the voice of Ella Baker, who brings the militantly feminine perspective of Truth, Tubman, and Wells-Barnett (at best marginal in the men's contributions) into the heart of the civil rights struggle.

FREDERICK DOUGLASS
COMMENTS FROM 1857, 1864, AND 1883

From 1857

I know, my friends, that in some quarters the efforts of colored people meet with very little encouragement. We may fight, but we must fight like the Sepoys of India, under white officers. This class of Abolitionists don't like colored celebrations, they don't like colored conventions, they don't like colored Anti-Slavery fairs for the support of colored newspapers. They don't like any demonstrations whatever in which colored men take a leading part. They talk of the proud Anglo-Saxon blood, as flippantly as those who profess to believe in the natural inferiority of races.

Your humble speaker has been branded as an ingrate, because he has ventured to stand up on his own right, and to plead our common cause as a colored man, rather than as a Garrisonian. I hold it to be no part of gratitude to allow our white friends to do all the work, while we merely hold their coats. Opposition of the sort now referred to, is partisan opposition, and we need not mind it. The white people at large will not largely be influenced by it. They will see and appreciate all honest efforts on our part to improve our condition as a people.

Let me give you a word of the philosophy of reform. The whole history of the progress of human liberty shows that all concessions yet made to her august claims, have been born of earnest struggle. The conflict has been exciting, agitating, all-absorbing, and for the time being, putting all other tumults to silence. It must do this or it does nothing. If there is no struggle there is no progress. Those who profess to favor freedom and yet deprecate agitation, are men who want crops without plowing up the ground, they want rain without thunder and lightning. They want the ocean without the awful roar of its many waters.

This struggle may be a moral one, or it may be a physical one, and it may be both moral and physical, but it must be a struggle. Power concedes nothing without a demand. It never did and it never will. Find out just what any people will quietly submit to and you have found out the exact measure of injustice and wrong which will be imposed upon them, and these will continue till they are resisted with either words or blows, or with both. The limits of tyrants are prescribed by the endurance of those whom they oppress. In the light of these ideas, Negroes will be hunted at the North, and held and flogged at the South so long as they submit to those devilish outrages, and make no resistance, either moral or physical. Men may not get all they pay for in this world, but they must certainly pay for all they get. If we ever get free from the oppressions and wrongs heaped upon us, we must pay for their removal. We must do this by labor, by suffering, by sacrifice, and if needs be, by our lives and the lives of others.

From 1864

President Lincoln introduced his administration to the country as one which would faithfully catch, hold, and return runaway slaves to their masters. He avowed his determination to protect and defend the slaveholder's right to plunder the black laborer of his hard earnings. Europe was assured by Mr. Seward that no slave should gain his freedom by this war. Both the President and the Secretary of State have made progress since then.

Our Generals, at the beginning of the war, were horribly Pro-Slavery. They took to slave-catching and slave-killing like ducks to water. They are now very generally and very earnestly in favor of putting an end to Slavery. Some of them, like Hunter and Butler, because they hate Slavery on its own account, and others, because Slavery is in arms against the Government.

The Rebellion has been a rapid educator. Congress was the first to respond to the instinctive judgment of the people, and fixed the broad brand of its reprobation upon slave-hunting in shoulder-straps. Then came very temperate talk about confiscation, which soon came to be pretty radical talk. Then came propositions for Border-State, gradual, compensated, colonized Emancipation. Then came the threat of a proclamation, and then came the proclamation. Meanwhile the Negro had passed along from a loyal spade and pickax to a Springfield rifle.

Haiti and Liberia are recognized. Slavery is humbled in Maryland, threatened in Tennessee, stunned nearly to death in Western Virginia, doomed in Missouri, trembling in Kentucky, and gradually melting away before our arms in the rebellious States.

The hour is one of hope as well as danger. But whatever may come to pass, one thing is clear: The principles involved in the contest, the necessities of both sections of the country, the obvious requirements of the age, and every suggestion of enlightened policy demand the utter extirpation of Slavery from every foot of American soil, and the enfranchisement of the entire colored population of the country. Elsewhere we may find peace, but it will be a hollow and deceitful peace. Elsewhere we may find prosperity, but it will be a transient prosperity. Elsewhere we may find greatness and renown, but if these are based upon anything less substantial than justice they will vanish, for righteousness alone can permanently exalt a nation.

I end where I began—no war but an Abolition war; no peace but an Abolition peace; liberty for all, chains for none; the black man a soldier in war, a laborer in peace; a voter at the South as well as at the North; America his permanent home, and all Americans his fellow-countrymen. Such, fellow-citizens, is my idea of the mission of the war. If accomplished, our glory as a nation will be complete, our peace will flow like a river, and our foundations will be the everlasting rocks.

From 1883

The Labor Question

Not the least important among the subjects to which we invite your earnest attention is the condition of the labor class at the South. Their cause is one with the labor classes all over the world. The labor unions of the country should not throw away this colored element of strength. Everywhere there is dissatisfaction with the present relation of labor and capital, and today no subject wears an aspect more threatening to civilization than the respective claims of capital and labor, landlords and tenants. In what we have to say for our laboring class we expect to have and ought to have the sympathy and support of laboring men everywhere and of every color.

It is a great mistake for any class of laborers to isolate itself and thus weaken the bond of brotherhood between those on whom the burden and hardships of labor fell. The fortunate ones of the earth, who are abundant in land and money and know nothing of the anxious care and pinching poverty of the laboring classes, may be indifferent to the appeal for justice at this point, but the laboring classes cannot afford to be indifferent. What labor everywhere wants, what it ought to have, and will some day demand and receive, is an honest day's pay for an honest day's work. As the laborer becomes more intelligent he will develop what capital he already possesses—that is the power to organize and combine for its own protection. Experience demonstrates that there may be a slavery of wages only a little less galling and crushing in its effects than chattel slavery, and that this slavery of wages must go down with the other.

There is nothing more common now than the remark that the physical condition of the freedmen of the South is immeasurably worse than in the time of slavery; that in respect to food, clothing, and shelter they are wretched, miserable, and destitute; that they are worse masters to themselves than their old masters were to them. To add insult to injury, the reproach of their condition is charged upon themselves. A grandson of John C. Calhoun, an Arkansas landowner, testifying the other day before the Senate Committee of Labor and Education, says the "Negroes are so indolent that they fail to take advantage of the opportunities offered them to procure the necessities of life; that there is danger of a war of races," etc., etc.

His testimony proclaims him the grandson of the man whose name he bears. The blame which belongs to his own class he shifts from them to the shoulders of labor. It becomes us to test the truth of that assertion by the light of reason, and by appeals to indisputable facts. Of course the landowners of the South may be expected to view things differently from the landless. The slaveholders always did look at things a little differently from the slaves, and we therefore insist that, in order that the whole truth shall be brought out, the laborer as well as the capitalist shall be called as witnesses before the Senate Committee of Labor and Education. Experience proves that it takes more than one class of people to tell the whole truth about matters in which they are interested on opposite sides, and we protest against the allowance of only one side of the labor question to be heard by the country in this case. Meanwhile, a little reason and reflection will in some measure bring out truth! The colored people of the South are the laboring people of the South. The labor of a country is the source of its wealth; without the colored laborer today the South would be a howling wilderness, given up to bats, owls, wolves, and bears. He was the source of its wealth before the war, and has been the source of its prosperity since the war. He almost alone is visible in her fields, with implements of toil in his hands, and laboriously using them today.

Let us look candidly at the matter. While we see and hear that the South is more prosperous than it ever was before and rapidly recovering from the waste of war, while we read that it raises more cotton, sugar, rice, tobacco, corn, and other valuable products than it ever produced before, how happens it, we sternly ask, that the houses of its laborers are miserable huts, that their cloths are rags, and their food the coarsest and scantiest? How happens it that the landowner is becoming richer and the laborer poorer?

The implication is irresistible—that where the landlord is prosperous the laborer ought to share his prosperity, and whenever and wherever we find this is not the case there is manifestly wrong somewhere.

This sharp contrast of wealth and poverty, as every thoughtful man knows, can exist only in one way, and from one cause, and that is by one getting more than its proper share of the reward of industry, and the other side getting less, and that in some way labor has been defrauded or otherwise denied of its due proportion, and we think the facts, as well as this philosophy, will support this view in the present case, and do so conclusively. We utterly deny that the colored people of the South are too lazy to work, or that they are indifferent to their physical wants; as already said, they are the workers of that section.

The trouble is not that the colored people of the South are indolent, but that no matter how hard or how persistent may be their industry, they get barely enough for their labor to support life at the very low point at which we find them.

✳   ✳   ✳

MARTIN DELANY
EXCERPTS FROM *THE CONDITION, ELEVATION, EMIGRATION, AND DESTINY OF THE COLORED PEOPLE OF THE UNITED STATES* (1852)

One part of the American people, though living in near proximity and together, are quite unacquainted with the other; and one of the great objects of the author is, to make each acquainted. Except the character of an individual is known, there can be no just appreciation of his worth; and as with individuals, so is it with classes.

The colored people are not yet known, even to their most professed friends among the white Americans; for the reason, that politicians, religionists, colonizationists, and abolitionists, have each and all, at different times, presumed to *think* for, dictate to, and *know* better what suited colored people, than they knew for themselves; and consequently, there has been no other knowledge of them obtained, than that which has been obtained through these mediums. Their history—past, present, and future, has been written by them, who, for reasons well known, which are named in this volume, are not their representatives, and, therefore, do not properly nor fairly present their wants and claims among their fellows. Of these impressions, we design disabusing the public mind, and correcting the false impressions of all classes upon this great subject. A moral and mental, is as obnoxious as a physical servitude, and not to be tolerated; as the one may, eventually, lead to the other. Of these we feel the direful effects.

If I'm designed your lordling's slave,
By nature's law designed;
Why was an independent wish
E'er planted in my mind?

One of our great temporal curses is our consummate poverty. We are the poorest people, as a class, in the world of civilized mankind—abjectly, miserably poor, no one scarcely being able to assist the other. To this, of course, there are noble exceptions; but that which is common to, and the very process by which white men exist, and succeed in life, is unknown to colored men in general. In any and every considerable community may be found, some one of our white fellow-citizens, who is worth more than all the colored people in that community put together. We consequently have little or no efficiency. We must have means to be practically efficient in all the undertakings of life; and to obtain them, it is necessary that we should be engaged in lucrative pursuits, trades, and general business transactions. In order to be thus engaged, it is necessary that we should occupy positions that afford the facilities for such pursuits. To compete now with the mighty odds of wealth, social and religious preferences, and political influences of this country, at this advanced stage of its national existence, we never may expect. A new country, and new beginning, is the only true, rational, politic remedy for our disadvantageous position; and that country we have already pointed out, with triple golden advantages, all things considered, to that of any country to which it has been the province of man to embark.

Every other than we, have at various periods of necessity, been a migratory people; and all when oppressed, shown a greater abhorrence of oppression, if not a greater love of liberty, than we. We cling to our oppressors as the objects of our love. It is true that our enslaved brethren are here, and we have been led to believe that it is necessary for us to remain, on that account. Is it true, that all should remain in degradation, because a part are degraded? We believe no such thing. We believe it to be the duty of the Free, to elevate themselves in the most speedy and effective manner possible; as the redemption of the bondman depends entirely upon the elevation of the freeman; therefore, to elevate the free colored people of America, anywhere upon this continent; forebodes the speedy redemption of the slaves. We shall hope to hear no more of so fallacious a doctrine—the necessity of the free remaining in degradation, for the sake of the oppressed. Let us apply, first, the lever to ourselves; and the force that elevates us to the position of manhood's considerations and honors, will cleft the manacle of every slave in the land.

A continuance in any position, becomes what is termed "Second Nature;" it begets an *adaptation* and *reconciliation* of *mind* to such condition. It changes the whole physiological condition of the system, and adapts man and woman to a higher or lower sphere in the pursuits of life. The offsprings of slaves and peasantry, have the general characteristics of their parents; and nothing but a different course of training and education, will change the character.

The slave may become a lover of his master, and learn to forgive him for continual deeds of maltreatment and abuse; just as the Spaniel would couch and fondle at the feet that kick him; because he has been taught to reverence them, and consequently, becomes adapted in body and mind to his condition. Even the shrubbery-loving Canary, and lofty-soaring Eagle, may be tamed to the cage, and learn to love it from habit of confinement. It has been so with us in our position among our oppressors; we have been so prone to such positions, that we have learned to love them. When reflecting upon this all-important, and to us, all-absorbing subject; we feel in the agony and anxiety of the moment, as though we could cry out in the language of a Prophet of old: "Oh that my head were waters, and mine eyes a fountain of tears, that I might weep day and night for the" degradation "of my people! Oh that I had in the wilderness a lodging place of wayfaring men; that I might leave my people, and go from them!"

The Irishman and German in the United States, are very different persons to what they were when in Ireland and Germany, the countries of their nativity. There their spirits were depressed and downcast; but the instant they set their foot upon unrestricted soil; free to act and untrammeled to move, their physical condition undergoes a change, which in time becomes physiological, which is transmitted to the offspring, who when born under such circumstances, is a decidedly different being to what it would have been, had it been born under different circumstances.

A child born under oppression, has all the elements of servility in its constitution; who when born under favorable circumstances has, to the contrary, all the elements of freedom and independence of feeling. Our children then, may not be expected to maintain that position and manly bearing—born under the unfavorable circumstances with which we are surrounded in this country—that we so much desire. To use the language of the talented Mr. Whipper, "they cannot be raised in this country, without being stoop shouldered." Heaven's pathway stands unobstructed, which will lead us into a Paradise of bliss. Let us go on and possess the land, and the God of Israel will be our God.

A Project for an Expedition of Adventure, to the Eastern Coast of Africa

Every people should be the originators of their own designs, the projector of their own schemes, and creators of the events that lead to their destiny—the consummation of their desires.

Situated as we are, in the United States, many, and almost insurmountable obstacles present themselves. We are four and a half millions in numbers, free and bond; six hundred thousand free, and three and a half millions bond.

We have native hearts and virtues, just as other nations; which in their pristine purity are noble, potent, and worthy of example. We are a nation within a nation; as the Poles in Russia, the Hungarians in Austria, the Welsh, Irish, and Scotch in the British dominions.

But we have been, by our oppressors, despoiled of our purity, and corrupted in our native characteristics, so that we have inherited their vices, and but few of their virtues, leaving us in character, really a *broken people*.

Being distinguished by complexion, we are still singled out—although having merged in the habits and customs of our oppressors—as a distinct nation of people; as the Poles, Hungarians, Irish, and others, who still retain their native peculiarities, of language, habits, and various other traits. The claims of no people, according to established policy and usage, are respected by any nation, until they are presented in a national capacity.

To accomplish so great and desirable an end, there should be held a great representative gathering of the colored people of the United States; not what is termed a National Convention, represented en masse, such as have been, for the last few years, held at various times and places; but a true representation of the intelligence and wisdom of the colored freemen; because it will be futile and an utter failure, to attempt such a project without the highest grade of intelligence.

We must Make an Issue, Create an Event, and Establish a National Position for Ourselves; and never may expect to be respected as men and women, until we have undertaken some fearless, bold, and adventurous deeds of daring, contending against every odds—regardless of every consequence.

* * *

SOJOURNER TRUTH
SPEECHES AT ANTISLAVERY CONFERENCES

Speech at Akron Convention (1851)
[Account written by Frances D. Gage]

The leaders of the movement trembled on seeing a tall, gaunt black woman in a gray dress and white turban, surmounted with an uncouth sunbonnet, march deliberately into the church, walk with the air of a queen up the aisle, and take her seat upon the pulpit steps. A buzz of disapprobation was heard all over the house, and there fell on the listening ear, "An abolition affair!" "Woman's rights and niggers!" "I told you so!" "Go it, darkey!"

I chanced on that occasion to wear my first laurels in public life as president of the meeting. At my request order was restored, and the business of the Convention went on. Morning, afternoon, and evening exercises came and went. Through all these sessions old Sojourner, quiet and reticent as the "Lybian Statue," sat couched against the wall on the corner of the pulpit stairs, her sun-bonnet shading her eyes, her elbows on her knees, her chin resting upon her broad, hard palms. At intermission she was busy selling the "Life of Sojourner Truth," a narrative of her own strange and adventurous life. Again and again, timorous and trembling ones came to me and said, with earnestness, "Don't let her speak, Mrs. Gage, it will ruin us. Every newspaper in the land will have our cause mixed up with abolition and niggers, and we shall be utterly denounced." My only answer was, "We shall see when the time comes."

The second day the work waxed warm. Methodist, Baptist, Episcopal, Presbyterian, and Universalist ministers came in to hear and discuss the resolutions presented. One claimed superior rights and privileges for man, on the ground of "superior intellect"; another, because of the "manhood of Christ; if God had desired the equality of woman, He would have given some token of His will through the birth, life, and death of the Savior." Another gave us a theological view of the "sin of our first mother."

There were very few women in those days who dared to "speak in meeting"; and the august teachers of the people were seemingly getting the better of us, while the boys in the galleries, and the sneerers among the pews, were hugely enjoying the discomfiture, as they suppose, of the "strong-minded." Some of the tender-skinned friends were on the point of losing dignity, and the atmosphere betokened a storm. When, slowly from her seat in the corner rose Sojourner Truth, who, till now, had scarcely lifted her head. "Don't let her speak!" gasped half a dozen in my ear. She moved slowly and solemnly to the front, laid her old bonnet at her feet, and turned her great speaking eyes to me. There was a hissing sound of disapprobation above and below. I rose and announced "Sojourner Truth," and begged the audience to keep silence for a few moments.

The tumult subsided at once, and every eye was fixed on this almost Amazon form, which stood nearly six feet high, head erect, and eyes piercing the upper air like one in a dream. At her first word there was a profound hush. She spoke in deep tones, which, though not loud, reached every ear in the house, and away through the throng at the doors and windows.

"Wall, chilern, whar dar is so much racket dar must be somethin' out o'kilter. I tink dat 'twixt de niggers of de Souf and de womin at de Norf, all talkin' 'bout rights, de white men will be in a fix pretty soon. But what's all dis here talkin' 'bout?

"Dat man ober dar say dat womin needs to be helped into carriages, and lifted ober ditches, and to hab de best place everywhar. Nobody eber helps me into carriage, or ober mud-puddles, or gibs me any best place!" And raising herself to her full height, and her voice to a pitch like rolling thunder, she asked.

"And a'n't I a woman? Look at me! Look at my arm! (and she bared her right arm to the shoulder, showing her tremendous muscular power). I have ploughed, and planted, and gathered into barns, and no man could head me! And a'n't I a woman? I could work as much and eat as much as a man—when I could get it—and bear de lash as well! And a'n't I a woman? I have borne thirteen chilern, and seen 'em mos' all sold off to slavery, and when I cried out with my mother's grief, none but Jesus heard me! And a'n't I a woman?

"Den dey talks 'bout dis ting in de head; what dis dey call it?" ("Intellect," whispered some one near). "Dat's it, honey. What's dat got to do wid womin's rights or nigger's rights? If my cup won't hold but a pint, and yourn holds a quart, wouldn't ye be mean not to let me have my little half-measure full?" And she pointed her significant finger, and sent a keen glance at the minister who had made the argument. The cheering was long and loud.

"Den dat little man in black dar, he say women can't have as much rights as men, 'cause Christ wan't a woman! Whar did your Christ come from?" Rolling thunder couldn't have stilled that crowd, as did those deep, wonderful tones, as she stood there with outstretched arms and eyes of fire. Raising her voice still louder, she repeated, "Whar did your Christ come from? From God and a woman! Man had nothin' to do wid Him." Oh, what a rebuke that was to that little man.

Turning again to another objector, she took up the defense of Mother Eve. I cannot follow her through it all. It was pointed, and witty, and solemn; eliciting at almost every sentence deafening applause; and she ended by asserting: "If de fust woman God ever made was strong enough to turn de world upside down all alone, dese women togedeer (and she glanced her eye over the platform) ought to be able to turn it back, and get it right side up again! And now dey is asking to do it, de man better let 'em." Long-continued cheering greeted this. "Bleeged to ye for hearin' on me, and now ole Sojourner han't got nothin' more to say."

Amid roars of applause, she returned to her corner, leaving more than one of us with streaming eyes, and hearts beating with gratitude. She had taken us up in her strong arms and carried us safely over the slough of difficulty turning the whole tide in our favor. I have never in my life seen anything like the magical influence that subdued the mobbish spirit of the day, and turned the sneers and jeers of an excited crowd into notes of respect and admiration. Hundreds rushed up to shake hands with her, and congratulate the glorious old mother, and bid her God-speed on her mission of "testifyin' agin concerning the wickedness of this 'ere people."

Speech at New York City Convention (1853)

Is it not good for me to come and draw forth a spirit, to see what kind of spirit people are of? I see that some of you have got the spirit of a goose, and some have got the spirit of a snake. I feel at home here. I come to you, citizens of New

York, as I suppose you ought to be. I am a citizen of the State of New York; I was born in it, and I was a slave in the State of New York; and now I am a good citizen of this State. I was born here, and I can tell you I feel at home here. I've been lookin' round and watchin' things, and I know a little mite 'bout Woman's Rights, too. I come forth to speak 'bout Woman's Rights, and want to throw in my little mite, to keep the scales a-movin', I know that it feels a' kind o' hissin' and ticklin' like to see a colored woman get up and tell you about things, and Woman's Rights. We have all been thrown down so low that nobody thought we'd ever get up again; but we have been long enough trodden now; we will come up again, and now I am here.

I was a-thinkin', when I see women contendin' for their rights, I was a-thinkin' what a difference there is now, and what there was in old times. I have only a few minutes to speak; but in the old times the kings of the earth would hear a woman. There was a king in the Scriptures; and then it was the kings of the earth would kill a woman if she come into their presence; but Queen Esther,* come forth, for she was oppressed, and felt there was a great wrong. And she said I will die or I will bring my complaint before the king. Should the king of the United States be greater, or more crueler, or more harder? But the king, he raised up his scepter and said: "Thy request shall be granted unto thee—to the half of my kingdom will I grant it to thee." Then he said he would hang Haman on the gallows he had made up high. But that is not what women come forward to contend. The women want their rights as Esther. She only wanted to explain her rights. And he was so liberal that he said, "the half of my kingdom shall be granted to thee," and he did not wait for her to ask, he was so liberal with her.

Now, women do not ask half of a kingdom, but their rights, and they don't get 'em.—When she comes to demand 'em; don't you hear how sons hiss their mothers like snakes, because they ask for their rights; and can they ask for anything less? The king ordered Haman to be hung on the gallows which he prepared to hang others; but I do not want any man to be killed, but I am sorry to see them so short-minded. But we'll have our rights; see if we don't; and you can't stop us from them; see if you can. You may hiss as much as you like, but it is comin'. Women don't get half as much rights as they ought to; we want more, and we will have it. Jesus says: "What I say to one, I say to all—watch!" I'm a-watchin'. God says: "Honor your father and your mother." Sons and daughters ought to behave themselves before their mothers, but they do not. I can see them a-laughin' and pointin' at their mothers up here on the stage. They hiss when an aged woman comes forth. If they'd been brought up proper they'd have known

---

*The Old Testament King Ahasuerus offered to fulfill any request made by his Jewish wife Esther, even if she asked for half of his kingdom. Esther asked for justice for her people. Prince Haman was slaughtering the Jews because he believed he had been insulted by the king's adviser, Mordecai. King Ahasuerus hanged Haman on the gallows Haman had built for Mordecai.

better than hissing like snakes and geese. I'm 'round watchin' these things, and I wanted to come up and say these few things to you, and I'm glad of the hearin' you give me. I wanted to tell you a mite about Woman's Rights, and so I came out and said so. I am sittin' among you to watch; and every once and awhile I will come out and tell you what time of night it is.

*   *   *

HARRIET TUBMAN
(1868)

There was one of two things I had a *right* to, liberty, or death; if I could not have one, I would have the other; for no man should take me alive; I should fight for my liberty as long as my strength lasted, and when the time came for me to go, the Lord would let them take me.

*   *   *

IDA B. WELLS-BARNETT
EXCERPTS FROM *SOUTHERN HORRORS:*
LYNCH LAW IN ALL ITS PHASES (1892)

From this exposition of the race issue in lynch law, the whole matter is explained by the well-known opposition growing out of slavery to the progress of the race. This is crystallized in the oft-repeated slogan: "This is a white man's country and the white man must rule." The South resented giving the Afro-American his freedom, the ballot box and the Civil Rights Law. The raids of the Ku-Klux and White Liners to subvert reconstruction government, the Hamburg and Ellerton, South Carolina, the Copiah County Mississippi, and the Lafayette Parish, Louisiana, massacres were excused as the natural resentment of intelligence against government by ignorance.

Honest white men practically conceded the necessity of intelligence murdering ignorance to correct the mistake of the general government, and the race was left to the tender mercies of the solid South. Thoughtful Afro-Americans with the strong arm of the government withdrawn and with the hope to stop such wholesale massacres urged the race to sacrifice its political rights for sake of peace. They honestly believed the race should fit itself for government, and when that should be done, the objection to race participation in politics would be removed.

But the sacrifice did not remove the trouble, nor move the South to justice. One by one the Southern States have legally (?) disfranchised the Afro-American, and since the repeal of the Civil Rights Bill nearly every Southern State has passed separate car laws with a penalty against their infringement. The race regardless of advancement is penned into filthy, stifling partitions cut off from smoking cars. All this while, although the political cause has been removed, the butcheries of black men at Barnwell, South Carolina, Carrolton, Mississippi, Waycross, Georgia, and Memphis, Tennessee, have gone on; also the flaying alive of a man in Kentucky, the burning of one in Arkansas, the hanging of a fifteen-year-old girl in Louisiana, a woman in Jackson, Tennessee, and one in Hollendale, Mississippi, until the dark and bloody record of the South shows 728 Afro-Americans lynched during the past 8 years. Not 50 of these were for political causes; the rest were for all manner of accusations from that of rape of white women, to the case of the boy Will Lewis who was hanged at Tullahoma, Tennessee, last year for being drunk and "sassy" to white folks.

These statistics compiled by the Chicago *Tribune* were given the first of this year (1892). Since then, not less than one hundred and fifty have been known to have met violent death at the hands of cruel bloodthirsty mobs during the past nine months.

To palliate this record (which grows worse as the Afro-American becomes intelligent) and excuse some of the most heinous crimes that ever stained the history of a country, the South is shielding itself behind the plausible screen of defending the honor of its women. This, too, in the face of the fact that only *one-third* of the 728 victims to mobs have been *charged* with rape, to say nothing of those of that one-third who were innocent of the charge. A white correspondent of the *Baltimore Sun* declares that the Afro-American who was lynched in Chestertown, Maryland, in May for assault on a white girl was innocent; that the deed was done by a white man who had since disappeared. The girl herself maintained that her assailant was a white man. When that poor Afro-American was murdered, the whites excused their refusal of a trial on the ground that they wished to spare the white girl the mortification of having to testify in court.

This cry has had its effect. It has closed the heart, stifled the conscience, warped the judgment, and hushed the voice of press and pulpit on the subject of lynch law throughout this "land of liberty." Men who stand high in the esteem of the public for christian character, for moral and physical courage, for devotion to the principles of equal and exact justice to all, and for great sagacity, stand as cowards who fear to open their mouths before this great outrage. They do not see that by their tacit encouragement, their silent acquiescence, the black shadow of lawlessness in the form of lynch law is spreading its wings over the whole country.

Men who, like Governor Tillman, start the ball of lynch law rolling for a certain crime, are powerless to stop it when drunken or criminal white toughs feel like hanging an Afro-American on any pretext.

Even to the better class of Afro-Americans the crime of rape is so revolting they have too often taken the white man's word and given lynch law neither the investigation nor condemnation it deserved.

They forget that a concession of the right to lynch a man for a certain crime, not only concedes the right to lynch any person for any crime, but (so frequently is the cry of rape now raised) it is in a fair way to stamp us a race of rapists and desperadoes. They have gone on hoping and believing that general education and financial strength would solve the difficulty, and are devoting their energies to the accumulation of both.

The mob spirit has grown with the increasing intelligence of the Afro-American. It has left the out-of-the-way places where ignorance prevails, has thrown off the mask, and with this new cry stalks in broad daylight in large cities, the centers of civilization, and is encouraged by the "leading citizens" and the press.

The South's Position

Henry W. Grady in his well-remembered speeches in New England and New York pictured the Afro-American as incapable of self-government. Through him and other leading men the cry of the South to the country has been "Hands off! Leave us to solve our problem." To the Afro-American the South says, "the white man must and will rule." There is little difference between the Ante-bellum South and the New South.

Her white citizens are wedded to any method however revolting, any measure however extreme, for the subjugation of the young manhood of the race. They have cheated him out of his ballot, deprived him of civil rights or redress therefore in the civil courts, robbed him of the fruits of his labor, and are still murdering, burning, and lynching him.

The result is a growing disregard of human life. Lynch law has spread its insidious influence till men in New York State, Pennsylvania, and on the free Western plains feel they can take the law in their own hands with impunity, especially where an Afro-American is concerned. The South is brutalized to a degree not realized by its own inhabitants, and the very foundation of government, law and order, are imperiled.

Public sentiment has had a slight "reaction" though not sufficient to stop the crusade of lawlessness and lynching. The spirit of Christianity of the great M. E. [Methodist Episcopal] Church was aroused to the frequent and revolting crimes against a weak people, enough to pass strong condemnatory resolutions at its General Conference in Omaha last May. The spirit of justice of the grand old party asserted itself sufficiently to secure a denunciation of the wrongs, and a feeble declaration of the belief in human rights in the Republican platform at Minneapolis, June 7th. Some of the great dailies and weeklies have swung into line declaring that lynch law must go. The President of the United States issued a proclamation that it be not tolerated in the territories over which he has jurisdiction. Governor Northern and Chief Justice Bleckley of Georgia have proclaimed against it. The citizens of Chattanooga, Tennessee, have set a worthy example in that they not only condemn lynch law, but her public men demanded a trial for Weems, the accused rapist, and guarded him while the trial was in progress. The trial only lasted ten minutes, and Weems chose to plead guilty and accept twenty-one years sentence, than invite the certain death which awaited him outside that cordon of police if he had told the truth and shown the letters he had from the white woman in the case.

Col. A. S. Colyar, of Nashville, Tennessee, is so overcome with the horrible state of affairs that he addressed the following earnest letter to the Nashville "American." "Nothing since I have been a reading man has so impressed me with the decay of manhood among the people of Tennessee as the dastardly submission to the mob reign. We have reached the unprecedented low level; the awful criminal depravity of substituting the mob for the court and jury, of giving up the jail keys to the mob whenever they are demanded. We do it in the largest cities and in the country towns; we do it in midday; we do it after full, not to say formal, notice, and so thoroughly and generally is it acquiesced in that the murderers have discarded the formula of masks. They go into the town where everybody knows them, sometimes under the gaze of the governor, in the presence of the courts, in the presence of the sheriff and his deputies, in the presence of the entire police force, take out the prisoner, take his life, often with fiendish glee, and often with acts of cruelty and barbarism which impress the reader with a degeneracy rapidly approaching savage life. That the State is disgraced but faintly expresses the humiliation which has settled upon the once proud people of Tennessee. The State, in its majesty, through its organized life, for which the people pay liberally, makes but one record, but one note, and that a criminal falsehood, 'was hung by persons to the jury unknown.' The murder at Shelbyville is only a verification of what every intelligent man knew would come, because with a mob a rumor is as good as a proof."

These efforts brought forth apologies and a short halt, but the lynching mania has raged again through the past three months with unabated fury.

The strong arm of the law must be brought to bear upon lynchers in severe punishment, but this cannot and will not be done unless a healthy public sentiment demands and sustains such action.

The men and women in the South who disapprove of lynching and remain silent on the perpetration of such outrages, are particeps criminis, accomplices, accessories before and after the fact, equally guilty with the actual law-breakers who would not persist if they did not know that neither the law nor militia would be employed against them.

Self-Help

In the creation of this healthier public sentiment, the Afro-American can do for himself what no one else can do for him. The world looks on with wonder that we have conceded so much and remain law-abiding under such great outrage and provocation.

To Northern capital and Afro-American labor the South owes its rehabilitation. If labor is withdrawn capital will not remain. The Afro-American is thus the backbone of the South. A thorough knowledge and judicious exercise of this power in lynching localities could many times effect a bloodless revolution. The white man's dollar is his god, and to stop this will be to stop outrages in many localities.

The Afro-Americans of Memphis denounced the lynching of three of their best citizens and urged and waited for the authorities to act in the matter and bring the lynchers to justice. No attempt was made to do so, and the black men left the city by thousands, bringing about great stagnation in every branch of business. Those who remained so injured the business of the street car company by staying off the cars, that the superintendent, manager, and treasurer called personally on the editor of the "Free Speech," asked them to urge our people to give them their patronage again. Other business men became alarmed over the situation and the "Free Speech" was run away that the colored people might be more easily controlled. A meeting of white citizens in June, three months after the lynching, passed resolutions for the first time, condemning it. *But they did not punish the lynchers.* Every one of them was known by name, because they had been selected to do the dirty work, by some of the very citizens who passed these resolutions. Memphis is fast losing her black population, who proclaim as they go that there is no protection for the life and property of any Afro-American citizen in Memphis who is not a slave.

The Afro-American citizens of Kentucky, whose intellectual and financial improvement has been phenomenal, have never had a separate car law until now. Delegations and petitions poured into the Legislature against it, yet the bill passed and the Jim Crow Car of Kentucky is a legalized institution. Will the great mass of Negroes continue to patronize the railroad? A special from Covington, Kentucky, says:

"Covington, June 13th.—The railroads of the State are beginning to feel very markedly, the effects of the separate coach bill recently passed by the Legislature. No class of people in the State have so many and so largely attended excursions as the blacks. All these have been abandoned, and regular travel is reduced to a minimum. A competent authority says the loss to the various roads will reach $1,000,000 this year."

A call to a State Conference in Lexington, Kentucky, last June had delegates from every county in the State. Those delegates, the ministers, teachers, heads of secret and others orders, and head of every family should pass the word around for every member of the race in Kentucky to stay off railroads unless obliged to ride. If they did so, and their advice was followed persistently the convention would not need to petition the Legislature to repeal the law or raise money to file a suit. The railroad corporations would be so affected they would in self-defense lobby to have the separate car law repealed. On the other hand, as long as the railroads can get Afro-American excursions they will always have plenty of money to fight all the suits brought against them. They will be aided in so doing by the same partisan public sentiment which passed the law. White men passed the law, and white judges and juries would pass upon the suits against the law, and render judgment in line with their prejudices and in deference to the greater financial power.

The appeal to the white man's pocket has ever been more effectual than all the appeals ever made to his conscience. Nothing, absolutely nothing, is to be gained by a further sacrifice of manhood and self-respect. By the right exercise of his power as the industrial factor of the South, the Afro-American can demand and secure his rights, the punishment of lynchers, and a fair trial for accused rapists.

Of the many inhuman outrages of this present year, the only case where the proposed lynching did *not* occur, was where the men armed themselves in Jacksonville, Florida, and Paducah, Kentucky, and prevented it. The only times an Afro-American who was assaulted got away has been when he had a gun and used it in self-defense.

The lesson this teaches and which every Afro-American should ponder well, is that a Winchester rifle should have a place of honor in every black home, and it should be used for that protection which the law refuses to give. When the white man who is always the aggressor knows he runs as great risk of biting the dust every time his Afro-American victim does, he will have greater respect for Afro-American life. The more the Afro-American yields and cringes and begs, the more he has to do so, the more he is insulted, outraged, and lynched.

The assertion has been substantiated throughout these pages that the press contains unreliable and doctored reports of lynchings, and one of the most necessary things for the race to do is to get these facts before the public. The people must know before they can act, and there is no educator to compare with the press.

The Afro-American papers are the only ones which will print the truth, and they lack means to employ agents and detectives to get at the facts. The race must rally a mighty host to the support of their journals, and thus enable them to do much in the way of investigation.

✳   ✳   ✳

BOOKER T. WASHINGTON
FROM 1884 SPEECH

Any movement for the elevation of the Southern Negro, in order to be successful must have to a certain extent the cooperation of the Southern whites. They control government and own the property—whatever benefits the black man benefits the white man. The proper education of all the whites will benefit the Negro as much as the education of the Negro will benefit the whites. The Governor of Alabama would probably count it no disgrace to ride in the same railroad coach with a colored man, but the ignorant white man who curries the Governor's horse would turn up his nose in disgust. . . . Brains, property, and character for the Negro will settle the question of civil rights. The best course to pursue in regard to the civil rights bill in the South is to let it alone; let it alone and it will settle itself. Good schoolteachers and plenty of money to pay them will be more potent in settling the race question than many civil rights bills and investigating committees.

Now, in regard to what I have said about the relations of the two races, there should be no unmanly cowering or stooping to satisfy unreasonable whims of Southern white men, but it is charity and wisdom to keep in mind the two hundred years' schooling in prejudice against the Negro which the ex-slave holders are called upon to conquer. A certain class of whites in the South object to the general education of the colored man on the ground that when he is educated he ceases to do manual labor, and there is no evading the fact that much aid is withheld from Negro education in the South by the states on these grounds. Just here the great mission of INDUSTRIAL EDUCATION coupled with the mental comes in. It "kills two birds with one stone," viz: secures the cooperation of the whites, and does the best possible thing for the black man. An old colored man in a cotton field in the middle of July lifted his eyes toward heaven and said, "De cotton is so grassy de work is so hard, and de sun am so hot, I believe this darky am called to preach." This old man, no doubt, stated the true reason why not a few enter school. Educate the black man, mentally and industrially, and there will be no doubt of his prosperity; for a race who has lived at all, and paid, for the last twenty years, 25 and 30 percent interest on the dollar advanced for food, with almost no education, can certainly take care of itself when educated mentally and industrially.

＊ ＊ ＊

W. E. B. DU BOIS
THE NIAGARA ADDRESS OF 1906

The men of the Niagara Movement coming from the toil of the year's hard work and pausing a moment from the earning of their daily bread turn toward the nation and again ask in the name of ten million the privilege of a hearing. In the past year the work of the Negro hater has flourished in the land. Step by step the defenders of the rights of American citizens have retreated. The work of stealing the black man's ballot has progressed and the fifty and more representatives of stolen votes still sit in the nation's capital. Discrimination in travel and public accommodation has so spread that some of our weaker brethren are actually afraid to thunder against color discrimination as such and are simply whispering for ordinary decencies.

Against this the Niagara Movement eternally protests. We will not be satisfied to take one jot or tittle less than our full manhood rights. We claim for ourselves every single right that belongs to a freeborn American, political, civil, and social; and until we get these rights we will never cease to protest and assail the ears of America. The battle we wage is not for ourselves alone but for all true Americans. It is a fight for ideals, lest this, our common fatherland, false to its founding, become in truth the land of the thief and the home of the Slave—a by-word and a hissing among the nations for its sounding pretentions and pitiful accomplishment.

Never before in the modern age has a great and civilized folk threatened to adopt so cowardly a creed in the treatment of its fellow-citizens born and bred on its soil. Stripped of verbiage and subterfuge and in its naked nastiness the new American creed says: Fear to let black men even try to rise lest they become the equals of the white. And this is the land that professes to follow Jesus Christ. The blasphemy of such a course is only matched by its cowardice.

In detail our demands are clear and unequivocal. First, we would vote; with the right to vote goes everything: Freedom, manhood, the honor of your wives, the chastity of your daughters, the right to work, and the chance to rise, and let no man listen to those who deny this.

We want full manhood suffrage, and we want it now, henceforth and forever.

Second. We want discrimination in public accommodation to cease. Separation in railway and street car, based simply on race and color, is un-American, undemocratic, and silly. We protest against all such discrimination.

Third. We claim the right of freemen to walk, talk, and be with them that wish to be with us. No man has a right to choose another man's friends, and to attempt to do so is an impudent interference with the most fundamental human privilege.

Fourth. We want the laws enforced against rich as well as poor; against Capitalist as well as Laborer; against white as well as black. We are not more lawless than the white race, we are more often arrested, convicted, and mobbed. We want justice even for criminals and outlaws. We want the Constitution of the country enforced. We want Congress to take charge of Congressional elections. We want the Fourteenth Amendment carried out to the letter and every State disfranchised in Congress which attempts to disfranchise its rightful voters. We want the Fifteenth Amendment enforced and no State allowed to base its franchise simply on color.

The failure of the Republican Party in Congress at the session just closed to redeem its pledge of 1904 with reference to suffrage conditions at the South seems a plain, deliberate, and premeditated breach of promise, and stamps that party as guilty of obtaining votes under false pretense.

Fifth. We want our children educated. The school system in the country districts of the South is a disgrace and in few towns and cities are the Negro schools what they ought to be. We want the national government to step in and wipe out illiteracy in the South. Either the United States will destroy ignorance or ignorance will destroy the United States.

And when we call for education we mean real education. We believe in work. We ourselves are workers, but work is not necessarily education. Education is the development of power and ideal. We want our children trained as intelligent human beings should be, and we will fight for all time against any proposal to educate black boys and girls simply as servants and underlings, or simply for the use of other people. They have a right to know, to think, to aspire.

These are some of the chief things which we want. How shall we get them? By voting where we may vote, by persistent, unceasing agitation, by hammering at the truth, by sacrifice and work.

We do not believe in violence, neither in the despised violence of the raid nor the lauded violence of the soldier, nor the barbarous violence of the mob, but we do believe in John Brown, in that incarnate spirit of justice, that hatred of a lie, that willingness to sacrifice money, reputation, and life itself on the altar of right. And here on the scene of John Brown's martyrdom we reconsecrate ourselves, our honor, our property to the final emancipation of the race which John Brown died to make free.

Our enemies, triumphant for the present, are fighting the stars in their courses. Justice and humanity must prevail. We live to tell these dark brothers of ours—scattered in counsel, wavering and weak—that no bribe of money or notoriety, no promise of wealth or fame, is worth the surrender of a people's manhood or the loss of a man's self-respect. We refuse to surrender the leadership of this race to cowards and trucklers. We are men; we will be treated as men. On this rock we have planted our banners. We will never give up, though the trump of doom find us still fighting.

And we shall win. The past promised it, the present foretells it. Thank God for John Brown! Thank God for Garrison and Douglass! Sumner and Phillips,

Nat Turner and Robert Gould Shaw,* and all the hallowed dead who died for freedom! Thank God for all those today, few though their voices be, who have not forgotten the divine brotherhood of all men, white and black, rich and poor, fortunate and unfortunate.

We appeal to the young men and women of this nation, to those whose nostrils are not yet befouled by greed and snobbery and racial narrowness: Stand up for the right, prove yourselves worthy of your heritage and whether born north or south dare to treat men as men. Cannot the nation that has absorbed ten million foreigners into its political life without catastrophe absorb ten million Negro Americans into that same political life at less cost than their unjust and illegal exclusion will involve?

Courage, brothers! The battle for humanity is not lost or losing. All across the skies sit signs of promise. The Slav is raising in his might, the yellow millions are tasting liberty, the black Africans are writhing toward the light, and everywhere the laborer, with ballot in his hand, is voting open the gates of Opportunity and Peace. The morning breaks over blood-stained hills. We must not falter, we may not shrink. Above are the everlasting stars.

* * *

MARCUS GARVEY
AFRICAN FUNDAMENTALISM (1925)

A Racial Hierarchy and Empire for Negroes.
Negro's Faith Must Be Confidence in Self,
His Creed: One God, One Aim, One Destiny

The time has come for the Negro to forget and cast behind him his hero worship and adoration of other races, and to start out immediately to create and emulate heroes of his own. We must canonize our own saints, create our own martyrs, and elevate to positions of fame and honor black men and women who have made their distinct contributions to our racial history. Sojourner Truth is worthy of the

---

*Along with Frederick Douglass, among the most prominent (white) abolitionists were William Lloyd Garrisson, Sen. Charles Sumner, and Wendell Phillips. Nat Turner led a violent slave uprising. Colonel Robert Gould Shaw commanded the Fifty-fourth Massachusetts Infantry (an African American unit) and was killed along with many of his men in the storming of Fort Wagner, South Carolina, in 1863.

place of sainthood alongside of Joan of Arc: Crispus Attucks and George William Gordon are entitled to the halo of martyrdom with no less glory than that of the martyrs of any other race. Toussaint L'Ouverture's brilliancy as a soldier and statesman outshone that of a Cromwell, Napoleon, and Washington; hence, he is entitled to the highest place as a hero among men. Africa has produced countless numbers of men and women, in war and in peace, whose luster and bravery outshine that of any other people. Then why not see good and perfection in ourselves? We must inspire a literature and promulgate a doctrine of our own without any apologies to the powers that be. The right is ours and God's. Let contrary sentiment and cross opinions go to the winds. Opposition to race independence is the weapon of the enemy to defeat the hopes of an unfortunate people. We are entitled to our own opinions and not obligated to or bound by the opinions of others.

A Peep at the Past

If others laugh at you, return the laughter to them; if they mimic you, return the compliment with equal force. They have no more right to dishonor, disrespect, and disregard your feeling and manhood than you have in dealing with them. Honor them when they honor you, disrespect and disregard them when they vilely treat you. Their arrogance is but skin deep and an assumption that has no foundation in morals or in law. They have sprung from the same family tree of obscurity as we have; their history is as rude in its primitiveness as ours; their ancestors ran wild and naked, lived in caves and in branches of trees, like monkeys, as ours; they made human sacrifices, ate the flesh of their own dead and the raw meat of the wild beast for centuries even as they accuse us of doing; their cannibalism was more prolonged than ours; when we were embracing the arts and sciences on the banks of the Nile their ancestors were still drinking human blood and eating out of the skulls of their conquered dead; when our civilization had reached the noonday of progress they were still running naked and sleeping in holes and caves with rats, bats, and other insects and animals. After we had already fathomed the mystery of the stars and reduced the heavenly constellations to minute and regular calculus they were still backwoodsmen, living in ignorance and blatant darkness.

Why Be Discouraged?

The world today is indebted to us for the benefits of civilization. They stole our arts and sciences from Africa. Then why should we be ashamed of ourselves? Their *modern improvements* are but *duplicates* of a grander civilization that we reflected thousands of years ago, without the advantage of what is buried and still hidden, to be resurrected and reintroduced by the intelligence of our generation and our posterity. Why should we be discouraged because somebody laughs at us today? Who can tell what tomorrow will bring forth? Did they not laugh at Moses, Christ, and Mohammed? Was there not a Carthage, Greece, and Rome? We see and have changes every day, so pray, work, be steadfast, and be not dismayed.

Nothing Must Kill the Empire Urge

As the Jew is held together by his *religion*, the white races by the assumption and the unwritten law of superiority, and the Mongolian by the precious tie of blood, so likewise the Negro must be united in one *grand racial hierarchy*. Our union must know no *clime, boundary, or nationality*. Like the great Church of Rome, Negroes the world over must practice one faith, that of Confidence in themselves, with One God! One Aim! One Destiny! Let no religious scruples, no political machination divide us, but let us hold together under all climes and in every country, making among ourselves a Racial Empire upon which "the sun shall never set."

Allegiance to Self First

Let no voice but your own speak to you from the depths. Let no influence but your own rouse you in time of peace and time of war; hear all, but attend only to that which concerns you. Your allegiance shall be to your God, then to your family, race, and country. Remember always that the Jew in his political and economic urge is always first a Jew; the white man is first a white man under all circumstances, and you can do no less than being first and always a Negro, and then all else will take care of itself. Let no one innoculate you with evil doctrines to suit their own conveniences. There is no humanity before that which starts with yourself. "Charity begins at home." First, to thyself be true, and "thou canst not then be false to any man."

We Are Arbiters of Our Own Destiny

God and Nature first made us what we are, and then out of our own created genius we make ourselves what we want to be. Follow always that great law. Let the sky and God be our limit and Eternity our measurement. There is no height to which we cannot climb by using the active intelligence of our own minds. Mind creates, and as much as we desire in Nature we can have through the creation of our own minds. Being at present the scientifically weaker race, you shall treat others only as they treat you; but in your homes and everywhere possible you must teach the higher development of science to your children; and be sure to develop a race of scientists par excellence, for in science and religion lies our only hope to withstand the evil designs of modern materialism. Never forget your God. Remember, we live, work, and pray for the establishing of a great and binding racial hierarchy, the founding of a racial empire whose only natural, spiritual, and political limits shall be God and "Africa, at home and abroad."

* * *

A. PHILIP RANDOLPH
ON RACE, CLASS, AND ECONOMICS

The Struggle for the Liberation of the Black Laboring Masses (1961)

In this mid–twentieth century black labor is one hundred years behind white labor. Black labor is behind white labor in the skilled crafts. They are behind in trade union organization. They are behind in workers' education. They are behind in employment opportunities.

Why? The answer is not because white labor is racially superior to black labor. Not because white labor is more productive than black labor.

In the race between black and white labor in American industry, black labor never had a chance. How could it be otherwise when Negro workers began as slaves while white workers began as free men, or virtually as free men?

In addition to a quarter of a thousand years of captivity in the labor system of chattel slavery, black labor, even after emancipation, has been a prisoner for a hundred years of a moneyless system of peonage, sharecropper-plantation-farm laborism, and a helpless and hopeless city-slum proletariat. . . .

No greater tragedy has befallen the working class anywhere in the modern world than that which plagues the working class in the South. Both white and black workers turned against their own class and gave aid to their enemy, the feudalistic-capitalist class, to subject them to sharper and sharper exploitation and oppression.

Verily, black and white workers did not fight each other because they hated each other, but they hated each other because they fought each other. They fought each other because they did not know each other. They did not know each other because they had no contact or communication with each other. They had no contact or communication with each other because they were afraid of each other. They were afraid of each other because each was propagandized into believing that each was seeking to take the jobs of the other.

By poisonous preachments by the press, pulpit, and politician, the wages of

Reprinted by permission from the A. Philip Randolph Institute.

both black and white workers were kept low and working conditions bad, since trade union organization was practically nonexistent. And, even today, the South is virtually a no-man's-land for union labor.

There is no remedy for this plight of the South's labor forces except the unity of the black and white working class. It is a matter of common knowledge that union organization campaigns, whether under the auspices of the old American Federation of Labor, or the younger Congress of Industrial Organizations, or the AFL-CIO, have wound up as miserable failures.

The reason is not only because the southern working class is divided upon a basis of race, but also because the AFL, the CIO, and the AFL-CIO never took cognizance of this fact. They never built their organization drives upon the principle of the solidarity of the working class. On the contrary, they accepted and proceeded to perpetuate this racial-labor more, the purpose of which was, and is, the perpetuation of segregation—the antithesis of trade union organization.

Thus, they sowed the winds of the division of the workers upon the basis of race, and now they are reaping the whirlwinds.

The leadership of the organized labor movement has at no time ever seriously challenged Jim Crow unionism in the South. White leaders of labor organizations, like white leaders of the Church, business, government, schools, and the press, marched together, under the banner of white supremacy, in the Ku Klux Klan, to put down and keep down by law or lawlessness, the Negro. . . .

While, before Emancipation, the Negro only had job security as a slave because he toiled for nothing, so, following Black Reconstruction, black freedmen labored within the framework of a peonage-sharecrop, labor-barter commissary system for, perhaps, a little more than nothing.

And, despite the Thirteenth, Fourteenth, Fifteenth Amendments, clear commitments to the protection of the freedmen, the Negro laboring masses have never fully broken through the barrier of the ethnic-labor mores of the South, which were hardened into a racially segregated order by the celebrated *Plessy* v. *Ferguson* decision of the U.S. Supreme Court of 1896. Moreover, like the proverbial locusts, the doctrine of least ethnic-labor costs, or a racial sub-wage differential, spread in every area of American industry.

Thus, Negro workers are not yet fully free in the South. By the same token, white workers in the South are not yet fully free, because no white worker can ever become fully free as long as a black worker is in southern Bourbon bondage. And as long as white and black workers in the South are not fully free, the entire working class, North, East, South, and West, is not and will not become fully free. There is no principle more obvious and universal than the indivisibility of the freedom of the workers regardless of race, color, religion, national origin, or ancestry, being based, as it were, upon the principle of least labor costs in a free market economy.

This is why the racial policies of the American Federation of Labor and Congress of Industrial Organizations have so devastatingly weakened, morally, organizationally, and politically, the American labor movement before the Congress, the public, and the world.

One has only to note that while trade unions, such as the Amalgamated Clothing Workers, Ladies' Garment Workers, and United Textile Workers, are building up decent wage rates and sound rules governing working conditions in New York, Massachusetts, Pennsylvania, and Illinois, corporate capital, highly sensitive to the least threat to high rates of profits and interest upon investments, promptly takes flight into the land of nonunion, low wage, low tax, race bias, mob law, and poor schools, namely, Dixie. Southern mayors, governors, and legislatures make special appeals in the northern press to industries to come South for nonunion, cheap labor.

But this anti–trade union condition in the South is labor's fault. It is the direct result of the fact that neither the old AFL, nor the CIO, nor the AFL-CIO ever came to grips with the racial-labor problem in the South. Instead of meeting the racial-labor issue head on, organized labor has always adopted a policy of appeasement, compromise, and defeatism. The evidence exists in the fact that it has recognized and accepted:

- The Jim Crow union
- The color bar in union constitutions, rituals, or exclusionary racial policies by tacit consent
- Racially segregated seniority rosters and lines of job progression
- Racial subwage differential
- Indifferent recognition, if not acceptance of the concept and practice of a "white man's job" and a "black man's job"
- Racial barriers against Negro participation in apprenticeship training programs
- Failure to demand Negro workers' participation in union democracy
- Racially segregated state conventions of the AFL-CIO in southern cities
- Racially segregated city central labor bodies of the AFL-CIO

Is there anyone so naive or cynical as to believe that these forms of race bias are not organizationally and economically disadvantageous to the black laboring masses? Not only has the long system of color caste condition in American industry thrust the Negro workers to the lowest rungs of the occupational hierarchy, but it tends to reinforce the accepted inferiority hereditary position of black labor, which drastically limits their economic mobility and viability.

Although not unaware of the fact that racial discrimination in trade unions affiliated to the AFL-CIO has existed for almost a century, no profound concern is now manifest by the leadership about this dreadful evil.

Instead of becoming aroused and disturbed about the existence of race bias in unions that affect employment opportunities and the economic status of the Negro worker, AFL-CIO leadership waves aside criticism of the movement's racial policies, as pure exaggeration unworthy of dispassionate examination.

Such was the reaction to a memorandum on race bias in trade unions, together with corrective proposals, I submitted to George Meany and the Executive Council at Unity House, Pennsylvania, June 1961.

Instead of giving the memorandum a painstaking, rational analysis to determine if it contained any meritorious suggestions, it became the occasion of voluminous rebuttal and attack upon, and censure of, myself.

The rebuttal was not only innocuous, barren and sterile of a single new, vital, creative and constructive idea with which to grapple with the menace of race segregation and discrimination, but was a distressingly vain effort to justify a "do little" civil rights record in the House of Labor. . . .

Just a word now about the objective effects and results of race bias in trade unions and industry in two major cities that are generally considered to be relatively liberal, New York and Detroit.

In New York City, as well as throughout the state, nonwhite persons make up a very large part of those who live in poverty; a poverty that is frequently related to discriminatory racial practices that force Negroes into a marginal position in the economy, even though opportunities may increase for other groups within the community.

The two major industries in New York City are garment manufacturing and printing and publishing. The printing and publishing industry alone employs more than 160,000 workers, or about 9 percent of the manufacturing labor force. In both garment manufacturing and printing, however, we find that Negroes and Puerto Ricans are concentrated in the low-paid, unskilled job classifications.

The Graduate School of Public Administration of Harvard University recently conducted a series of case studies in New York metropolitan manufacturing and concluded that in the New York garment industry Negroes and Puerto Ricans "were largely to be found in the less skilled, low-paid crafts and in shops making the lower priced lines, and in this industry their advancement to higher skills is not proceeding very rapidly. In the higher skilled coat and suit industry the new ethnic groups have hardly made an appearance."

The New York metropolitan region has 20 percent of the nation's employment in printing and publishing. In a survey made by the NAACP of Negro employment on the seven major New York City newspapers we find that, with the exclusion of building service and maintenance, less than 1 percent of those employed on the seven major newspapers are Negroes. Virtually all of the Negroes that are employed on these newspapers are within the white-collar jurisdiction of the New York Newspaper Guild.

We estimate that less than one-half of 1 percent of those currently employed in the newspaper crafts outside of the Guild's jurisdiction are Negroes. This includes printing pressmen, compositors, photoengravers, stereotypers, paper handlers, mailers, and delivery drivers.

In the past decade very little progress has been made in eliminating the traditional pattern of Negro exclusion and discrimination in the Plumbers and Pipe Fitters Union; the Iron and Structural Steel Workers; the Plasterers and Lathers; the Sheet Metal Workers; the Boiler Makers; the Carpenters, as well as the Bricklayers, Masons, and Plasterers Union, and others.

In New York City, Negro waiters and bellboys are more noted by their absence than presence in the hotels and restaurants except, perhaps, in a token form at some banquets. However, Negroes are members of the Hotel and Restaurant Employees Union. One will need the proverbial microscope to discover a Negro bartender anywhere in the city except in a Negro community.

Negro motion picture operators have no job mobility. They are chiefly confined to the second-class motion picture theatres in Negro communities where they receive a subwage differential paid operators in this class of theatre.

At present there is a broad exclusion of Negro youth from major apprenticeship programs jointly conducted by industrial management and labor unions in the City of New York. For many occupations the only way a worker can be recognized as qualified for employment is to complete the apprenticeship training program. This is true for the printing trades, among machinists and metal workers, the construction industry, and others.

The role of the labor union in these occupations is decisive because the trade union usually determines who is admitted into the training program and, therefore, who is admitted into the union. This is especially true when the union controls access to employment.

In the New York metropolitan area there are many apprenticeship training programs in the building trades. Apprenticeship programs provide essential training for a wide variety of skills in their important area of the region's economy. These include apprenticeship programs for asbestos workers, electrical workers, glaziers, ironworkers, latherers, painters, plumbers, and sheet metal workers.

A recent study by the NAACP clearly indicates that less than 1 percent of the apprentices in the construction industry throughout the nation are Negroes. Unfortunately, the number of Negroes in apprenticeship training programs in the New York construction industry differs little from the national pattern.

The lack of apprentice-trained Negro craftsmen directly affects the economic standing of Negroes as a whole. Data indicates that craftsmen command substantially higher incomes than unskilled workers. If, then, Negroes are not employed in such occupations in large numbers, a potential source of high income is removed from this group. When this is coupled with other income limitations it becomes apparent why Negroes constitute a permanently depressed segment of American society.

Excerpts from the foreword to Negroes and Jobs (1968)

Despite progress toward social and political equality, the Negro worker finds that his relative economic position is deteriorating or stagnating. The desperation and frustration that this paradoxical situation engenders is responsible for much of the militance and impatience of the current civil rights revolution. And this militance will not abate. Long ago, during Reconstruction, the Negro learned the cruel lesson that social and political freedom cannot be sustained in the midst of economic insecurity and exploitation. He learned that freedom requires a material foundation. Recent civil rights gains are based largely on the economic progress the Negro made in the 1940s and early 1950s and these gains could be canceled out by the economic stagnation that has characterized Negro communities since 1953.

Automation and technological change are destroying tens of thousands of unskilled and semiskilled jobs to which Negroes have traditionally been relegated. Meanwhile, centuries of discrimination and exploitation have deprived Negro workers of the education and training required by the new skilled jobs which are opening up. Thus, we find that approximately 25 percent of the long-term unemployed are black Americans and that as unemployment becomes increasingly structural, the Negro is increasingly rendered economically useless. And this at a time when there is a shortage of highly skilled technical and professional workers. These skilled workers are so much in demand that they work overtime and enjoy high standards of living while millions of other workers are unemployed, underemployed, or unemployable. These millions are creating what the great Swedish economist Gunnar Myrdal has described as a vast "underclass" in American society. They are the pariahs, the untouchables, the exiles in our economy.

The Negro is trapped in this underclass, trapped in the growing slums and ghettoes of the big cities, while the more prosperous white workers are migrating to the pleasant suburbs. A racial and occupational separation is taking place which dooms our aspirations for integrated housing and schools. In fact, residential and educational segregation is actually increasing in our metropolitan centers. Deprived of decent integrated education, how are Negro youth to acquire the skills demanded by our technically advancing economy?

In the past few years the rumblings from the Negro underclass have exploded into thunderous and wildly destructive violence, from the tenements of Harlem to the slums of Cleveland and Watts. It serves no purpose simply to denounce the riots without understanding their causes. Of this much we can be certain: if those causes are not identified and uprooted, radically and finally, we will be courting disaster in this country. . . .

I have spent all of my life in the labor and civil rights movements, which is to say that I have spent a lifetime in search of solutions to the problem of race and the problem of jobs. In the early days, the task, so far as I was concerned, was a relatively simple one: I could—had to—concentrate exclusively on helping Negroes to break into the job market from which they were almost totally excluded. The situation today is somewhat different. As the economy has become more sophisticated and complex, both in its methods of production and in its relation to the total American labor force, the problems of securing wider employment opportunities for Negroes has ultimately become connected with the problem of finding wider employment opportunities for all the poor. Therefore, it is no longer possible to make the struggle for jobs exclusively a Negro struggle. As Michael Harrington has remarked in his essay "The Economics of Protest," one of the main responsibilities of the Negro struggle is "a concern with the question of full employment. And this is an 'integrated' task, for it is clearly impossible to provide jobs for Negroes while leaving whites behind. The issue will be resolved on a national basis for all."

The Negro is not alone in the vicious circle in which he finds himself. Many white workers are also caught short by the profound transformations our economy is undergoing. The problem of these workers, black and white, is social as well as economic, since social justice and economic reform are intertwined in our time. If we are to speak for the needs of all these poor Americans, we must understand that the Negro protest is today but the first rumblings of the under-class. As the Negro has taken to the streets, so will the unemployed of all races take to the streets. Thus, to discuss the civil rights revolution is to write the agenda of labor's unfinished revolution in this country.

* * *

PAUL ROBESON
On W. E. B. Du Bois (1965)

Casting my mind back, my first clear memory of Dr. Du Bois was my pride in his recognized scholarship and authority in his many fields of work and writing. In high school and at college our teachers often referred us to standard reference works on sociology, race relations, Africa, and world affairs. I remember feeling great pride when the books and articles proved to be by our Dr. Du Bois, and often loaned these to my fellow students, who were properly impressed by his universally respected and acknowledged authority.

Reprinted by permission from The Lawrence Jordan Agency, 345 West 121st Street, New York, NY 10027.

We Negro students joined the NAACP, which Dr. Du Bois helped to organize and build; we read religiously *The Crisis*, of which he was editor for so many years, and in which he wrote clearly, constructively, and militantly on the complex problems of the American scene, on the Negro question, on Africa, and on world affairs. He called upon the American people, and particularly upon the whole labor movement, to understand the need for unity in the struggle of the working masses, including the Negro, for a decent standard of living.

We spoke of Dr. Du Bois as Our Professor, the Doctor, the Dean, with great respect, paid close attention to his pronouncements, and many of us followed him proudly marching down New York's Fifth Avenue in a protest parade led by the NAACP for civil rights.

Dr. Du Bois talked and wrote and marched for civil rights. He insisted upon first-class citizenship for all Americans, upon full equality of opportunity, dignity, legal rights for us all. And he directed universal interest and attention to our Negro history and our rich African ancestry, to give us solid background for our struggle.

All this was way back many, many years ago, long before I graduated from college in 1919. Our good doctor, this great man, understood our situation, and our world, and was often a lone but clarion voice pointing out the urgent need for change.

Dr. Du Bois was a distinguished historian as well as a social scientist. We often talked about the wealth and beauty of our folk heritage, particularly about Negro music, which he loved and found deeply moving. He often stressed the importance of this special contribution to American culture. We had interesting discussions about the likeness of our Negro folk music to many other folk musics throughout the world.

Our professor was not only a great and recognized scholar, he was also our most distinguished statesman. His knowledge of world affairs, his founding of the Pan-African Congress, his continuing work in many capitals of the world for African independence, made him widely known and respected abroad, and beloved in Africa. His book *The World and Africa* was one of the first important books on modern postwar Africa, and helped to point out and focus attention on the continuing exploitation of Africa by the "free world."

We of the Council on African Affairs were very fortunate and proud when Dr. Du Bois joined our organization as chairman in 1949. His knowledge, experience, and wisdom, together with our very able and devoted executive secretary, Dr. Alphaeus Hunton, helped us to make some meaningful contribution to the struggle of the African People, particularly in South Africa.

Fifteen years ago, when we built the Negro newspaper *Freedom*, under the very fine editorship of our friend and colleague, the late Louis Burnham, Dr. Du Bois was one of our very frequent and most brilliant contributors. His clear, forthright, informative articles on Africa, on the Negro in America, on the changing world situation, added stature to our publication.

Association, discussion, and work with this great man were always richly rewarding.

Probably as a result of his research and work in sociology, his close scientific observance of American history and social scene, his keen and continuing interest in Africa and in international affairs, Dr. Du Bois became a strong supporter of socialism as a way of life. He followed the rise of the Soviet Union with understanding and appreciation, and made friends with the whole socialist world.

He welcomed not only their rejection of racism, but also, as a social scientist, he appreciated their constructive and practical interest in, and effective governmental activity for the welfare of the vast majority of the people. Dr. Du Bois said many times that he believed the 1917 Russian Revolution was the turning point in modern history, and was of first importance in the shaping of a new world with the emergence of many other socialist lands.

So that it was logical and deeply moving when, in 1961—having the whole world picture in focus—Dr. Du Bois became a member of the Communist Party of the United States, and still later became a welcome and honored citizen of Ghana, in his beloved Africa. He followed with deep concern the independence struggles in various parts of Africa, and knew that these struggles must be won, so that Africa and the African people could develop their great potential.

With his brilliant mind, his far-reaching education, his scholarly academic background, Dr. Du Bois was nevertheless a very much down-to-earth human being, with a delightful and ready wit, a keen and mischievous sense of humor, and enjoyed life to the full. I especially remember his gay spontaneous laughter.

And I remember particularly a wonderful Thanksgiving dinner at his home in Grace Court in Brooklyn about ten years ago. He had invited some guests from the United Nations, because he knew they had heard and read about Thanksgiving, but had no personal experience and understanding of this special American holiday. So this was as typical a Thanksgiving dinner and evening as he and his wife, Shirley, could make it, with the good Doctor a gay and witty host, explaining everything step by step—from turkey and cranberry sauce to pumpkin pie and early American history. After the delicious dinner, over coffee and brandy before the log fire burning in the spacious living room fireplace, he spoke of Frederick Douglass, whose portrait hung over the mantel, and of his place in American history. That day is a happy and cherished memory.

I also remember so well the political campaigning of Dr. Du Bois when he was candidate of the American Labor Party of New York for the U.S. Senate. In the usual free-for-all scramble which American political campaigns involve, Dr. Du Bois always remained calm and dignified. He never descended to shrill attack or name-calling, but discussed the real issues with brilliant speeches in which he combined his keen intelligence and trenchant humor. All of us worried about how he, at the age of eighty-two and seemingly fragile, would withstand the grueling pace of the campaign. But Dr. Du Bois took care of his health as intelligently as he did everything else, and those who planned meetings at which he would speak knew that if he was scheduled for 10 P.M. for half an hour, then no matter what the unpredictable state of the meeting, at ten o'clock precisely Dr. Du Bois would walk onto the platform, speak brilliantly for half an hour, rest a while, then go on his way.

The more Dr. Du Bois observed and understood world events, the more he recognized that peace was a prime issue in this nuclear age. And so, typically, he became associated with peace movements all over the world, and worked actively for peace. In 1949 he became chairman of the Peace Information Center here in our country, and was later indicted, tried, and acquitted for his leadership in work for peace.

When Dr. Du Bois and Shirley came to London in 1958, we were living in a flat in Maida Vale. Soon after their arrival Eslanda and I went to Moscow for a long visit and turned our flat over to the Du Boises. We were very happy when they told us they had enjoyed their stay there, and we had thus helped to make their London visit comfortable. After they left we felt we should put a plate on the door saying "Dr. Du Bois slept here."

My last memory of Dr. Du Bois is in London, in less happy circumstances, in 1962. The Doctor, then ninety-four years old and very ill, had been brought to London for a very serious operation. He was tired and weak, and we worried about how he could stand the ordeal.

I was ill in a London nursing home at the time, and felt very sad and helpless about the Doctor's condition. So that when my wife, who visited him regularly in the hospital, told me that he wanted very much to see me and had asked especially for me, I got up and went to London University Hospital and we spent some time together. Ill as he was, he told me about his work on the Encyclopedia Africana; we talked about the progress of the Negro revolt at home in America, about the power and influence of the socialist world, about the marvelous coming-of-age of the African people.

I visited him once again in the hospital, and was delighted and greatly relieved to find him miraculously improving. This was in August 1962.

While I remained in the London nursing home, still ill, Dr. Du Bois recovered from his operation, got up, and with Shirley traveled to Switzerland where he rested in the sun, went to Peking where they attended the October Celebration, on to Moscow where they attended the November Celebration, and back again to London in late November, where Dr. Du Bois visited *me* in the nursing home! He gave a fascinating account of his trip and experiences, which he had enjoyed immensely.

That was the last time I saw him. He and Shirley went on to Ghana where a marvelous welcome awaited them.

My cherished memories of Dr. Du Bois are his brilliant and practical mind, his intellectual courage and integrity, his awareness of the world and of our place in it—which helped to make us all also aware. His fine influence on American thinking and on Negro thinking will continue to be incalculable. We admired, respected, appreciated, and followed him because he was clear and forthright, because he was militant with a fighting strength and courage based upon wide knowledge, great wisdom, and experience. I remember, too, his deep kindness.

Dr. Du Bois was and is in the truest sense an American leader, a Negro leader, a world leader.

✳ ✳ ✳

BAYARD RUSTIN
EXCERPT FROM IN MEMORY OF A. PHILIP RANDOLPH (1979)

Our Chief, Phil Randolph, was for me father, uncle, adviser, defender. And as we pay tribute to him, we must not lose sight of his human qualities. It is in these qualities that we understand his life.

Mr. Randolph was a successful and uniquely gifted labor and civil rights activist, precisely because he was a sensitive, unselfish, and dignified human being. He did not study organizational behavior, nor tactical skills, nor social sciences to inspire and create great movements for justice. Rather, his leadership flowed from the depth of his humanity. It flowed from his understanding of the human condition.

His modesty, his integrity, his generosity, and his unshakeable dedication won for him loyalty—and, yes, mostly love—of his comrades in the trade union movement and of his brothers and sisters. We who worked for the Chief never served him out of a sense of coercion or fear, but out of a sense of love and a need to share his very deep commitment.

As an illustration of his gentle leadership style, I like to recall an incident which occurred more than thirty years ago. In 1948, some young militants including myself had a serious tactical disagreement with Mr. Randolph. After lengthy and delicate negotiations, he secured an agreement from President Harry Truman to issue an executive order banning segregation in the military. Because Truman finally complied with the Chief's central demand, a planned march on Washington was canceled. But we young militants wanted to proceed with the demonstration with an additional demand—the release of a number of black prisoners. Mr. Randolph however had given his solemn word to Truman and refused to abrogate his agreement.

Thinking ourselves more militant and wiser than the Chief, we held a press

Reprinted by permission of the A. Philip Randolph Institute.

conference at 10 A.M. to denounce him and Truman. At 4 P.M. on the same day, Mr. Randolph held a press conference to explain his position and gently chide us for being unwise and mistaken. He issued no condemnation; he said nothing in anger; he never questioned our motives.

Because of our disagreements at the time, I foolishly avoided Mr. Randolph for nearly two and a half years. Finally, I decided that he had been right all along, and I went to see him. Rather than sternly lecturing me or expecting an apology, he simply looked up from his desk, smiled at me in his unique way, and calmly said, "Bayard, where have you been? I needed you. We have work to do."

Just as his leadership sprang from his humanity, so did his political philosophy. As a young man, he saw and felt the ugly reality of racial oppression that was to him an abomination. The irrationality and cruelty of oppression offended him deeply. And early in his life when he was a mere solitary, powerless individual, he swore to challenge this affront to humanity.

He was also disturbed by the deplorable conditions of American workers, white as well as black. He understood that people subjected to the indignities of arbitrary employer power could never be fully human, nor fully free. He knew that powerless workers could uplift themselves only by uniting in democratic trade unions, the only effective instruments for economic liberation then and now. He thus rejected elitist approaches like W. E. B. Du Bois's emphasis on the "Talented Tenth," and modern-day movements for "black capitalism." Likewise, he rejected separatist strategies whether they originated with Marcus Garvey in the 1920s or forty years later with figures like H. Rap Brown, Stokely Carmichael, or the Black Panthers.

From his youth, he saw that industrial capitalism created enormous inequalities between people who labored long hours under intolerable conditions and those who lived in luxury from inherited wealth or profits. He believed that an economic system motivated by insecurity, greed, and ruthless competition debased everything in that society in a fundamental way.

He also understood the terror and the depravity of absolute power wielded by totalitarian elites. He saw how men like Stalin and Hitler could trample on the most basic human rights of the individual and commit crimes against humanity. And he was aware that systems based on total power constitute a threat to freedom and justice everywhere.

Thus while rejecting religious intolerance, worker exploitation, and unbridled capitalism, the Chief never embraced totalitarianism and always was distressed fundamentally by those who in one breath denounced oppression in America and tolerated slavery in totalitarian states.

He believed in democratic socialism, the political system which was the foundation of his strategy and tactics in the trade union movement and in the civil rights movement and which combined with his intelligence, his integrity, and his complete lack of sentimentality helped him reject the fads, the easy answers, and the separatist illusions that had too frequently plagued movements for liberation.

This philosophy provided as well a basis for universal moral concern which compelled his resistance to any tendency anywhere in the world which defended unjust acts in the name of justice or which excused wrongdoing—either by blacks or whites—because it was done in the name of some particular freedom, or in the name of democracy, or of anticolonialism, or of racial liberation, or of any other cause. He was a consistent man.

As a gentle but iron-willed radical, the Chief's commitments were boundless. His concerns flowed to every facet of the human condition. He was a true partisan, that is a partisan for all humanity, regardless of race, religion, or nationality. The Chief taught us that the struggle for any right is linked to the struggle for all rights.

The Chief's universality is clearly seen in his worldview. Way back in 1942, he urged me and others to devote our energy to a struggle on behalf of Japanese Americans who were detained during World War II.

Later, he urged us to become personally involved with the independence movements of and sent some of us to India, Ghana, Nigeria, Zambia, Kenya, and Tanzania. In 1953 he helped create the first committee in America against apartheid. When the civil rights movement began growing in the South, he asked many of us to join the struggle with Dr. Martin Luther King Jr.

More recently, he offered enthusiastic encouragement as we began the difficult task of organizing the black Americans to support Israel. Later he asked me to take the lead in doing something useful for the thousands of defenseless refugees fleeing the brutal, totalitarian regimes in Vietnam, Cambodia, and Laos. Even a few days before his death, he emphasized to me the urgency of assisting the many refugees from Haiti who are reaching our shores in search of freedom.

Even in his final days with us, his concern and compassion were alive and strong. The flame of his humanity still burned strongly even as his physical condition weakened with each passing day.

* * *

ELLA BAKER
THE BLACK WOMAN IN THE CIVIL RIGHTS STRUGGLE (1969)

I think that perhaps because I have existed much longer than you and have to some extent maintained some degree of commitment to a goal of full freedom

Reprinted from *Ella Baker: Freedom Bound*, by Joanne Grant, John Wiley & Sons, 1998. Used by permission.

that this is the reason Vincent Harding invited me to come down as an exhibit of what might possibly be the goal of some of us to strive toward—that is, to continue to identify with the struggle as long as the struggle is with us.

I was a little bit amazed as to why the selection of a discussion on the role of black women in the world. I just said to Bernice Reagon that I have never been one to feel great needs in the direction of setting myself apart as a woman. I've always thought first and foremost of people as individuals . . . [but] wherever there has been struggle, black women have been identified with that struggle. During slavery there was a tremendous amount of resistance in various forms. Some were rather subtle and some were rather shocking. One of the subtle forms was that of feigning illness. . . . One of the other forms of resistance which was perhaps much more tragic and has not been told to a great extent is the large number of black women who gave birth to children and killed them rather than have them grow up as slaves. There is a story of a woman in Kentucky who had borne thirteen children and strangled each of them with her own hands rather than have them grow up as slaves. Now this calls for a certain kind of deep *commitment* and *resentment. Commitment* to freedom and deep *resentment* against slavery.

I would like to divide my remaining comments into two parts. First, the aspect that deals with the struggle to get into the society, the struggle to be a part of the American scene. Second, the struggle for a different kind of society. The latter is the more radical struggle. In the previous period, the period of struggling to be accepted, there were certain goals, concepts, and values such as the drive for the "Talented Tenth." That, of course, was the concept that proposed that through the process of education black people would be accepted in the American culture and they would be accorded their rights in proportion to the degree to which they qualified as being persons of learning and culture. . . .

[There was] an assumption that those who were trained were not trained to be *part* of the community, but to be *leaders* of the community. This carried with it another false assumption that being a leader meant that you were separate and apart from the masses, and to a large extent people were to look up to you, and that your responsibility to the people was to *represent* them. This means that the people were never given a sense of their own values. . . . Later, in the 1960s, a different concept emerged: the concept of the right of the people to participate in the decisions that affected their lives. So part of the struggle was the struggle toward intellectualism [which] so often separated us so far from the masses of people that the gulf was almost too great to be bridged.

The struggle for being a part of the society also led to another major phase of the civil rights struggle. That was the period in which legalism or the approach to battling down the barriers of racial segregation through the courts which was spearheaded by the National Association for the Advancement of Colored People. . . . We moved from the question of equal educational opportunity in terms of teachers' salaries into another phase: equality in travel accommodations. . . . One of the young persons who was part of the first efforts to test [segregated travel] was Pauli Murray. Pauli Murray and I were part of a committee that was organized to try to go into the South to test Jim Crow in bus travel. But the decision was made that only the men could go. . . . I had just finished a tour of duty with the NAACP and had ridden a lot of Jim Crow buses and wanted very much to go, but I guess it was decided that I was too frail to make such a journey.

I think the period that is most important to most of us now is the period when we began to question whether we really wanted in. Even though the sit-in movement started off primarily as a method of getting in, it led to the concept of questioning whether it was worth trying to get in. The first effort was to be able to sit down at the lunch counters. When you look back and think of all the tragedy and suffering that the first sit-iners went through you begin to wonder, Why pay a price like that for the privilege of eating at lunch counters? There were those who saw from the beginning that the struggle was much bigger than getting a hamburger at a lunch counter. There were those who saw from the beginning that it was part of the struggle for full dignity as a human being. So out of that came two things that to me are very significant. First, there was the concept of the trained finding their identity with the masses. Another thing that came out of it at a later period was that of leadership training. As the young people moved out into the community and finally were able to be accepted, they began to discover indigenous leaders. . . .

Around 1965 there began to develop a great deal of questioning about what is the role of women in the struggle. Out of it came a concept that black women had to bolster the ego of the male. This implied that the black male had been treated in such a manner as to have been emasculated both by the white society and black women because the female was the head of the household. We began to deal with the question of the need of black women to play the subordinate role. I personally have never thought of this as being valid because it raises the question as to whether the black man is going to try to be a man on the basis of his capacity to deal with issues and situations rather than be a man because he has some people around him who claim him to be a man by taking subordinate roles.

I don't think you could go through the freedom movement without finding that the backbone of the support of the movement were women. When demonstrations took place and when the community acted, usually it was some woman who came to the fore. . . .

I think at this stage the big question is, What is the American society? Is it the kind of society that either black women or black men or anyone who is seeing a dignified existence as a human being that permits people to grow and develop according to their capacity, that gives them a sense of value, not only for themselves, but a sense of value for other human beings. Is this the kind of society that is going to permit that? I think there is a great question as to whether it can become that kind of society. . . .

In order for us as poor and oppressed people to become a part of a society that is meaningful, the system under which we now exist has to be radically changed. This means that we are going to have to learn to think in *radical* terms. I use the term radical in its original meaning—getting down to and understanding the root cause. It means facing a system that does not lend itself to your needs and devising means by which you change that system. That is easier said than done. But one of the things that has to be faced is, in the process of wanting to change that system, how much have we got to do to find out who we are, where we have come from, and where we are going. About twenty-eight years ago I used to go around making speeches, and I would open up my talk by saying that there was a man who had a health problem and he was finally told by the doctor that they could save his sight or save his memory, but they couldn't save both. They asked him which did he want and he said, "Save my sight because I would rather see where I am going than remember where I have been." I am saying as you must say, too, that in order to see where we are going, we not only must remember where we've been, but *we must understand where we have been.* This calls for a great deal of analytical thinking and evaluation of methods that have been used. We have to begin to think in terms of where do we really want to go and how can we get there.

Finally, I think it is also to be said that it is not a job that is going to be done by all the people simultaneously. Some will have to be in cadres, the advanced cadres, and some will have to come later. But one of the guiding principles has to be that we cannot lead a struggle that involves masses of people without getting the people to understand what their potentials are, what their strengths are.

II.

DIMENSIONS OF THE
BLACK LIBERATION STRUGGLE

The leader of the National Association for the Advancement of Colored People (NAACP), W. E. B. Du Bois, in the aftermath of World War I gave succinct expression (in columns in the NAACP journal *Crisis*, entitled "Pan-Africa" and "Of Giving Work") to what would be key elements in the radical wing of the black liberation movement. While favoring an uncompromising struggle for equal rights for African Americans, he was not simply advocating integration of blacks into the existing white society. Rather, he was calling for the radical restructuring of that society—in part by black Americans who maintained their identification with African culture and with African resistance to imperialism and colonial oppression, at the same time challenging the capitalist power structure of white America.

Speaking from the standpoint of radical black nationalism on a Philadelphia radio show, Malcolm X critically surveyed the state of the civil rights movement in 1964, touching on the themes Du Bois had advanced years earlier. Martin Luther King Jr. did the same not long before his death in 1968, proposing in "Where Do We Go from Here?" radical directions for the civil rights struggle. The strength, energies, and conceptualizations of women had been central to that struggle, and aspects of this contribution are indicated in the article by Septima Clark (who served on the staff of the Highlander Folk School and the Southern Christian Leadership Conference) and the interview with Ella Baker (who was a key organizer for the NAACP, the Southern Christian Leadership Conference [SCLC], and the Student Non-Violent Coordinating Committee [SNCC]).

Whatever its limitations, the civil rights movement of 1954–68 was a powerful force for social change in the United States. Its richness and continuing relevance are suggested in the essay by historian Vincent Harding. A more critical note is struck by political scientist Adolph Reed, comparing the relative quiescence of the twentieth century's last three decades to the earlier years of insurgency.

W. E. B. DU BOIS
EXCERPTS FROM *PAN-AFRICA* (1919)
AND *OF GIVING WORK* (1920)

Pan-Africa

Europe had begun to look with covetous eyes toward Africa as early as 1415 when the Portuguese at the Battle of Ceuta gained a foothold in Morocco. Thereafter Prince Henry of Portugal instituted the series of explorations which resulted not only in the discovery of Cape Verde, the Guinea Coast, and the Cape of Good Hope, but by 1487 gave to Portugal the possession of a very fair slice of the African East Coast. This was the beginning of the Portuguese Colonies of Guinea, Angola, and East Africa. Other European nations, France, Holland, Spain, England, and Denmark, followed and set up trading stations along the African coast whose chief reason for existence was the fostering of the slave trade.

But the partition of Africa as we know it is much more recent and begins with the founding in 1884 of the Congo Free State whose inception was so zealously fostered by Leopold of Belgium and which in 1908 was annexed to Belgium. The "scramble" for African colonies was on and within a quarter of a century Africa was virtually in the hands of Europe.

In this division the British Empire gained a network of possessions extending from the Anglo-Egyptian Sudan down to South Africa with valuable holdings on the east coast and in Somaliland. France came next with an actually larger area, but with a smaller population. Her spoils reached from Morocco and Algeria, including the Algerian Sahara, to the French Congo, and on the eastern coast comprised Madagascar and French Somaliland. Germany, who was late in entering the game of colonization, contrived nonetheless to become mistress of four very valuable colonies, Togoland, Kamerun, South-West Africa, and East Africa. Italy's and Spain's possessions were relatively unimportant, embracing for the former, Eritrea and Italian Somaliland, and for the latter Rio de Oro and the Muni River settlements.

This was the state of affairs when the war broke out in 1914. In Africa the only independent states were the Republic of Liberia, and the Kingdom of Abyssinia which, according to history, has been independent since the days of Menelek, the reputed son of Solomon and the Queen of Sheba. The number of souls thus under the rule of aliens, in the case of England, France, Germany, and Belgium, amounted to more than 110,000,000. During the course of the war Germany lost all four of her African colonies with a population estimated at 13,420,000. It is the question of the reapportionment of this vast number of human beings which has started the Pan-African movement. Colored America is indeed involved.

> *If we do not feel the chain*
> *When it works another's pain,*
> *Are we not base slaves indeed*
> *Slaves unworthy to be freed?*

Colonial Imperialism in Africa

The suggestion was made that these colonies which Germany lost should not be handed over to any other nation of Europe but should, under the guidance of *organized civilization*, be brought to a point of development which shall finally result in autonomous states. This plan met with criticism and ridicule. Let the natives develop along their own lines and they will "go back," has been the cry. Back to what, in Heaven's name?

Is a civilization naturally backward because it is different? Outside of cannibalism, which can be matched in this country, at least, by lynching, there is no vice and no degradation in native African customs which can begin to touch the horrors thrust upon them by white masters. Drunkenness, terrible diseases, immorality, all these things have been the gifts of European civilization. There is no need to dwell on German and Belgian atrocities, the world knows them too well. Nor have France and England been blameless. But even supposing that these masters had been models of kindness and rectitude, who shall say that any civilization is in itself so superior that it must be superimposed upon another nation without the expressed and intelligent consent of the people most concerned. The culture indigenous to a country, its folk customs, its art, all this must have free scope or there is no such thing as freedom for the world.

The truth is, white men are merely juggling with words—or worse—when they declare that the withdrawal of Europeans from Africa would plunge that continent into chaos.

What Europe, and indeed only a small group in Europe, wants in Africa is not a field for the spread of European civilization, but a field for exploitation. They covet the raw materials—ivory, diamonds, copper, and rubber in which the land abounds, and even more do they covet cheap native labor to mine and produce these things. Greed, naked, pitiless lust for wealth and power, lie back of all of Europe's interest in Africa and the white world knows it and is not ashamed.

Any readjustment of Africa is not fair and cannot be lasting which does not consider the interests of native Africans and peoples of African descent. Prejudice, in European colonies in Africa, against the ambitious Negro is greater than in America, and that is saying much.

But with the establishment of a form of government which shall be based on the concept that Africa is for Africans, there would be a chance for the colored American to emigrate and to go as a pioneer to a country which must, sentimentally at least, possess for him the same fascination as England does for Indian-born Englishmen.

Not Separatism

This is not a "separatist" movement. There is no need to think that those who advocate the opening up of Africa for Africans and those of African descent desire to deport colored Americans to a foreign land. Once for all, let us realize that we are Americans, that we were brought here with the earliest settlers, and that the very sort of civilization from which we came made the complete adoption of Western modes and customs imperative if we were to survive at all. In brief, there is nothing so indigenous, so completely "made in America" as we. It is as absurd to talk of a return to Africa, merely because that was our home 300 years ago, as it would be to expect the members of the Caucasian race to return to the fastnesses of the Caucasus Mountains from which, it is reputed, they sprang.

But it is true that we as a people are not given to colonization, and that thereby a number of essential occupations and interests have been closed to us which the redemption of Africa would open up. To help bear the burden of Africa does not mean any lessening of effort in our own problem at home. Rather it means increased interest. For any ebullition of action and feeling that results in an amelioration of the lot of Africa tends to ameliorate the condition of colored peoples throughout the world. And no man liveth to himself.

Of Giving Work

"We give you people work and if we didn't, how would you live?"

The speaker was a southern white man. He was of the genus called "good." He had come down from the Big House to advise these Negroes, in the forlorn little church which crouched on the creek. He didn't come to learn, but to teach. The result was that he did not learn, and he saw only that blank, impervious gaze which colored people know how to assume; and that dark wall of absolute silence which they have a habit of putting up instead of applause. He felt awkward, but he repeated what he had said, because he could not think of anything else to say:

"We give you people work, and if we didn't, how would you live?"

And then the old and rather ragged black man arose in the back of the church and came slowly forward and as he came, he said:

"And we gives you homes; and we gives you cotton; and we makes your land worth money; and we waits on you and gets your meals and cleans up your dirt. If we didn't do all those things for you, how would you live?"

The white man choked and got red, but the old black man went on talking:

"And what's more: we gives you a heap more than you gives us and we's getting mighty tired of the bargain—"

"I think we ought to give you fair wages," stammered the white man.

"And that ain't all," continued the old black man, "We ought to have something to say about your wages. Because if what *you* gives us gives *you* a right to say what we ought to get, then what *we* gives you gives *us* a right to say what you ought to get; and we're going to take that right *some day*."

The white man blustered:

"That's Bolshevism!" he shouted.

And then church broke up.

✳   ✳   ✳

MALCOLM X
ACTION THAT WILL GET RESULTS (1964)

[On March 20, 1964, shortly after his break from Elijah Muhammad's Nation of Islam, Malcolm X was a guest on Joe Rainey's Philadelphia radio show, *Listening Post*. Beginning with a prepared statement, he called on all black organizations and leaders to form a united front to "find a common approach, common solution to a common problem," and described his new organization, Muslim Mosque, Incorporated. This was an organization committed to black nationalism,

Reprinted from *Malcolm X as They Knew Him*, ed. David Gallen (New York: Carroll & Graf, 1992). Used with permission.

racial solidarity, and what he viewed as militant and effective action—including self-defense in the face of racist attacks. What is presented here are portions of the discussion, which followed that statement, as transcribed from FBI files after an agent of the FBI recorded the program.]

JOE RAINEY: Well, number one, the emphasis that you're placing on self-defense is contrary to the belief that many people advance in relation to taking an aggressive side. In other words what you're advocating is self-defense. You're not advocating that people buy guns and start shooting up places, are you?

MALCOLM X: No, all I said was, if you notice, in areas where the government is either unable or unwilling, then it's time for the so-called Negro to be a man as others are men and defend himself. If you read the Constitution, Article II, from the original amendments, the Bill of Rights, it says this: "A well-regulated militia being necessary to the security of a free state, the right of the people to keep and bear arms shall not be infringed." We're not telling anybody to break the law, but we're telling the so-called Negroes to read the Constitution, and in the context of his constitutional rights he should do whatever is necessary to defend himself, especially since the government itself has proven its inability or else its unwillingness to come to the rescue and defend our people when they are being unjustly attacked. . . .

[Rainey asked about boxer and Muslim Cassius Clay (who would soon be known as Muhammad Ali), who was facing the possibility of being drafted into the U.S. Army.]

I think any black man today who is twenty-two and who faces the possibility of being drafted into an army to fight for a philosophy that has fallen short where he's concerned, that man is really faced with a grave question. And almost every young, so-called Negro today when it comes time for him to be drafted asks himself what is he being drafted for. What does he have to fight for? The young generation is asking that question. Now preceding generations were supposed to be militant and all that, but they allowed themselves to be drafted to fight for something that they never received. And I think that most youth today—that is, among our people—are asking themselves just what are they fighting for, what did their fathers fight for, what did their uncles fight for. And if they didn't get what they fought for, how does this present generation know that it will get what it's being called upon to fight for? And not only that, if these young Negroes aren't allowed to fight in Mississippi, it says here in the news that just came out where the Klan is burning Negroes, shooting Negroes, terrorizing Negroes, and then these Negro leaders are telling these young Negroes to turn the other cheek, be nonviolent, and love their enemy. Well, you got the young generation now thinking, and they are asking themselves why should they be nonviolent in Mississippi and allow this government to draft them and send them to be violent in South Vietnam or in Germany somewhere. If it's right to be violent abroad, it's right to be violent at home. And if it's right to be nonviolent at home, then the government should expect these young Negroes to be nonviolent when it comes time to be drafted.

JOE RAINEY: You made some mention a little earlier relative to your desire to work with a number of other organizations in their program. Am I quoting it correctly now when I say that? Just exactly what do you mean in view of the fact that you have in the past differed with some of the philosophies as advanced by such organizations as the NAACP, the organization of Dr. King, the Student Nonviolent Coordinating Committee? You have disagreed in the past with their philosophy; are you now approving of what they do?

MALCOLM X: No. Krushchev and John F. Kennedy disagreed with each other on philosophy, but they were able to exchange wheat with each other. And if white people with differences can get together I think it's time for us so-called Negroes to submit. Some of our differences can be submitted, and we can get together in areas that we have in common. And if the Honorable Elijah Muhammad has always said that in areas where we can work with the so-called civil rights groups without compromising our religious philosophy we should get our heads together. So I was involved just this week in the school boycott in New York, *not* because I believe in integration but I am against segregation. I realize that the segregated school system produces crippled children that are crippled when it comes to education. So my involvement in the boycott is that I agree with the civil rights leaders that it is an inferior education. And, therefore, I will work with them in this particular field against a segregated school system. But at the same time they believe in integration and I believe in separation. Where we don't agree we won't bring that up. We only bring up where we do agree, and once we eliminate that we'll get to our disagreements later.

Both of us believe that quality education is needed in the so-called Negro community. Now we disagree on integration, but we agree on quality education. We believe that the so-called Negro schools should have better facilities, that we should have better teachers, that we should have better books. Where we agree let us work toward trying to bring that about, but where we disagree, again on integration, let's not bring that up.

So all I have said to these civil rights groups is start at the things where we can agree and let's get together on that, and leave the things where we don't agree in the closet until a later date.

JOE RAINEY: What has been the reaction of the leaders of the groups that you have mentioned recently: the NAACP, the Urban League, King's group, and so forth. How have they reacted?

MALCOLM X: Well, I was in Chester, Pennsylvania, a week ago tomorrow, Saturday; I was involved in a conference in which a cross section of civil rights leaders were represented. Gloria Richardson was there, Landry who headed the school boycott in Chicago was there, several others. Stanley Branche hosted the meeting, of Chester. The young chap from down in Maryland where they had so much trouble a few weeks ago, there was a cross section represented, and they agreed to form a group called ACT. The initials mean nothing; the word is what they are using, ACT. And this organization is going to be free to act whenever, wherever, whatever men are necessary to get a job done, and Landry of Chicago was chosen as the chariman. It was quite a milestone. I believe in the whole struggle. And I was invited to address the group, and my address was designed to show them that as long as they call themselves a civil rights group and fight the battle at a civil rights level they are alienating much of the assistance that they could get. But if they would expand the entire civil rights struggle to a human rights level where different members of the United Nations can step in and lend their support, in fact, they put it on a level by which the groups can take it to the United Nations Committee on Human Rights. They actually make it a much broader battle, and they get help from many quarters. . . .

[Rainey asked about Malcolm X's new organization, The Muslim Mosque, Incorporated.]

MALCOLM X: The strangest thing is I have gotten a flood of mail from student groups from coast to coast, expressing a desire to become active with us, and although we have Islam as our religion, black nationalism is our political philosophy. Our social philosophy is black nationalism, our economic philosophy is black nationalism, which means that the political philosophy of black nationalism means that the so-called Negro controls the politics and the politicians of his own community. The economic philosophy of black nationalism means that our people should be reeducated into the importance of economics and the importance of controlling the economy in the community in which we live. And the social so that we can create jobs for our own kind instead of having to boycott and picket and beg the white man to give us jobs. And the social philosophy of black nationalism involves the emphasis upon the culture of the black man, which will be designed for us to connect with our cultural roots, to restore the racial dignity necessary for us to love our own kind and be in unity and harmony with our own kind and strike at the evils and vices that strike at the moral fiber of our own community and our own society. The social philosophy of black nationalism encourages the black man to elevate his own society instead of trying to force himself into the unwanted presence of the white society. . . . Usually in the past Muslims have kept their politics to themselves. But you'll find there's a lot of young Muslims who want action and who are aggressive, who are progressive, who have an education and who want to take part in these things to uplift the standard of the so-called Negro community.

JOE RAINEY: What sort of action do they want?

MALCOLM X: Action that will get results, any kind of action that will get results. If a man wants freedom, he shouldn't be confined to certain tactics. Freedom is something that's so dear that someone who doesn't have it should reserve the right to use whatever technique or tactic that is necessary to bring about this freedom.

If George Washington and Jefferson and Hamilton and Patrick Henry and the founding fathers of this country had been confined to certain tactics, why these people wouldn't even have a country. This would still be England or New England.

A FEMALE LISTENER: Would you ask Malcolm X for me if he intends to hold any public speaking rallies here in Philadelphia any time soon, and if he intends to set up any headquarters here. Thank you.

MALCOLM X: The Muslim Mosque, Incorporated, which is presently headquartered in New York, will definitely be here in Philadelphia also. There are a large number of our people who have already expressed the desire to organize into groups to work in conjunction with those of us who are organizing in New York. We are interested in all people. We don't care whether you are a Christian or a Jew or a gentile or whatever the case may be; if you are fed up with the conditions that the black people are suffering in this country, and you want to take an active part, then we are interested in helping you organize so that we can get together, work together, and get the problem solved.

A MALE LISTENER: All of us are people who support in all respects Malcolm's traditions on the freedom movement. I would like to ask him two questions. First, what are his feelings concerning the issue in which Robert Williams of Monroe raised the issues that he did raise. And second, I feel that there are differences among the various groups, different meanings to the freedom movement, of radical organizations which are predominantly white, which he feels give—that is, does he feel that some radical groups are more amenable to his position than others?

MALCOLM X: Concerning Robert Williams, who is a very good friend of mine who was exiled to Cuba, primarily because he was teaching the so-called Negroes in I think it's South Carolina, Monroe, or North Carolina, to defend themselves, he was exiled down to Cuba. He made some mistakes. For one thing, all of the civil rights groups united against him. All of the integrationist groups united against him. They allowed themselves to be used by the government against Robert Williams. Well, this was two or three years ago, and most of our people today are becoming more mature. Many of our people who were, say, fourteen four years ago are eighteen today, and a whole new world of thought has opened up unto them as they mature toward this higher age level. You know, just a new thinking period and I have gotten response, as I say, from high school students as well as college students, all of whom are changing in their outlook in this whole struggle. So that we feel that we are well on the popular side or that we have the masses on our side when we come to the conclusion that it is time to take a stand on these injustices. Robert Williams was just a couple years ahead of his time; but he laid a good groundwork, and he will be given credit in history for the stand that he took prematurely.

Now we don't think that our stand is premature. We think that now things have gotten to the point, especially behind the March on Washington last year, which was probably the century's greatest fizzle and probably the most unproductive move that was ever made by so many people.

JOE RAINEY: Why do you call it a fizzle?

MALCOLM X: Fizzle—what did it produce? They went down, they sang some songs, they marched around. They went and marched between the feet of two dead presidents, Lincoln and, what's his name, Washington. They carried signs, they shouted. When they left Washington the civil rights bill hadn't passed yet. In fact . . .

JOE RAINEY: Well, it hasn't passed yet, but a lot of people are going to claim the civil rights bill, when it passes, if it does, that it would not have passed if it had not been for the March on Washington.

MALCOLM X: Well, Mr. Rainey, I was in Washington at the time of the march, and I heard the leaders talking about, this was in August, I heard the leaders talking, saying to each other we will be back. And they said we'll be back in September. September passed, October passed, November passed, the president passed, December passed, the year passed, and the bill itself hasn't passed yet. So everything has passed except that which is supposed to help Negroes. So the march was a fizzle. In fact, I heard Bayard Rustin on a radio program in New York a couple weeks ago pointing out that someone had challenged him concerning what the march had produced. His explanation was this: that since last year in June and July and August there was so much talk about the potential violence and explosion, he said that once everybody began to look toward the march in August this would channel their frustrations. And the march in itself was an escape valve permitting the Negro to give vent to his feelings, which automatically nullified or neutralized that explosive potential. So what Bayard was saying was the March on Washington was successful due to that it stopped the explosion, but it didn't give the Negro anything that the march was supposed to produce. And so this is why I say that.

And now concerning the gentleman's other question about all these white groups, the white groups that want to help can help, but they can't join. The white man who wants to join in with Negroes does nothing but castrate the effort of those Negroes; when whites join Negro groups, they aren't joining the Negroes and they end up by controlling the group that the Negro is supposed to be controlling. The day of whites at the helm of Negro movements is long gone. It's over. So we the Muslim Mosque, Incorporated, are interested in establishing a movement that will be under the complete control and the direction of black people themselves. And eventually the young ones, the new generation, that doesn't have a stake in this present structure and therefore they don't mind doing whatever is necessary to change the structure. Most of the older generation of Negroes have a stake. They have crumbs that they get from that structure, and therefore they are not trying to change it. They are trying to be accepted into the same old crumby or corrupt. But the youth, the young generation, wants to fix it where it cannot any longer exploit and suppress us.

※ ※ ※

MARTIN LUTHER KING JR.
WHERE DO WE GO FROM HERE? (1967)

Now, in order to answer the question, "Where do we go from here?" which is our theme, we must first honestly recognize where we are now. When the Constitution was written, a strange formula to determine taxes and representation declared that the Negro was 60 percent of a person. Today another curious formula seems to declare that he is 50 percent of a person. Of the good things in life, the Negro has approximately one half those of whites. Of the bad things of life, he has twice those of whites. Thus half of all Negroes live in substandard housing. And Negroes have half the income of whites. When we view the negative experiences of life, the Negro has a double share. There are twice as many unemployed. The rate of infant mortality among Negroes is double that of whites, and there are twice as many Negroes dying in Vietnam as whites in proportion to their size in the population.

In other spheres, the figures are equally alarming. In elementary schools, Negroes lag one to three years behind whites, and their segregated schools receive substantially less money per student than the white schools. One-twentieth as many Negroes as whites attend college. Of employed Negroes, 75 percent hold menial jobs.

This is where we are. Where do we go from here? First, we must massively assert our dignity and worth. We must stand up amidst a system that still oppresses us and develop an unassailable and majestic sense of values. We must no longer be ashamed of being black. The job of arousing manhood within a people that have been taught for so many centuries that they are nobody is not easy.

Even semantics have conspired to make that which is black seem ugly and degrading. In Roget's *Thesaurus* there are 120 synonyms for blackness and at least 60 of them are offensive, as for example, blot, soot, grim, devil, and foul. And there are some 134 synonyms for whiteness and all are favorable, expressed in such words as purity, cleanliness, chastity, and innocence. A white lie is better than a black lie. The most degenerate member of a family is a "black sheep." Ossie Davis has suggested that maybe the English language should be reconstructed so that teachers will not be forced to teach the Negro child 60 ways to despise himself, and thereby perpetuate his false sense of inferiority, and the white child 134 ways to adore himself, and thereby perpetuate his false sense of superiority.

The tendency to ignore the Negro's contribution to American life and to strip him of his personhood is as old as the earliest history books and as contemporary as the morning's newspaper. To upset this cultural homicide, the Negro must rise up with an affirmation of his own Olympian manhood. Any movement for the Negro's freedom that overlooks this necessity is only waiting to be buried. As long as the mind is enslaved, the body can never be free. Psychological freedom, a firm sense of self-esteem, is the most powerful weapon against the long night of physical slavery. No Lincolnian emancipation proclamation or Johnsonian civil rights bill can totally bring this kind of freedom. The Negro will only be free when he reaches down to the inner depths of his own being and signs with the pen and ink of assertive manhood his own emancipation proclamation. And, with a spirit straining toward true self-esteem, the Negro must boldly throw off the manacles of self-abnegation and say to himself and to the world, "I am somebody. I am a person. I am a man with dignity and honor. I have a rich and noble history. How painful and exploited that history has been. Yes, I was a slave through my foreparents and I am not ashamed of that. I'm ashamed of the people who were so sinful to make me a slave." Yes, we must stand up and say, "I'm black and I'm beautiful," and this self-affirmation is the black man's need, made compelling by the white man's crimes against him.

Another basic challenge is to discover how to organize our strength in terms of economic and political power. No one can deny that the Negro is in dire need of this kind of legitimate power. Indeed, one of the great problems that the Negro confronts is his lack of power. From old plantations of the South to newer ghettos of the North, the Negro has been confined to a life of voicelessness and power-lessness. Stripped of the right to make decisions concerning his life and destiny he has been subject to the authoritarian and sometimes whimsical decisions of this white power structure. The plantation and ghetto were created by those who had power, both to confine those who had no power and to perpetuate their pow-erlessness. The problem of transforming the ghetto, therefore, is a problem of power—confrontation of the forces of power demanding change and the forces of power dedicated to the preserving of the status quo. Now power properly understood is nothing but the ability to achieve purpose. It is the strength required to bring about social, political, and economic change. Walter Reuther defined power one day. He said, "Power is the ability of a labor union like the UAW [United Auto Workers] to make the most powerful corporation in the world, General Motors, say, 'Yes' when it wants to say 'No.' That's power."

Now a lot of us are preachers, and all of us have our moral convictions and con-cerns, and so often have problems with power. There is nothing wrong with power if power is used correctly. You see, what happened is that some of our philosophers got off base. And one of the great problems of history is that the concepts of love and power have usually been contrasted as opposites—polar opposites—so that love is identified with a resignation of power, and power with a denial of love.

It was this misinterpretation that caused Nietzsche, who was a philosopher of the will to power, to reject the Christian concept of love. It was this same mis-interpretation which induced Christian theologians to reject the Nietzschean phi-losophy of the will to power in the name of the Christian idea of love. Now, we've got to get this thing right. What is needed is a realization that power without love is reckless and abusive, and love without power is sentimental and anemic. Power at its best is love implementing the demands of justice, and jus-tice at its best is power correcting everything that stands against love. And this is what we must see as we move on. What has happened is that we have had it wrong and confused in our own country, and this has led Negro Americans in the past to seek their goals through power devoid of love and conscience.

This is leading a few extremists today to advocate for Negroes the same destructive and conscienceless power that they have justly abhorred in whites. It is precisely this collision of immoral power with powerless morality which con-stitutes the major crisis of our times.

We must develop a program that will drive the nation to a guaranteed annual income. Now, early in this century this proposal would have been greeted with ridicule and denunciation, as destructive of initiative and responsibility. At that time economic status was considered the measure of the individual's ability and talents. And, in the thinking of that day, the absence of worldly goods indicated a want of industrious habits and moral fiber. We've come a long way in our understanding of human motivation and of the blind operation of our economic system. Now we realize that dislocations in the market operations of our economy and the prevalence of discrimination thrust people into idleness and bind them in constant or frequent unemployment against their will. Today the poor are less often dismissed, I hope, from our consciences by being branded as inferior or incompetent. We also know that no matter how dynamically the economy develops and expands, it does not eliminate all poverty.

The problem indicates that our emphasis must be twofold. We must create full employment or we must create incomes. People must be made consumers by one method or the other. Once they are placed in this position we need to be concerned that the potential of the individual is not wasted. New forms of work that enhance the social good will have to be devised for those for whom traditional jobs are not available. In 1879 Henry George anticipated this state of affairs when he wrote in *Progress and Poverty*:*

> The fact is that the work which improves the condition of mankind, the work which extends knowledge and increases power and enriches literature and elevates thought, is not done to secure a living. It is not the work of slaves driven to their tasks either by the task, by the taskmaster, or by animal necessity. It is the work of men who somehow find a form of work that brings a security for its own sake and a state of society where want is abolished.

Work of this sort could be enormously increased, and we are likely to find that the problems of housing and education, instead of preceding the elimination of poverty, will themselves be affected if poverty is first abolished. The poor transformed into purchasers will do a great deal on their own to alter housing decay. Negroes who have a double disability will have a greater effect on discrimination when they have the additional weapon of cash to use in their struggle.

Beyond these advantages, a host of positive psychological changes inevitably will result from widespread economic security. The dignity of the individual will flourish when the decisions concerning his life are in his own hands, when he has the means to seek self-improvement. Personal conflicts among hus-

---

*Henry George (1839–1897) was the father of the single-tax system, which he set forth in his *Progress and Poverty*, published in 1879. The book argued that the land belonged to society, which created its value and properly taxed that value, not improvements on the land.

bands, wives, and children will diminish when the unjust measurement of human worth on the scale of dollars is eliminated.

Now our country can do this. John Kenneth Galbraith said that a guaranteed annual income could be done for about twenty billion dollars a year. And I say to you today, that if our nation can spend thirty-five billion dollars a year to fight an unjust, evil war in Vietnam, and twenty billion dollars to put a man on the moon, it can spend billions of dollars to put God's children on their own two feet right here on earth.

Now, let me say briefly that we must reaffirm our commitment to nonviolence. I want to stress this. The futility of violence in the struggle for racial justice has been tragically etched in all the recent Negro riots. Yesterday, I tried to analyze the riots and deal with their causes. Today I want to give the other side. There is certainly something painfully sad about a riot. One sees screaming youngsters and angry adults fighting hopelessly and aimlessly against impossible odds. And deep down within them, you can see a desire for self-destruction, a kind of suicidal longing.

Occasionally Negroes contend that the 1965 Watts riot and the other riots in various cities represented effective civil rights action. But those who express this view always end up with stumbling words when asked what concrete gains have been won as a result. At best, the riots have produced a little additional antipoverty money allotted by frightened government officials, and a few water-sprinklers to cool the children of the ghettos. It is something like improving the food in the prison while the people remain securely incarcerated behind bars. Nowhere have the riots won any concrete improvement such as have the organized protest demonstrations. When one tries to pin down advocates of violence as to what acts would be effective, the answers are blatantly illogical. Sometimes they talk of overthrowing racist state and local governments and they talk about guerrilla warfare. They fail to see that no internal revolution has ever succeeded in overthrowing a government by violence unless the government had already lost the allegiance and effective control of its armed forces. Anyone in his right mind knows that this will not happen in the United States. In a violent racial situation, the power structure has the local police, the state troopers, the National Guard and, finally, the army to call on—all of which are predominantly white. Furthermore, few if any violent revolutions have been successful unless the violent minority had the sympathy and support of the nonresistant majority. Castro may have had only a few Cubans actually fighting with him up in the hills, but he could never have overthrown the Batista regime unless he had the sympathy of the vast majority of Cuban people.*

---

*In 1956 Fidel Castro landed on the coast of Cuba in the vessel *Gramma*, to overthrow the despot Fulgencio Batista. Twelve men survived the counterattack and went on to lead the Cuban people to victory over Batista, who fled the island on New Year's Day 1959, which ushered in the Cuban revolutionary victory.

It is perfectly clear that a violent revolution on the part of American blacks would find no sympathy and support from the white population and very little from the majority of the Negroes themselves. This is no time for romantic illusions and empty philosophical debates about freedom. This is a time for action. What is needed is a strategy for change, a tactical program that will bring the Negro into the mainstream of American life as quickly as possible. So far, this has only been offered by the nonviolent movement. Without recognizing this we will end up with solutions that don't solve, answers that don't answer, and explanations that don't explain.

And so I say to you today that I still stand by nonviolence. And I am still convinced that it is the most potent weapon available to the Negro in his struggle for justice in this country. And the other thing is that I am concerned about a better world. I'm concerned about justice. I'm concerned about brotherhood. I'm concerned about truth. And when one is concerned about these, he can never advocate violence. For through violence you may murder a murderer but you can't murder murder. Through violence you may murder a liar but you can't establish truth. Through violence you may murder a hater, but you can't murder hate. Darkness cannot put out darkness. Only light can do that.

And I say to you, I have also decided to stick to love. For I know that love is ultimately the only answer to mankind's problems. And I'm going to talk about it everywhere I go. I know it isn't popular to talk about it in some circles today. I'm not talking about emotional bosh when I talk about love, I'm talking about a strong, demanding love. And I have seen too much hate. I've seen too much hate on the faces of sheriffs in the South. I've seen hate on the faces of too many Klansmen and too many White Citizens Councilors in the South to want to hate myself, because every time I see it, I know that it does something to their faces and their personalities and I say to myself that hate is too great a burden to bear. I have decided to love. If you are seeking the highest good, I think you can find it through love. And the beautiful thing is that we are moving against wrong when we do it, because John was right, God is love. He who hates does not know God, but he who has love has the key that unlocks the door to the meaning of ultimate reality.

I want to say to you as I move to my conclusion, as we talk about "Where do we go from here," that we honestly face the fact that the movement must address itself to the question of restructuring the whole of American society. There are forty million poor people here. And one day we must ask the question, "Why are there forty million poor people in America?" And when you begin to ask that question, you are raising questions about the economic system, about a broader distribution of wealth. When you ask that question, you begin to question the capitalistic economy. And I'm simply saying that more and more, we've got to begin to ask questions about the whole society. We are called upon to help the discouraged beggars in life's marketplace. But one day we must come to see that an edifice which produces beggars needs restructuring. It means that questions must be raised. You see, my friends, when you deal with this, you begin to ask the question, "Who owns the oil?" You begin to ask the question, "Who owns the iron ore?" You begin to ask the question, "Why is it that people have to pay water bills in a world that is two-thirds water?" These are questions that must be asked.

Now, don't think that you have me in a "bind" today. I'm not talking about communism.

What I'm saying to you this morning is that communism forgets that life is individual. Capitalism forgets that life is social, and the kingdom of brotherhood is found neither in the thesis of communism nor the antithesis of capitalism but in a higher synthesis. It is found in a higher synthesis that combines the truths of both. Now, when I say question the whole society, it means ultimately coming to see that the problem of racism, the problem of economic exploitation, and the problem of war are all tied together. These are the triple evils that are interrelated.

If you will let me be a preacher just a little bit—One night, a juror came to Jesus and he wanted to know what he could do to be saved. Jesus didn't get bogged down in the kind of isolated approach of what he shouldn't do. Jesus didn't say, "Now Nicodemus, you must stop lying." He didn't say, "Nicodemus, you must stop cheating if you are doing that." He didn't say, "Nicodemus, you must not commit adultery." He didn't say, "Nicodemus, now you must stop drinking liquor if you are doing that excessively." He said something altogether different, because Jesus realized something basic—that if a man will lie, he will steal. And if a man will steal, he will kill. So instead of just getting bogged down in one thing, Jesus looked at him and said, "Nicodemus, you must be born again."

He said, in other words, "Your whole structure must be changed." A nation that will keep people in slavery for 244 years will "thingify" them—make them things. Therefore they will exploit them, and poor people generally, economically. And a nation that will exploit economically will have to have foreign investments and everything else, and will have to use its military might to protect them. All of these problems are tied together. What I am saying today is that we must go from this convention and say, "America, you must be born again!"

So, I conclude by saying again today that we have a task and let us go out with a "divine dissatisfaction." Let us be dissatisfied until America will no longer have a high blood pressure of creeds and an anemia of deeds. Let us be dissatisfied until the tragic walls that separate the outer city of wealth and comfort and the inner city of poverty and despair shall be crushed by the battering rams of the forces of justice. Let us be dissatisfied until those that live on the outskirts of hope are brought into the metropolis of daily security. Let us be dissatisfied until slums are cast into the junk heaps of history, and every family is living in a decent sanitary home. Let us be dissatisfied until the dark yesterdays of segregated schools will be transformed into bright tomorrows of quality, integrated education. Let us be dissatisfied until integration is not seen as a problem but as an opportunity to participate in the beauty of diversity. Let us be dissatisfied until men and women, however black they may be, will be judged on the basis of the content of their character and not on the basis of the color of their skin. Let us be dissatisfied. Let us be dissatisfied until every state capitol houses a governor who will do justly, who will love mercy, and who will walk humbly with his God. Let us be dissatisfied until from every city hall, justice will roll down like waters and righteousness like a mighty stream. Let us be dissatisfied until that day when the lion and the lamb shall lie down together, and every man will sit under his own vine and fig tree and none shall be afraid. Let us be dissatisfied. And men will recognize that out of one blood God made all men to dwell upon the face of the earth. Let us be dissatisfied until that day when nobody will shout "White Power!"—when nobody will shout "Black Power!"—but everybody will talk about God's power and human power.

I must confess, my friends, the road ahead will not always be smooth. There will be still rocky places of frustration and meandering points of bewilderment. There will be inevitable setbacks here and there. There will be those moments when the buoyancy of hope will be transformed into the fatigue of despair. Our dreams will sometimes be shattered and our ethereal hopes blasted. We may again with tear-drenched eyes have to stand before the bier of some courageous civil rights worker whose life will be snuffed out by the dastardly acts of blood-thirsty mobs. Difficult and painful as it is, we must walk on in the days ahead with an audacious faith in the future. And as we continue our charted course, we may gain consolation in the words so nobly left by that great black bard who was also a great freedom fighter of yesterday, James Weldon Johnson:

> Stony the road we trod,
> Bitter the chastening rod
> Felt in the days
> When hope unborn had died.
>
> Yet with a steady beat,
> Have not our weary feet
> Come to the place
> For which our fathers sighed?
>
> We have come over the way
> That with tears hath been watered.
> We have come treading our paths
> Through the blood of the slaughtered,

Out from the gloomy past,
Till now we stand at last
Where the bright gleam
Of our bright star is cast.

Let this affirmation be our ringing cry. It will give us the courage to face the uncertainties of the future. It will give our tired feet new strength as we continue our forward stride toward the city of freedom. When our days become dreary with low-hovering clouds of despair, and when our nights become darker than a thousand midnights, let us remember that there is a creative force in this universe, working to pull down the gigantic mountains of evil, a power that is able to make a way out of no way and transform dark yesterdays into bright tomorrows. Let us realize the arc of the moral universe is long but it bends toward justice.

Let us realize that William Cullen Bryant is right: "Truth crushed to earth will rise again." Let us go out realizing that the Bible is right: "Be not deceived, God is not mocked. Whatsoever a man soweth, that shall he also reap." This is for hope for the future, and with this faith we will be able to sing in some not too distant tomorrow with a cosmic past tense, "We have overcome, we have overcome, deep in my heart, I did believe we would overcome."

* * *

SEPTIMA P. CLARK
EDUCATION AND EMPOWERMENT (1964)

The teacher wrote "Citizen" on the blackboard. Then she wrote "Constitution" and "Amendment." Then she turned to her class of thirty adult students.

"What do these mean, students?" she asked. She received a variety of answers, and when the discussion died down, the teacher was able to make a generalization.

"This is the reason we know we are citizens: Because it's written in an amendment to the Constitution."

An elderly Negro minister from Arkansas took notes on a yellow legal pad. A machine operator from Atlanta raised his hand to ask another question.

This was an opening session in an unusual citizenship education program that is held once each month at Dorchester Center, McIntosh, Georgia, for the purpose of helping adults help educate themselves.

In a five-day course, those three words became the basis of a new education in citizenship for the Negroes and whites who attended the training session. Each

Reprinted from *To Redeem a Nation: A History and Anthology of the Civil Rights Movement*, ed. Thomas R. West and James W. Mooney, Brandywine Press, 1993. Used with permission.

participant left with a burning desire to start their own Citizenship Education schools among their own communities.

The program now being sponsored by the Southern Christian Leadership Conference has resulted in the training of more than eight hundred persons in the best methods to stimulate voter registration back in their home towns. Their home towns comprising eleven southern states from eastern Texas to northern Virginia. The program was transferred to SCLC from The Highlander Folk School in Monteagle, Tennessee.

I learned of Highlander in 1952 but attended my first workshop in 1954. In 1955 I directed my first workshop and did door-to-door recruiting for the school. Unable to drive myself I found a driver for my car and made three trips from Johns Island, South Carolina, to Monteagle, Tennessee. On each trip six islanders attended and were motivated. They became literate and are still working for liberation.

In 1954 in the South, segregation was the main barrier in the way of the realization of democracy and brotherhood. Highlander was an important place because Negroes and whites met on an equal basis and discussed their problems together.

There was a series of workshops on Community Services and Segregation; Registration and Voting; and Community Development. Then it became evident that the South had a great number of functional illiterates who needed additional help to carry out their plans for coping with the problems confronting them. Problems such as the following: Six-year-old Negro boys and girls walking five miles on a muddy road in icy, wet weather to a dilapidated, cold, log cabin schoolhouse in most of the rural sections of the south. In cities like Charleston, South Carolina, children of that same tender age had to leave home while it was yet dark, 7:00 A.M., to attend an early morning session and vacate that classroom by 12:30 P.M. for another group in that same age bracket which would leave at 5:30 P.M. for home (nighttime during the winter months). These children would pass white schools that had regular school hours and fewer children enrolled. The Negro parents accepted this for many years. They did not know what to do about it. They had to be trained.

Highlander had always believed in people and the people trusted its judgement and accepted its leadership. It was accepted by Negroes and whites of all religious faiths because it had always accepted them and made them feel at home. The staff at Highlander knew that the great need of the South was to develop more people to take leadership and responsibility for the causes in which they believed. It set out on a program designed to bring out leadership qualities in people from all walks of life.

Adults from all over the South, about forty at a time, went there for the specific purpose of discussing their problems. They lived together in rustic, pleasant, rural surroundings on the top of the Cumberland plateau in a number of simple cabins around a lake, remote from business and other affairs that normally demand so much attention and energy. Though of different races and often of greatly contrasting economic or educational backgrounds, they rarely felt the tension that such differences can cause and if they did, as it occurred sometimes, it was never for long. They soon became conscious of the irrelevance of all such differences. Each person talked with people from communities with problems similar to those of his own. Each discussed both formally and informally the successes and difficulties he had had in his efforts to solve these problems in various ways.

The participants of the workshops included community leaders and civic-minded adults affiliated with agencies and organizations. They had a common concern about problems but no one knew easy solutions. The issues then as now were among the most difficult faced by society. The highly practical discussions at the workshops challenged their thinking which in turn helped them to understand the difficulties and in most cases steps were suggested towards a solution. They found out that it was within their power to take the steps necessary to meet with members of school boards. In Charleston County they asked for new schools and buses to transport their children. They staged a boycott to get rid of double sessions. *They won!* The immense value of a willingness to take responsibility and to act becomes clear when one sees what others have done, apparently through this willingness alone.

Prior to the Supreme Court's decision of 1954 [*Brown* v. *Board of Education of Topeka, Kansas*] the Negro communities of the South would have been characterized as uncoordinated, made up of groups whose interests diverged or conflicted. Today one can say that the school-integration issue has served to mobilize and unify the groups. The present psychological health of Negro leaders is good. Such things as an official ballot handed to Negro leaders in Alabama, on which is engraved a rooster crowing "white supremacy," will not weaken their determination nor courage to be free. They have amassed funds, sent men to the Justice Department, and took their gerrymandering cases to the courts. Today they are registering to vote. The registrars are not hiding in the bank vaults any more. Literacy means liberation.

✻ ✻ ✻

ELLA BAKER
ORGANIZATION WITHOUT DICTATORSHIP (1966)

Q. What is the basic goal of SNCC [Student Nonviolent Coordinating Committee]?

A. To change society so that the have-nots can share in it.

Q. Could you discuss in detail SNCC's move from the sit-ins to other things?

A. In the early days, there was little communication, except on a highly personal basis, as between friends and relatives, in the sit-in movement. I had originally thought of pulling together 120–125 sit-in leaders for a leadership training conference—but the rate of speed of the sit-ins was so rapid and the response so electrifying, both North and South, that the meeting ended up with 300 people. Many colleges sent representatives; there was a great thrust of human desire and effort. The first sit-in took place February 1, 1960; the meeting in Raleigh was around April 17, 1960, for three days. Nineteen colleges above the Mason-Dixon Line sent representatives, most of them white. There were so many northerners that at the meeting it was decided that northerners could not participate in decision making. This decision was made sort of by mutual agreement after discussion, because the northerners recognized that the thrust of the action came from the South. They had been drawn magnetically to the movement because of their great admiration for the wonderful, brave southerners. The southerners wanted it that way, at that meeting, because of the divergent levels of political thinking both within the northern group and between the North and the politically unsophisticated Deep South. (There were many representatives from Georgia, Louisiana, Alabama, although only token representation from Mississippi.) There was an outstanding leadership group from Nashville. It was a basic insecurity that caused the South to keep the North out of decision making. The North and South used different terminology, had trouble communicating. This has cropped up again in SNCC. It became more subdued in the summer of '64 when there was a real program to be carried out.

Q. What else was decided on at the meeting?

A. That the coordinating group (SNCC) was not to be part of any other organization. Some tried to make it the student arm of SCLC [Southern Christian Leadership Conference], which had put up the few dollars to hold the meeting. They decided that it was too early to fix the structure of the organization, but the feeling was that it ought to be independent from adults.

Moreover, some of those who took part (I realize in retrospect) saw a basic difference in the role of leadership in the two organizations. In SCLC, the organ-

Reprinted from *To Redeem a Nation: A History and Anthology of the Civil Rights Movement,* ed. Thomas R. West and James W. Mooney, Brandywine Press, 1993. Used with permission.

ization revolved around King; in SNCC, the leadership was group-centered (although I may have had some influence). Southern members of the movement were somewhat in awe of each other. There was a feeling that it was the "dawn of a new era," that something new and great was happening and that only they could chart the course of history. A strong equalitarian philosophy prevailed. There was a belief you could just go into an area and organize if you had had no leadership experience. SNCC rejected the idea of a God-sent leader. A basic goal was to make it unnecessary for the people to depend on a leader, for them to be strong themselves. SNCC hoped to spread into a big movement, to develop leadership from among the people. . . .

Q. What is SNCC's basic goal, that makes it unique?

A. The NAACP, Urban League, etc., do not *change* society, they want to get in. It's a combination of concern with the black goal for itself and, beyond that, with the whole society, because this is the acid test of whether the outs can get in and share in equality and worth. By worth, I mean creativity, a contribution to society. SNCC defines itself in terms of the blacks but is concerned with all excluded people.

Q. Has there been a change in SNCC's goal over time?

A. During the sit-in movement, we were concerned with segregation of public accommodations. But even then we recognized that that was only a surface goal. These obvious "irritants" had to be removed first; this was natural. Some people probably thought this in itself would change race relations; others saw deeper.

Q. Would you tell in detail how SNCC's policy changed after the sit-ins?

A. From the start, there were those who knew sitting-in would not bring basic changes. Youngsters who had not thought it through had not bargained with the intractable resistance of the power structure. The notion of "appeals to the conscience" assumed that there is a conscience, and after a while the question began to be raised, *is* there a conscience? Students, because they were most out front in the movement, began to see this and its political connotations. People began asking who *really* controlled things. The realization arose in Georgia that the rural areas had control because of the county unit system and that change had to be in the direction of political action. The NAACP had long been conducting voter action through the courts. In the process of internal communications, the question of the vote arose. SNCC people began to go to Washington to talk to the attorney general, at first about Interstate Commerce [Commission rulings]. Kennedy [attorney general] tried to sell them on the idea of voter registration. . . .

Some people in SNCC thought voter registration was it; others liked the nonviolent resistance effort and feared that it would be sacrificed to voter registration. It was later decided that you couldn't possibly have voter registration without demonstrations. . . .

Q. How were whites in SNCC dealt with before the summer of '64?

A. It was not a major problem. Anybody who wanted to help was welcomed. After '64 the problem arose not in terms of whites but in terms of the right of the individual to make his own decisions in SNCC (this was Freedom High).

At a staff meeting in November '64, the issue of structure versus nonstructure arose. Some wanted structure; others thought the real genius of SNCC was in the scope given to the original organizer. Some people said nobody should ever be fired. I thought this was unrealistic, that people were thinking in terms of a small closed society. It was a tragedy . . . people finding their personal need was not SNCC's purpose.

Old radicals have a saying: "You can't make the new world and live in it, too." The young people in SNCC wanted to live in it, too. This was all part of a general thing about young people not conforming. At first we dressed in work clothes in order to identify with those with whom we were working, but later this became a part of our *right* to identity.

Q. Was the Freedom High connected with the white-black problem?

A. I'm not sure. I think maybe it was—because there were more whites in Freedom High, especially whites who felt their talents hadn't been well used, for reasons of their philosophy or their psychological problems. In those days, resentment against whites came not from black nationalism but from a feeling that it was the whites who brought in these ideas (Freedom High) and who perhaps had trouble accepting leadership.

Freedom High was an effort to develop a nucleus of the "pure" in which you could disregard the outside world.

The sense of community was pervasive in the black community as a whole, I mean especially the community that had a sense of roots. This community had been composed to a large extent by relatives. Over the hill was my grandfather's sister who was married to my Uncle Carter, and up the grove was another relative who had a place. So it was a deep sense of community. I think these are the things that helped to strengthen my concept about the need for people to have a sense of their own value, and *their* strengths, and it became accentuated when I began to travel in the forties for the National Association for the Advancement of Colored People. Because during that period, in the forties, racial segregation and discrimination were very harsh. As people moved to towns and cities, the sense of community diminished. A given area was made up of people from various and sundry other areas. They didn't come from the same place. So they had to *learn* each other, and they came into patterns of living that they had not been accustomed to. And so whatever deep sense of community that may have been developed in that little place that I spoke of, didn't always carry over to the city when they migrated. They lost their roots. When you lose that, what will you do next. You *hope* that you begin to think in terms of the *wider* brotherhood. . . .

I guess revolutionary is relative to the situations that people find themselves in, and whatever their goals are, and how many people are in agreement that this is a desired goal. The original four kids who sat down in Greensboro, North Carolina, I'm confident that they had little or no knowledge of the revolutionary background that people talk about when they speak of changing the society by way of socialism or communism. They were youngsters who had a very simple reaction to an inequity. When you're a student with no money, and you go buy what you need like your paper or your pencils, where do you go? The five-and-ten-cent store. At least you could then, because the prices were not quite as disproportionate as they are now. These two had been talking with a dentist, a black dentist who apparently had some experience with the earlier days of the formation of the Congress of Racial Equality (CORE). They were able to talk with him about their frustrations, going in there, spending all their little money, and yet not being able to sit and buy a five-cent Coke. That was a rather simple challenge as you look back. They decided they were going to do something about it, and so they sat down. Then some others followed their actions. A sister who had a brother in school in another town, her town had already sat in. She might call and ask, why doesn't his school sit in? This was the communication link, plus the media. They sat, and the others came and sat, and it spread. I guess one of the reasons it spread was because it was simple, and it struck home to a lot of young people who were in school.

It hadn't gone on so long before I suggested that we call a conference of the sit-inners to be held in Raleigh. It was very obvious to the Southern Christian Leadership Conference that there was little or no communication between those who sat in, say, in Charlotte, North Carolina, and those who eventually sat in at some other place in Virginia or Alabama. They were motivated by what the North Carolina four had started, but they were not in contact with each other, which meant that you couldn't build a sustaining force just based on spontaneity.

My estimate was that the conference would bring together a couple hundred of the young leadership. I had not hoped for such large numbers of adults who came. These adults were part and parcel of groups such as the Montgomery bus boycott. They also may have been relating to the organizing first steps of SCLC, which had been officially established but had not expanded very much.

We ended up with about three hundred people. We had insisted that the young people be left to make their own decisions. Also, we provided for those who came from outside the South to meet separately from those who came from the sit-in areas, because the persons who came from say, New York, frequently had had wider experience in organizing and were too articulate. In the initial portion of the conference, the southern students had the right to meet, to discuss, and to determine where they wanted to go. It wasn't my idea to separate the northern and southern students. I hesitated to project ideas as pointedly as that, but those who had worked closely with me knew that I believed very firmly in the right of the people who were under the heel to be the ones to decide what action they were going to take to get from under their oppression. As a group, basically, they were the black students from the South. The heritage of the South was theirs, and it was one of oppression. Those who came from the other nineteen schools and colleges and universities up North didn't have the same oppression, and they were white. They were much more erudite and articulate, farther advanced in the theoretical concepts of social change. This can become overwhelming for those who don't even understand what you're talking about and feel put down.

The Southern Christian Leadership Conference felt that they could influence how things went. They were interested in having the students become an arm of SCLC. They were most confident that this would be their baby, because I was their functionary and I had called the meeting. At a discussion called by the Reverend Dr. King, the SCLC leadership made decisions who would speak to whom to influence the students to become part of SCLC. Well, I disagreed. There was no student at Dr. King's meeting. I was the nearest thing to a student, being the advocate, you see. I also knew from the beginning that having a woman be an executive of SCLC was not something that would go over with the male-dominated leadership. And then, of course, my personality wasn't right, in the sense I was not afraid to disagree with the higher authorities. I wasn't one to say, yes, because it came from the Reverend King. So when it was proposed that the leadership could influence the direction by speaking to, let's say, the man from Virginia, he could speak to the leadership of the Virginia student group, and the assumption was that having spoken to so-and-so, so-and-so would do what they wanted done, I was outraged. I walked out.

✳ ✳ ✳

VINCENT HARDING
ONE FINAL, SOARING HOPE:
BUILDING THE CAMPGROUNDS OF RENEWAL (1990)

As an adviser to the filmmaking team, I was privileged to see some of the earliest working images of the *Eyes on the Prize* series. Ever since then, I've been obsessed, sometimes overwhelmed, by a relentless vision, a wild and soaring hope: What if we could get some of our young sisters and brothers off the most dangerous streets, out of the drug-related traps of quick, apparently easy, bloodied money, away from the flashy, destructive models (both human and automotive), apart from their lethal weapons and their beepers, out of the crippled and often crippling schools, freed from the brutalizing cycle of the criminal justice system. If, with the help of these films, we could create and discover together a new set of personal, family, and social options for their lives. If.

Yes, I think, if we could perhaps find a way to convince a dozen, or twenty, or fifty of them, along with their most supportive, least-despairing grandmothers, uncles, parents—whoever is ready to risk a new beginning, to provide the needed support. If we could journey together with such a group to John's Island or to Lincoln University, or to a campground in the Maine or Michigan woods, or even to a monastery or retreat center on the Pacific coast. And there, here, wherever, if we could gather the young people and some of their family members, together with half a dozen other serious, centered, creatively mature women and men to play, to work (perhaps even to meditate and pray), and to watch *Eyes on the Prize*, it might be possible to begin to break the deadly cycle.

In such a setting, with the fresh air of life intoxicating us, with demanding work to engage and reward us, with time for play and quietness, it might be possible to discover together a set of new life-affirming possibilities for some of them, for some of us. Indeed, in such an unfamiliar setting we might even stumble upon new models of teaching, learning, and hope, and set them loose across this nation like dancing tongues of fire, networks of purifying flame.

But first, before the fire: After the first few difficult, exploratory days, I see us sitting together, watching one segment of *Eyes* each day, discussing the films in small groups, working with the images and messages formally and informally, during meals and work and play. I hear us, feel us, moving continually toward the key questions: What did these earlier, historic experiences mean for the people who lived through them, and what meaning can we make for ourselves now, and in the days that follow these, the daunting days when we must leave this hidden place?

(By the way, I think I would begin with a group of African American young

Reprinted from *Hope and History*, by Vincent Harding (New York: Orbis Books, 1990). Used with permission.

people. Part of my reasoning is based on the fact that so much of the trouble of the larger society bursts out harder, sharper, clearer among them. I would begin there, too, because they are often in greatest, most vivid need, with so few resources available to them. I think I would start there because so many of the role models on the screen become fully accessible, perhaps inescapable, for them. Of course, I would also begin among such youngsters and their families because my own life experiences as a child of Harlem and the South Bronx have so often brought me so close to where they are, and I simply cannot pass them by. And yet, having thought and said all that, I still hesitate, for I am not fully at peace with such logical conclusions. Rather, I see and feel the powerful arguments for a multiracial gathering on our campground of renewal. It might be predominantly black, but rich in other experiences of struggle and hope, especially among peoples of color. So I continue to wrestle with this part of the vision. Meanwhile, I trust I have already made it clear in the earlier essays how many ways there are for us to use the same materials to open new possibilities for all young people and their families, whatever their color and condition. Regardless of where I begin on the campground, my basic assumption of universal application remains the same.)

This is not the place to try to elaborate on the discussions, debates, and profound explorations that I know would emerge from these workshops in the woods, these vacations from the streets. (I say I *know* only because, like some of you, I have spent time among young persons such as these, opened opportunities—occasionally with a segment of *Eyes*—for their voices, fears, hopes, and wonderings to be heard. And the depths to which they have taken the discussions have often been stunning.) But could we begin here to imagine some of the ways in which elements of both parts of the *Eyes on the Prize* series might be brought together in serious engagement with the hard realities of their lives?

Early in the process, whatever else happened, we would surely introduce them to Mose Wright, allow them to begin to imagine what Mississippi had been like for him, let our young friends and their families talk about his real alternatives when the killers came to the door for his grandnephew, Emmett Till, reflect together on the sources of this man's courage when he pointed to Milam and Bryant in the open court. For some of the older family members these scenes may dislodge harsh and hidden memories of their own southern-based childhoods, or of summers spent sequestered in the crevices between the beauty and terror of that land. Perhaps some of them will remember with loving appreciation their own Mose Wrights, men and women of great, rough-hewn dignity, caught in hard and threatening places, striving to maintain integrity, safety, and sanity. And what discussions of family and womanhood might flow out of the consideration of Mamie Till Bradley, and of *her* mother, and their firm determination to open their sorrow and indignation to the world?

In the same way it would be crucial for Rosa Parks (perhaps even in person) to be present for them, to help them learn—some for the first time—the meaning of living with and against Jim Crow, and the great risks and brutal costs that were necessary before its legal realities could be eliminated, just in time for them to be born (free from the terrible constraints that their foreparents knew, but now tragically imprisoned in lives that have not yet found anything to be free *for*). Let them watch King and ask why he left the relative security of his middle-class Baptist pastorate to risk his own life and the safety of his family to respond to the compelling, freedom-seeking call of the rising people. And certainly, we can begin to savor the kinds of struggles that could take place among us when we explore together King's stirring invitation to the way of collective nonviolent resistance, and his little family's early personal decision to give up the gun they had kept in their house for protection. Was that part of their own movement toward freedom? And what does such freedom mean now for the gun-filled streets of Dorchester, of Lawndale, of L.A.? Is there any place for courageous, persistent nonviolent soldiers in our own time?

The questions abound. Would our young people grasp the great daring and high hopes of the sit-ins and freedom rides? Could we introduce them to role-playing to demonstrate the disciplined courage that it took for young women and men to refuse to allow their opponents to set the familiar agendas of violence-for-violence? Who would play the roles of the courageous white students who came to risk their lives and shed their blood in the cause? It would be revealing to hear the discussion in the role-play groups concerning the decisions and commitments which finally led the Nashville contingent of college students who had given leadership to the 1960 sit-ins there to go forward again in 1961, determined to reclaim for democracy the brutal ground of the Montgomery, Alabama, bus station. The question of what our young people and their family members think they might have done later, with the mob surrounding the church, would certainly provoke intense and moving responses. At some point someone, perhaps one of the grandmothers present, could also call our attention to all those "square" Christian women in that endangered church building, many with their flowered hats and white gloves on, bravely singing "Leaning on the Everlasting Arms." What would they make of that? What do we make of it? (Remembering that powerful church scene, I can hardly wait to see who will volunteer to play the role of Fred Shuttlesworth, beaten and bombed in the freedom cause more than once, courageously, foolhardily, pushing his way from the outside, through the mob and the police, clearing the path for himself and James Farmer to join the beleaguered folks on the inside. How do you explain that from the South Bronx or from Grand Boulevard in Detroit?) Will there be anyone in the families to testify to the ways in which religion can empower, encourage, and discipline people to walk through fire on the way to freedom?

Then, for the young people who have asked us, seriously, sadly, "And who was Malcolm the Tenth, anyway?" this would present a marvelous opportunity. Here, perhaps, is a life that allows them (us?) no excuses, no escapes. Detroit Red, child of a cruelly broken home, experienced with destructive white enemies and paternalistic helpers, exposed to a wild life on the streets, dope user and dealer, immersed in crime of many kinds, with memories of seven long years in prison. And out of it all emerges a man transformed (one of a growing company for whom prison becomes a fiery furnace for annealing and conversion), a man who, in the words of poet Robert Hayden, "became much more than there was time for him to be." What will they (we) do with Malcolm, with the Muslims, with the world of Islam, with El-Hajj Malik? More important, what will we do with *them*, the children of Malcolm, the offspring of Malik who gather with us in the woods? Will someone help them, guide them to receive all the gifts brought by *Eyes*, help them perhaps to claim for themselves the time that Malcolm did not have? Will they find tough, loving, compassionate teachers, as Malcolm eventually did? Will there be relatives to share new life with them? And who will answer the other questions: Does our society—and its teachers—look forward to the second coming of many Malcolms, many Martins, many Ella Bakers and Fannie Lou Hamers? And what is the future of this nation if there is no space, no time for the women- and men-children of the streets to find their truest maturity, their temporarily hidden redemptive purpose, identity, and hope?

Once more, questions abound, even as we imagine our young folks and their families watching the encounter between C. T. Vivian and Sheriff Jim Clark and his deputies on the steps of the courthouse in Selma. What empowers a black man in 1965 to stand in front of a group of white law officers (with all the terrible history of such encounters written in his bones) and lecture them on the meaning of the Nuremberg tribunals and on personal accountability for their consciences? And how did C. T. get up again from the ground after taking a combination punch and billy stick blow? How did he stand, refusing to run, refusing to be quiet, indeed insisting on paraphrasing Winston Churchill ("What kind of people are you?") to the threatened, threatening keepers of Selma's old law and order?

What will be their responses when *Eyes on the Prize* helps to make it clear that C. T. rising from the ground, that the people returning to the Edmund Pettus Bridge, armed only with courage, to face again the officers who had recently beaten them to the earth, that Viola Liuzzo singing a freedom song as she saw the assassins' car approaching her vehicle on the road, that Jimmy Lee Jackson dying for his mother and his people—that these and many more are all part of the price that was paid for the expansion of their possibilities beyond the limits of the streets? (Of course, they will also see eventually that all these were part of the path of human courage, sacrifice, and hope that made it possible for their hero, Jesse Jackson, to have a podium from which he could speak to the world. Indeed, what we all eventually discover is that the same spirit, the same courage, the same sacrifice, the same hope also made it possible for Nelson Mandela to emerge from twenty-seven years in prison as the unofficial president of South Africa.) When they discover the costs that others have paid to begin to break open certain doors for them, will they begin to revision themselves and their best possibilities?

It may be that we will be faced with even more piercing, probing questions when we move with our young friends and their families into the *Eyes II* presentation of some of the northern phases of the great struggle for democracy. To share their responses to the fury of the white mobs of the Chicago suburbs, the burning of Detroit, and the rise of the Panthers will surely be worth all the effort it will take to develop the setting. For the opportunities those stories provide for ventilation, reflection, and powerful revisioning are unlimited. The conversations across generational lines will likely be invaluable, both upsetting and healing. We may wonder, for instance, about what differences they will see between the defiance of the system that Fred Hampton of the Chicago Panthers represented and that of the leading drug dealers in their communities. Will they recognize differences between the guns of the Panthers and the guns of the gangs? Perhaps even more important, will they see the similarities? Do we?

Of course, the camp will not be complete without the marvelous scenes of Muhammad Ali. Perhaps it will be necessary to include a set of boxing gloves (very well padded ones, of course) in our equipment. If we are able to get past that stage, it will be good to see our young people, male and female, respond to Ali, absorb the significant levels of personal and racial meaning that flow beneath his marvelous humor. In fact, there may even be time to re-enact the earthshaking Ali–Maynard Jackson engagement from *Eyes II*. What better way for them to be introduced to the positive possibilities of inspired and inspiring electoral politics, to the world that the movement helped open up for Shirley Chisholm, Jesse Jackson, Harold Washington, David Dinkins, Douglas Wilder, and many more. If we could encourage them to add their own names to the longer list, if together we could imagine their faces on some future screen of honor, a great dream might begin to rise.

But there is one other segment of *Eyes* that must be seen at the retreat, one less dreamlike sequence for this quiet place of revisioning. Attica. Here the intention will not be to frighten but to bring into focus for frank discussion the world of the prison and the role it has played in our lives as African American people. It will not be an unfamiliar territory for some of our extended family, but it needs to be seen again. Perhaps Frank "Big Black" Smith could visit the camp, could be heard and seen and touched in discussions and basketball games. Perhaps he could simply tell his story, like a great big uncle whose love for them is palpable, who seeks to call them away from the paths of self-destruction to the unmistakably creative powers inherent in their lives.

Imagining the presence of our brother from Attica sets loose scores of other possibilities, suggests many other visitors. I wonder how our extended family would respond to the inspiriting, compassionate presence of Sonia Sanchez and Gwendolyn Brooks and others like them. Would the group understand the calls from Amiri Baraka, Angela Davis, and Haki Madhubuti, from June Johnson and Ben Chavis, calls to rethink the choices they have made, to consider far better uses for their lives? Who knows? June's powerful, dangerous, and courageous experiences as a teenage freedom fighter in Mississippi, as a committee worker for democracy now, just may come through.

Perhaps when they hear the Last Poets and recognize some of the movement foundations for rap and hip-hop, perhaps they will respond to the calling from their roots, dare to write some poetry of their own, explore the deeper, hidden fountains of their humanity. Perhaps when our discussions of the series open them to Nkrumah and Nyerere, to Winnie and Nelson Mandela, and to the great world of explosive democratic aspirations beyond these shores, it may be they will find even more heroes, new models, new hopes. And what then? When the struggles engendered by *Eyes* begin to rage within the deep places of their lives, someone will need to be present for them. That is why we invited the families. That is why we came ourselves. Thus we are reminded that when we determine to explore the most profound levels of human experiences and possibilities, the role of the teacher is expanded in grand and awesome ways. We become part of the extended family, part of the healing company of witnesses.

Then, in the wildness of my dreams, after we have seen the entire *Eyes on the Prize* series together, the students would be asked to write letters to both the living and the departed makers of that history. They are asked especially to write to the people who meant something to them as they watched the films, to people who raised fundamental questions or great hopes for them. So hours would be given to the sometimes painful task, perhaps now made a bit more bearable by new motivation, a sense of great relevance, and the presence of compassionate teachers and supportive relatives. Letters to Mrs. Parks, to Angela Davis, to Medgar Evers, to Dr. King, to James Chaney and his courageous passengers in the station wagon, Goodman and Schwerner, to James Reeb, Huey Newton, Unita Blackwell, Fred Shuttlesworth, Mose Wright and the nuns on their way to Selma (on their way to new freedoms and new challenges in their own lives), to Coretta King and Jo Ann Robinson, to the men of Attica, to Ella Baker and Fred Hampton, to Paul Robeson, and many more. They would be asked to write letters from their hearts to the men and women who kept their eyes on the prize for themselves and for us. The only prescribed part of the letters would be an expression of gratitude for what the addressees did, gave, created, and envisioned on behalf of us all. The rest of the letter would be whatever they wanted to say, ask, present.

This is more than an exercise. It is meant to call the young people into communion with their black and white ancestors in the struggle for a more humane American nation. It assumes that we are less than human when we do not acknowledge those who prepared the way for us, often at great cost, when we do not give thought to how we shall help clear the path for others yet unborn Something tells us that one of the deep wounds of the life of the streets (indeed, these wounds are inflicted on streets and malls of many colors and classes in this nation) is that the young people have been separated from both their past and their future, leaving a vast and aching void, often to be filled with nothing more than the most destructive values of the society. *Eyes on the Prize* opens a way for such young people to reenter the humanizing flow of history, to consider the possibility that there is purpose and meaning for their lives far beyond the terror and temptations of their immediate situation.

Actually, as the vision soars, the letters are answered by both the living and the dead. (Creative, sensitive teachers can often serve as exciting amanuenses.) As a matter of fact, as indicated above, I envision many of the long-distance runners of this post–World War II freedom struggle, the prize-seekers and creators, coming to where the young people are, listening to them, sharing with them, encouraging them to believe that there are real alternatives for their lives.

However, it may be that some of the most important letters, the most crucial encounters, will be closer at hand. Somewhere in the campground process, after we have tried to learn, teach, model, and encourage the uses of silence, the power of mediation, the many varieties of prayer and reflection, the therapies of gratitude, at such points new visions may arise. Some young people may make new discoveries concerning their families, will see in this setting great strengths and feel deep love that they had not been free to recognize before. Here, we would encourage not only letters of gratitude and rethinking, but specific acts of appreciation directed toward those family members who have come to share the experience, who have offered so much teaching from their own lives. Small gifts created and given, flowers presented, poems and rap songs composed and shared in honor of those who have stood by them. Letters written to those who wanted to come but could not. Actions that might have seemed unthinkable before may now be recognized as pathways toward the expansion of our hearts, toward the healing and building of our humanity.

As a result, as a cause of such actions, one other level of communion will likely open to us. We will probably discover together and alone the healing, empowering spirit that lives within us all, the force that is always with us, the great connective presence which eventually draws us to such deep levels of our being that we cannot easily escape our rendezvous with all other life and existence. For many of us on the campground, such discovery (or rediscovery) may lead to a new path, may allow us to recognize that we are all capable of the kind of magnificent lives that have flashed before us on the screen. In the presence of this discovery, poems and songs, letters and love dances to ourselves, to the divine within us, to the life force in the trees and skies, lakes and flowers, rocks and earth will surely and appropriately overflow.

This is the healing creativity that our fractured, searching world now exhibits and requires everywhere. As we begin to discover it in the midst of the extended healing family, as we experience restructuring of our selfhood along with others, hope begins to grow. As a result, coming to the end of the retreat, preparing to leave the campground, some of our young people and their family members may be filled with certain understandable questions and concerns about how and where they can best nurture the seeds they have newly discovered within themselves. Some members of the community of hope will sense a need for fresh beginnings. Perhaps they will want to find new settings where they may prepare themselves more fully for their eventual return to the streets of their youth, equipped with skills, courage, hope, and direction, ready to be present for others like themselves, already building new campgrounds in their minds.

And this may be the point at which the wildest hope of all rises out of the series. For I would think and dream that there might be women and men and families who are working on their own development and who see their present role in the historic movement as one of opening themselves and their settings to such young people, to families of new beginnings. When some members of our campground community decide that they really want to try a new start, find a point of entry into the kind of life-affirming history they have seen in *Eyes,* and when they are convinced that they must have an alternative setting in which to begin again, I look for many hands, arms, lives to open wide.

At this point I have no idea where such a vision ends and "reality" begins. Perhaps such things no longer matter. It may be that all we need to know is that there are tremendous healing, transformative powers bound up in *Eyes on the Prize,* waiting to be released into the lives of even those persons we consider most desperately at risk in our society. It may be that all we need to hear now is that there are hidden campgrounds of hope and many creative resources waiting for committed teachers, teachers who are ready to call forth the impossible, from ourselves and everyone else.

Clearly, my rudimentary vision of how all this might happen is only a suggestion, an invitation to thousands of teachers everywhere to create your own settings, your own campgrounds of renewal, to form your own extended family, to take your own risks—to experience great joy.

✳ ✳ ✳

ADOLPH REED JR.
WHY IS THERE NO BLACK POLITICAL MOVEMENT? (1998)

The question itself, no doubt, is already a provocation. Even as I pose it, I can imagine loud objections to its obvious presumptions. It's easy to anticipate a list of examples to the contrary: from the hip-hop nation to the Million Man and Woman Marches to the current plans to organize a Black Radical Congress; from the black women who mobilized in support of Anita Hill to Jesse Jackson's Rainbow Coalition, Inc., and Operation PUSH; from various local mobilizations to the Congressional Black Caucus, the Urban League, the Southern Christian Leadership Conference, and the NAACP; from a plethora of nominal (both single-issue and multipurpose) coalitions to independent parties and candidacies to nationalist and other sects. So, before going any further, I should clarify the presumptions and why I ask the question. The rub lies in what one means by a "political movement."

What I mean is a force that has shown a capability, over time, of mobilizing popular support for programs that expressly seek to alter the patterns of public policy or economic relations. There simply is no such entity in black American life at this point.

I can also imagine objections to this notion of politics—protestations that say it is too narrow; that it overlooks the deeper significance of what Robin Kelley, following political scientist James Scott, has usefully summarized as "infrapolitics": the region of "daily confrontations, evasive actions, and stifled thoughts." Hogwash. Twenty years after Reaganism took hold and twenty-three years after Maynard Jackson, Atlanta's first black mayor, summarily fired nearly two thousand striking black sanitation workers with no rooted opposition from the black community, it's time for us to face some brute realities.

Sure, there's infrapolitics—there always is, and there always will be; wherever there's oppression, there's resistance. That's one of the oldest slogans on the left. But it's also a simple fact of life. People don't like being oppressed or exploited, and they respond in ways that reflect that fact. That and a buck fifty will get you on the subway. "Daily confrontations" are to political movements as carbon, water, and oxygen are to life on this planet. They are the raw material for movements of political change, and expressions of dissatisfaction that reflect the need for change, but their presence says nothing more about the potential for such a movement to exist, much less its actuality.

At best, those who romanticize "everyday resistance" or "cultural politics" read the evolution of political movements teleologically; they presume that those conditions necessarily, or even typically, lead to political action. They don't. Not

any more than the presence of carbon and water necessarily leads to the evolution of *Homo sapiens*. Think about it: infrapolitics is ubiquitous, developed political movements are rare.

At worst, and more commonly, defenders of infrapolitics treat it as politically consequential in its own right. This idealism may stem from a romantic
confusion, but it's also an evasive acknowledgement of the fact that there is no
real popular political movement. Further, it's a way of pretending that the mission movement is not a problem—that everyday, apolitical social practices are a
new, maybe even more "authentic," form of politics.

This evasive tendency links up with much deeper and broader reflexes in
black political life and masks a defeatist strain in black activism.

This defeatism stems from an impossible position that black organizers have
locked themselves into for nearly all of this century: the "brokerage" model of
politics. Under this strategy, political action centers on the claim to express the
unified interests of black Americans as a single, corporate entity. It's ultimately
a form of high-level negotiation; its main practice is assuming the voice of a
putatively coherent black community and projecting it toward policymakers.

This political style emerged at a time in which disfranchisement and white
supremacy severely limited possibilities for popular participation. However, its
origins in the black elite made it easy to overlook the significance of that limitation. The strategy was accompanied by a highborn sense of duty among the
elite—a responsibility to guide a rank-and-file population thought to be in need
of uplift as much as opportunity. And there was no shortage of energetic, middle-
class "Race Leaders" prepared to accept the burden of speaking for the mute
masses. Thus the old quip that any black person with a clean suit and five dollars
in his pocket imagined himself a Negro leader.

This form of politics reigns across the black ideological spectrum. It defines
the terms of debate along that Left-Right axis—a debate propelled by claims to
legitimacy of spokesmanship shaped within a rhetoric of authenticity (claims, it
should be said, that are directed largely at a white audience). Criticism of Ward
Connerly, Clarence Thomas, or the Harvard Afro-American Studies Dream
Team, for instance, focuses at least as much on their supposed distance from "the
community" as on the substance of their ideas.

This is a corporatist argument—born of brokerage-style politics—not a populist one. Even as it comes dressed in invocations of "the people" or "the
masses," this is not an approach that leads to popular mobilization. Rather, the
Race Leader principle—and its pursuit of a vague notion of black unity—under-
cuts the discussion that could actually help stimulate a genuine movement. The
"people" don't get to speak; they are spoken for. This is true by definition
because "the people" exist only as an idea.

What exists in reality, though, is a broad variety of black individuals with an array of concerns and interests that converge and diverge, crosscut and overlap from issue to issue. A politics that insists on unity, and representation of an idealized collective, hinders mobilization precisely because its reflex is to diminish the significance of these differences.

Instead, the current activist model subordinates debate over political diversity in favor of establishing "unity." This, in turn, means generating political programs that combine laundry lists of issues that bow to arbitrarily defined constituencies, and sets of least-common-denominator particulars that symbolize generically racial interests and outrages—such as church burnings and police brutality—that demonstrate the persistence and extent of racism.

But the concerns that the vast majority of black people experience the vast majority of the time are not about those outrages and large, symbolic issues (for instance, defense of affirmative action and majority-minority legislative districts). This is not to say that people don't care about those issues or that they aren't important. They are not, however, the kinds of issues on which a sustained popular movement can be built. They are too remote from ordinary individuals' daily experience to generate either intense, active support over time or the kind of dialogue that fuels political education.

The result is a notion of black leadership—"authentic" leadership—that substitutes for popular mobilization. It's a model that assumes categories of leader and led. The myth of the organic black community, moreover, makes it unnecessary to be troubled over questions regarding democratic representation—such as how to achieve accountability of spokespersons; how to stimulate and safeguard open debate; how to define plausible constituencies. These and other such issues are entirely absent from a black political discourse that conceptualizes democracy only in corporatist terms—as a condition that exists between the black community and others, not as a matter of serious interest within black political life itself.

A telling indication of how far the existing black politics is from such concerns is the general unwillingness to anchor political action in the creation of membership organizations—that is, groups with clearly identified constituencies that are, at least in principle, empowered to pass and execute judgment on leaders' actions. Nationally, only the NAACP is governed by its membership. Operation PUSH and the National Rainbow Coalition are mere banners for Jesse Jackson to speak in front of. Even the main products of the high period of political activism in the 1960s—the Student Nonviolent Coordinating Committee, Congress on Racial Equality, and Southern Christian Leadership Conference— were not mass-membership organizations.

My point is not that those specific groups should have structured themselves on a popular membership basis; they did the work they were created to do in epic political circumstances and did it effectively. However, the limitations of a politics—especially a movement politics—that doesn't take account of the need to stimulate popular participation have come home to roost dramatically in the subsequent history of the SCLC, the only one of those organizations to survive visibly into the present. That has been a story of decline, spiraling ever further downward into nostalgia and nepotism.

More radical, even avowedly Marxist or revolutionary, organizations have been no more inclined to concentrate on organizing concrete constituencies into membership organizations. Groups from the 1960s and 1970s—the Black Panther Party, Black Workers Congress, National Black Assembly, African Liberation Support Committee—and the more recent attempts to create black united fronts all have been either cadre organizations (organizations of organizers) or coalitions of such organizations. The latter, which amount to little more than stacks of letterhead, give the illusion of a broad, popular base by equating breadth of representation with the length of the list of paper organizations.

This politics creates a particular conundrum for radicals, for whom the idea of connectedness to a popular constituency is a paramount goal. Opportunism is often employed as a tactic to paper over the problem.

As a case in point, nationalist activists organized an Afro-Caribbean International Festival of Life held in Chicago's Washington Park, principal location for South Side cookouts and family reunions, on July 4. Ever since the Black Power era, black Americans' celebration of the Fourth [of July] has been something of a thorn in the side for radicals, an apparent indication of how little headway our theoretical critiques have made in the population. In that context there are two ways to read the international festival. On the one hand, it could be a strategy for presenting an alternative to the Fourth of July imagery; staging a big event where people are congregating anyway seems like a reasonable way to distribute the message. On the other hand, the festival could be an attempt to claim to speak for a large gathering by jumping out in front of it and controlling the only microphone.

Kwanzaa, Maulana Ron Karenga's mid-1960s invention, was perhaps the prototype of this self-deluding flimflam. For years, radicals had been trying to sell a critique of Christmas as a destructively consumerist and inappropriately Eurocentric celebration. Kwanzaa was an attempt to co-opt the ritual of midwinter celebration that the majority of black Americans were unwilling to give up. Less obviously, it was an admission of failure to sell an alternative view of the world that would make Christmas unappealing. Instead, Kwanzaa merely creates a mythology that paints Christmas black without really upsetting conventional practices.

From this perspective Kwanzaa belongs to the same family of evasions as claims about infrapolitics and the brokerage school of political action. All of them rely on the pretension to express the concerns of people who don't have any say in the matter. In the 1980s, Jesse Jackson figured out how to work this pretense through the mass media. Louis Farrakhan pushed its evolution in the 1990s with a strategy of giving speeches to packed civic auditoriums. Because in that format he is the only one empowered to speak, Farrakhan is able to claim that the lively, packed audiences both endorse his politics and represent a larger, mass base.

The Million Man March was this strategy's culminating moment, and radicals' defenses of this event underscore the proliferation of evasive politics. They also suggest its ultimate sources and why it seems so hard to break out of it. The defenses basically amount to a claim that the march should be separated from the man—that those who attended did so for multifarious reasons and didn't necessarily embrace Farrakhan's program.

The defense is hollow. The second claim is no doubt true, just as it was true of the 1963 March on Washington, anti-Vietnam War demos, and every other large gathering. The key fact about the Million Man March was that Farrakhan got to set the agenda, control the terms of discussion, and project himself as its leader. Those radicals who support and defend his rally dispute his claim by projecting other objectives onto the assembled throng. But even if one accepts this explanation, the throng remains an undifferentiated, mute mass—the repository of the interpretations of others who presume to speak on its behalf.

We'll never be able to create the kind of movement we need until we can break with the mystifications and opportunism that tie activism to the bankrupt brokerage model of politics. The only possibly successful strategy is one based on genuinely popular, deliberative processes and concrete, interest-based organizing that connects with people's daily lives.

III.

THE U.S. LEFT AND ANTIRACISM

The passionate vision, energy, and commitment of many on the American Left impacted powerfully on antiracist struggles in the United States. Analytical tools and organizational skills drawn from socialist and communist traditions—personified in a number of black and "white" activists—became essential elements in these struggles in the twentieth century.*

Essential elements of the basic left-wing orientation have included:

- the acceptance of the rich diversity of humanity and—at the same time—of an essential equality among people;
- the belief that each and every person has a right to dignity and freedom;
- the view that the oppressed must struggle to overcome their own oppression;

---

*We are not able to add a similar section in this volume on "The U.S. Right and Antiracism," unfortunately, because that area on the political spectrum has no equivalent history of antiracist struggle—in fact, as we've noted, the political Right to a large extent has been inclined toward an acceptance, in some cases even a vigorous promulgation, of racist ideology.

An examination of conservative histories and anthologies (Russell Kirk's *The Conservative Mind* and *The Portable Conservative Reader*, William F. Buckley's *American Conservative Thought in the Twentieth Century*, and George H. Nash's *The Conservative Intellectual Movement in America Since 1945*) reveal little but discomfort or hostility toward efforts to advance African American rights.

In recent decades, some personalities among the conservatives have explicitly rejected racism and have argued that it can and should be transcended (though not, of course, in ways that would upset capitalism). Among these have been nonwhite conservatives such as George Schuyler in the 1950s and 1960s, and more recently Thomas Sowell and Dinesh D'Souza. Rather than assuming prominent roles in antiracist struggles, however, they have preferred to function as sharp critics of such struggles.

- the critique of capitalist economic dynamics as generating various forms of oppression, with the various forms of oppression therefore being interconnected;
- the understanding of racial justice and economic justice as being necessarily linked, and that these goals can only be achieved through a profound power struggle between oppressed and oppressors;
- the conviction that the multiracial working-class majority constitutes a force that can establish rule by the people over the economy.

The best-publicized of the left-wing involvements in struggles for racial justice was that of the Communist Party, whose association with the powerful regime and world movement generated by the Russian Revolution led by V. I. Lenin and Leon Trotsky in 1917 gave it great attractive power. That organization was seen as "un-American" by conservatives and reactionaries from the time of its 1919 founding during the Red Scare period, and as being aligned with their nation's enemies by a majority of Americans during the later Cold War era. This guaranteed that any real and imagined connections of Communism with the struggle for black rights were played up by white racists in order to discredit the civil rights and black liberation movements. Some partisans of black rights have told the story differently—as worthy struggles into which the Communists intervened to play a manipulative and self-serving role (for example, Wilson Record in *Race and Radicalism* and Harold Cruse in *The Crisis of the Negro Intellectual*). More recent scholarship, perceptively explored by Alan Wald, has provided evidence of a more complex and fruitful interaction.

Another left-wing current was the small but important split-off from the Communist movement that was influenced by the ideas of Trotsky. The Trotskyists sought to defend revolutionary principles from the authoritarian and often opportunistic policies fostered in the Communist mainstream by the USSR's dictator Joseph Stalin. One of the most significant Trotskyist leaders for a number of years was the famed Afro-Caribbean intellectual C. L. R. James, whose classic and influential perspective—summarized in "The Revolutionary Answer to the Negro Problem in the United States"—is accompanied here by a sketch, authored by Steve Bloom and David Finkel, of this current's interaction with the black liberation struggle.

The outstanding member of the Socialist Party to play a role in the black liberation struggle was A. Philip Randolph. He and his cothinker Chandler Owen were tagged "the Lenin and Trotsky of Harlem" in the early 1920s, but he stayed with the Socialist Party and by the decade's end he had become a founder and longtime president of the influential Brotherhood of Sleeping Car Porters. In 1966, under the auspices of the newly established A. Philip Randolph Institute, *A Freedom Budget for All Americans* was produced, shaped by Randolph in conjunction with other Socialist Party personalities, such as Michael Harrington, Bayard Rustin, and Tom Kahn, with assistance from economists such as Leon Keyserling. It projected economic and social policies that would eliminate poverty and the economic underpinnings of racism within a ten-year period. Although it claimed this could be done while leaving the fundamental structure of capitalism intact, it was seen as far too radical by both Democratic and Republican politicians and was rejected out of hand by both the Johnson and Nixon administrations.

An important influence emerging in the 1960s and 1970s was the Communist current associated with the Chinese Revolution of 1949 and its leader Mao Zedong. Often blended with Pan-Africanist and black nationalist perspectives, Maoism's attraction and influence were felt by many black activists and intellectuals. Amiri Baraka (previously known as LeRoi Jones)—internationally famous poet, playwright, and critic—was among the most prominent figures in this milieu, and his essay "The Revolutionary Tradition in African American Literature" combines his political and literary sensibilities into an illuminating intellectual survey.

Representing a different variant of the black nationalist–Maoist synthesis, the Black Panther Party exerted a powerful influence from the late 1960s through the mid-1970s before succumbing to a lethal combination of sometimes murderous government repression and sometimes murderous self-destructiveness. (Different aspects of the story can be found in the primary documents gathered in Philip Foner's *The Black Panthers Speak*, in the devastating journalistic critique *Shadow of the Panther* by Hugh Pearson, and in the reflective anthology *Liberation, Imagination, and the Black Panther Party*, edited by Kathleen Cleaver and George Katsiaficas.) Some of its most positive qualities are captured in the 1966 "Black Panther Manifesto," presented here.

Seeking a more classically Marxist orientation in the black industrial working class was the League of Revolutionary Black Workers, whose position paper "Labor History and the League's Labor Program" gives a sense of the organization's approach—far more combative toward existing union structures than was the case with most other currents on the Left. Like the Black Panthers, however, this organization did not last beyond the 1970s. (Indeed, by the 1980s Maoism in the United States collapsed, and throughout that decade the other major currents on the Left—Communist, Socialist, Trotskyist—had each experienced severe fragmentation and general decline.)

Reflecting on the historical experience in which she had participated as a black nationalist, a well-known member of the Communist Party, and a supporter of the Black Panthers, Angela Davis's "Black Nationalism: The Sixties and the Nineties" suggests the continuing relevance of the left-wing contribution to the struggle for racial justice.

✳　✳　✳

ALAN WALD
AFRICAN AMERICANS, CULTURE, AND COMMUNISM:
NATIONAL LIBERATION AND SOCIALISM (2000)

[This review essay deals with the following works: *The Cry Was Unity: Communists and African Americans, 1917–1936*, by Mark Solomon (Jackson, Mississippi: University Press of Mississippi, 1998); *Old Negro, New Left: African American Writing and Communism between the Wars*, by William J. Maxwell (New York: Columbia University Press, 1999); *Popular Fronts: Chicago and African American Cultural Politics, 1935–46*, by Bill V. Mullen (Urbana and Chicago: University of Illinois Press, 1999); *The New Red Negro: The Literary Left and African American Poetry, 1930–1946*, by James Edward Smethurst (New York: Oxford University Press, 1999).]

Part I

From the early 1920s until the late 1950s, the U.S. Communist movement was a significant pole of attraction in African American political and cultural life. Only a few prominent African American poets, fiction writers, playwrights, and critics—such as novelist Richard Wright—publicly boasted of party membership. Yet it seems likely that Margaret Walker, Lance Jeffers, Claude McKay, John Oliver Killens, Julian Mayfield, Alice Childress, Shirley Graham, Lloyd Brown, John Henrik Clarke, William Attaway, Frank Marshall Davis, Lorraine Hansberry, Douglas Turner Ward, Audre Lorde, W. E. B. Du Bois, and Harold Cruse were among those organizationally affiliated in individualized ways.

A list of other African American cultural workers who were, to varying degrees and at different points, fellow travelers, would probably include Ralph Ellison, Chester Himes, Sterling Brown, Langston Hughes, Paul Robeson, Theodore Ward, Countee Cullen, James Baldwin (as a teenager), Richard Durham, Alain Locke, Willard Motley, Rosa Guy, Sarah Wright, Jessie Fausett, Owen Dodson, Ossie Davis, Dorothy West, Marion Minus, Robert Hayden, Waring Cuney, and Lonne Elder III.

For five decades, students of the Left have had access to the reasons why some black cultural and intellectual figures were eventually dismayed by Communism, through novels such as Chester Himes's *The Lonely Crusade* (1947), Ralph Ellison's *Invisible Man* (1952), and Richard Wright's *The Outsider* (1953), reinforced by Harold Cruse's brutal polemic *The Crisis of the Negro Intellectual* (1967).

Less available were richly documented, independently critical, yet compelling explanations of just how and why the Communist movement wielded the

Reprinted from *Against the Current* 84 (January–February 2000): 23–29 and 86 (May–June 2000): 27–34. Used with permission.

attractive power that it did, despite all the obvious disadvantages of being regarded as a "communist" for blacks as well as whites. Then, during the 1980s, two scholarly works began to promote a rethinking of the relationship of blacks to reds: Mark Naison's *Communists and Harlem during the Depression* (1983), and Robin D. G. Kelley's *Hammer and Hoe: Alabama Communists during the Great Depression* (1990).

Now we have four new books in 1998–99 that constitute a quantum leap forward in our ability to understand what was achieved by this symbiotic relationship, and what has been lost in one-sided assaults upon the legacy of Communist-led antiracist struggles by McCarthyites, Cold War liberals, and some of the Communist movement's Left critics, as well as by that movement's incapacity to understand and fairly represent its own remarkable history in the 1930s and 1940s.

The focus of three of the books is on culture, but together they provide a wealth of new detail and conceptual propositions that need to be critically assimilated by those committed to building an interracial movement for social transformation.

The indispensable foundation for appreciating this body of new scholarship is Mark Solomon's stunning narrative of the absorption of revolutionary black nationalists and other black radicals into the post–World War I Communist movement. His highly nuanced and finely researched *The Cry Was Unity* treats the consequences of this comingling for the development of Communist ideology and activity from the early 1920s through the first year of the Popular Front.

Solomon, a retired history professor from Simmons College, is in a unique situation to assess the experience. He has been a participant in the antiracist and radical movement since he was a teenager in the early Cold War years, and is the author of an earlier published doctoral dissertation from Harvard University called *Red and Black: Communism and Afro-Americans, 1929–1935* (1988).

Solomon's approach is deftly elaborated in a short introduction explaining his motivations for recreating the story of how the Communist movement "broke free from isolation and ideological abstractions to achieve a significant place in the battle for racial justice." In contrast to recent liberal discussions, such as President Clinton's "conversation on race," Solomon is pledged to review the early history of the antiracist Left because

> The pivotal issues then were neither tactical nor sentimental; they involved the basic character of American society. Capitalism's cornerstone was seen to have been laid by slavery and fortified by racism. Therefore, the achievement of equality implied the ultimate transformation of the nation's economic and social foundation. (xviii)

On the one hand, Solomon's book seeks to elaborate the "theory" of national oppression and the road to liberation worked out by U.S. Communists, black and white, in their first decade and a half. On the other, his aim is equally to explore the practical activities against which the evolving theory was tested as this heroic, interracial organization rose up against white supremacism "with unprecedented passion as an indispensable requirement for achieving social progress" (xviii).

Most impressive is the way that Solomon triangulates the development of Communist theory and practice by examining black Marxist activists and theorists, the national Communist Party institutions, and the influence of Comintern (Communist International) policy. In contrast to those who favor the "top-down" or "bottom-up" approaches to Communist historiography, Solomon presents us with what might be called a "force field" approach in which different elements gain hegemony at various points and under certain circumstances.

The fact that Comintern hegemony might be shown to be paramount over a period of decades and at moments of crisis does not negate how important it was for a group of black party women in Harlem to raise an issue (unknown to the Soviet party) for debate and discussion. Without that latter—the local vitality—the attractiveness of the party would be inexplicable (which certainly seems to be the case in many extant narratives of party history).

In rich detail, Solomon's book covers the period of nearly two decades from the founding of Cyril Briggs's magazine the *Crusader* after World War I to the launching of the party-led National Negro Congress in 1936. Thus he follows Communist policy through three phases: from the view of a "colorblind" class outlook, to the theory of nationality, to the broadly based "Negro-labor alliance."

The overall structure of the book is divided into three components, recalling the traditional Hegelian triad. The initial five chapters review the efforts of the first black Communists to formulate a policy, their interaction with a vision of the Communist International, and the development of a theory (the view of African Americans as "a nation within a nation") and an organization (the American Negro Labor Congress) to realize this project.

Part II presents another six chapters, this time focused on the 1929–33 era of the ultra-revolutionary "Third Period." Solomon convincingly demonstrates his rather disconcerting view that unrealistic visions, aspirations, and demands frequently motivated the most heroic projects. From this perspective he discusses the astonishing courage of party practice in the Deep South, and struggles against eviction, hunger, and lynching.

The book marches to a climax at the beginning of the Popular Front when, at last, in Solomon's judgment, the foundation of black/labor unity is established. This is achieved through the success of Peoples Front policy in Harlem and the creation of the National Negro Congress, a multiracial organization under black leadership. Within this daunting framework, Solomon presents many discrete episodes worthy of at least a brief survey.

Pioneer African American Communists

From the very first sentences of the first chapter, Solomon meticulously corrects the record of previous writings on blacks and Communism, with the kind of scrupulous research only possible from the pen of a scholar committed to learning what really happened because the record matters for life and death struggles.

For example, contrary to earlier studies claiming that no blacks were present at the founding of the U.S. Communist movement—and an alternative version that two attended—Solomon documents that only Otto Huiswood, born in the Dutch West Indies (now called Surinam) was present. Huiswood would have been joined by his comrade from the left wing of the Socialist Party, Arthur P. Hendricks, who was born in British Guiana; but Hendricks had just died of tuberculosis. (Possibly Huiswood's presence was not noticed by some who wrote reports on the meeting due to his light color.)

Although the two militants, and many who would join them, were Caribbean-born, Solomon views the pioneer cadre of U.S. black Communism as a genuine Harlem-based alliance of immigrants from colonized nations and U.S.-born men and women. The former tended to have a greater class and anti-imperialist awareness, and a more "assertive psychological makeup" (4), along with a greater degree of formal education.

It is significant that initially, black revolutionists tended to gravitate around their own institutions, especially the Peoples Educational Forum in Harlem. One group—Huiswood, Richard B. Moore, Lovett Fort-Whiteman, and Grace Campell—soon joined the new Communist movement when the left wing of the Socialist Party was purged. Another group—Frank Crosswaith, A. Philip Randolph, and Chandler Owen—remained with the Socialists.

An additional important figure, Cyril Briggs, also from the Caribbean (he was born on the island of Nevis), was a journalist for Harlem's *Amsterdam News*. Briggs was much inspired by the Easter Rebellion in Ireland and committed to the prospects of a decolonized Africa. He launched the *Crusader* in December 1918, a dynamic organ of the "New Negro Crowd" that advocated "a renaissance of Negro culture and power throughout the world" (6).

Over the next six months Briggs's journal began drawing the links between capitalism and imperialism, and "projecting a shared proletarian identity between black and white workers as the counterweight to the dominant system" (7). In Solomon's words, Briggs "merged black nationalism with revolutionary socialism and introduced the twentieth century global revolutionary tide to America" (7).

One of Briggs's signal contributions was that he devoted himself to solving the riddle of contradiction between a separate black national destiny and achieving unity with Euro-American workers. The first organizational expression of this perspective was Briggs's formation of the African Blood Brotherhood (ABB) in the fall of 1919, which was led by Caribbean-born radicals (with many World War I veterans in its ranks) and would grow to a membership of about 3,500.

The ABB was clearly independent of the Communist movement at the outset. The various Communist factions were too busy vying for the Moscow franchise to pay attention, and Briggs was simultaneously influenced by an Afro-Centric movement called the Hamitic League, as well as by the rituals (pass-words, secrecy, oaths) of the Irish Sinn Fein.

By 1921, when the ABB declared the *Crusader* its public organ and also gained some notoriety for its association with the armed resistance of blacks against white attacks in Oklahoma, its leadership had evolved to pro-Communism.

According to correspondence located by Solomon in Comintern archives, Briggs was recruited to the party by Caribbean poet Claude McKay. This was facilitated by McKay's having introduced Briggs to a couple of Euro-American Communists with a special interest in black liberation—the famous cartoonist from Texas, Robert Minor, and the Jewish American firebrand Rose Pastor Stokes. These two were affiliated with the "Goose Caucus," which advocated parallel communist parties, one to be legal and aboveground, while the other party would remain secret and underground.

Still, more important than organizational affiliation is the manner in which Briggs creatively projected strategies and visions for liberation. Blending a strong "sense of African identity and national culture with Leninist internation-alism," he formulated arguments to combine a struggle for an "independent Negro State" (which might be in Africa, although not necessarily) in the process of fighting for a "universal Socialist Cooperative Commonwealth."

Briggs admitted that the independent black state might not be the ideal route, but that it was understandably necessary in light of the need for "peoples of African descent" to "reclaim their distinct political and cultural heritage." To put it bluntly, "the Negro has been treated so brutally in the past by the rest of humanity that he may be pardoned for now looking at the matter from the view-point of the Negro than from that of a humanity that is not humane" (13).

The liberation of African Americans and the struggle for socialism world-wide was theorized by Briggs as an alliance in which a distinct black agenda remained viable and central. With Briggs's Communist membership, this pro-gram was further clarified so as to provide a clear alternative to the politics of middle-class reform organizations. Briggs promoted a dramatic switch in the objectives of the African American liberation movement away from assimilation into the bourgeois order and toward a goal of socialist transformation. He also urged that the class composition of black leadership be proletarian and no longer middle class, and that African Americans ally with Euro-American workers instead of white liberals.

Briggs and his comrades were well aware that racism was widespread in the

Euro-American working class, and of the history of blacks being betrayed by false white friends in the past. Thus he held that the Left was obligated to aggressively educate against white supremacism in order to facilitate an alliance.

Analogous notions of African American autonomy and alliances also carried over to the predominant attitude of Briggs and his associates toward the Russian revolution. Solomon observes:

> The embrace of communism carried with it a promising connection with Soviet power as indispensable ally, patron, and spiritual guide. For the new black Communists the Soviets were an exhilarating source of strength, pride, hope, and respect for black interests. Heretofore anonymous men and women would now have an international stage where they would be taken seriously and where power was manifest and at the disposal of the black liberation struggle. The greatness of Bolshevik power—as an anti-imperialist force, as liberator of labor, as cleanser and avenger of racism, as faithful ally—became an ardent belief and defining point of the African Blood Brotherhood. (16)

Finally, Briggs certainly believed that, in the long run, Euro-American workers would come to recognize their commonality of interests with blacks. Yet he also held that, if blacks were to devote themselves to the class struggle, there had to be an "acid test of white friendship"—which was the acceptance by Euro-Americans of the right of black armed self-defense, even if such defense resulted in the killing of whites (17).

A Nation within a Nation

Solomon argues that the pro-Communist evolution of the African Blood Brotherhood profoundly affected the American Communists. A result was the ultimate transformation of the left-wing "color blind" view of race that prevailed in the early 1920s in both the Communist Labor Party and the Communist Party, most of which fused into the United Communist Party (UCP) in 1920.* Leaders of the UCP did listen to and learn from the ABB, and their publications and resolutions began to resemble ABB ideas, with one exception—the Euro-Americans omitted the need to fight racism within their political party itself.

It is also true that the May 1921 convention that finally unified all Communist factions did not reflect the new alliance in the composition of its delegates

---

*Solomon's narrative runs counter to the version that, on orders from Lenin, the UCP briefly assigned a member named Zack Kornfeder to link up to radical blacks in Harlem. Solomon could find no evidence of such a command in the Moscow archives and no knowledge of such an episode among Lenin scholars. Thus he makes a compelling case that this is part of the Cold War mythology exaggerating Comintern control of U.S. Communists and downplaying the autonomous contribution of U.S. blacks.

nor in resulting resolutions. Still, Solomon quotes from internal discussion documents (written under pseudonyms) that show a rich understanding of the complex strategic issues that needed to be addressed.

For example, there was now a recognition that the black population could not be won over by abstract ideological professions of good will; Communists would have to respond specifically to the "black ideology" that had developed due to white racist exclusionism. They would also have to "humanize" their political dealings with African Americans, and fight aggressively for specific reforms (such as voting rights in the South) crucial to allowing blacks to create their own conditions for developing activity and consciousness.

Simultaneously, Briggs was involved in a bitter battle with black nationalist leader Marcus Garvey. Solomon talks candidly of Briggs's collaboration with the federal government's case against Garvey's Universal Negro Improvement Association (which continually published the claim that Briggs was actually a European, until Briggs took legal action). Moreover, destruction of the Garvey movement became the obsession of the *Crusader*.*

In this clash, Solomon sees central themes in the U.S. black radical tradition. Briggs held to the view that "racial consciousness alone was not enough to win freedom in the modern world, where power was based partially on race but centrally on corporate, class, national, and military forces"; thus he championed alliances with progressive forces around a common interest in socioeconomic restructuring (28).

Garvey, although anticolonialist and anti-imperialist, in his determination to create a separate African-based territory, refused alliances with forces aimed at challenging those very seats of power. Believing that, in the last analysis, white workers would side with white bosses against blacks, Garvey alternatively attempted to negotiate with governments and even racist forces who likewise favored separation of the "races."

Nevertheless, the Communists would continue to see the ranks of the Garvey movement as a radicalized milieu from which potential recruits might be garnered.

Toward Self-Determination

In a chapter called "The Comintern's Vision," Solomon explains how the Leninist notion of the necessary alliance of working-class and national liberation movements as "a linked social process" was closer to that of the former ABB members than the ideas of early Euro-American Communists such as John Reed.

At the 1922 Fourth Congress of the Comintern, in response to presentations

---

*Robert Minor, the white Texan (but a militant antiracist) in charge of "Negro Work" for the party, differed with Briggs and argued that defending Garvey against government persecution was the more appropriate strategy.

by McKay and Huiswood, a multinational Negro Commission was set up under Huiswood's direction (and with McKay as a guest participant). This body viewed the African diaspora peoples in the framework of colonialism, with black Americans poised to play a key role in a global struggle requiring Communist backing of all movements of blacks opposed to capitalism and imperialism.

This perspective probably set the stage for the slogan of "Self-determination in the Black Belt" (which was a region of the South with majority black population) adopted by U.S. communists six years later. Although McKay departed from the conference en route to a stance as an independent radical (eventually converting to Catholicism before his death), Huiswood would become the first black member of the Central Committee of the U.S. party, now headquartered in Chicago.

A new figure emerging to prominence by the mid-1920s was Lovett Fort-Whiteman, an African American who had studied at Tuskegee, and who was closely associated with Robert Minor. Fort-Whiteman pursued earlier efforts to get the Comintern to back U.S. black Communists in internal U.S. policy by forwarding the first concept of an American Negro Labor Congress.

Fort-Whiteman also developed the argument that blacks perceive oppression as stemming from race more than class, and that such persecution had bonded blacks of all economic strata together. Marxism had to be recast to address this unique psychology, and practical work required a dual focus on both the South and problems specific to the great migration in the North (such as the housing crisis in urban ghettos).

Thus, in preparing for the 1925 American Negro Labor Congress (ANLC), Huiswood, Moore, and others pleaded for the involvement of black Communists on all party committees responsible for the gathering, for the party not to push itself aggressively, and for literature that took into account the special psychology of the black proletariat.

This was ignored, and the event—which had only thirty-three accredited delegates—had a majority white audience who were entertained by Russian ballet and theater groups but no black artists. For the next year the organization stumbled along until a shake-up in which Moore replaced Fort-Whiteman as leader. (The latter departed for the Soviet Union, where he would teach for a while and then be imprisoned and die in a labor camp.)*

Moore's leadership introduced a less sectarian phase of community and union work. Even followers of Lovestone's faction (near the end of its reign) now favored dumping the ANLC, although their alternative was direct party recruitment. But the advent of the Comintern's Third Period following the Sixth

---

*It is unfortunate that Solomon says so little about the fate of Fort-Whiteman in light of his importance to the narrative. If the information contained in Harvey Klehr et al., *The Soviet World of American Communism* (New Haven: Yale, 1998), pp. 218–27, is accurate, no assessment of the African American Left's association with the USSR can be complete without a fuller discussion of the events and their significance.

Comintern Congress ended any hope for a broader political strategy, due to its campaign against "social fascism" (the theory that Socialist parties were fascist in practice) and for United Front from Below.

Solomon is especially critical of the Third Period for its ideological rigidity; he believes that the political line was really about Stalin's fight to dominate the Soviet party and the Comintern, one that would be "ultimately drenched in Soviet blood" (68). He is also distressed by evidence of party members (almost all white and largely foreign-born in the early years) speaking an alien political language, and occasionally using "internationalism" to undermine racial priorities.

Moreover, he is dismayed at what he sees as arrogant and thoughtless efforts to substitute workers for the traditional middle-class leaders, accompanied by a blindness to the resentment expressed by African Americans aspiring to assemble their own agendas.

At the Sixth Congress of the Comintern no veteran black Communists were present. Instead, the U.S. party was represented by a young student at the Lenin school, Harry Haywood.

Haywood was influenced by a Siberian named Charles Nasanov, who had lived in the United States and saw U.S. blacks as an oppressed nation with the right to self-determination. He and Haywood shared the view that historical circumstances (slavery, betrayal of Reconstruction, imperialism) had prevented blacks from joining whites in a single nation, resulting in a distinct cultural and psychological makeup.

Garveyism was regarded as an expression of authentic national strivings that would arise again—only next time Communists should be in the leadership. Such an approach broke free at last from class-reductionist dogmas that relegated the antiracist struggle to second place. Rather, the black movement was regarded as inherently revolutionary yet also an indispensable ally of the working class.

Haywood had no support in the early stages of the debate; but gradually it became evident that the Comintern leadership favored an alteration in party policy toward African Americans. The amended resolution provided "an ostensible middle ground . . . based on the concept of a racial *and* national question— with *national* switching places with *racial* in parentheses" (77).

When the official resolutions appeared in 1928 and 1930, they explained a difference in the Communist policy in the North and South of the United States. In the North, where blacks were a national minority, the struggle would be for social and political equality; in the South, where blacks held a majority in certain regions (the Black Belt), the African American nationality had the right to secede and form a separate republic if it so desired.

If a revolution were successful in the larger nation, however, Communists would urge the black population to remain. (If blacks did opt to secede, Euro-Americans might reside in the black republic with minority rights.)

Nevertheless, Solomon's opinion is that the nation thesis is flawed. While Lenin was accurate in recognizing nationalist feelings among the black population, he thought that these would be undermined by the expansion of the capitalist economy (industrialization, migration) because the economy was inseparable from that of the larger nation. Communist defenders of the nation thesis such as James Allen believed that capitalism, having advanced as far as it would, was imprisoning the African American peasantry in the region with no escape except social revolution.*

Yet Solomon is impressed with the effects of "self-determination" on party practice. In everyday life it meant that Communists believed in the right of oppressed people to choose their own future, and the party throwing itself wholeheartedly into antiracist struggles. As a concept it meant the end of the subordination of race to class and paying close attention to all issues—cultural as well as political—that affected African America.

Solomon concludes that "national oppression" is the appropriate terminology for describing what happened to black Americans.

There were contradictions, of course, to carrying out such a policy under the delusions of the Third Period. Communists held that revolution was on the agenda, so they crudely exposed liberal compromisers as social fascists, and they marched in parades under slogans urging defense of the USSR. Yet such fervent belief enabled the same Communists, Euro-American and black, to brave police clubs—and bullets—as they organized election rallies, antilynching protests, funerals for martyred comrades, and fought back against evictions and police brutality in the streets of Harlem.

Likewise, the Communists' revolutionary dual union, the National Miners Union (NMU), took strong antiracist actions. In Pennsylvania, the NMU convinced black miners to join striking white miners, and in Kentucky convinced white miners to desegregate the strike kitchen. Most famously, the Communist-led National Textile Workers Union emphasized antiracism in its leadership of the Gastonia Strike in North Carolina.

This was followed by a heroic campaign to organize the South, an effort that Solomon believes had been hampered by the party's adherence to an earlier theory (when Jay Lovestone was in the leadership of the party) holding that the rural South was a reserve of reaction. The new efforts resulted in the creation of a union of sharecroppers in Alabama, as well as impressive organizing activities in the face of murderous harassment in Tennessee, Louisiana, Mississippi, and elsewhere.

The party's steadfast opposition in the 1930s to any form of racial segregation, at a time when it was tolerated by liberals and other progressives, was also

---

*After 1935 the slogan was deemphasized during the Popular Front, and then abandoned in 1943 (by party leader Earl Browder), revived in 1946 (following the expulsion of Browder), and buried in 1958.

an outgrowth of its assessment of the party's failure to make gains in the 1920s. Solomon says that the party came to the conclusion that "racial segregation and the savaging of black identity represented both an institutional foundation for American capitalism and its weak point."

Thus the toleration of any form of racism only bolstered capitalism and "wounded its most potent foes." The party had to create an internal culture qualitatively different from radical or liberal movements that "extended a hand to blacks while allowing in [their] own structures the very circumstances that engendered inequality" (128).

Hence the party promoted a view of race chauvinism as the ultimate evil. Antiblack racism served the ruling class; Euro-Americans could only purify themselves of its stink by personally engaging in militant "struggles against Negro oppression," which would also be a step toward dismantling the legitimate distrust by blacks of whites (131).

Moreover, one could not expect blacks to unite with Communists without taking steps to counter the special oppression of blacks. One Jewish party leader, Israel Amter, demanded that all white Communists should be prepared to violently avenge any insult against blacks, even at the risk of death.

The center of CP [Communist Party] and Young Communist League life became the interracial dance, even when it antagonized the larger community. A more theatrical approach was the occasional mass trial of a party member accused of racist behavior; this was carried out for purposes of public education.

Solomon compellingly recapitulates the antiracist arguments developed by Communists, who tried to go beyond older appeals to "morality, abstract justice, and 'healing' through 'understanding.'" Instead, Communists emphasized changing power relationships in the interests of all the dispossessed.

Rather than appealing to sentimentality and guilt, the effort was to win over white workers on the basis of their own needs. This was possible because working-class whites could never achieve what they wanted as long as racial division persisted. Instead of being "pitied or patronized," blacks were to be "welcomed as indispensable allies in the battle to change the world" (146).

This meant that whites should respect black history and culture, as well as understand that the prerequisite for unity was black self-organization and autonomous leadership.

A Legacy of Struggle

Among the most inspiring aspects of Solomon's research is his chronicle of the efforts of party members to fight racism on every front, starting with campaigns against hunger and eviction. He provides portraits of many female and male activists, vignettes of martyrdom, and describes heroism by blacks and whites.

The result of such selfless work was that thousands of blacks joined unemployment councils, and hundreds applied for party membership and signed up for the party's legal defense auxiliary, International Labor Defense.

Simultaneously, an interracial culture emerged. In the late 1920s "Negro Weeks" were launched by Briggs to celebrate revolutionary heroes such as Toussaint L'Ouverture and Denmark Vesey. Whites did go into black communities and serve on black publications, but usually in subordinate positions under the supervision of black Communists. What was expected of these whites was a record of fighting racism and respecting the abilities of blacks.

In the early 1930s, the American Negro Labor Congress (ANLC), which regarded anticapitalism as a basis of the antilynching movement, collapsed and was followed by the League of Struggle for Negro Rights (LSNR). The new party-led organization saw the campaign against lynching as the major manifestation of national oppression within its larger agenda of demands for justice.

Nevertheless, as an organization that was openly pro-Communist, the LSNR was somewhat in competition for space with the party itself, and the Unemployed Councils occupied available space, too. Even when the LSNR developed its own leadership with Langston Hughes as honorary president, and an official membership of ten thousand, it did not reach much beyond the party's influence.

In contrast, the party's response to the Scottsboro case (when nine black youths were framed on rape charges in Alabama) was a breakthrough vindicating Communists' claims to sincerity about antiracism. Throughout the country activists, white and black, gave their all to the slogan "they shall not die!" Such activity was possible because they were imbued with the belief that the fate of the defendants was linked inextricably to their own lives.

Nevertheless, Solomon is harshly critical of the CP's sectarian policy toward middle-class allies—he even endorses criticisms of the "united front from below" policy made by the expelled Lovestone group. However, he refutes the claims that the Communists wanted the nine youths to die as martyrs, and believes that charges about the Communists' inflammatory conduct toward the courts "were overstated and deflected attention from a racist judicial system" (203).

There was constant party-led antiracist activity throughout the early 1930s. The candidacy of African American James Ford on the CP ticket, the running of dozens of other black Communist candidates, and the defense of Angelo Herndon, charged with insurrection for leading a demonstration in Atlanta, were important developments. There were also numerous strikes in which the party played a role where race issues were important—St. Louis, Chicago, San Joaquin Valley, San Francisco, Birmingham, Louisiana, and so forth.

Moreover, Harlem became a centerpiece for antiracist activity, especially when U.S.-born black party leader James Ford took control and Briggs and Moore were eased out. The latter tended to emphasize race issues more emphatically, and were sometimes accused of blaming white workers more than the bosses; but they defended themselves by insisting that forging unity should be more of a white responsibility than a black one.

Solomon's biggest criticism of the party in this era is its conviction that it deserved sole leadership of the black movement due to its possession of the correct revolutionary program. As long as the party spoke of establishing "hegemony over the Negro liberation struggle itself," it would often antagonize those who questioned or opposed it and would negate its own claims to be fighting for self-determination (205).

Thus Solomon ends the book with a chapter and a half devoted to the development of the Popular Front, which he regards as a positive advance away from this posture. In his view, the dropping of Third Period sectarianism primarily meant the opportunity to work with liberals and Socialists cooperatively, as well as taking a friendlier attitude toward churches, professional organizations, and so on. Some of the tactical flexibility was shown in holding together an alliance against the invasion of Ethiopia, and in the CP's intervention into the 1935 "Harlem Riot" (272).

The culminating event for Solomon is the founding of the National Negro Congress, launched in Chicago in 1936. It was preceded by broad discussions and impressive organizational groundwork under the leadership of John P. Davis, a nonpublic Communist. The perspective was for "a multiracial organization under black leadership, working to build a Negro-labor alliance and advance civil rights on a wide front." At the same time, Solomon cites internal CP material to show that Davis had the view that the CP should control the NCC to "guarantee its breadth and democratic character" (303).

This raises a question, which Solomon never clearly answers, about the exact nature of the party's understanding of "self-determination" when it came to trusting an independent black leadership. In any event, the organization was launched with over eight hundred delegates from 551 organizations that claimed to represent as many as three million people. In a striking effort to demonstrate sincerity about the new unity, the party's old socialist rival, A. Philip Randolph, was elected president.

Part II

William Maxwell's 254-page *New Negro, Old Left: African American Writing and Communism between the Wars* (including a handsome thirteen-page insert of photographs and illustrations) puts cultural flesh on the organizational and political scaffolding constructed by Mark Solomon. It also reconfigures in startlingly new ways the entire terrain of 1920s–1930s left-wing cultural production.

Maxwell's focus is on the movement of a number of African American writers from a background of "New Negro" and "Harlem Renaissance" experiences toward the Communist movement in the interwar period. His unique orientation emphasizes a mutual indebtedness, a two-way channel "between radical Harlem and Soviet Moscow, between the New Negro renaissance and proletarian literature." This interchange is the reason why the explanation for such a development "cannot be pursued without acknowledging both modern black literature's debt to Communism and Communism's debt to modern black literature."

Moreover, the importance of the Harlem/Moscow transit in black cultural history also explains the reason why the disillusionment of a handful of African American leftists was expressed so fervently after the 1930s and has received so much attention.

Maxwell's emphasis on "black volition" and the "interracial education of the Old Left" corresponds to Solomon's research; but Maxwell aims to enhance our understanding of African American and "white" modern literature as well as radicalism.

Included among the misrepresentations of the relationship of "New Negro" (the term for militants in the Harlem Renaissance days) and "Old Left" refuted by Maxwell, are the preeminent readings of novels by Richard Wright and Ralph Ellison that view the relationship of the Left to African Americans as one of manipulation; black nationalist interpretations of the faults of earlier black writing that are usually attributed to the malign influence of the white left; the claims of black feminist and "vernacular" critics that the Communist tradition posited a hostility to black folk materials; and the ironic exclusion of the black/Left relationship from recent arguments in literary theory about "mulatto modernism."

Maxwell's objection to these earlier treatments of the black/Left cultural relation is not due to a disagreement with the dismay of some of the critics about the Left's illusions in the Stalin regime—a dismay that Maxwell shares. His dissent is because of the failure of these earlier critics to recognize that the association had as great an impact on changing the U.S. Communist movement's culture and politics and vice versa.

Maxwell's effort to recuperate African American agency in the relationship is based on his observation that black pro-Communists were independently zealous in their support of what they took to be Soviet policy in the USSR and internationally; that neither black nor white literary Communists took "dictation from Moscow"; and that earlier narratives of this symbiotic relationship have been too immersed in the Cold War fixation on evidence of "white seduction and betrayal of black mouthpieces."

Moreover, what Maxwell calls "black Communist initiative" is supported by the most compelling trend in historical and literary scholarship of the recent era, such as the aforementioned books by Robin Kelley and Mark Naison (5).

This is a trend to which Maxwell wants to make additions and corrections, primarily by extending the time line backward from the 1930s. To Maxwell, the 1920s comprises the crucial moment when historical forces such as the Great Migration of blacks to urban centers, and the Harlem Renaissance's pioneering of "black routes into international modernity," produced a "black working-class protagonist" as a means by which socialism might be African Americanized in the form of joining Marxism and the "vernacular culture of the descendants of African slaves" (6–7).

The resulting negotiations between black militants moving toward Communism and the Communist institutions themselves can best be traced through literary-cultural expressions, especially the advent of "proletarian literature" and the party's construction of a view of African America as a nation within a nation.

Maxwell's first and by far longest chapter begins the revision of the post–World War I cultural landscape through an examination of the poet-lyricist Andy Razaf, whose writings are used to present him "as a partial product and gauge of the place of black bolshevism within the cultural field of the Harlem Renaissance" (15). Razaf, who had a special feeling for the experience of "service" work (he had held jobs such as operating an elevator), wrote first for Cyril Briggs's *Crusader* and then for midtown music publishers.

Maxwell's view contrasts with those of Harold Cruse, George Hutchinson, and others, who hold that an attraction to Communism destroyed the potential evolution of the renaissance—or else that the renaissance came about by displacing post–World War I black militancy. Razaf, however, expresses an important trend of mostly Caribbean immigrants around the *Crusader* who saw the new black renaissance within a field of class relationships affected by the international crisis of capitalism and the impact of the Russian Revolution. Indeed, part of the attraction to Moscow was based on a conviction that the Soviet leadership would assist the "special interests" of U.S. blacks in relation to the Left.

The *Crusader* view was that, with the Harlem Renaissance as a cultural center, the new urban African Americans (including Caribbean immigrants) would continue the struggle launched by black World War I veterans, escalating it even into the international arena. Maxwell sees the efforts of Howard University professor Alain Locke to promote his interpretation of the renaissance as partly in competition with the pro-Bolshevik trend; he also regards the version fostered by the group around W. E. B. Du Bois, which emphasized spirituals as the central black musical achievement, as missing the boat in its failure to appreciate Razaf's focus on blues, jazz, films, broadcasting, and vaudeville.

Chapter 2 returns initially to the *Crusader* to examine its favorite poet, Claude McKay, and his book *The Negroes in America* (1923), as an example of the way in which blacks shaped Communist policy. Maxwell, from the perspective now established, provides compellingly fresh interpretations of McKay's poems "If We Must Die" and "The White City."

McKay's experiences in the USSR are also recounted, after which Maxwell offers an important interpretation of McKay's long-neglected one-hundred-page Marxist treatise on black America. In particular, McKay viewed white workers as having developed a white supremacist "race-consciousness" on their own to defend privilege, and also in response to having assimilated a complex social psychology of black sexuality rooted in the agricultural labor of early colonies in the South.

McKay's antidotes to racism involve "the modern upsurge of black culture" (including sports) and "white feminism" (which needs to recognize that the "protective" role of white men against alleged black rapists is posited on misogyny). Maxwell's case is strong that "McKay's pre-echo of more recent, more exclusively academic work in African American history, whiteness studies, cultural studies, and a post-Soviet Marxism without guarantees is valuable for its challenges as well as its flattering symmetries" (88).

Moreover, Maxwell provides evidence of the little-known text's influence on the Bolshevik leadership (especially Trotsky) and the role of its author's ideas in preparing for the Black Belt nation thesis.

The third chapter shifts to McKay's coeditor on the Marxist *Liberator*, the Jewish American writer Mike Gold, especially Gold's "antiminstrel show," *Hoboken Blues* (1927), which reinforces from another angle a blending of Communist proletarian literature and the Harlem Renaissance. Maxwell observes that Gold's manifesto "Towards Proletarian Art" parallels Alain Locke's "New Negro" perspective of drawing sustenance from the common people and soil.

He also notes that under Gold's editorship, the *Liberator* offered McKay's poetry collection *Harlem Shadows* as a subscription premium, characterized as a work of proletarian internationalism. Moreover, Maxwell believes that Gold's 1923 book on *The Life of John Brown* is "an oblique reference" to his and McKay's collaboration.

Using careful textual analysis of primary documents, Maxwell shows that Gold's famous puritanical attacks on Harlem cabaret culture in the 1930s Communist press were similar to those of Du Bois, and that Gold held a positive view of certain black-specific cultural traditions rooted in spirituals, writings by Frederick Douglass, and perhaps noncommercial jazz.

This is a crucial corrective to those (especially Hutchinson, North, and Cruse) who misread selected conjunctural writings of Gold as the defining antirenaissance moment of the Left. It is also a useful entrée to Maxwell's reading of Gold's *Hoboken Blues* (1927) as an effort to temporarily elude white identity and participate in the Harlem Renaissance. Although Maxwell pulls no punches in noting paternalistic and ineffective aspects of the drama, he makes a powerful case that Gold's play is antiminstrel in that it "embraces the identification of African Americans with preindustrial values yet rejects the moment of censure and the imprisonment of these values within a rigidly racialized and rapidly fading arcadian memory" (119).

In mulling over Gold's surprising celebration of a nonproletarian protagonist, Maxwell considers the views expressed on "the race question" in light of McKay's opinions, and concludes that "McKay's simultaneous possession of the garlands of revolutionary and New Negro poetry is the standard of aesthetic achievement that Gold's play covets, a play that poses Sam's [the black protagonist's] renaissance in Harlem as a lesson in proletarian revolution and a lesson to proletarian art" (120).

That Gold would later (in *The Hollow Men*, 1941) counterpoise proletarianism as the negation of decadent New Negroism cannot erase the view here and in other places of a "considerable harmony" that paved the way for a "depression-era reemergence of the position in the renaissance field that spliced New Negro and working-class insurrection, a position that took a low profile during the second half of the 1920s but never vanished . . ."(122).

Moreover, Maxwell observes that a less selective examination of Gold's achievement than that offered by Gold-bashers suggests that his proletarianism was a "'normal' modernism" in its "scramble of interracial attraction and aversion" (123). Once again, we have evidence that the Left's theory and practice (in this instance, Gold's view of proletarian art) evolved from a multifaceted dialogue with the cultural renaissance in Harlem.

Chapter 4 is a turning point in the book, not only for its shift to the 1930s but also for introducing a gender critique of the communist tendency to masculinize the very prospect of interracial radicalism. Maxwell's focus is on the effort by the Left to deconstruct the "triangular lynch myth" that involves a black male rapist, white female victim, and white male protector; this in turn produced a homosocial "antilynch triangle" premised on the interracial bonding of male proletarians against a misogynist view of white female accusers.

Maxwell traces the function of such triangular mythologies (Right and Left), culminating in a consideration of Langston Hughes's Scottsboro writings. He concludes by considering the corrective work of black Communist Louise Thompson, whose "reportage" managed to write "a way through Scottsboro's paired triangles against the exclusions of both the rape-lynch and the antilynch trios" (149).

The fifth chapter is the first of two focused on Richard Wright. Here Maxwell claims that Wright's views of a black southern nation, following Communist theory, resembled that of novelist Zora Neale Hurston's anthropological approach influenced by the work of Franz Boaz. This analysis is a continuation of Maxwell's method of challenging oversimplified oppositions.

Maxwell also effectively reconstructs Wright's career as a Communist, and the particular attraction of Stalin as a member of an oppressed minority group. He then compares a number of texts by Hurston and Wright from the late 1930s to demonstrate the degree to which they shared sympathy for the rural black folk under assault from the Great Migration.

The final chapter compares the "antibuddy" narratives of Wright's famous *Native Son* and his radical friend Nelson Algren's novel *Somebody in Boots*. These narratives of failed male bonding comprise sympathetic but informative critiques of the Communist project of interracialism. But Maxwell's fresh and cogent contextualized rethinking of the novels is now enriched by a continuous backward look at previous discussions of the Harlem Renaissance/Marxist connections, the "interracial triangles" of the cultural discourse around Scottsboro, and the debate around rural southern folk culture.

New Negro, Old Left demands the attention not only of those who wish to be informed about the history of the African American Left, the Harlem Renaissance, and proletarian literature, but also those seeking to gain an understanding of the potential relevance of contemporary critical arguments from scholars such as Eric Lott, David Roediger, Pierre Bourdieu, Eve Sedgewick, Hazel Carby, George Hutchinson, Michael North, Michael Rogin, Robin Wiegman, and others.

Indeed, the book is so rich and pithy, so full of complex allusions (very often expressed through humorous "signifying" on phrases familiar mainly to those working in the fields), that its most important weakness may be that it is written in a style that will limit accessibility to the very large and diversified audience that the book deserves. Yet careful readings and rereadings of *New Negro, Old Left* are worth the effort, for this is without doubt a pathbreaking and clarifying advance in our understanding of African American literature, modernity, and the Left.

What is especially sound and convincing in this achievement stems from Maxwell's thorough grounding in prior scholarship—his working through the arguments of predecessors in order to correct and advance them. This approach is most evident in Maxwell's insistence on rigorously historicizing and contextualizing conventional bifurcations and oppositions in order to demonstrate that, in the world of living cultural practice, various texts and careers do not fit into the prevailing narratives that have previously dominated the discourse of the black/Left interaction.

Repeatedly Maxwell demonstrates how selective quotations—from Mike Gold in relation to the Harlem Renaissance, from Wright in relation to Hurston—create false paradigms. Yet Maxwell's method is not to reverse these paradigms, only to rethink them in terms of the actual aims, activities, and views of the protagonists.

Often this requires our holding several contradictory opinions in mind at the same time—for example, in regard to Gold's opinions about jazz and black culture, or the profound misogyny of much of the most admirable antiracist discourse. We come away from the experience with a more authentic apprehension of the ambiguities of cultural practice, even at the expense of losing some of those little boxes by means of which we had neatly classified earlier relationships.

Poets on the Left

Different in form, but complementary in content, James Smethurst's *The New Red Negro* is a powerful narrative of the evolution of a single genre. It is also a long-overdue truth-telling that documents central links between African American poetry and the Communist Left. Thus it corrects the work of earlier scholars who have treated the Left associations of black poets in terms of anti-Communist conventions and cliches that Smethurst deftly demolishes.

The book also rebuts those cultural historians who are intellectual prisoners of diminished narratives of twentieth-century literature that isolate literary radicalism of "The Thirties" as a decade-limited "moment," rather than understanding it as a crucial stage in a longer-term, midcentury development.

This very ambitious book tries to argue a complex challenge to prevailing views of the evolution of African American poetry, revise conventional notions of literary classification, offer a theory for the various emphases in form and content of a range of black poets over several decades, counter institutionalized amnesia about the seriousness and subtleties of political engagements, and speculate on the long-term impact of this midcentury experience. Each aspect of the project is carried out with an impressively lucid writing style and a highly polished means of documentation. (Smethurst's footnotes alone require meticulous study.)

The basic thesis of Smethurst's book is that the evolving ideology and institutions of the U.S. Communist cultural movement played a substantial role in shaping the form and content of African American poetry in the 1930s and 1940s. The primary poets in the study are Sterling Brown, Langston Hughes, Gwendolyn Brooks, Countee Cullen, Owen Dodson, Robert Hayden, Melvin Tolson, and Margaret Walker; attention is also paid to Waring Cuney, Frank Marshall Davis, Richard Wright, and several others.

While the range of relationships to Communist ideology and organizations among this group is diverse, Smethurst finds the influence most evident in the specificities of the gendered folk-street voice of much of this poetry, a result of a kind of "yoking" together of "cultural nationalism, integrationism, and internationalism within a construct of class struggle" (10).

Once the leading poetry of the decade is discussed in this context, one can then gain new insight into such complex matters as the poetry's relation to rural and urban forms of African American popular culture, and the interrelations between "high" and "vernacular" art.

Smethurst's introduction incisively reviews the previous scholarship on black poetry in the 1930s and 1940s, as well as drawbacks to extant memoirs of and scholarship about the cultural Left. Among Smethurst's most convincing points are his sensible explanation of the ill effects of the tendency to separate the 1930s from the 1940s in regard to periodization, and his emphasis on the crucial mixing of "high" and "low" culture.

Less convincing is the assertion that the U.S. Communist cultural leadership welcomed the 1920s modernist revolution in literary form and sensibility. In my view, this assessment contradicts the writings of the most authoritative party critics: V. J. Jerome, John Howard Lawson, Milton Howard, A. B. Magil, Samuel Sillen.

It would have been sufficient to observe that perhaps party critics did not recognize African American or more "populist" versions of modernism for what they were, and that they held a double standard when it came to the treatment of writers who had or had not expressed dismay over the repressive nature of the Soviet regime.

Chapter 1 presents a kind of overview of the origin and evolution of black writers and Communism from the post–World War I era. This is a vivid summary of some familiar episodes that also integrates new information and insights into the narrative.

Smethhurst's characterization of the Communist approach to the "national question" as providing "a paradigm" with which African American writers felt comfortable is impressive. The chapter additionally contains a fabulous review of Communist cultural institutions (mainly journals) in relation to black writers, as well as provocative considerations of masculinity and gender in recreating the "folk voice" before and during the Popular Front.

Chapter 2 concentrates on the work of Sterling Brown, beginning with a fine recontextualization of his writing in relation to the Communist Left as well as a useful explanation of Brown's distinction between a "Harlem" and "New Negro" renaissance. Smethurst's observations about the parallels between Brown's cultural project and the Communists' evolving orientation are also exciting.

Equally noteworthy, the argument proves its mettle in the consideration of the poetry, starting with Smethurst's astute commentary on the poem "Southern Road" and continuing through a striking comparison of Brown's and Alain Locke's views of the respective contributions of Harlem and rural folk culture to the "New Negro" renaissance.

Chapter 3 reconsiders Langston Hughes in relation to the Communist Left. Although the story has been told before in biographies by Arnold Rampersad and Faith Berry, Smethurst manages to provide an impressively fresh version due perhaps to a more nuanced understanding of the Communist project.

The consideration of voice in the poetry is informative, and the discussion of Hughes's "Scottsboro Limited" is a fine contribution toward rehabilitating Hughes's 1930s cultural work. Smethurst concludes that Hughes's ability to ultimately establish a genuine base in the African American reading public was intimately connected with his "engagement with the aesthetics of the Popular Front" (115).

In his fourth chapter, Smethurst switches the mode from a focus on individual writers to a thematic survey using categories such as "The Folk Documentary" and three versions of "Narratorial Consciousness." Among the writers treated in this framework are Richard Wright, Lucy Mae Turner, Frank Marshall Davis, Waring Cuney, Countee Cullen, and Ida Gerling Athens. The strategy results in stimulating and compelling readings of many texts.

Chapter 5 inaugurates the consideration of the late 1930s and first half of the 1940s when poetic styles of the Depression era evolve to what Smethurst calls "neomodernism" (which comes in "popular" and "high" varieties). Here we have Langston Hughes discussed as an exemplar of the former, with sensitive readings of poems of the 1940s and a suggestive argument about Hughes as a forerunner of the black arts movement of the 1960s.

Chapter 6 treats Gwendolyn Brooks as the paradigmatic figure of "high" neomodernism. It begins with a much-needed challenge to prevailing images of Brooks's alleged distance from the Left. Smethurst then shows how Brooks develops a heroic female subject in her poetry.

Chapter 7 repeats the effective strategy of the first half of the book by reviewing a range of black poets (Margaret Walker, Robert Hayden, Melvin Tolson, and Owen Dodson) in light of the paradigms established in the preceding studies of Hughes and Brooks, as well as in relation to topics discussed in the first part of the book.

Smethurst frames his interpretations with a brief historical discussion of the transformation of the prevailing folk ethos between the 1930s and 1940s from South to urban North and West. This extraordinary volume concludes with suggestive observations about the implications of this cultural history for black poets of the 1950s and after, and, more briefly, in relation to the phenomenon of the "New American Poetry" in the 1950s.

The Companion Front

Bill Mullen's *Popular Fronts* is distinguished by his intense focus on one particular arena of political and cultural antiracist struggle and black art—the city of Chicago, from the advent of the Popular Front to the Cold War. For this project he applies Yale professor Michael Denning's appropriation of the concept of "The Cultural Front" as the term of choice for leftists who saw "culture as one arm, or front, of a widening campaign for social, political, and racial equality" (2).

Although others besides Communists used that term, Mullen believes that the expression became especially important after the call for the People's Front coalition. The call precipitated a shift from a proletarian revolutionary culture to a "people's culture" for the purpose of extending the country's democratic heritage.

The brilliance of Mullen's approach is that he gives a concreteness to this general development. This is the same virtue found in the work of Solomon, Maxwell, and Smethurst, and it is the one that makes all the difference.

The concern at this stage in scholarship is not merely exposing the proclamations of official Comintern documents to lay bare the *realpolitik* motivating political twists and turns (something in regard to which the four authors represent a range of views). Mullen demonstrates that, whatever the intentions of Kremlin or CP bureaucrats, Chicago as a vibrant city had its own local history of Left antiracist activism that received a special stamp in early 1936. At that time the National Negro Congress (NNC) was launched through the presence of nearly a thousand delegates from twenty-eight states, to an audience of an additional four thousand. One of its themes was advancement of culture and cultural workers, alongside political demands.

This event introduced to Chicago a style of politics and culture that took root. By the 1940s many of the themes, slogans, demands, and cultural icons of this would-be "Negro People's Front" were virtually hegemonic on the South Side; the *Chicago Defender,* for example, without ever referring to the Communists or other Left organizations, frequently presented the race-and-class-based radicalism of the Communist Party.

Although the CP as a whole suffered an enormous crisis at the time of the Hitler-Stalin Pact, and even abandoned the Popular Front orientation for a period, black party members in Chicago continued to forge an alliance with the *Defender* and with black liberal forces across the country to launch a famous boycott of the film *Gone With the Wind*.

Simply put, Mullen's book aims to be a corrective to earlier treatments of the Popular Front. It answers not only the negative ones that show a condescending attitude toward the accommodating politics and cultural strategies of the time; it also augments the positive ones that treat Euro-American culture primarily and fail to grasp that there existed a "companion front" for African Americans. The appeal of this companion front was so strong that it lasted far longer than the official party policy and helped to shape antiracist struggle in the black community up to the present.

The specificity of Chicago provides a unique testing ground, for Chicago has been the site of a recent revival of cultural scholarship that had hitherto been debilitated by a failure to understand the African American cultural Left beyond the canonical figure of Richard Wright.

Mullen's view is that what is usually called the 1930s–40s "Chicago Renaissance" is actually "the fruit of an extraordinary rapprochement between African American and white members of the U.S. Left around debate and struggle for a new 'American Negro' culture," a "black and interracial cultural radicalism, best described and understood as a revised if belated realization of the Communist Party's 1936 aspiration for a Negro People's Front" (6).

On the one hand, "the 1936 opening of Chicago's black 'cultural front' represented both a culmination and a new beginning for African American engagement of and revision within the U.S. Left." On the other, "Chicago's cultural 'renaissance' and the CPUSA's Popular Front/Negro People's Front ... were events that were historically mutually constitutive and in many ways unthinkable in separation" (6).

The roots of revolutionary Marxism in Chicago's South Side (which by the mid-1930s was the largest concentration of blacks in the United States after Harlem) can be traced back to World War I; Mullen cites the *Whip* and the Free Thought Society as the "genesis" of the local branch of the African Blood Brotherhood.

Subsequently, organizations such as the League of Struggle for Negro Rights, American Negro Labor Congress, United Front Scottsboro Committee, and the National Unemployed Councils were "crucial chapters in black Chicago and the white-dominated Communist Party's reconsideration and reconstitution of each other" (7).

Mullen assesses the radical politics of Chicago as combining two elements: a broad interracial Popular Front on one hand, and a "companion" Negro People's Front in Chicago on other. The latter is understood by Mullen as a "climactic 'black' moment in the history of U.S. radicalism when African American political culture actively and willingly engaged, revived, reformed, and deployed 'Communism' in a manner generally consistent with official party policy, yet primarily derived from and utilized in relation to the 'objective conditions' of life in Black Metropolis" (8).

These elements include a responsiveness to both the proletarian component of the population (men working in stockyards and steel mills; women as domestics) as well as its middle and upper classes aspiring to become "players" in the democratic capitalist system and its culture. A special emphasis on black churches was included as well.

Perhaps more emphatically than Smethurst, Mullen argues that the African American cultural Left prior to 1936 had been moving autonomously in a manner that would form a symbiotic relationship with the double Popular Front thrust.

Writers, artists, and intellectuals such as Margaret Burroughs, Fern Gayden, Alice Browning, Theodore Ward, Gwendolyn Brooks, Horace Cayton, St. Clair Drake, Charles White, Margaret Walker, and Frank Marshall Davis were evolving in that direction; they would make that orientation visible not only through individual writings but also through the "Negro in Illinois" project of the Illinois Federal Writers Project, the South Side Community Center, the Associated Negro Press, the *Chicago Defender*, and *Negro Story*.

Moreover, at moments when the Communist Party seemed to diverge from the larger project it had helped to engender—especially during World War II—this trend not only continued but deepened and creatively developed certain aspects.

In particular, Mullen holds that in Chicago the black cultural Left "constituted among the most aesthetically and politically complex black art of the century, challenging the commonly shared assumption that Popular Front art universally succumbed to an ameliorated populist aesthetics or a mawkish sentimentality" (11).

None of this is to deny that there were tensions in the companion front; part of Mullen's story is of the struggles between the members of the "black bourgeoisie" who ultimately controlled cultural institutions, and the militants who participated in them. Mullen takes note of the fact that very often radical ideas were disguised to appease the black patronage class as much as to evade FBI surveillance.

Ultimately, the Chicago Renaissance was ended in practical terms through a combination of flight—in some cases flight into exile, in other cases into a black bourgeois intellectual life.

The seven chapters of Mullen's book aspire to map out the political, cultural, and geographical landscape of the companion front from the mid-1930s through World War II. He begins with a striking revision of Richard Wright's contribution to the phenomenon; by documenting Wright's atypicality, Mullen both gains a clearer perspective on his achievement and helps bring back into vision the many other cultural workers, institutions, and activities hitherto obscured.

The second, third, and fourth chapters treat key institutions of the renaissance and Negro People's Front. Foremost is the *Chicago Defender,* which after 1940 not only covered the pro-Communist Left sympathetically but hired editors and writers from that milieu. In contrast, the South Side Community Arts Center is noted for its interracial alliances among cultural workers.

Negro Story, published from 1944 to 1946, is reclaimed as helping to "foreground the short story as a genre for black radical voicing" through its blend of the tradition of "proletarian literature" and the racialized wartime experiences of black women (16).

Shifting gears in the fifth and six chapters, Mullen turns to literary analysis of short fiction and poetry of the 1940s. In the case of the former, the fiction record of *Negro Story* shows the "critical amnesia" which allowed the establishment of a select group of major black writers to obscure their roots in the companion front and the contributions of lesser-known writers. In regard to Brooks, especially "A Street in Bronzeville," Mullen offers an extraordinary interpretation of her writing as an "unsystematic feminist skepticism" of Left culture within a radical framework, even as Brooks herself has denied any past association with the Left.

Mullen's final chapter and his postscript focus on the combined effects of McCarthyism, postwar political splintering (due to the absence of a common struggle against international fascism), embourgeoisement, and the liberalizing of formerly radical institutions, for the legacy of the companion front experience.

Building a New Interracial Left

These four books definitively establish the Communist-led antiracist movement in mid-century as fundamental for any future interracial socialist Left. This is not to dismiss the substantial literature documenting the mistakes and delusions of the Communist movement—especially its reprehensible policies in World War II (including support of Japanese internment, opposition to the "Double V" campaign, and collaboration with the federal government's suppression of the civil liberties of Trotskyists).

Rather, it is to conclude that this unconscionable record only problematizes but does not negate the palpable achievements recorded in these remarkable books. Together they embody a series of "lessons" that might be carried over as the starting point of any radical movement in the new millennium.

In addition, there are the methodological contributions of this literature to ongoing considerations about the cultural and political history of the Left.

Three of the most important lessons might be summarized as follows:

• First, as we have seen from the experiences of the Communist movement in the 1920s, militancy, devotion to class struggle, and a fervent belief in equality are inadequate to build an interracial movement. The nature of racism as both material and ideological oppression requires that socialist organizations and projects take special measures in order to transform their membership composition and their relationship to the struggle of people of color.

It is not enough to preach the need for unity and promise fair treatment. Black history is replete with examples of betrayals by "white friends," and Communists were correct in understanding why there was the need for black leadership of autonomous black struggles.

• Second, the Communist movement, prodded by the arguments of black revolutionaries from the Left nationalist movement, as well as by the Communist International, developed a basic theory to explain both the historical reasons why "special measures" must be taken, as well as to suggest what these measures should be.

That theory is basically the view of "national oppression," as opposed to the stance that the issue to be addressed is simply racism (dislike of people who look different), injustice, and so forth. Understanding African Americans as a nationality helps explain why nationalism of various forms has been an ongoing feature of the struggle, and why revolutionaries should not oppose this nationalist struggle but find ways to relate to it in order to assist its evolution in a radical, anticapitalist, and internationalist direction.

The development of a proletarian-led nationalist movement with an internationalist vision is probably the prerequisite to a unified movement for socialism—a stage over which Marxists may not be able to leap.

The Communists chose to put this theory into practice by building a working-class movement in two complementary areas: on the one hand, they struggled for an integrated CIO, that put the cause of antiracism among its priorities; on the other, they promoted a black-led labor movement with a broad social agenda, culminating in the National Negro Congress after 1936.

(Here it is worth mentioning that the precise decision-making procedures in the NNC are not fully discussed, and Solomon believes that at least one public leader was a secret party member. So the record of how, exactly, the party maintained influence in an "independent" black-led organization remains to be explored.)

From this perspective, it becomes clear why forms of affirmative action (such as taking special measures to insure that all barriers are removed from advancement to leadership of African Americans) are necessary *within* as well as *without* a socialist organization; why black members should be the leaders in areas of black work, but also in the general political life of the group; why cultural and psychological issues are of crucial importance; why "integration" or "assimilation" into the racist house of capitalism is an inadequate solution; and why an organization's membership must be reeducated to understand the complex and subtle ways in which paternalism and white privilege can exist despite one's best intentions. (Recent scholarship has especially emphasized how the choice of European ethnic groups to identify as "white" assisted, and still reinforces, the racist order.)

In regard to this last point, the Communists were especially effective in demonstrating to their own membership the truth that the struggle against racism is in everyone's interest, not just that of African Americans.

Euro-American members came to see that their own best hope for the future was interconnected with black liberation, to the point of supporting black self-defense against other Euro-Americans. In general, antiracism became the duty of every Communist, not just black members.

- A third lesson from the Communist experience suggests the manner in which substantial numbers of African Americans will possibly come to join a socialist organization.

Some, of course, may join out of individual friendship with members who have won their confidence on the job, as neighbors, or in a common struggle. However, if the organization adheres to the kind of attitudes promoted by the

Communists, broader layers of the most politicized vanguard of the black struggle will come increasingly to respect the socialist movement; eventually cadres will enter, first by ones and twos, and then these will come to play the key role in the recruitment of thousands more. (But it is also the duty of Euro-American socialists to themselves actively assist in this effort to change the composition of the organization.)

With an organization, like the Communist Party, willing to defend the black population from exploitation in general—not just around obvious "political" cases, but against police brutality, eviction—the culture of the movement will become increasingly hospitable to people of color.

The Dream of Cyril Briggs

Of course, these four books begin—but they hardly end—the crucial discussions that need to take place in regard to the above "lessons," a discussion in which a new generation of activists and Marxist scholars of all colors and both genders will have to participate along with veterans.

For example, one of the themes most stressed by Solomon is the central role of ideology, vision, and a unified organization. In fact, even false visions and a relatively undemocratic military command–type organization seem to have the ability to empower antiracist activists. Solomon's own point of reference here is the mistaken view that the Black Belt in the South was the basis of a potential black republic.*

However, there is also the issue of just how empowering was the false view that the Soviet Union represented a genuine step forward into the socialist future, a country in which workers' rights were supposedly defended and racism virtually expunged.

Clearly the belief that the beginning of a new world already existed gave much self-confidence to a struggling group of black and Euro-American Communists in an adversarial position. But what about a balance sheet measuring these benefits against the deficits of having a mostly false dream, and adjusting national political priorities to the needs of a foreign dictatorship?

Even if one puts aside (for the moment) all the complex debates about whether Communist policies in Germany, Spain, the colonies, etc., actually

---

*It's worth noting that Solomon's opinion is that, even in those periods when the Communists' view was clearly that the Black Belt republic was not a "given" but that the choice was up to the black population, such a strategy was inappropriate. This raises the ongoing question of the meaning of self-determination. For example, after the late 1930s the Trotskyist view was consistently that the issue of a separate state must be settled by the oppressed nationality itself, which could, in fact, opt for a land-based separate state even if socialists thought this was unworkable or undesirable. How can one talk of "self-determination" if certain options for self-rule by people of color are ruled out in advance by the white majority?

advanced or retarded antifascism and socialist movements, we need to ask ourselves: in the long run, were the gains of a self-comforting illusion worth the betrayal of idealistic rank-and-file party members by leaders who banked their reputations on false information about the Stalin regime?

Was it worth the long-term discrediting of Marxism among millions who, to this day, identify socialism with the Stalinist horror?

In addition, the ongoing controversy about the politics of the Popular Front is raised implicitly and explicitly in these writings. By and large, the view of Solomon—that local practice was the crucial test for the black movement; that the Third Period was at best a trial run to learn firsthand the futility of sectarianism—seems to be vindicated by the three other scholars.

Still, since Solomon ends in 1936, and Maxwell and Smethurst are primarily focused on cultural practice, only Mullen explicitly treats the Popular Front throughout its two phases (before and after the Hitler-Stalin Pact) as both a high point and something of a model to be emulated. And he does this in a nuanced fashion, emphasizing the semiautonomy of the companion front.

Nevertheless, Mullen tends to treat the Popular Front orientation through euphemisms such as "coalitionist politics" (6). Since no critic of Popular Front politics ever objected to coalitions—indeed, the Trotskyist and Left socialist critics were for coalition politics in the days when the CP was for a "United Front from Below"—this formula is likely to be seen by those skeptical of the Popular Front as sidestepping the hardest and more troubling questions.

On what basis should one develop alliances with nonsocialist and non-working-class forces so as to advance the struggle on all fronts, building for the day when authentic economic and political reconstruction are truly on the agenda? In my view, it is impossible to reach a final judgment on the actual degree of autonomy of the companion front during World War II without a candid, comparative appraisal of the CP's practice on a national level (and its international positions).

Finally, there is the issue of the uniqueness of the modern African American liberation movement as a paradigm for a "new" twentieth-century social movement requiring a rethinking of classical Marxist projections about the likely course of social advance.

Many of the points of analysis about African American "national oppression" seem appropriate not only to other populations of oppressed nationalities in land areas of the United States historically linked to these groups (especially Chicanos, Puerto Ricans, and Native Americans), but also to a number of non-European immigrant nationalities (Latinos from Latin America, Asian Americans, Caribbeans) and even to women.

To what extent is the declaration of a "national oppression" decisive to the recognition of the legitimacy of autonomous struggles, self-leadership, the need for affirmative action, the recognition of the importance of psychological and cultural issues?

Is it possible that one aspect of Communist theoretical work (and corresponding practical intervention) in relation to African Americans is that it simply instigated a rethinking of narrower interpretations of Marxism, a rethinking that is necessary for socialists of future generations to eventually realize the liberatory dreams of Cyril Briggs and all who came after?

❋   ❋   ❋

C. L. R. JAMES
EXCERPTS FROM THE REVOLUTIONARY ANSWER TO THE NEGRO PROBLEM IN THE UNITED STATES (1948)

The decay of capitalism on a world scale, the rise of the CIO [Congress of Industrial Organizations] in the United States, and the struggle of the Negro people have precipitated a tremendous battle for the minds of the Negro people and for the minds of the population in the United States as a whole over the Negro question. During the last few years certain sections of the bourgeoisie, recognizing the importance of this question, have made a powerful theoretical demonstration of their position, which has appeared in *The American Dilemma*, by Gunnar Myrdal, a publication that took a quarter of a million dollars to produce. Certain sections of the sentimental petty bourgeoisie have produced their spokesmen, one of whom is Lillian Smith. That has produced some very strange fruit, which however has resulted in a book which has sold some half a million copies over the last year or two. The Negro petty bourgeoisie, radical and concerned with communism, has also made its bid in the person of Richard Wright, whose books have sold over a million copies. When books on such a controversial question as the Negro question reach the stage of selling half a million copies it means that they have left the sphere of literature and have now reached the sphere of politics. . . .

We can compare what we have to say that is new by comparing it to previous positions on the Negro question in the socialist movement. The proletariat [working class], as we know, must lead the struggles of all the oppressed and all those who are persecuted by capitalism. But this has been interpreted in the past— and by some very good socialists, too—in the following sense: the independent struggles of the Negro people have not got much more than an episodic value and, as a matter of fact, can constitute a great danger not only to the Negroes themselves, but to the organized labor movement. The real leadership of the Negro

---

This essay is reprinted from a report with which James presented a resolution on "the Negro question" to the 1948 Convention of the Socialist Workers Party.

struggle must rest in the hands of organized labor and of the Marxist party. Without that the Negro struggle is not only weak, but is likely to cause difficulties for the Negroes and dangers to organized labor. This, as I say, is the position held by many socialists in the past. Some great socialists in the United States have been associated with this attitude.

We, on the other hand, say something entirely different.

We say, number one, that the Negro struggle, the independent Negro struggle, has a vitality and a validity of its own; that it has deep historic roots in the past of America and in present struggles; it has an organic political perspective, along which it is traveling, to one degree or another, and everything shows that at the present time it is traveling with great speed and vigor.

We say, number two, that this independent Negro movement is able to intervene with terrific force upon the general social and political life of the nation, despite the fact that it is waged under the banner of democratic rights, and is not led necessarily either by the organized labor movement or the Marxist party. We say, number three, and this is the most important, that it is able to exercise a powerful influence upon the revolutionary proletariat, that it has got a great contribution to make to the development of the proletariat in the United States, and that it is in itself a constituent part of the struggle for socialism. In this way we challenge directly any attempt to subordinate or to push to the rear the social and political significance of the independent Negro struggle for democratic rights. That is our position. It was the position of Lenin thirty years ago. It was the position of Trotsky, which he fought for during many years. It has been concretized by the general class struggle in the United States, and the tremendous struggles of the Negro people. It has been sharpened and refined by political controversy in our movement, and best of all it has had the benefit of three or four years of practical application in the Negro struggle and in the class struggle by the Socialist Workers Party during the past few years.

Now if this position has reached the stage where we can put it forward in the shape that we propose, that means that to understand it should be by now simpler than before; and by merely observing the Negro question, the Negro people, rather, the struggles they have carried on, their ideas, we are able to see the roots of this position in a way that was difficult to see ten or even fifteen years ago. The Negro people, we say, on the basis of their own experiences, approach the conclusions of Marxism. And I will have briefly to illustrate this as has been shown in the resolution.

First of all, on the question of imperialist war. The Negro people do not believe that the last two wars, and the one that may overtake us, are a result of the need to struggle for democracy, for freedom of the persecuted peoples by the American bourgeoisie. They cannot believe that.

On the question of the state, what Negro, particularly below the Mason-

Dixon Line, believes that the bourgeois state is a state above all classes, serving the needs of all the people? They may not formulate their belief in Marxist terms, but their experience drives them to reject this shibboleth of bourgeois democracy.

On the question of what is called the democratic process, the Negroes do not believe that grievances, difficulties of sections of the population, are solved by discussions, by voting, by telegrams to Congress, by what is known as the "American way."

Finally, on the question of political action, the American bourgeoisie preaches that Providence in its divine wisdom has decreed that there should be two political parties in the United States, not one, not three, not four, just two; and also in its kindness, Providence has shown that these two parties should be one, the Democratic Party and the other, the Republican, to last from now until the end of time.

That is being challenged by increasing numbers of people in the United States. But the Negroes more than ever have shown it—and any knowledge of their press and their activities tells us that they are willing to make the break completely with that conception. . . .

As Bolsheviks we are jealous, not only theoretically but practically, of the primary role of the organized labor movement in all fundamental struggles against capitalism. That is why for many years in the past this position on the Negro question has had some difficulty in finding itself thoroughly accepted, particularly in the revolutionary movement, because there is this difficulty—what is the relation between this movement and the primary role of the proletariat—particularly because so many Negroes, and most disciplined, hardened, trained, highly developed sections of the Negroes, are today in the organized labor movement.

First, the Negro struggles in the South are not merely a question of struggle of Negroes, important as those are. It is a question of the reorganization of the whole agricultural system in the United States, and therefore a matter for the proletarian revolution and the reorganization of society on socialist foundations.

Second, we say in the South that although the embryonic unity of whites and Negroes in the labor movement may seem small and there are difficulties in the unions, yet such is the decay of southern society and such the fundamental significance of the proletariat, particularly when organized in labor unions, that this small movement is bound to play the decisive part in the revolutionary struggles that are inevitable.

Third, there are one and a quarter million Negroes, at least, in the organized labor movement.

On these fundamental positions we do not move one inch. Not only do we not move, we strengthen them. But there still remains in question: what is the relationship of the independent Negro mass movement to the organized labor movement? And here we come immediately to what has been and will be a very puzzling feature unless we have our basic position clear.

Those who believed that the Negro question is in reality, purely and simply, or to a decisive extent, merely a class question, pointed with glee to the tremendous growth of the Negro personnel in the organized labor movement. It grew in a few years from 300,000 to 1 million; it is now 1.5 million. But to their surprise, instead of this lessening and weakening the struggle of the independent Negro movement, *the more the Negroes went in the labor movement, the more capitalism incorporated them into industry, the more they were accepted in the union movement. It is during that period, since 1940, that the independent mass movement has broken out with a force greater than it has ever shown before.*

That is the problem that we have to face, that we have to grasp. We cannot move forward and we cannot explain ourselves unless we have it clearly. And I know there is difficulty with it. I intend to spend some time on it, because if that is settled, all is settled. The other difficulties are incidental. If, however, this one is not clear, then we shall continually be facing difficulties which we shall doubtless solve in time.

Now Lenin has handled this problem and in the resolution we have quoted him. He says that the dialectic of history is such that small independent nations, small nationalities, which are powerless—get the word, please—*powerless*, in the struggle against imperialism *nevertheless* can act as one of the ferments, one of the bacilli, which can bring onto the scene the real power against imperialism—the socialist proletariat.

Let me repeat it please. Small groups, nations, nationalities, themselves powerless against imperialism, nevertheless can act as one of the ferments, one of the bacilli which will bring onto the scene the real fundamental force against capitalism—the socialist proletariat.

In other words, as so often happens from the Marxist point of view from the point of view of the dialectic, this question of the *leadership* is very complicated.

What Lenin is saying is that although the fundamental force is the proletariat, although these groups are powerless, although the proletariat has got to lead them, it does not by any means follow that they cannot do anything until the proletariat actually comes forward to lead them. *He says exactly the opposite is the case.*

They, by their agitation, resistance, and the political developments that they can initiate, can be the means whereby the proletariat is brought onto the scene.

Not always, and every time, not the sole means, but one of the means. That is what we have to get clear.

Now it is very well to see it from the point of view of Marxism which developed these ideas upon the basis of European and Oriental experiences. Lenin and Trotsky applied this principle to the Negro question in the United States. What we have to do is to make it concrete, and one of the best means of doing so is to dig into the history of the Negro people in the United States, and to see the relationship that has developed between them and revolutionary elements in past revolutionary struggles.

For us the center must be the Civil War in the United States and I intend briefly now to make some sharp conclusions and see if they can help us arrive at a clearer perspective. Not for historical knowledge, but to watch the movement as it develops before us, helping us to arrive at a clearer perspective as to this difficult relationship between the independent Negro movement and the revolutionary proletariat. The Civil War was a conflict between the revolutionary bourgeoisie and the Southern plantocracy. That we know. That conflict was inevitable. But for twenty to twenty-five years before the Civil War actually broke out, the masses of the Negroes in the South, through the Underground Railroad, through revolts, as Aptheker has told us, and by the tremendous support and impetus that they gave to the revolutionary elements among the abolitionists, absolutely prevented the reactionary bourgeoisie—revolutionary later—absolutely prevented the bourgeoisie and the plantocracy from coming to terms as they wanted to do. In 1850 these two made a great attempt at a compromise. What broke that compromise? It was the Fugitive Slave Act. They could prevent everything else for the time being, but they could not prevent the slaves from coming, and the revolutionaries in the North from assisting them. So that we find that here in the history of the United States such is the situation of the masses of the Negro people and their readiness to revolt at the slightest opportunity, that as far back as the Civil War, in relation to the American bourgeoisie, they formed a force which *initiated* and *stimulated* and *acted as a ferment*.

That is point number one.

Point number two. The Civil War takes its course as it is bound to do. Many Negroes and their leaders make an attempt to get incorporated into the Republican Party and to get their cause embraced by the bourgeoisie. And what happens? The bourgeoisie refuses. It doesn't want to have Negroes emancipated. Point number three. As the struggle develops, such is the situation of the Negroes in the United States, that the emancipation of the slaves becomes an absolute necessity, politically, organizationally, and from a military point of view.

The Negroes are incorporated into the battle against the South. Not only are they incorporated here, but later they are incorporated also into the military government which smashes down the remnants of resistance in the Southern states. But, when this is done, the Negroes are deserted by the bourgeoisie, *and there falls upon them a very terrible repression.*

That is the course of development in the central episode of American history.

Now if it is so in the Civil War, we have the right to look to see what happened in the War of Independence. It is likely—it is not always certain—but it is *likely* that we shall see there some *anticipations* of the logical development which appeared in the Civil War. They are there. The Negroes begin by demanding their rights. They say if you are asking that the British free you, then we should have our rights, and furthermore, slavery should be abolished. The American bourgeoisie didn't react very well to that. The Negroes insisted—those Negroes who were in the North—insisted that they should be allowed to join the Army of Independence. They were refused.

But later Washington found that it was imperative to have them, and four thousand of them fought among the thirty thousand soldiers of Washington. They gained certain rights after independence was achieved. Then sections of the bourgeoisie who were with them deserted them. And the Negro movement collapsed. We see exactly the same thing but more intensified in the populist movement. There was a powerful movement of one and one quarter of a million Negroes in the South (the Southern Tenant Farmers' Association). They joined the populist movement and were in the extreme left wing of this movement, when populism was discussing whether it should go on with the Democratic Party or make the campaign as a third party. The Negroes voted for the third party and for all the most radical planks in the platform. They fought with the populist movement. But when populism was defeated, there fell upon the Negroes between 1896 and about 1910 the desperate, legalized repression and persecution of the Southern states.

Some of us think it is fairly clear that the Garvey movement came and looked to Africa because there was no proletarian movement in the United States to give it a lead, to do for this great eruption of the Negroes what the Civil War and the populist movement had done for the insurgent Negroes of those days. And now what can we see today? Today the Negroes in the United States are organized as never before. There are more than half a million in the NAACP, and in addition to that, there are all sorts of Negro groups and organizations—the churches in particular—*every single one of which is dominated by the idea that each organization must in some manner or another contribute to the emancipation of the Negroes from capitalist humiliation and from capitalist oppression.* So that the independent Negro movement that we see today and which we see growing before our eyes is nothing strange. It is nothing new. *It is something that has always appeared in the American movement at the first sign of social crisis.*

It represents a climax to the Negro movements that we have seen in the past. From what we have seen in the past, we would expect it to have its head turned toward the labor movement. And not only from a historical point of view but today concrete experience tells us that the masses of the Negro people today look upon the CIO with a respect and consideration that they give to no other social or political force in the country. To anyone who knows the Negro people, who reads their press—and I am not speaking here specially of the Negro workers— if you watch the Negro petty bourgeoisie—reactionary, reformist types as some of them are in all their propaganda, in all their agitation—whenever they are in any difficulties, you can see them leaning toward the labor movement. As for the masses of Negroes, they are increasingly prolabor every day. So that it is not only Marxist ideas; it is not only a question of Bolshevik-Marxist analysis. It is not only a question of the history of Negroes in the United States.

The actual concrete facts before us show us, and anyone who wants to see, this important conclusion, that the Negro movement logically and historically and concretely is headed for the proletariat. That is the road it has always taken in the past, the road to the revolutionary forces. Today the proletariat is that force. And if these ideas that we have traced in American revolutionary crises have shown some power in the past, such is the state of the class struggle today, such the antagonisms between bourgeoisie and proletariat, such, too, the impetus of the Negro *movement toward the revolutionary forces*, which we have traced in the past, is stronger today than ever before. So that we can look upon this Negro movement not only for what it has been and what it has been able to do—we are able to know as Marxists by our own theory and our examination of American history that it is headed for the proletarian movement, that it must go there. There is nowhere else for it to go. And further we can see that if it doesn't go there, the difficulties that the Negroes have suffered in the past when they were deserted by the revolutionary forces, those will be ten, one hundred, ten thousand times as great as in the past. The independent Negro movement, which is boiling and moving, must find its way to the proletariat. If the proletariat is not able to support it, the repression of past times when the revolutionary forces failed the Negroes will be infinitely, I repeat infinitely, more terrible today.

Therefore our consideration of the independent Negro movement does not lessen the significance of the proletarian—the essentially proletarian—leadership. Not at all. It includes it. We are able to see that the mere existence of the CIO, its mere existence, despite the fakery of the labor leadership on the Negro question, as on all other questions, is a protection and a stimulus to the Negroes. We are able to see and I will show in a minute that the Negroes are able by their activity to draw the revolutionary elements and more powerful elements in the proletariat to their side. We are coming to that. But we have to draw and emphasize again and again this important conclusion. If—and we have to take these theoretical questions into consideration—if the proletariat is defeated, if the CIO is destroyed, then there will fall upon the Negro people in the United States such a repression, such persecution, comparable to nothing that they have seen in the past. We have seen in Germany and elsewhere the barbarism that capitalism is capable of in its death agony. The Negro people in the United States offer a similar opportunity to the American bourgeoisie. The American bourgeoisie have shown their understanding of the opportunity the Negro question gives them to disrupt and to attempt to corrupt and destroy the labor movement.

But the development of capitalism itself has not only given the independent Negro movement this fundamental and sharp relation with the proletariat. It has created Negro proletarians and placed them as proletarians in what were once the most oppressed and exploited masses. But in auto, steel, and coal, for example, these proletarians have now become the vanguard of the workers' struggle and have brought a substantial number of Negroes to a position of primacy in the struggle against capitalism. The backwardness and humiliation of the Negroes that shoved them into these industries is the very thing which today is bringing them forward, and they are in the very vanguard of the proletarian movement from the very nature of the proletarian struggle itself. Now, how does this complicated interrelationship, the Leninist interrelationship express itself? Henry Ford could write a very good thesis on that if he were so inclined.

The Negroes in the Ford plant were incorporated by Ford: first of all he wanted them for the hard, rough work. I am also informed by the comrades from Detroit he was very anxious to play a paternalistic role with the Negro petty bourgeoisie. He wanted to show them that he was not the person that these people said he was—Look! he was giving Negroes opportunities in his plant. Number three, he was able thus to create divisions between whites and Negroes that allowed him to pursue his antiunion, reactionary way.

What has happened within the last few years that is changed? The mass of the Negroes in the River Rouge plant, I am told, are one of the most powerful sections of the Detroit proletariat. They are leaders in the proletarian struggle, not the stooges Ford intended them to be.

Not only that, they act as leaders not only in the labor movement as a whole but in the Negro community. It is what they say that is decisive there. Which is very sad for Henry. And the Negro petty bourgeois have followed the proletariat. They are now going along with the labor movement: they have left Ford, too. It is said that he has recognized it at last and that he is not going to employ any more Negroes. He thinks he will do better with women. But they will disappoint him, too. . . .

Let us not forget that in the Negro people, there sleep and are now awakening passions of a violence exceeding, perhaps, as far as these things can be compared, anything among the tremendous forces that capitalism has created. Anyone who knows them, who knows their history, is able to talk to them intimately, watches them at their own theaters, watches them at their dances, watches them in their churches, reads their press with a discerning eye, must recognize that although their social force may not be able to compare with the social force of a corresponding number of organized workers, the hatred of bourgeois society and the readiness to destroy it when the opportunity should present itself, rests among them to a degree greater than in any other section of the population in the United States.

✳ ✳ ✳

STEVE BLOOM AND DAVID FINKEL
HISTORICAL NOTES ON TROTSKYISM AND BLACK STRUGGLE (2000)

I. Brief Sketch Regarding the Socialist Workers Party (Bloom)

A concern with the question of black liberation goes back to the earliest days of the Trotskyist movement in the United States. Leaders of the Communist League of America [CLA] (the initial grouping created by Left oppositionists expelled from the Communist Party in 1928) initiated a series of discussions with Trotsky on this subject beginning with their very first meeting, in Prinkipo, Turkey, shortly after Trotsky's exile from the USSR. With Trotsky's assistance the movement in the United States came to view "the Negro question" in the general context of Lenin's approach to the right of oppressed nations to self-determination. One specific issue had to do with the CP's insistence on calling for the creation of an independent nation in the "Black Belt" south. Trotsky and his U.S. comrades came to the conclusion that this should be a question for the black population itself to decide, not something which a working-class revolutionary party ought to insist on as part of its own platform. (The transcribed text of these discussions is included in the pamphlet *Leon Trotsky on Black Nationalism and Self-Determination* published by Pathfinder Press.)

One central idea clearly distinguished the record of the CLA, and later the Workers Party and Socialist Workers Party [SWP] (until its degeneration).* Black people in the United States should not subordinate their struggle to any other social or political agenda. Thus when the CP, during World War II, was urging both the trade unions and the black movement to "wait" until the war was over to press their demands (in order not to undermine the U.S. military alliance with the USSR), the SWP vigorously defended and supported the March on Washington movement organized by A. Phillip Randolph, for example.

During the civil rights movement of the 1950s the SWP participated (modestly, due to its small size) in the predominant, nonviolent wing of the struggle. But it also established a relationship with Robert Williams who, in Monroe, North Carolina, combined a local NAACP branch with a chapter of the National Rifle Association, actively arming the black community for self-defense against KKK violence. The party helped to organize a defense committee against the inevitable government attack on Williams, and Williams later became a sponsor of the Fair Play for Cuba Committee, which the SWP was instrumental in launching.

---

*The Workers Party of the United States was created in 1935 through a fusion of the CLA and the American Workers Party led by A. J. Muste. This organization entered the Socialist Party of America for a short time, then forming the Socialist Workers Party in 1938, which for a number of years was the leading Trotskyist group in the United States. The SWP abandoned Trotskyism in the early 1980s after mass expulsions engineered by a younger leadership.

The party also developed a special relationship with Malcolm X during the early part of the 1960s. The *Militant* printed his speeches and reported on his organizing activities in a supportive way, unlike most groups on the socialist Left. Malcolm was invited to speak at SWP forums. George Breitman, then one of the editors at the party's publishing house, worked to get Malcolm's ideas into book and pamphlet form so that they could be widely distributed. To this day, young people interested in Malcolm know the name of George Breitman, and know about the relationship the SWP, and *Militant* newspaper, established with Malcolm (though most do *not* know that the SWP which is around today is a different party from what it was then).

It was during this period of the early–mid-1960s that the SWP, again with Breitman's leadership, developed the theory of combined revolution in the United States as a special application of Lenin's approach to the national question and Trotsky's theory of permanent revolution. The coming American revolution according to this concept, would be two revolutions taking place simultaneously: (1) a working-class revolution for socialism, and (2) a black revolution for national liberation. Though there would obviously be connections between them—due to the overwhelmingly working-class character of the black community if for no other reason—each of these struggles would unfold according to its own dynamics, with its own forms of mass mobilization, its own set of demands, and its own leadership. But neither could succeed alone. Each needed the other in order to overthrow their common enemy—the U.S. ruling class.

This theory guided the general approach of the party to developments in the black struggle during the next decade or so. The party was generally supportive of black nationalism as an ideology. A distinction was made between revolutionary nationalism, which was political and could help the movement to develop, and a purely cultural nationalism, which could not. Manifestations of cultural identity were, of course, essential for the development of any political movement among black people. But an effort to *substitute* cultural expression for a political movement was understood to be a diversion.

The party welcomed and defended the movement for community control of the schools in New York City in 1968, again distinguishing itself from most other groups on the Left. It's relationship with the Black Panther Party [BPP], however, was much more contradictory. While seeing considerable potential in this formation—especially at the outset—the political weaknesses of the Panthers (a tendency toward extreme ultraleft rhetoric, a fetishization of armed struggle, and a tendency to wave Mao's "Little Red Book" as a substitute for real political discussion) created barriers to close collaboration. The SWP participated actively in defense campaigns around figures like Huey Newton, Eldridge Cleaver, and other Panther political prisoners, but never established much of a political relationship with the BPP.

Later, during the 1970s, the party attempted to make connections with and build support for the movement around school busing as a means for desegregation, with mixed success.

Unlike the CP or various Maoist groups the SWP never recruited a large number of black cadre. There was always a modest layer of comrades, and they played important roles in the party. Some extremely prominent black activists—such as C. L. R. James—spent time as members of the organized Trotskyist movement. But the numbers never came close to the broader percentage of blacks in the population as a whole. There was some complacency about this in the party, at least from the 1960s onward. In part that attitude probably flowed from the theory that the black struggle was something which had to develop with its own dynamics, separate from (even if connected with) the working-class struggle. The party was theoretically in favor of building a multinational revolutionary organization. But until there was a simultaneous upsurge of both the workers' movement and the black community which could lay the basis for overcoming the racial division that society itself imposes, it was generally considered unlikely that this could become a reality.

As the SWP degenerated its attitude toward all organizations and movements outside of itself became much more instrumentalist (how can we use this particular group or political development to advance our own sectarian agenda) rather than collaborative and supportive. This inevitably had a negative affect on the party's reputation and relationship with black activists and movements.

II. A Brief Sketch Regarding the International Socialists (Finkel)

The following hastily drafted notes are intended to assist both with historical background and present-day orientation on antiracist work and recruitment. Steve Bloom has prepared notes reflecting the SWP experience, hence most of the historical material here reflects the "slant" of the International Socialists' [IS] perspective. (Most of the founding members of Solidarity in 1986 came from currents that had been through some part of the IS or SWP experience.)

I stress also that this is "informal," that is, not footnoted or precisely documented. Some highly relevant presentations were also given at the Solidarity Midwest Women's Retreat. I am in the process of checking to see which of these are, or could be put, in writing. This history is worth summarizing, in my view, because it helps situate our organization and to show that the problems we confront are not new ones.

Background

It is obviously impossible to treat the history of the U.S. Left and antiracism without reference to the Communist Party. Fortunately Alan Wald has dealt with this in his essay, which should be read along with the sources that Alan cites.

The central and irreplaceable contribution of the early CP was to supersede the politics of the old Debsian left wing of the Socialist Party on the issue of race, which held that racism was an evil of the capitalist system that should be fought unconditionally, but that the socialist movement "had no special program" to offer to the black population apart from the general struggle for socialism. (Meanwhile the SP right wing included various racists, anti-Chinese, prowar nationalist and other types.)

Heavily influenced by Lenin's writings on the National Question and the early Communist International, as well as its alliance with Cyril Briggs and the African Blood Brotherhood, the CP moved toward an understanding of black oppression and struggle in the United States as having a national dynamic as well as being central to the U.S. proletarian revolution. This legacy remained central for those revolutionary Marxists who broke (or were purged) from the CP over the various crimes of Stalinism.

It is easy to see major defects in the particular theory of the "Black Belt" in the South seen by the CP as the material basis for a black nation. Even by the late 1920s when this conception was put forward, it had been profoundly undermined by mechanization of agriculture, which displaced massive amounts of farm labor and accelerated the northward migration of black labor. Further, black nationalism in real life attained greater footholds in northern urban centers than in the South, precisely because in the North the black community felt both its potential power and the horrible effects of a racist capitalist economy.

Nonetheless the theorization of a black nation was clearly onto something important. Rather than the sterile exercise of demanding that a people fit into some preset "objective criteria" (territory, common language, culture, etc.) for their claims to nationhood to be regarded as "legitimate" (to be decided by whom??), intelligent materialists should begin by recognizing the reality of national consciousness (whether partly or fully developed) and explore the material realities that have produced that consciousness.

Debates on theory and perspective in the Marxist Left on the black struggle tend to revolve around two models as poles of attraction. This was definitely reflected in the IS experience.

The first of these views the African American population as "overwhelmingly proletarian in composition," including the most heavily exploited part of the working class. The second sees the distinctive historical experience and culture of African Americans as constituting a separate nation (or nationality, depending on how these inexact terms are defined) within the U.S. ("American") nation-state.

In fact, both of these theoretical models capture important parts of reality—yet are inadequate by themselves. Anything close to an adequate theoretical understanding requires a complex synthesis. It is also important to understand how, in U.S. society as a whole, white-supremacist ideology for the first time in history has been officially discredited both in the elite and popular culture, and yet the deep structure of institutional racism remains deeply entrenched.

The relevance of both models has been modified but not negated by developments of the past, say, fifty years. Thus, despite the enormous expansion of a black middle class and openings for African American entrepreneurship, the fundamentally working-class character of the black community is demonstrated by the growing weight of African American workers in the union movement. At the same time, the end of formal segregation has not weakened the desire for African American self-organization.

We have learned that black self-organization, including nationalism, are not to be seen in opposition to the struggle for full equality and integration. They are both aspects of a freedom struggle. This may sound simple enough, but the process of understanding it is not so easy! After all, it is not only white leftists who have trouble getting the point—the greatest U.S. revolutionary of our time, Malcolm X, only in the last few years of his life realized the true significance of the civil rights movement as going far beyond simple integrationist goals, precipitating his break from the separatist-abstentionist sectarianism of the Nation of Islam.

In the U.S. revolutionary Marxist tradition this synthetic understanding was best articulated by the current around C. L. R. James in the course of its complex organizational trajectory in the 1940s through the Trotskyist movement (Socialist Workers Party and Workers Party). Within the WP this view emerged as a minority as against the majority perspective authored by Ernest Rice McKinney, who was a party leader as well as a trade unionist and an important civil rights organizer in his own right.

Prior to the 1940 SWP-WP split McKinney was the first black member of the SWP Political Committee. Hence the theoretical debate took place in both groups over a fairly extended period. The McKinney/WP majority view can be summed up as a struggle for full equality (i.e., a basic democratic demand), to be fought for by means of proletarian struggle and ultimately won through socialist revolution. Thus McKinney saw a natural revolutionary alliance between the black struggle for equality and the newly powerful industrial union movement, which could only come to fruition if the CIO undertook its responsibility to be the champion of all antiracist struggles.

In this context, black nationalism was seen as an understandable, yet backward defensive response to the fact that white workers and the union movement had not taken on their antiracist responsibilities. Nationalism or separatism in itself could accomplish nothing and would only divert the consciousness of any black workers it could influence by aligning them with a dependent and feeble black petit bourgeoisie. (It should be recalled that Henry Ford in particular had enlisted black ministers to use their influence against black support for union organizing.)

James's insight was to recognize that independent black self-organization, arising from the national dynamics of the black struggle, could play not a diversionary but a vanguard role not only for African Americans but for the whole class struggle. (This was seen as a potential arising, for example, from black self-defense against murderous white mobs in the Detroit 1943 riot.) The black working class would play a leadership role in the "American revolution" as both a class and national vanguard.

In this context, recognizing the right of black self-determination became important, including the right of separation as a principle regardless of whether the physical-territorial separation of the black population was seen as desirable or even practical. The McKinney view rejected this position as a diversionary irrelevance. For James it was essential to recognize and uphold the black national struggle against oppression (not only segregation). I think we can apply this understanding to many present-day campaigns around, for example, affirmative action, the demand for reparations for slavery and racial oppression, etc.

The civil rights and black power movements were powerful stimulants to the emergence of the 1960s New Left and the organized socialist currents that developed during the period. It is fair to say that with or without the adoption of formal resolutions, all our currents had recognized the superiority of an approach that embraced the central importance of independent black self-organization. (In the IS experience it must be admitted that a lot of mimeograph ink was spilled in the not particularly successful attempt to figure out whether this actually represented "nationalism" or something else. It is horribly easy to become entangled in debates over abstractions.)

The IS and its predecessor grouping (the Independent Socialist Clubs [ISC]) were clear on a number of key issues: in defense of black power, support of community control of education in New York City against the racist and disastrous Shanker-led teachers' strike there (1969), and principled support for the Black Panther Party. In fact the Berkeley ISC was instrumental in forging an alliance between the Panthers and the Peace and Freedom Party, which should be recounted in more detail.

When the IS formed in 1969 and began discussing industrial union perspectives, we saw the possibility of an alliance with the emerging Panther caucuses and RUM [Revolutionary Union Movement] groups in auto in California and Detroit, respectively. By the time we located ourselves in Detroit and began to get some auto implantation, the obstacles to this hopeful perspective proved to be overwhelming.

The first big problem of course was the weakness and inexperience of our own group. Second, the League of Revolutionary Black Workers (successor of the RUMs) was greatly weakened by its isolation and had undergone a sectarian evolution. Third, the UAW bureaucracy (and corporate management as well) had learned the dangers of black rank-and-file insurgency and had applied its most sophisticated techniques of co-optation and repression. The latter climaxed in 1973 when the Doug Fraser leadership mobilized cadres of union officials with the help of police to smash up a wildcat strike at Mack Avenue, ending a series of plant walkouts over heat, intolerable conditions, and arbitrary discipline. Finally, the recession of 1974–75 wiped out the spirit of militant resistance in the inner-city plants, which frankly has never recovered.

During this same period the IS had to confront the question of school busing and the white backlash against it. This was a hard issue and initially uncomfortable for us, especially for those laboring under certain illusions that putting forward a revolutionary program of "classwide demands" was the road to interracial unity, because busing affected working-class whites while leaving the elites untouched. If nothing else the busing issue brought home the raw realities of white racism in America. . . .

In Detroit and in a new branch we had formed in Louisville, the IS became active in busing defense activities. Comrades who were centrally involved in that work should be encouraged, indeed compelled to write up the experience, which I believe has never really been done to the necessary extent.

Finally, perhaps most important, the mid-1970s IS "turn to agitation" and intensified industrialization effort did actually lead to recruitment of black rank-and-file workers. I have not attempted to check the numbers, but I believe that during this period several dozen black workers passed through the group—not a huge number, but enough to represent a meaningful experience—although most of them briefly. (The number might have been close to one hundred, a figure which probably includes members of our youth group, the Red Tide—though this may be an overestimate.)

The problem was that we mistakenly believed, in keeping with our general expectation of rapid worker radicalization (we failed to realize that the possibility of this had been snuffed out, not accelerated, by the mid-1970s slump), that recruitment of a small number of working class militants would be rapidly followed by others, producing a proletarian transformation of our group. Important note: it wasn't that we didn't want these recruits to be leaders of our organization—indeed, we had illusions about how quickly this could be accomplished, and very little understanding of how to do it.

Instead, workers who joined discovered themselves in an environment pretty much totally alien to their fellow workers, families, and communities—black workers most of all. Our woefully underdeveloped cadre development structures only contributed to their rapid departure.

I believe that there are critical lessons to be learned here both about the possibility of recruiting worker militants, both black and white, and the difficulties of retaining them in what will continue to be a small revolutionary group.

In any case, for the purposes of this informal history, I don't think there is much to be added from the last five or six years of the IS when we were more or less attempting to maintain our work in the unions and a presence in the movements while barely holding ourselves together. I hope that the above history and that of other currents now present in Solidarity can help to inform a discussion of our present tasks.

❋   ❋   ❋

A. PHILIP RANDOLPH INSTITUTE
A FREEDOM BUDGET FOR ALL AMERICANS (1966)

Introduction

The "Freedom Budget" spells out a specific and factual course of action, step by step, to start in early 1967 toward the practical liquidation of poverty in the United States by 1975. The programs urged in the "Freedom Budget" attack *all* of the major causes of poverty—unemployment and underemployment; substandard pay; inadequate social insurance and welfare payments to those who cannot or should not be employed; bad housing; deficiencies in health services, education, and training; and fiscal and monetary policies which tend to redistribute income regressively rather than progressively. The "Freedom Budget" leaves no room for discrimination in any form, because its programs are addressed to *all* who need more opportunity and improved incomes and living standards—not just to some of them. . . .

Why Do We Call This a "Freedom Budget"?

The language evokes the struggle of the civil rights movement, its vision of social justice and equality, its militant determination that these goals be rapidly and forthrightly achieved. This is the vision and determination that underlies the "Freedom Budget" and must propel any genuine war on poverty. The moral issues in this war are no less compelling than those of the battle against racism.

Reprinted by permission from the A. Philip Randolph Institute.

We call this a "Freedom Budget" in recognition that poverty and deprivation, as surely as denial of the right to vote, are erosive of human freedom and democracy. In our affluent nation, even more than in the rest of the world, economic misery breeds the most galling discontent, mocking and undermining faith in political and civil rights. Here in these United States, where there can be no economic nor technological excuse for it, poverty is not only a private tragedy but in a sense a public crime. It is above all a challenge to our morality.

We call this a "Freedom Budget" because it embodies programs which are essential to the Negro and other minority groups striving for dignity and economic security in our society. But their legitimate aspirations cannot be fulfilled in isolation. The abolition of poverty (almost three-quarters of whose U.S. victims are white) can be accomplished only through action which embraces the totality of the victims of poverty, neglect, and injustice. Nor can the goals be won by segmental or ad hoc programs alone; there is need for welding such programs into a unified and consistent program. . . .

In the economic and social realm, no less than in the political, justice too long delayed is justice denied. We propose and insist that poverty can and therefore must be abolished within ten years. . . .

Who, only a few short years ago, would have acknowledged the "political feasibility" of the tremendous legislative victories of the civil rights movement in our own day?

There breakthroughs were not won by those who thought narrowly of what was "politically feasible," but by those who placed the moral issues squarely before the American people. Having stated the issues clearly, they forged a mighty coalition among the civil rights and labor movements, liberal and religious forces, students and intellectuals—the coalition expressed in the historic 1963 March on Washington for Jobs and Freedom.

Social progress is always the trusteeship of those battling constantly to lift the level of "political feasibility." A nation can decay, as all history shows, if the level of "feasibility" is kept too far below what is required to survive and advance. We must ask, not only what is feasible by whom, but also what is needed by whom.

To the full goals of the 1963 march the "Freedom Budget" is dedicated. Within this coalition of conscience the strength must be mobilized for the implementation of this "Freedom Budget" for all Americans.

A. Philip Randolph

The "Freedom Budget" in Brief

Basic Objectives

The seven basic objectives of the "Freedom Budget" are these:

(1) *To restore full employment as rapidly as possible*, and to maintain it thereafter, for all able and willing to work, and for all whom adequate training and education would make able and willing.

(2) *To assure adequate incomes for those employed.*

(3) *To guarantee a minimum adequacy level of income to all those who cannot or should not be gainfully employed.*

(4) *To wipe out the slum ghettos, and provide a decent home for every American family, within a decade.*

(5) *To provide, for all Americans, modern medical care and educational opportunity up to the limits of their abilities and ambitions, at costs within their means.*

(6) *To overcome other manifestations of neglect in the public sector, by purifying our airs and waters, and bringing our transportation systems and natural resource development into line with the needs of a growing population and an expanding economy.*

(7) *To unite sustained full employment with sustained full production and high economic growth.*

The Key Role of our Federal Government

The "Freedom Budget" is a call to action. But the response to this call must take the form of national programs and policies, with the federal government exercising that leadership role which is consistent with our history, our institutions, and our needs. The six prime elements in this federal responsibility are now set forth.

(1) *Beginning with 1967, the President's Economic Reports should embody the equivalent of a "Freedom Budget."* These reports should quantify ten-year goals for full employment and full production, for the practical liquidation of U.S. poverty of 1975, for wiping out the slum ghettos, and indeed for each of the seven basic objectives set forth in the "Freedom Budget."

(2) *The bedrock civilized responsibility rests with our federal government to guarantee sustained full employment.*

(3) *The federal government should exert the full weight of its authority toward immediate enactment of a federal minimum wage of $2.00 an hour, with coverage extended to the uppermost constitutional limits of federal power.*

(4) *A new farm program, with accent upon incomes rather than prices, should focus upon parity of income for farmers and liquidation of farm poverty by 1975.*

(5) *To lift out of poverty and also above deprivation those who cannot or should not be employed, there should be a federally initiated and supported guaranteed annual income, to supplement rather than to supplant a sustained full-employment policy at decent pay.*

(6) *Fiscal and monetary policies should be readjusted to place far more weight upon distributive justice.*

The "Economic Growth Dividend"

We cannot enjoy what we do not produce. The "Freedom Budget" recognizes that all of the goals which it sets must be supported by the output of the U.S. economy. This output should grow greatly from year to year, under policies designed to assure sustained maximum employment, production, and purchasing power in accord with the objectives of the Employment Act of 1946.

The "Freedom Budget" does not contemplate that this "economic growth dividend" be achieved by revolutionary nor even drastic changes in the division of responsibility between private enterprise and government under our free institutions. To illustrate, in 1965, 63.7 percent of our total national production was in the form of private consumer outlays, 16.5 percent in the form of private investment, and 19.8 percent in the form of public outlays at all levels for goods and services. Under the "higher" goals in the "Freedom Budget," these relationships in 1975 would be 63.5 percent, 16.9 percent, and 19.6 percent.

But while the "Freedom Budget" will not be regarded as socialistic, it is indeed socially minded. It insists that we must make deliberate efforts to assure that, through combined private and public efforts, a large enough proportion of this "economic growth dividend" shall be directed toward the great priorities of our national needs: liquidation of private poverty, restoration of our cities, abolition of the slum ghettos, improvement of rural life, and removal of the glaring deficiencies in facilities and services in "the public sector" of our economy. The "Freedom Budget" thus has moral as well as materialistic purposes.

Responsibilities of the Federal Budget

The following table reveals the "Freedom Budget" proposals for the federal budget (measured in 1964 dollars).

These proposals for the federal budget will seem excessive only to those who do not appreciate the growing productive powers of the U.S. economy, under conditions of sustained full employment and full production.

Looked at even more broadly, the whole program set forth in the "Freedom Budget" would not subtract from the income of anyone. It would facilitate progress for practically all, but with accent upon the dictates of the social conscience that those at the bottom of the heap should make relatively the most progress.

	1967 (Actual)		1970		1975	
	Total Bil. $	$ Per Capita	Total Bil. $	$ Per Capita	Total Bil. $	$ Per Capita
All Federal Outlays	104.1	521.79	135.0	645.93	155.0	685.84
National Defense, Space Technology All International	64.6	323.77	77.5	370.82	87.5	387.17
All Domestic Programs	39.5	198.04	57.5	275.12	67.5	298.67
Economic Opportunity Program	1.5	7.39	3.0	14.36	4.0	17.70
Housing and Community Development	0.1	0.57	3.4	16.03	3.8	16.81
Agriculture and Natural Resources	5.9	29.75	10.5	50.24	12.0	53.10
Education	2.6	13.10	7.0	33.49	9.5	42.04
Health Services and Research	3.3	16.74	4.8	22.97	7.0	30.97
Public Assistance; Labor, Manpower, and Other Welfare Services	4.4	21.92	6.6	31.58	7.5	33.18

The Role of the American Negro in the "Freedom Budget"

The "Freedom Budget" Will Benefit All

In one sense the American Negro, relative to his numbers, has an unusually large stake in a "Freedom Budget." When unemployment is excessive, the rate tends to be more than twice as high among Negroes as others. Viewing U.S. multiple-person families in 1964, 37.3 percent of the nonwhites lived in poverty with annual incomes under $3,000, contrasted with only 15.4 percent of the whites. About 14 percent of the nonwhite families had incomes between $1,000 and $2,000, contrasted with 5.4 percent of the whites. And 7.7 percent of the nonwhite families had incomes below $1,000, contrasted with only 2.7 percent of the whites. Among unattached individuals, 52.3 percent of the nonwhites lived in poverty with annual incomes under $1,500, contrasted with 40.5 percent of the whites; and 35.8 percent of the nonwhites were below $1,000, contrasted with 24.4 percent of the whites.

Thus, the only reason why the Negro will benefit relatively more than others from the liquidation of excess unemployment and poverty is not because he is a Negro, but rather because he is at the bottom of the heap.

Aside from this dismal phenomenon, which is a liability rather than an asset to the Negro, others will benefit far more in absolute numbers through achievement of the goals of the "Freedom Budget." There are far more unemployed among whites than among nonwhites. In 1964, 6.6 million white families and 4.2 million white unattached individuals lived in poverty, contrasted with 1.8 million nonwhite families and 0.9 million nonwhite unattached individuals.

The "Freedom Budget" in Relation to Civil Rights

There is an absolute analogy between the crusade for civil rights and liberties and the crusade which the "Freedom Budget" represents. This is because the "Freedom Budget" would achieve the freedom from economic want and oppression, which is the necessary complement to freedom from political and civil oppression. And just as the progress thus far made on the front of civil rights and liberties has immeasurably strengthened the entire American political democracy, so will the "Freedom Budget" strengthen immeasurably our entire economic and social fabric.

The Negro's greatest role on both of these fronts is not as a beneficiary, but rather as a galvanizing force. Out of his unique suffering, he has gone a long way toward awakening the American conscience with respect to civil rights and liberties. The debt which the whole nation owes him will be increased many times, as he helps to win the battle against unemployment and poverty and deprivation.

✳   ✳   ✳

AMIRI BARAKA
THE REVOLUTIONARY TRADITION
IN AFRO-AMERICAN LITERATURE (1984)

Speaking about the general ghettoized condition of Afro-American literature within the framework of so-called American literature, Bruce Franklin, a professor at the Newark branch of Rutgers University, had this to say in the *Minnesota Review*:

Reprinted from *The LeRoi James/Amiri Baraka Reader*, by Amiri Baraka. Copyright © 2000 by Amiri Baraka. Appears here by permission of the publisher, Thunder's Mouth Press.

If we wish to continue to use the term "American Literature," we must either admit that we mean white American literature or construe it to include the literature of several peoples, including the Afro-American nation. The latter course leads to a fundamental redefinition of American literature, its history, and the criteria appropriate to each and every American literary work. For the viewpoint of oppressed people can then no longer be excluded from the criticism and teaching of American literature. . . . The most distinctive feature of United States history is Afro-American slavery and its consequences. This truth is at the heart of our political, economic, and social experience as a nation-state. It is also at the heart of our *cultural* experience, and therefore the slave narrative, like Afro-American culture in general, is not peripheral but central to American culture.

These words are so important because Franklin calls attention to not only the fact that what is called American literature is basically the literature of certain white men, but he also points out the importance to American culture and life itself of Afro-American life and culture in this country. But if we look at the standard history of American literature—Franklin points to the *Literary History of the United States* by Spiller, Thorp, Johnson, Canby, Ludwig, and Gibson, a college standard, in its 4th revised edition in 1974—we find, in its 1,555 pages of small print, four black writers, [Charles W.] Chesnutt, [Paul Laurence] Dunbar, [Langston] Hughes, and [Richard] Wright—and in the section on literature produced by the South during the Civil War, they devote three chapters, and discuss such literary giants as Hugh Legaré, William Wirt, and George Fitzhugh, author of *Cannibals All!* or *Slaves without Masters*. There is no mention of the slave narrative or slave poetry. There is no mention of William Wells Brown, the nineteenth-century black novelist and playwright. They do not even mention Frederick Douglass!! So we must face the essential national chauvinism of what is taught as American literature, even the "white part" of it, so that in many instances the anthologies and survey courses that we learn literature from are the choice of or have been influenced to a great extent by some of the most reactionary elements in American society. We have been raised up in literature too often on right-wing anthologies and the standards of right-wing critics, pushing conservative and reactionary literature, playing down progressive and revolutionary forces, and almost outright excluding oppressed nationalities and minorities and women.

It was the rebellions of the sixties, explosions in 110 U.S. cities, that created the few black studies and Afro-American studies departments that exist today. At the same time, these uprisings created the agonizingly small space that Afro-American literature takes up in the canon of academic and commercial written culture. A few authors got "walk-on" roles, to paraphrase Franklin again.

First we must understand the basic distortion that is given to all American literary history and official reflections of American life and culture. This is obviously because the literary establishment, and the academic establishment, far from being independent, represent in the main the ideas and worldview of the rulers of this country. These ideas, and the institutions from which they are mashed on us, constitute merely the superstructure of this society, a superstructure that reflects the economic foundations upon which it is built, the material base for U.S. life and culture, monopoly capitalism. So that in the main what is taught and pushed as great literature, or great art, philosophy, etc., are mainly ideas and concepts that can help maintain the status quo, which includes not only the exploitation of the majority by a capitalist elite, but also national oppression, racism, the oppression of women, and the extension of U.S. imperialism all over the world.

Afro-American literature as it has come into view, fragmented by chauvinism and distorted by the same reactionary forces that have distorted American literature itself, has indeed been laid out in the same confusing and oblique fashion. A method intended to hide more than it reveals, a method that wants to show that at best Afro-American literature is a mediocre, and conservative, reflection of the mediocre and conservative portrait that is given of all American literature.

In Afro-American literature for instance we have been taught that its beginnings rest with the writings of people like Phyllis Wheatley and Jupiter Hammon. Ms. Wheatley writing in the eighteenth century is simply an imitator of Alexander Pope. It was against the law for black slaves to learn to read or write, so Ms. Wheatley's writings could only come under the "Gee whiz, it's alive" category of Dr. Frankenstein checking out his new monster! Also Wheatley's writing abounds with sentiments like "Twas mercy brought me from my pagan land," evincing gratitude in slavery—that the European slave trade had actually helped the Africans by exposing them to great European culture: which be the monster remarking how wise, how omniscient be her creator!

Hammon is, if possible, even worse. In his stiff doggerel are such great ideas as slavery was good for us Africans because it taught us humility—so when we get to heaven we'll know how to act around God. Pretty far out! (Both were privileged Northern house servants reflecting both their privilege and their removal and isolation from the masses of African/Afro-American slaves.)

But these two are pushed as Afro-American literature simply as a method of showing off trained whatnots demonstrating the glory of the trainer. But this is not the beginnings of Afro-American literature as a genre.

The black people of this country were brought here in slavery chains on the ships of rising European capitalism. It is impossible to separate the rise of capitalism, the industrial revolution, the emergence of England and later America as world powers, from the trade in Africans. And from their initial presence as commodities initiating world trade through the triangular trade route of slaves to the New World, raw materials to England, and manufactured goods to Africa for the African feudal ruling class who had sold the other Africans into slavery, black life has contributed to and animated Anglo-American life and culture. But a formal, artifact-documented presence could easily be denied slaves. African culture was banned by the slave masters as *subversive*. Christianity was used first as a measure of civilization (if you weren't a Christian you weren't civilized—the papal bull states, it's cool to enslave non-Christians) but later it was used as a pacifier and agency for social control (its present function). The development of a *specifically* Afro-American culture must wait for the emergence of the Afro-American people, the particular nationality composed of Africans transformed by the fact and processes of slavery into an American people of African descent.

The most practical artifacts of that culture are the tools and environment of day-to-day living. In these practical pursuits are found the earliest Afro-American art—artifactual reflections of the life of that people. Music, because it is most abstract and could not therefore be so severely limited and checked by slave culture, must be the earliest of the "nonpractical" arts to emerge (although a work song is to help one work!): the work song, chants, hollers, the spiritual, eventually the blues.

Afro-American literature rises as a reflection of the self-conscious self-expression of the Afro-American people, but to be an Afro-American literature, truly, it must reflect, in the main, the ideological and sociocultural portrait of that people! The Wheatleys and Hammons reflect the ideology of Charlie McCarthy in relationship to Edgar Bergen. (Is that before anybody's time?)

The celebration of servitude is not the ideological reflection of the Afro-American masses, but of their tormentors.

In the slave narratives, the works of Frederick Douglass, Henry Bibb, Moses Roper, Linda Brent, William Wells Brown, the Krafts, Henry "Box" Brown, and others, Solomon Northrup, James Pennington, etc., are found the beginnings of a genuine Afro-American written literature. Here are the stirring narratives of slave America, the exploits and heroism of resistance and escape, the ongoing struggle and determination of that people to be free. Beside this body of strong, dramatic, incisive, democratic literature where is the literature of the slavemasters and -mistresses? Find it and compare it with the slave narratives and say which has a clearer, more honest, and ultimately more artistically powerful perception of American reality! (Yes, there are William Gilmore Simms, John Pendleton Kennedy, Augustus B. Longstreet, and George Washington Harris, touted as outstanding writers of the white, slave South.) But their writing is unreadable, even though overt racists like Allen Tate and the Southern Agrarians prated about the slave South as a "gracious culture despite its defects." Those defects consisted in the main of millions of black slaves, whose life expectancy at maturity by the beginning of the nineteenth century in the Deep South was seven years. One of the main arguments, as Bruce Franklin points out in *The Victim as Criminal and Artist*, for black slavery was that the blacks could do the manual labor "for which they were best suited . . . leaving their owners free to create a fine, elegant, and lasting culture" (28). But check it out. At best such artistic efforts representing this so-called lasting culture are embarrassing satires, the efforts of the Southern Agrarians to represent them as something else notwithstanding.

The slave narratives are portraits of a people in motion, and they come into being as creations of the economic, social, and political life of the United States. The early part of the nineteenth century was marked by an intensification of slavery and by the taking away of the limited civil rights of free blacks as well. This was because slavery did not die out toward the end of the eighteenth century as was predicted. With the creation of the cotton gin, to the feudalistic or patriarchal slavery imposed on blacks was now added capitalist exploitation. Karl Marx points out in *Capital* that once cotton became an international commodity, no longer used only in U.S. domestic markets, blacks were not only tied for life to domestic slavery, but now had added to their inhuman burden the horrors of having to produce *surplus value*, as a kind of slave and proletarian in combination. The seven-year life expectancy came about "down river" in the Black Belt cotton region because the slavemasters discovered that working slaves to death and then replacing them was more profitable than letting them live to grow old, less productive but still eating, wearing clothes, and taking up space!

This period of intense repression is when Afro-American literature emerges. It is also the period when the resistance of the Afro-American people intensifies. It is now that Gabriel Prosser, Denmark Vesey, Nat Turner, lead their uprisings and rebellions, and Harriet Tubman develops the Underground Railway.

At the approach of the Civil War, there is also another strong movement in Afro-American literature, the pre–Civil War revolutionary black nationalists: David Walker, the activists Henry Highland Garnet, Charles Lenox Remond, C. H. Langston, as well as William Wells Brown, an escaped slave who became the first black playwright and novelist. It is a literature sparked by protest, an anti-slavery literature, a fighting oral literature, that even when it was written was meant to be proclaimed from the lecterns and pulpits of the North and circulated secretly to inspire the black slaves in the South. These were black abolitionists, damning slavery in no uncertain terms, proclaiming death to slavery, and calling for rebellion from the slaves. This was not upper-class white abolitionism, morally outraged but politically liberal. (The most genuine of the white abolitionists was John Brown—he knew what to do about slavery, wage armed struggle against it!) These were black revolutionists, some like Langston even calling for black people to seize the land they toiled upon because it was only that land that provided a practical basis for the survival and development of the Afro-American people!

Usually in discussing Afro-American literature, teachers of literature combine the Wheatleys and Hammons with perhaps Douglass's narrative, and maybe

Brown's novel *Clotel*. The other slave narratives and the pre–Civil War black revolutionary nationalists are largely ignored or their importance diminished. Charles Chesnutt, who lamented that quality black folks had to be lumped together with the ignorant black masses, is pushed as a kind of father of black literature. Next, Paul Laurence Dunbar and James Weldon Johnson are raised to the top rank, but an analysis of the content of these men's works is made vague or one-sided. We are not aware perhaps that for all the positive elements of Dunbar's work, his use of dialect, which is positive insofar as it is the language of the black masses, is negative in the way that Dunbar frequently uses it only in the context of parties, eating, and other "coonery." Most of Dunbar's "serious" poetry is not in dialect.

Dunbar was deeply conservative, and his short story "The Patience of Gideon" shows a young slave, Gideon, who is put in charge of the plantation as the massa goes off to fight the Civil War. Gideon stays despite the masses of slaves running away as soon as massa leaves. Even Gideon's wife-to-be pleads with him to leave, but he will not. He has made a promise to massa, and so even his woman leaves him, alone with his promise to the slavemaster.

J. W. Johnson's quandary was how to create a "high art" out of Afro-American materials, not completely understanding that "high art" is by definition slavemaster, bourgeois art and that what was and is needed by all artists, or by those artists who intend for their works to serve the exploited and oppressed majority in this country, is that they be artistically powerful and politically revolutionary!

Johnson's *Autobiography of an Ex-Colored Man* tells of that quandary in social terms, with his protagonist existing in a never-never land between black and white and finally deciding because he is shamed and humiliated and horrified by the lynching of a black man that he cannot be a member of a race so disgraced. He disappears among the whites, forsaking art for commerce, pursuing the white lady of his heart!

The real giant of this period, the transitional figure, the connector between nineteenth-century Reconstruction and the new literary giants of the twentieth century and the Harlem Renaissance, is W. E. B. Du Bois. His *Souls of Black Folk*, which issued an ideological challenge to the capitulationist philosophy of Booker T. Washington, is the intellectual and spiritual forerunner of the writings of the renaissance. Du Bois's *Black Reconstruction* remains the most important work on the Reconstruction period done by an American. He was a social scientist, historian, as well as novelist, poet, and political activist. He founded black theatrical troupes like Krigwa Players, organized international conferences of black activists as leader of the Pan-Africanist movement, led social movements in the United States like the Niagara Movement and the NAACP, was a fighting literary editor, and his works of historical and sociological analysis are among the greatest written by an American. He studied and wrote about all aspects of black life and its connection with Africa and the slave trade. He was a socialist by 1910, and at the end of his life, inspired by and inspiring the African Independence movements, residing in Nkrumah's Ghana, he became a communist. It is not possible to understand the history of ideas in the United States without reading Du Bois. Not to know his work is not to have a whole picture of Afro-American literature, sociology, history, and struggle and is to have a distorted view of American life in general.

Langston Hughes's manifesto, "The Negro Artist and the Racial Mountain" (1926), is not possible without Du Bois and his total rejection of American racial paternalism and cultural aggression. The Harlem Renaissance is simply the flowering of a twentieth-century Afro-American intelligentsia reflecting the motion of black people in America. It reflects a peasant people in motion out of the South toward the urban North to serve as cheap labor (a developing proletariat) for the developing U.S. imperialism cut off from its European immigrants by the coming of World War I. It is a literature of the new city dwellers having left their rural pasts. It is a literature of revolt, it is anti-imperialist, and fights the cultural aggression that imperialism visits upon its colonial and nationally oppressed conquests—first by reflecting and proclaiming the beauty and strengths of the oppressed people themselves. By showing the lives of the people themselves in all its rawness, deprivation, and ugliness. By showing them to themselves. It is a revolutionary nationalist literature at its strongest, especially the works of Claude McKay and Langston Hughes. It reflects the entrance into the twentieth century of Afro-American people and the United States in general. It is the sensibility of the Afro-American nation that developed after the destruction of the Reconstruction governments (and the period of Reconstruction was the most democratic period in U.S. life)—the sensibility that survived the dark repression of the 1880s and 1890s, when the northern industrial capitalists no longer needed blacks to stabilize the South while the Wall Street conquerors stripped the southern plantation aristocrats of economic and political independence, so now the northern capitalists sold blacks back into near slavery with the Hayes-Tilden Compromise of 1876, to crush black political life with the Ku Klux Klan lynching, the black codes, segregation, and outright fascism!

The Harlem Renaissance influenced black culture worldwide, but it all reflected the fact that all over the world, oppressed nations and colonial peoples were intensifying their struggle against imperialism. In Haiti, where the United States invaded in 1915, there was the *Indigisme* movement; in Puerto Rico it was called *Negrissmo*, in Paris, Senghor, Cesaire, and Damas called it *Negritude* and cited McKay and Hughes as their chief influences!

One aspect of the Harlem Renaissance in the "Roaring Twenties" as part of "the Jazz Age" was the stirring anti-imperialism—another part (showing how the bourgeoisie tries to transform everything to its own use) was the cult of exoticism and commercializers and, often pathological, bourgeois "patrons" of the "New Negro" made of this cultural outpouring. This was the period, Hughes said, when "the Negro was in vogue."

But by the beginning of the thirties, after the crash of 1929 and the Great Depression—only one of many cyclical recessions, the bust part of the boom-bust cycle pointing toward the eventual destruction of capitalism—the exotic part of the renaissance was over. The philanthropists turned to other pursuits and, just as in factories where blacks are the last hired and the first fired, the literary flowering as manifested by American publishers came to an end!

In the Depression thirties the revolutionary ideas of the Russian Bolsheviks, of Marx, Engels, Lenin, and Stalin, had enormous influence on U.S. intellectuals. It was apparent that capitalism could not solve the problems of the exploited majority, let alone of black people, and that the U.S. bourgeoisie was unfit to rule society. Black writers also show this influence, mostly as it was transmitted by the *then* revolutionary Communist Party USA [CPUSA]. The works of Hughes and McKay especially show this influence, and even though Hughes later copped out before the inquisitors of the HUAC [House Un-American Activities Committee], a collection of his thirties writings, *Good Morning, Revolution*, is must reading to get at his really powerful works.

Richard Wright was one of the most publicized and skilled black writers of the 1930s and 1940s. His early works, *Uncle Tom's Children, Native Son, Black Boy*, including the long-suppressed section of his book called *American Hunger*, are among the most powerful works written by any American writer of the period. Wright was, even more than Hughes, influenced by Marxist-Leninist ideology, though Wright's individualism and idealism finally sabotaged him. He joined the CPUSA when he got to Chicago. (He came in from the John Reed Club, an anti-imperialist writers' organization. And if one believes *American Hunger*, the careerist aspects of this move, getting his early works published by the Communists, etc., are not insubstantial.) Wright had just come from Memphis when he joined and he remained a member of the CPUSA until 1944. It was at this point ironically that the CP, burdened by opportunist reactionary leadership, sold out the black liberation movement by liquidating the correct revolutionary slogans "Liberation for the black nation! Self-determination for the Afro-American nation in the Black Belt South!" The CP even liquidated itself, temporarily becoming the Communist Political Association, "a nonparty movement following the ideals of Washington, Jefferson, Lincoln, and Tom Paine." But Wright's individualism and petit bourgeois vacillation had begun to isolate him from the party years before, though the errors and opportunism of CP leadership must be pointed out.

Many of the Left, anti-imperialist, revolutionary, Marxist, and even pro-Soviet ideas that grew to such prominence in the thirties were sustained into the forties because the United States by then had joined a united front with the Soviet Union against fascism. But by the fifties U.S. world dominance (which was enhanced by the fact of its emerging unscathed from World War II) dictated that it launch a cold war against the Soviet Union to try to dominate a world market. World War II had allowed the insurgent colonial peoples to grow even stronger as the imperialists fought each other, and in 1949 the Chinese communists declared the People's Republic of China. This occasioned an attempted blockade and isolation of China as well by the United States and resulted in the Korean "police action." This was accompanied by intense ideological repression inside the United States itself, as McCarthyism emerged: the modern capitalist inquisition to purge all Left and Marxist and anti-imperialist influences from American intellectual life!

Hughes copped out before HUAC, said he would not do it again, and told James Eastland that all U.S. citizens had equality. A tragedy! Wright fled to France and became an existentialist. Another event with tragic overtones. Du Bois was indicted as an agent of a foreign power and went abroad for an extended period. Robeson was persecuted and driven to his death as Jackie Robinson testified against him at HUAC. Powerful writers like Theodore Ward were covered with mountains of obscurity.

With the defection of the CPUSA to reformism, culminating in its 1957 pronouncement that it was now seeking socialism via the ballot in a "peaceful transition to socialism" and that the road to socialism was integration not revolution, the late 1940s and the 1950s were marked by a "reevaluation" of Wright's works. Both James Baldwin and Ralph Ellison spuriously condemned protest literature, and the general tone put out by well-published "spokespersons for black people" was that it was time to transcend the "limitations" of race and that Afro-American writing should disappear into the mainstream like *Lost Boundaries*. Baldwin of course later refutes his own arguments by becoming a civil rights spokesman and activist, and by the sixties with *Blues for Mr. Charlie* he had even begun to question the nonviolent, passive pseudorevolution put forward by the black bourgeoisie through its most articulate spokesman, Dr. Martin Luther King. And this is exactly the point in time when Ralph Ellison is put forward by the bourgeoisie as the most notable Afro-American writer!

Ralph Ellison's *Invisible Man* was the classic work of the fifties in restating and shifting the direction of Afro-American literature. The work puts down both nationalism and Marxism, and opts for *individualism*. This ideological content couched in the purrs of an obviously elegant technique was important in trying to steer Afro-American literature away from protest, away from the revolutionary concerns of the 1930s and early 1940s, and this primarily is the reason this work and its author are so valued by the literary and academic establishments in this country. Both Ellison and Baldwin wrote essays dismissing or finding flaws in Wright's ultimate concern in his best work.

But the fifties civil rights movement was also superseded by the people's rapid intensification of the struggle in the sixties, and black literature like everything else was quick to show this. Malcolm X emerged to oppose the black bourgeois line of nonviolent passive resistance, which duplicates the reformist anti-Marxists of the CPUSA in their "nonviolent transition to socialism." Where the black bourgeoisie had dominated the black liberation movement in the fifties with the aid of the CPUSA and the big capitalists themselves, in the sixties Malcolm X came forward articulating the political line of the black majority, self-determination, self-respect, and self-defense, and struggled out in the open against the civil rights line of the black bourgeoisie, who could see black people beaten and spit on and bombed in churches, and whose only retaliation would be to kneel in the dust and pray.

Just as Malcolm's influence turned the entire civil rights movement around, for example, the student movement, which was SNCC, to the militance of Stokely Carmichael and Rap Brown, so the whole movement changed radically. The black bourgeoisie were no longer in control of the movement, and from civil rights we were talking next about self-defense, and then after Rap Brown about rebellion, to revolution itself.

All these moves were reflected by black literature, and they are fundamentally movements and thrusts by the people themselves, that the literature bears witness to and is a reflector of. The black arts movement of the sixties basically wanted to reflect the rise of the militancy of the black masses as represented by Malcolm X. Its political line, at its most positive, was that literature must be a weapon of revolutionary struggle, that it must serve the black revolution. And its writers, Askia Muhammad Toure, Larry Neal, Clarence Reed, Don Lee, Sonia Sanchez, Carolyn Rodgers, Welton Smith, Marvin X, Henry Dumas, Gaston Neal, Clarence Franklin, Ben Caldwell, Ed Bullins, Ron Milner, Mari Evans, etc., its publications, its community black arts theaters, its manifestos and activism, were meant as real manifestations of black culture—black art as a weapon of liberation.

On the negative side, the black arts movement, without the guidance of a scientific revolutionary organization, a Marxist-Leninist communist party, was like the black liberation movement itself, left with spontaneity. It became embroiled in cultural nationalism, bourgeois nationalism, substituting mistrust and hatred of white people for scientific analysis of the real enemies of black people, until by the middle seventies a dead end had been reached that could only be surmounted by a complete change of worldview, ideology.

It is my view that this is exactly what is going on today in many places in the country. Afro-American literature is going through the quantitative changes necessary to make its qualitative leap back into the revolutionary positivism of the 1930s and the positive aspect of the black arts 1960s. For certain, the literature will always be a reflection of what the people themselves are, as well as a projection of what they struggle to become. The Afro-American nation is an oppressed nation, and its people, whether in the Black Belt land base of that nation or as an oppressed nationality spread out around the rest of the nation-state, still face a revolutionary struggle. That nation is still oppressed by imperialism, and its liberation and self-determination can only be gained through revolution. The next wave of Afro-American literature, of a genuine people's literature, will dramatically record this.

* * *

BLACK PANTHER PARTY
THE BLACK PANTHER MANIFESTO (1966)

1. *We want freedom. We want power to determine the destiny of our black community.* We believe that black people will not be free until we are able to determine our destiny.

2. *We want full employment for our people.* We believe that the federal government is responsible and obligated to give every man employment or a guaranteed income. We believe that if the white American businessman will not give full employment, then the means of production should be taken from the businessmen and placed in the community so that the people of the community can organize and employ all of its people and give a high standard of living.

3. *We want an end to the robbery by the CAPITALIST of our black community.* We believe that this racist government has robbed us and now we are demanding the overdue debt of forty acres and two mules. Forty acres and two mules was promised one hundred years ago as restitution for slave labor and mass murder of black people. We will accept the payment in currency which will be distributed to our many communities. The Germans are now aiding the Jews in Israel for the genocide of the Jewish people. The Germans murdered six million Jews. The American racist has taken part in the slaughter of over fifty million black people, therefore, we feel that this is a modest demand that we make.

4. *We want decent housing, fit for shelter of human beings.* We believe that if the white landlords will not give decent housing to our black community, then the housing and the land should be made into cooperatives so that our community, with government aid, can build and make decent housing for its people.

5. *We want education for our people that exposes the true nature of this decadent American society. We want education that teaches us our true history*

Reprinted by permission from the Dr. Huey P. Newton Foundation.

and our role in the present-day society. We believe in an educational system that will give to our people a knowledge of self. If a man does not have knowledge of himself and his position in society and the world, then he has little chance to relate to anything else.

6. *We want all black men to be exempt from military service.* We believe that black people should not be forced to fight in the military service to defend a racist government that does not protect us. We will not fight and kill other people of color in the world who, like black people, are being victimized by the white racist government of America. We will protect ourselves from the force and violence of the racist police and the racist military, by whatever means necessary.

7. *We want an immediate end to POLICE BRUTALITY and MURDER of black people.* We believe we can end police brutality in our black community by organizing black self-defense groups that are dedicated to defending our black community from racist police oppression and brutality. The Second Amendment to the Constitution of the United States gives a right to bear arms. We therefore believe that all black people should arm themselves for self-defense.

8. *We want freedom for all black men held in federal, state, county and city prisons and jails.* We believe that all black people should be released from the many jails and prisons because they have not received a fair and impartial trial.

9. *We want all black people when brought to trial to be tried in court by a jury of their peer group or people from their black communities, as defined by the Constitution of the United States.* We believe that the courts should follow the U.S. Constitution so that black people will receive fair trials. The Fourteenth Amendment of the U.S. Constitution gives a man a right to be tried by his peer group. A peer is a person from a similar economic, social, religious, geographical, environmental, historical, and racial background. To do this the court will be forced to select a jury from the black community from which the black defendant came. We have been, and are being tried by all-white juries that have no understanding of the "average reasoning man" of the black community.

10. *We want land, bread, housing, education, clothing, justice, and peace. And as our major political objective, a United Nations–supervised plebiscite to be held throughout the black colony in which only black colonial subjects will be allowed to participate, for the purpose of determining the will of black people as to their national destiny.* When, in the course of human events, it becomes necessary for one people to dissolve the political bands which have connected them with another, and to assume, among the powers of the earth, the separate and equal station to which the laws of nature and nature's God entitle them, a decent respect to the opinions of mankind requires that they should declare the causes which impel them to the separation.

We hold these truths to be self-evident, that all men are created equal; that they are endowed by their Creator with certain inalienable rights; that among these are life, liberty, and the pursuit of happiness. *That, to secure these rights, governments are instituted among men, deriving their just powers from the consent of the governed; that, whenever any form of government becomes destructive of these ends, it is the right of the people to alter or to abolish it, and to institute a new government, laying its foundation on such principles, and organizing its powers in such form, as to them shall seem most likely to effect their safety and happiness.* Prudence, indeed, will dictate that governments long established should not be changed for light and transient causes; and, accordingly, all experience hath shown, that mankind are more disposed to suffer, while evils are sufferable, than to right themselves by abolishing the forms to which they are accustomed. *But, when a long train of abuses and usurpations, pursuing invariably the same object, evinces a design to reduce them under absolute despotism, it is their right, it is their duty, to throw off such government, and to provide new guards for their future security.*

* * *

LEAGUE OF REVOLUTIONARY BLACK WORKERS
GENERAL POLICY STATEMENT, LABOR HISTORY, AND THE LEAGUE'S LABOR PROGRAM (1971)

As the betrayal of blacks became more of a reality, and capitalism became entrenched in the society, white labor became more outrageous. Strikes were numerous and most of them were against the hiring of black workers. Observe the following list of strikes from 1882 to 1900. . . . [The list shows over eighty strikes of "white" workers against the hiring of black workers, against being "forced" to work with black workers, calling for the firing of black workers, etc.]

Aside from the fact that white workers were racist, we can't ignore the fact that the rise of imperialism worked hand in glove with buttressing the demands of the white labor. In essence, white workers had the following ideals:

American labor talked of spiritualism of labor; talked of merging labor with the rising monopoly class, the class that was brutally exploiting blacks, whites, and the world; spoke for the annexation of other territories.

This was the level of consciousness of the white worker and many times their leaders; he ignored slavery, refused to acknowledge the blacks as vanguard in struggles, fought for expansion of slavery and concomitant to this, worked hand in hand for the rise of imperialism.

It's important to understand that the move by America to annex Santo

Reprinted from *Inner-City Voice* (the official organ of the League of Revolutionary Black Workers) 3 (February 1971): 10–12.

Domingo, Philippines, and other places enhanced the polarization between black and white workers. The support of the capitalist system by the white worker granted them certain privileges that blacks were and still are denied. . . .

The one outstanding factor at this point is that as long as white workers think of themselves as white workers or white middle or lower class, they will be counter to the struggle, and will retain white consciousness as opposed to class consciousness. To think in those terms means a struggle for the decaying privileges that buttress the system of racism and exploitation instead of for the liberation of all working people.

It is without question that white labor will be forced to shift gears. Currently, however, the liberation struggle of blacks is moving at a quickening pace. It is our contention that the key to the black liberation struggle lies with the black workers.

As previously stated, the black liberation struggle is part and parcel of a world struggle of the oppressed against the oppressor. However, we must carefully scrutinize which groups in the struggle are the most important in changing a society and stopping its functioning the way it is. That is the group most able, due to their position in production, to lead and carry on the revolutionary struggle.

We say black workers, but this group must be defined better. There are many "workers" among our people, like small shop owners, professionals, service workers, and also the factory and mine workers. It is the latter group that we speak of as the backbone of the revolutionary forces. Specifically the mine and factory workers, because they do the jobs that grant the most profits to capitalists, the ruling class.

Auto plants, mine companies, chemical corporations, steel, aluminum, etc., all make their billions at the expense of foundry, assembly, etc., workers, all of whom work for far below the wages they should get in relation to work done and, in fact, do most of their work so the owners can pocket the profits.

These blacks comprise the majority of the workers among the black working class. It is also significant to note that this class is the most organized group. The organization of black labor dates back to the late 1860s and early 1870s, as a direct result of manipulative use by the monopoly capitalist class of white labor's racism.

Aside from numbers, organization, viability, and strength, this group (along with all workers in the plants and mines) is in direct conflict with the owners of the means of production. Just as the peasant in South America, the black mine worker in Africa, the worker in Europe, are the backbones of production in their countries, blacks have been and still are, the backbone of exploitative labor in this country. . . .

Overall Position of Black Workers

Even based on government statistics, the position of the black worker in the labor force is clear. In 1970 the total civilian labor force was approximately 84,617,000 with a total black force of 9,560,000 or 10.1 percent of the total labor force. The total labor force represents a 59.6 percent participation rate by the entire white population and a 62.4 percent participation rate by the total black population.

Unemployed statistics show that there are 2,214,000 or 3.1 percent of the white labor force out of work as compared to 523,000 or 6.1 percent of the black labor force out of work.

In concluding the findings of these tables we state that black workers make up a significant section of the reserve army of the unemployed and that the rate of unemployed among black workers is twice as high as that amongst whites. The labor participation rate percentage categories demonstrate that blacks as a people, are more of an integral part of the proletariat than whites and would even have a greater labor participation rate if jobs were not so hard for blacks to find.

Tables further indicate that black workers are disproportionately located in blue-collar and service-worker positions. In blue-collar positions black workers are mainly operatives and laborers working on the hottest, dirtiest, and most dangerous jobs. In this category black workers comprise 23 percent or nearly one-quarter of all positions. Figures fail to present an adequate picture in the industries and plants like Dodge Main, Eldon Avenue, Ford Rouge, etc., black workers make up 70 to 85 percent of the workforce and have the ability to bring all production to a halt, by methods of closing down the hot dirty foundries, steel mills, and production plants. Whites working in the operatives and laborer category are able to gain the fruits of their white-skinned privileged positions by being placed in the easiest jobs such as stock chasing, transportation, and light assembly positions, leaving black workers to make up only 3.1 percent of all apprenticeship positions, which is directly related to the lack of upward mobility from the operative blue-collar sector. In the skilled-trades sector black workers once again are heavily concentrated in dirty, hard positions; they comprise 12.3 percent of all masons, tilesetters, and stonecutters, 22.8 percent of all plasterers, lathers, and cement finishers placing them at the bottom of the building trades. Black workers make up 23.8 percent of all furnacemen, smelters, and pourers, and 25 percent of all metal molders are found in the smog and polluted air of the foundries.

To the contrary, the percentage of white craftsmen and foremen is double that of blacks and a definite product of white-skinned privilege which degrades black workers, especially in the area of promotions.

One half of the white working force is employed in white-collar positions, as compared to one quarter of the black working population. But even in these categories [blacks] perform the hardest and steady physical work; 11 percent of black workers in this sector are tied to low clerical positions categorized by low pay and constant physical work. Black workers are employed to such a degree in the clerical sector that, once again, they are essential to many industries and have the power also to bring all work to a standstill.

In the service sector black workers are employed three times to the degree of whites and have a near monopoly in household services. Whites working the service sector enjoy the luxuries of homes of the ruling class barons and earn lucrative salaries for their services; mainly the management and overseeing of black service workers.

In the farm-worker sector, black workers perform mainly the migrant employment categorized by next to slave wages and subhuman living conditions by the families of those involved. While whites in this sector are mainly owners of the land and the farm products being produced.

The tables finally show that black workers are systematically excluded from all decision-making positions—judges, lawyers, and administrators and are left virtually in a powerless position not only in industry on the job, but also at home in the black community. Black workers find themselves as paupers as the white-skinned privilege outside the places of work takes the form of white racist domination in order to maintain the resolute privileged position occupied by white racist, antiblack, and backward administrators who only carry out those policies which are in opposition to the interests of blacks.

Because of the positions which blacks occupy as workers, which are characterized generally by hard work and low pay, they are forced into a position of perpetual suffering, economically. The wives of black workers are very often forced to take extra employment in order to meet basic family needs.

Economic Situation of Black Workers

Categories in which white workers are heavily concentrated are areas of highest pay and power. Professional positions, categories in which whites are employed heavily, represent the areas of highest pay. Management and skilled positions in which whites are employed up to five times the degree of blacks, also, are the recipients of high pay scales.

In comparison, the economic position of black workers, in their areas of highest concentration, blue-collar service, lower clerical and farm workers, represent the lowest position of the wage scale. The combination of the dual oppression of black workers of the hardest, dirtiest jobs, and at the same time, receiving the lowest pay, has had the effect of raising their political consciousness more and more to the point of open class war at the point of production. The struggle of black workers has been systematically stifled by the overall political economy of poverty. The ruling class has systematically dressed up the realities under which black workers live. Through constant streams of propaganda, in the form of advertisements, they have been able to some degree, to foster false hopes and dreams in the minds of black workers. The educational system has perpetuated false notions in terms of understanding the fundamental characteristics of life under monopoly capitalism.

Both the unions and the companies have denied blacks the knowledge of the fundamentals for organizing techniques and propaganda skills, which has fostered strong feelings of individualism and personal gain.

The ruling class has acted as though it was seriously addressing itself to the problem of black workers by extending its rolls of nonproductive employees in order to have more troops to dupe the already confused and unorganized black workers. The companies have created hard-core programs and backed certain community organizations and propagandized heavily about them via the mass media. They have mixed repressive techniques with soft-lined measures in order to crush and stifle rebellion simultaneously. Many reform groups and civil rights organizations have attempted to gain purely economic reforms without addressing the importance of the political economy of poverty. The monopoly capitalist class has to maintain a system of strict poverty domestically. It cannot afford to spend the billions of dollars thrown away annually on imperialist wars here, at home, for fear of it changing the objective power relationships between itself and the proletariat. During a few lucrative months during 1966, before the rising inflationary prices and high taxes had begun to deplete the wage gains of workers, it became necessary for many companies to stop paying afternoon-shift workers on Thursday, which has been a long ago established standard, because over half of the workers would not come to work the following Friday. Once black workers had earned enough to meet their immediate objective necessities, the extra day gave them time to explore organizing methods or hire organizers to buy guns which they, in turn, could use in their struggles against the ruling class.

The monopoly corporations have placed great emphasis on the political aspect of the economy of poverty. They have done everything possible except slow down the level of production and raise the economic level of workers, which is the reality which has sparked class struggle amongst black workers inside basic industry.

So that reality still exists, black workers are the main producers in this society. It is the bare hands of black workers which turn raw materials into finished products. They are transforming those raw materials far out of proportion to what statistics show they are producing in increasingly greater numbers as production becomes harder and faster. Black workers are toiling under more and more severe working conditions while black children and wives go hungry because of the low wages, inflationary prices, and increased taxes. They exist as the most oppressed and exploited section of the proletariat and have the power to bring all of industry to a screeching halt. Their only hope can be seen through open class war and the potential of carrying out a Black General Strike, which would bring the entire U.S. productive capacity and its monopoly capitalist owners to their demise.

* * *

ANGELA Y. DAVIS
BLACK NATIONALISM: THE SIXTIES AND THE NINETIES (1991)

Initially, I had planned to discuss masculinist dimensions of black nationalism and cultural challenges to male supremacy in the work of the Blueswomen, since my current work revolves around ways of retrieving possible cultural histories of African American women. But my preliminary reflections on the kindred character of black nationalism(s) and ideologies of male dominance during the sixties led me to consider an autobiographical approach. Therefore, I will attempt to revisit my own experience with the nationalisms of the sixties and to suggest ways in which contemporary black popular culture may have been unduly influenced by some of the more unfortunate ideological convergences of that era.

I begin with some thoughts on the impact of Malcolm X's nationalist oratory on my own political awakening, which I would later think of in terms similar to Frantz Fanon's description of the coming to consciousness of the colonized in *The Wretched of the Earth.*

I remember the moment when I first felt the stirrings of "nationalism" in my—as I might have articulated it then—"Negro Soul." This *prise de conscience* occurred during a lecture delivered by Malcolm X at Brandeis University, where I was one of five or six black undergraduates enrolled. I might have said that I felt "empowered" by Malcolm's words—except that the notion of power had not yet been understood in a way that separated the exercise of power from the subjective emotions occasioned by an awareness of the possibility of exercising it. But I recall that I felt extremely good—I could even say I experienced that joy that Cornel West talked about—momentarily surrounded by, feeling nurtured and caressed by black people who, as I recall, seemed to have no particular identity other than that they were black.

This invitation to join an empowering, but abstract community of black people—this naïve nationalist consciousness—was extended to me in a virtually all-white setting. It was a strange, but quite logical, reversal. Having grown up in one of the most segregated cities in the South, I had never personally known a white person in my hometown. The only one with whom I remember having any contact was the Jewish man who owned the grocery store in our neighborhood. White people lived across the street from my family's house, but we literally lived on the border separating black from white and could not cross the street on which our house was located. Because of the mandatory character of the black community in which I grew up, I came to experience it as somewhat suffocating and desperately sought a way out.

Now, finally, on the other side of this feeling evoked in me by the offensive nationalist rhetoric of Malcolm X—offensive, both because he offended the white people in attendance and because he was ideologically on the offensive—I was able to construct a psychological space within which I could "feel good about myself." I could celebrate my body (especially my nappy hair, which I always attacked with a hot comb in ritualistic seclusion), my musical proclivities, and my suppressed speech patterns, among other things. But I shared these feelings with no one. It was a secret thing—like a collective, fictive playmate. This thing distanced me from the white people around me while simultaneously rendering controllable the distance I had always felt from them. It also meant that I did not have to defer to the mandatoriness of my Negro community back home. As a matter of fact, as a result of this experience into which Malcolm's words launched me, I felt a strengthening of the ties with the community of my birth.

This nationalist appeal of the early Malcolm X, however, did not move me to activism—although I had been something of an activist since the age of thirteen. I didn't particularly feel the need to *do* anything. It ended for me where it began—in changing the structure of my feeling. Don't get me wrong. I really needed that. I needed it at least as much as I would later need the appeal of the image of the leather-jacketed, black-bereted warriors standing with guns at the entrance to the California legislature. (I saw that image in a German newspaper while studying with Theodor Adorno in Frankfurt.) That image, which would eventually become so problematic for me, called me home. And it directed me into an organizing frenzy in the streets of South Central Los Angeles.

In a sense, the feeling that Malcolm had conjured in me could finally acquire a mode of expression—collective, activist, and, I hoped, transformative. Except that once I arrived in southern California—with contacts I had gotten from Stokely Carmichael, whom I met, along with Michael X, in London at a "Dialectics of Liberation" conference—my inquiries and enthusiasm were interpreted as a desire to infiltrate local black organizations. After all, I had just gotten off the boat from Europe. I had to be CIA or something. But, eventually, I did embark upon an exploration of some of the nationalisms of the era. I found out, during my initial contacts, that Ron Karenga's group was too misogynist (although I would not have used that word then). Another organization I found too middle class and elitist. Yet another fell apart because we, women, refused to be pushed to the back of the bus. And even though we may have considered the feminism of that period white, middle class, and utterly irrelevant, we also found compulsory male leadership utterly unacceptable.

Today, I realize that there is no simple or unitary way to look at expressions of black nationalism or essentialism in contemporary cultural forms. As my own political consciousness evolved in the sixties, I found myself in a politically oppositional stance to what some of us then called "narrow nationalism." As a Marxist, I found issues of class and internationalism as necessary to my philosophical orientation as inclusion in a community of historically oppressed people of African descent. But, at the same time, I needed to say "black is beautiful" as much as any of the intransigent antiwhite nationalists. I needed to explore my African ancestry, to don African garb, and to wear my hair natural as much as the blinder-wearing male supremacist cultural nationalists. (And, by the way, I had no idea my own "natural" would achieve its somewhat legendary status; I was simply emulating other sisters.)

My relationship to the particular nationalism I embraced was rooted in political practice. The vortex of my practice was always the progressive, politicized black community—though I frequently questioned my place as a black woman in that community, even in the absence of a vocabulary with which to pose the relevant questions. Within the Communist Party, "black" was my point of reference—which did not prevent me from identifying with the multiracial working class and its historical agency. I am not suggesting that the negotiation of that relationship was not fraught with many difficulties, but I do know that I probably would not have joined the Communist Party at that time if I had not been able to enter the party through an all-black collective in Los Angeles called the Che-Lumuma Club.

The sisters who were my closest comrades, in SNCC, in the Black Panther Party, in the Communist Party, fought tenaciously—and we sometimes fought tenaciously among ourselves—for our right to fight. And we were sometimes assisted in this by sympathetic men in these organizations. We may not have been able to talk about gendered racism, "sexuality" may have still meant sexiness, homophobia, as a word, may not yet have existed, but our practice, I can say in retrospect, was located on a continuum that groped and zigzagged its way toward this moment of deliberation on the pitfalls of nationalism and essentialism.

I revisit my own history here to situate myself, in this current exploration of postnationalism, as a revolutionary activist during an era when nationalist and essentialist ideas about black people and the black struggle in the United States crystallized in such a way as to render them capable of surviving in the historical consciousness of people of African descent throughout the diaspora, but especially in the collective imagination of large numbers of African American youth today. Perhaps we might make a similar observation about the Garveyism of the 1920s, but, among other things, the undeveloped state of—and forced exclusion from—both media technology and popular historical consciousness prevented us from later being inspired in the same way as by those slogans and images of the late sixties.

Today, of course, young people are explicitly inspired by what they know about Malcolm X and the Black Panther Party. And I find myself in a somewhat problematic position because my own image appears now and then in visual evocations of this nationalist impulse that fuel the advocacy of revolutionary change in contemporary hip-hop culture. These days, young people who were not even born when I was arrested often approach me with expressions of awe and disbelief. On the one hand, it is inspiring to discover a measure of historical awareness that, in our youth, my generation often lacked. But it is also unsettling. Because I know that almost inevitably my image is associated with a certain representation of black nationalism that privileges those particular nationalisms with which some of us were locked in constant battle.

What I am trying to suggest is that contemporary representations of nationalism in African American and diasporic popular culture are far too frequently reifications of a very complex and contradictory project that had emancipatory moments leading beyond itself. For example, my own first major activist effort as a budding "nationalist" was the construction of an alliance with Chicano students and progressive white students in San Diego for the purpose of demanding the creation of a college we called Lumumba-Zapata. It is the only college in the University of California, San Diego system that is identified today by its number—Third College—rather than by a name.

A further example: look at the issue of the Black Panther Party newspaper in the spring of 1970 in which Huey Newton wrote an article urging an end to verbal gay bashing, urging an examination of black male sexuality, and calling for an alliance with the developing gay liberation movement. This article was written in the aftermath of Jean Genet's sojourn with the Black Panther Party, and Genet's *Un Captif Amoureux* reveals suppressed moments of the history of sixties nationalism.*

Such moments as these have been all but eradicated in popular representations today of the black movement of the late sixties and early seventies. And I resent that the legacy I consider my own—one I also helped to construct—has been rendered invisible. Young people with "nationalist" proclivities ought, at least, have the opportunity to choose which tradition of nationalism they will embrace. How will they position themselves en masse in defense of women's rights and in defense of gay rights if they are not aware of the historical precedents for such positionings?

With respect to the exclusion of such progressive moments in the sixties' history of black nationalism, the mass media is not the sole culprit. We also have to look at the institutions that package this history before it is disseminated by the media—including some of the academic sites occupied by obsolete and inveterate nationalists. Furthermore, we need to look at who packages the practice. The only existing mass black organization that can claim the so-called

---

*Jean Genet, *Un Captif Amoureux* (Paris: Gallimard, 1986); translated as *Prisoner of Love* (London: Pan Books, 1989).

authority of having been there during the formative period of contemporary black nationalism, and therefore, of carrying forth Malcolm X's legacy is the Nation of Islam. Who is working with gang members in South Central Los Angeles today? Who is trying, on an ongoing basis, to end the violence and to bring warring gangs together in dialogue? Why is the rap artist, Paris, who calls himself the Black Panther of Rap, a member of the Nation of Islam? Why is Ice Cube studying with the Nation? Impulses toward collective political practice are being absorbed, in this instance, by a movement that accords nationalism the status of a religion.

As enthusiastic as we might be about the capacity of hip-hop culture to encourage oppositional consciousness among today's young people, it some-times advocates a nationalism with such strong misogynist overtones that it mil-itates against the very revolutionary practice it appears to promote. Where is the door—or even the window—opening onto a conception of political practice?

Where cultural representations do not reach out beyond themselves, there is the danger that they will function as surrogates for activism, that they will con-stitute both the beginning and end of political practice. I always go back to Marx's eleventh Feuerbach Thesis because, as Cornel [West] would say, it brings me joy: "Philosophers have interpreted the world in various ways. The point, however, is to change it."

IV.

INTERSECTIONS OF RACE, ETHNICITY, CLASS, AND GENDER

This set of readings dealing with intersections brings together a number of different voices that magnify and deepen many of the issues raised elsewhere in this volume.

Audre Lorde was a left-wing black lesbian feminist poet—and much more. These multiple identities are explored and interwoven in her vibrantly personal and political essay "Age, Race, Class, and Sex."

The concept of "whiteness" plays an important part in that analysis—a concept elaborated by radical labor historian David Roediger in his key essay "From the Social Construction of Race to the Abolition of Whiteness." June Jordan—poet and essayist—suggests the centrality of women in forging the majority that will be capable of achieving these twin goals. The poetic prose of celebrated writer Alice Walker, in "The Right to Life," fuses identities of race, gender, and class into a powerful challenge to multiple forms of oppression. Like many other poetic works, this contribution from 1989 lights up new pathways of thought and struggle.

The fact that black liberation is intimately connected to a multicultural struggle for a better future comes through in essays of Japanese American scholar Ronald Takaki and African American scholar Manning Marable. And black labor organizer Saladin Muhammed, describing more than two decades of work by the southern-based Black Workers for Justice, suggests ways in which these struggles continue into the twenty-first century.

AUDRE LORDE
AGE, RACE, CLASS, AND SEX: WOMEN REDEFINING DIFFERENCE (1980)

Much of western European history conditions us to see human differences in simplistic opposition to each other: dominant/subordinate, good/bad, up/down, superior/inferior. In a society where the good is defined in terms of profit rather than in terms of human need, there must always be some group of people who, through systematized oppression, can be made to feel surplus, to occupy the place of the dehumanized inferior. Within this society, that group is made up of black and Third World people, working-class people, older people, and women.

As a forty-nine-year-old black lesbian feminist socialist mother of two, including one boy, and a member of an interracial couple, I usually find myself a part of some group defined as other, deviant, inferior, or just plain wrong. Traditionally, in American society, it is the members of oppressed, objectified groups who are expected to stretch out and bridge the gap between the actualities of our lives and the consciousness of our oppressor. For in order to survive, those of us for whom oppression is as American as apple pie have always had to be watchers, to become familiar with the language and manners of the oppressor, even sometimes adopting them for some illusion of protection. Whenever the need for some pretense of communication arises, those who profit from our oppression call upon us to share our knowledge with them. In other words, it is the responsibility of the oppressed to teach the oppressors their mistakes. I am responsible for educating teachers who dismiss my children's culture in school. Black and Third World people are expected to educate white people as to our humanity. Women are expected to educate men. Lesbians and gay men are expected to educate the heterosexual world. The oppressors maintain their position and evade responsibility for their own actions. There is a constant drain of energy which might be better used in redefining ourselves and devising realistic scenarios for altering the present and constructing the future.

Institutionalized rejection of difference is an absolute necessity in a profit economy which needs outsiders as surplus people. As members of such an economy, we have *all* been programmed to respond to the human differences between us with fear and loathing and to handle that difference in one of three ways: ignore it, and if that is not possible, copy it if we think it is dominant, or destroy it if we think it is subordinate. But we have no patterns for relating across our human differences as equals. As a result, those differences have been misnamed and misused in the service of separation and confusion.

Certainly there are very real differences between us of race, age, and sex. But it is not those differences between us that are separating us. It is rather our refusal to recognize those differences, and to examine the distortions which result from our misnaming them and their effects upon human behavior and expectation.

Racism, the belief in the inherent superiority of one race over all others and thereby the right to dominance. Sexism, the belief in the inherent superiority of one sex over the other and thereby the right to dominance. Ageism. Heterosexism. Elitism. Classism.

It is a lifetime pursuit for each one of us to extract these distortions from our living at the same time as we recognize, reclaim, and define those differences upon which they are imposed. For we have all been raised in a society where those distortions were endemic within our living. Too often, we pour the energy needed for recognizing and exploring difference into pretending those differences are insurmountable barriers, or that they do not exist at all. This results in a voluntary isolation, or false and treacherous connections. Either way, we do not develop tools for using human difference as a springboard for creative change within our lives. We speak not of human difference, but of human deviance.

Somewhere, on the edge of consciousness, there is what I call a *mythical norm*, which each one of us within our hearts knows "that is not me." In America, this norm is usually defined as white, thin, male, young, heterosexual, Christian, and financially secure. It is with this mythical norm that the trappings of power reside within this society. Those of us who stand outside that power often identify one way in which we are different, and we assume that to be the primary cause of all oppression, forgetting other distortions around difference, some of which we ourselves may be practicing. By and large within the women's movement today, white women focus upon their oppression as women and ignore differences of race, sexual preference, class, and age. There is a pretense to a homogeneity of experience covered by the word *sisterhood* that does not in fact exist.

Unacknowledged class differences rob women of each others' energy and creative insight. Recently a women's magazine collective made the decision for one issue to print only prose, saying poetry was a less "rigorous" or "serious" art form. Yet even the form our creativity takes is often a class issue. Of all the art forms, poetry is the most economical. It is the one which is the most secret, which requires the least physical labor, the least material, and the one which can be done between shifts, in the hospital pantry, on the subway, and on scraps of surplus paper. Over the last few years, writing a novel on tight finances, I came to appreciate the enormous differences in the material demands between poetry and prose. As we reclaim our literature, poetry has been the major voice of poor, working-class, and colored women. A room of one's own may be a necessity for writing prose, but so are reams of paper, a typewriter, and plenty of time. The actual requirements to produce the visual arts also help determine, along class lines, whose art is whose. In this day of inflated prices for material, who are our sculptors, our painters, our photographers? When we speak of a broadly based women's culture, we need to be aware of the effect of class and economic differences on the supplies available for producing art.

As we move toward creating a society within which we can each flourish, ageism is another distortion of relationship which interferes without vision. By ignoring the past, we are encouraged to repeat its mistakes. The "generation gap" is an important social tool for any repressive society. If the younger members of a community view the older members as contemptible or suspect or excess, they will never be able to join hands and examine the living memories of the community, nor ask the all-important question, "Why?" This gives rise to a historical amnesia that keeps us working to invent the wheel every time we have to go to the store for bread.

We find ourselves having to repeat and relearn the same old lessons over and over that our mothers did because we do not pass on what we have learned, or because we are unable to listen. For instance, how many times has this all been said before? For another, who would have believed that once again our daughters are allowing their bodies to be hampered and purgatoried by girdles and high heels and hobble skirts?

Ignoring the differences of race between women and the implications of those differences presents the most serious threat to the mobilization of women's joint power.

As white women ignore their built-in privilege of whiteness and define *woman* in terms of their own experience alone, then women of color become "other," the outsider whose experience and tradition is too "alien" to comprehend. An example of this is the signal absence of the experience of women of color as a resource for women's studies courses. The literature of women of color is seldom included in women's literature courses and almost never in other literature courses, nor in women's studies as a whole. All too often, the excuse given is that the literatures of women of color can only be taught by colored women, or that they are too difficult to understand, or that classes cannot "get into" them because they come out of experiences that are "too different." I have heard this argument presented by white women of otherwise quite clear intelligence, women who seem to have no trouble at all teaching and reviewing work that comes out of the vastly different experiences of Shakespeare, Molière, Dostoyevsky, and Aristophanes. Surely there must be some other explanation.

This is a very complex question, but I believe one of the reasons white women have such difficulty reading black women's work is because of their reluctance to see black women as women and different from themselves. To examine black women's literature effectively requires that we be seen as whole people in our actual complexities—as individuals, as women, as human—rather than as one of those problematic but familiar stereotypes provided in this society in place of genuine images of black women. And I believe this holds true for the literatures of other women of color who are not black.

The literatures of all women of color recreate the textures of our lives, and many white women are heavily invested in ignoring the real differences. For as long as any difference between us means one of us must be inferior, then the recognition of any difference must be fraught with guilt. To allow women of color to step out of stereotypes is too guilt provoking, for it threatens the complacency of those women who view oppression only in terms of sex.

Refusing to recognize difference makes it impossible to see the different problems and pitfalls facing us as women.

Thus, in a patriarchal power system where whiteskin privilege is a major prop, the entrapments used to neutralize black women and white women are not the same. For example, it is easy for black women to be used by the power structure against black men, not because they are men, but because they are black. Therefore, for black women, it is necessary at all times to separate the needs of the oppressor from our own legitimate conflicts within our communities. This same problem does not exist for white women. Black women and men have shared racist oppression and still share it, although in different ways. Out of that shared oppression we have developed joint defenses and joint vulnerabilities to each other that are not duplicated in the white community, with the exception of the relationship between Jewish women and Jewish men.

On the other hand, white women face the pitfall of being seduced into joining the oppressor under the pretense of sharing power. This possibility does not exist in the same way for women of color. The tokenism that is sometimes extended to us is not an invitation to join power; our racial "otherness" is a visible reality that makes that quite clear. For white women there is a wider range of pretended choices and rewards for identifying with patriarchal power and its tools.

Today, with the defeat of ERA [Equal Rights Amendment], the tightening economy, and increased conservatism, it is easier once again for white women to believe the dangerous fantasy that if you are good enough, pretty enough, sweet enough, quiet enough, teach the children to behave, hate the right people, and marry the right men, then you will be allowed to coexist with patriarchy in relative peace, at least until a man needs your job or the neighborhood rapist happens along. And true, unless one lives and loves in the trenches it is difficult to remember that the war against dehumanization is ceaseless.

But black women and our children know the fabric of our lives is stitched with violence and with hatred, that there is no rest. We do not deal with it only on the picket lines, or in dark midnight alleys, or in the places where we dare to verbalize our resistance. For us, increasingly, violence weaves through the daily tissues of our living—in the supermarket, in the classroom, in the elevator, in the clinic and the schoolyard, from the plumber, the baker, the saleswoman, the bus driver, the bank teller, the waitress who does not serve us.

Some problems we share as women, some we do not. You fear your children will grow up to join the patriarchy and testify against you, we fear our children will be dragged from a car and shot down in the street, and you will turn your backs upon the reasons they are dying.

The threat of difference has been no less blinding to people of color. Those of us who are black must see that the reality of our lives and our struggle does not make us immune to the errors of ignoring and misnaming difference. Within black communities where racism is a living reality, differences among us often seem dangerous and suspect. The need for unity is often misnamed as a need for homogeneity, and a black feminist vision mistaken for betrayal of our common interests as a people. Because of the continuous battle against racial erasure that black women and black men share, some black women still refuse to recognize that we are also oppressed as women, and that sexual hostility against black women is practiced not only by the white racist society, but implemented within our black communities as well. It is a disease striking the heart of black nationhood, and silence will not make it disappear. Exacerbated by racism and the pressures of powerlessness, violence against black women and children often becomes a standard within our communities, one by which manliness can be measured. But these woman-hating acts are rarely discussed as crimes against black women.

As a group, women of color are the lowest paid wage earners in America. We are the primary targets of abortion and sterilization abuse, here and abroad. In certain parts of Africa, small girls are still being sewed shut between their legs to keep them docile and for men's pleasure. This is known as female circumcision, and it is not a cultural affair as the late Jomo Kenyatta insisted, it is a crime against black women.

Black women's literature is full of the pain of frequent assault, not only by a racist patriarchy, but also by black men. Yet the necessity for and history of shared battle have made us, black women, particularly vulnerable to the false accusation that antisexist is antiblack. Meanwhile, woman hating as a recourse of the powerless is sapping strength from black communities, and our very lives. Rape is on the increase, reported and unreported, and rape is not aggressive sexuality, it is sexualized aggression. As Kalamu ya Salaam, a black male writer points out, "As long as male domination exists, rape will exist. Only women revolting and men made conscious of their responsibility to fight sexism can collectively stop rape."*

Differences between ourselves as black women are also being misnamed and used to separate us from one another. As a black lesbian feminist comfortable with the many different ingredients of my identity, and a woman committed to racial and sexual freedom from oppression, I find I am constantly being

---

*From Kalamu ya Salaam, "Rape: A Radical Analysis, and African American Perspective," *Black Books Bulletin* 6, no. 4 (1980).

encouraged to pluck out some one aspect of myself and present this as the meaningful whole, eclipsing or denying the other parts of self. But this is a destructive and fragmenting way to live. My fullest concentration of energy is available to me only when I integrate all the parts of who I am, openly, allowing power from particular sources of my living to flow back and forth freely through all my different selves, without the restrictions of externally imposed definition. Only then can I bring myself and my energies as a whole to the service of those struggles which I embrace as part of my living.

A fear of lesbians, or of being accused of being a lesbian, has led many black women into testifying against themselves. It has led some of us into destructive alliances, and others into despair and isolation. In the white women's communities, heterosexism is sometimes a result of identifying with the white patriarchy, a rejection of that interdependence between women-identified women which allows the self to be, rather than to be used in the service of men. Sometimes it reflects a die-hard belief in the protective coloration of heterosexual relationships, sometimes a self-hate which all women have to fight against, taught us from birth.

Although elements of these attitudes exist for all women, there are particular resonances of heterosexism and homophobia among black women. Despite the fact that woman-bonding has a long and honorable history in the African and African American communities, and despite the knowledge and accomplishments of many strong and creative women-identified black women in the political, social, and cultural fields, heterosexual black women often tend to ignore or discount the existence and work of black lesbians. Part of this attitude has come from an understandable terror of black male attack within the close confines of black society, where the punishment for any female self-assertion is still to be accused of being a lesbian and therefore unworthy of the attention or support of the scarce black male. But part of this need to misname and ignore black lesbians comes from a very real fear that openly women-identified black women who are no longer dependent upon men for their self-definition may well reorder our whole concept of social relationships.

Black women who once insisted that lesbianism was a white woman's problem now insist that black lesbians are a threat to black nationhood, are consorting with the enemy, are basically unblack. These accusations, coming from the very women to whom we look for deep and real understanding, have served to keep many black lesbians in hiding, caught between the racism of white women and the homophobia of their sisters. Often, their work has been ignored, trivialized, or misnamed, as with the work of Angelina Grimke, Alice Dunbar-Nelson, Lorraine Hansberry. Yet women-bonded women have always been some part of the power of black communities, from our unmarried aunts to the amazons of Dahomey.

And it is certainly not black lesbians who are assaulting women and raping children and grandmothers on the streets of our communities.

Across this country, as in Boston during the spring of 1979 following the unsolved murders of twelve black women, black lesbians are spearheading movements against violence against black women.

What are the particular details within each of our lives that can be scrutinized and altered to help bring about change? How do we redefine difference for all women? It is not our differences which separate women, but our reluctance to recognize those differences and to deal effectively with the distortions which have resulted from the ignoring and misnaming of those differences.

As a tool of social control, women have been encouraged to recognize only one area of human difference as legitimate, those differences which exist between women and men. And we have learned to deal across those differences with the urgency of all oppressed subordinates. All of us have had to learn to live or work or coexist with men, from our fathers on. We have recognized and negotiated these differences, even when this recognition only continued the old dominant/subordinate mode of human relationship, where the oppressed must recognize the masters' difference in order to survive.

But our future survival is predicated upon our ability to relate within equality. As women, we must root out internalized patterns of oppression within ourselves if we are to move beyond the most superficial aspects of social change. Now we must recognize differences among women who are our equals, neither inferior nor superior, and devise ways to use each others' difference to enrich our visions and our joint struggles.

The future of our earth may depend upon the ability of all women to identify and develop new definitions of power and new patterns of relating across difference. The old definitions have not served us, nor the earth that supports us. The old patterns, no matter how cleverly rearranged to imitate progress, still condemn us to cosmetically altered repetitions of the same old exchanges, the same old guilt, hatred, recrimination, lamentation, and suspicion.

For we have, built into all of us, old blueprints of expectation and response, old structures of oppression, and these must be altered at the same time as we alter the living conditions which are a result of those structures. For the master's tools will never dismantle the master's house.

As Paulo Freire shows so well in *The Pedagogy of the Oppressed*,* the true focus of revolutionary change is never merely the oppressive situations which we seek to escape, but that piece of the oppressor which is planted deep within each of us, and which knows only the oppressors' tactics, the oppressors' relationships.

Change means growth, and growth can be painful. But we sharpen self-definition by exposing the self in work and struggle together with those whom we

---

*New York: Seabury Press, 1970.

define as different from ourselves, although sharing the same goals. For black and white, old and young, lesbian and heterosexual women alike, this can mean new paths to our survival.

✳   ✳   ✳

DAVID ROEDIGER
FROM THE SOCIAL CONSTRUCTION OF RACE
TO THE ABOLITION OF WHITENESS (1992)

A telling joke that has made the rounds among African American scholars comments on the distance between academic trends in writing on race and life in the "real world." "I have noticed," the joke laments, "that my research demonstrating that race is merely a social and ideological construction helps little in getting taxis to pick me up late at night." The humor here is sufficiently ironic that the joke does not signal a rejection of the idea that the social construction of race is worth talking and writing about, but it does focus attention on the fact that race may be more easily demystified on paper than disarmed in everyday life.

The problem raised by the "taxi joke" is a part of the broader questioning of recent critical scholarship on the grounds that its professed attempts to be popular and political have not yielded results that have proven useful in stemming the tide of reaction in the United States. Among the most sweeping critics of the "new scholarship," there is a tendency to regard its lack of immediate political impact as proof that not only postmodernist studies, but also scholarly works emphasizing race and gender, are at best frivolously apolitical and at worst obscenely hypocritical in their radicalism. Such attacks demand an answer, both because they at times score effectively in criticisms of the hyperacademicized jargon filling recent writing and because radical intellectuals should want to be held to a standard of political engagement. It would be easy to show that the critics of the new scholarship themselves often lack any coherent politics beyond a vague populism or a longing for a kind of Marxism that is unlikely to survive in a world in which women and people of color increasingly form the core of both the working class and the Left. Similarly, it would be easy to argue that it is unfair to expect a small number of university teachers to influence the habits of America's cabdrivers. What is harder, but necessary, is for those of us who believe that recent scholarship does make some modest contribution to radical change to be far more specific about how this is so and about the political implications of our work.

Reprinted from *Towards the Abolition of Whiteness*, by David Roediger. Copyright © 1994. Used by permission of Verso Books. This article is based on a keynote address given during Socialist Week at Iowa State University in the fall of 1992 before the presidential election of that year.

In taking up this challenge, I want to focus here particularly on the political implications of the idea that race is given meaning through the agency of human beings in concrete historical and social contexts, and is not a biological or natural category. The development of this insight constitutes a major achievement of recent scholarship and one broadly established across disciplinary lines. Students might learn this lesson in biology through the writings of Stephen Jay Gould or Donna Haraway; in history via Alexander Saxton's and Edmund Morgan's penetrating studies or Barbara Fields's seminal essays; in sociology from Richard Williams; in literature courses from the works of Toni Morrison or Hazel Carby; in women's studies from bell hooks or Vron Ware; in religious studies from Cornel West; or in African American studies by reading Sterling Stuckey's indispensable *Slave Culture*. Poststructuralist theory has enriched the work of some of these scholars and more fully informed the studies by Eric Lott, Colette Gullaumin, and Coco Fusco, all of which open important discussions in the "denaturing" of race.

Students who come to understand that race is given meaning within human society rather than within DNA codes are thus often putting together what they have learned in a number of areas. It often takes a good while for the insight to click. Even among Left-inclined students, the idea that race is natural is so ingrained that there is an assumption that liberal and even radical education must be trying to teach that race is not very important, but nonetheless is a material reality. When students do "get it," they are often tremendously enthusiastic. Seeing race as a category constantly being struggled over and remade, they sense that the possibilities of political action in particular and human agency in general are vastly larger than they had thought. They reflect on the manner in which structures of social oppression have contributed to the tragic ways that race has been given meaning. They often come to indict those structures. To the limited, but important, extent to which these things happen, one small corner of the extravagant *Reader's Digest/New Republic* nightmares regarding what goes on in "politically correct" American higher education is happily made flesh.

But as important as this transformation is, it sometimes proves more satisfying as a guide to making a way through seminars than through the rest of the day. As the joke that begins this chapter suggests, for all its insubstantiality race is a very powerful ideology. If students hope that the potency of race will give way simply because they can offer a strong intellectual demystification of the concept, they will quickly be disappointed. More important, the insight that race is socially constructed is so sweeping that by itself it implies few specific political conclusions. In the absence of a large student movement or class movement in which they might test directions to proceed from general insight to specific actions, students whose eyes have been opened concerning race may turn up in the Clinton campaign, with its emphasis on bringing all Americans together.

They may end up in small socialist sects, whose general acceptance of race as a natural category is balanced by an eager insistence that race is also manipulated and given prominence by employers and politicians seeking to divide workers—an insistence that makes for an argument that sounds like a thorough demystification of race based on the understanding of class. On campus, students who have been enlightened regarding race may be found agitating for the expansion of African American studies, because they appreciate the ways that racial ideology has conditioned history and daily life. Conversely, they may argue that anything race-specific is illusory and dangerous. Or those challenging the existence of race as a natural category may argue a hodge-podge of political positions. *Newsweek*'s special section on the Los Angeles rebellions of 1992, for example, takes the enlightened view that the "very concept of race" may be "a relic," which is "scientifically spurious" since "there is no such thing as 'black,'" and "white . . . does not define a race." The article then more or less randomly offers a thoroughly familiar and confused set of remedies for the urban crisis, emphasizing tax incentives to business, workfare, free enterprise zones, self-help, family values, and beefed up police forces.

Obviously, no amount of writing by radical intellectuals can stand in for a freedom movement in which ideas can be tested. But it nonetheless is incumbent on those of us who have argued that seeing race as socially constructed is a vital intellectual breakthrough to suggest where we think that breakthrough may lead politically. This introduction begins with a short travelogue of examples from England and Africa. This section is designed to show that the idea that race is socially constructed broadly "works," by helping powerfully to clarify important issues, but that it does not, by itself, settle the question of what political direction to take in matters of race and class. Returning to the United States, the chapter critiques attempts to minimize emphasis on allegedly "divisive" or "illusory" racial issues in American political struggles. It argues that the central political implication arising from the insight that race is socially constructed is the specific need to attack *whiteness* as a destructive ideology rather than to attack the concept of race abstractly. While acknowledging a tragic past and significant roadblocks to the creation of working-class nonwhiteness, the essay concludes that consciousness of whiteness also contains elements of a critique of that consciousness and that we should encourage the growth of a politics based on hopeful signs of a popular giving up on whiteness.

Transatlantic Notes on the Social Construction of Race

It is not possible to travel far without encountering vivid evidence that race is a socially constructed ideology rather than a biologically determined category. In Ghana's Ashanti region, where this is being written, we are greeted on the streets by children who chant, *"Oburoni koko maakye."* English-speaking Ashantis often translate this as "Red white man, good morning." Similarly, *oburoni wawu*, the term for used Western clothing, is charmingly translated as "the white men, they have died." However, *oburoni* derives from *Aburokyere*, the Akan word for "from across the waters," and is thus not the equivalent of Euro-American usages of *white*. The many Chinese, Koreans, and Japanese now in Ghana are generally also termed *oburoni*. But in discussing translation Ashantis will point out that this is not just because they are "from across the sea" but because they "are white"—that is, they are perceived as looking and acting like Europeans and Americans. African American visitors present an intriguing case because they literally have crossed the waters to reach Ashanti. In most cases today only the fairest of such visitors would be called *oburoni*. But in the recent past there apparently was some tendency to apply the term to them according to its original derivation. Thus it is intriguing in a number of ways that British listeners to Malcolm X's talks in Ghana on his celebrated pilgrimage to Mecca tell me that Ghanaians expressed surprise to them that an *oburoni* could say such things. Indeed one listener recalls hearing Malcolm described as a *white man* with astonishing ideas. Whatever strong elements of playfulness run through such characterizations, they ought to alert us to the complexity and the reality of the social construction of race.

Other transatlantic experiences demonstrate the ways the social construction of race enters politics. In 1984, when we lived in the London borough of Brent, immigrants and descendants of immigrants of many nationalities often called themselves "blacks," because that "racial" category came close to becoming what A. Sivanandan's brilliant work has characterized as a "political color" of the oppressed. Asian Indians, Pakistanis, Malaysians, Turks, Chinese, Bangladeshis, Arabs, and even Cypriots and some Irish so identified themselves. While on a movement-approved speaking tour in South Africa in 1989, we noted how consistently opponents of apartheid exposed the government-created "mixed race" category of *coloreds* as an ideological creation, by always taking care to use the term "so-called coloreds." Many among the "so-called colored" population insisted that they were in fact *Africans*. On the same visit to South Africa, the son of an African laborer in the Cape Town harbor told a story that further wonderfully illustrates how race is a created, and recreated, ideology. "WHITES ONLY" signs, according to the father, appeared historically on the Cape Town waterfront only after literally minded white U.S. seamen avoided "EUROPEANS ONLY" facilities.

Each of these examples is valuable in showing that the insight that race is socially constructed is apt and important. But they are also useful in pushing our discussions toward the complexities of how such knowledge might be applied politically. If extended, or probed, each example raises its own problems. For instance, we need to reflect on the fact that since the early 1980s the initiatives toward building a pan-black identity among the British oppressed have been stalled and even dismantled, amidst a sharp resurgence of ethnic particularism. How should political activists, armed with the knowledge that race is a mutable, ideological category, evaluate this change? Was it the inevitable result of trying to build resistance based on the "illusion" of "political color"? Is ethnic particularism, a more historic if not more "real" identity, bound to outlast an invented tradition of common blackness? Or, as Sivanandan forcefully maintains, was the real possibility of unifying the exploited around the class- and race-based consciousness of "political color" subverted by deliberate state policy and by opportunism among ethnic leaders?

Similar problems attend the South African example. In my early talks there, I eagerly attempted to extend the phrase "so-called colored" to all racial constructions, and spoke of "so-called whites" and "so-called blacks." As a way to force consideration of the fact that these were also historically created categories this was perhaps a justifiable strategy. As a contribution to political debate in the freedom movement in South Africa it was less apposite. The best militants there were arguing for thorough programs of affirmative action in the schools, the movement structures, and the larger society, holding that the way to nonracialism includes a consideration of race. I offered a formulation that could comfort those who thought that a nonracial future could be created by dismissing race-based politics and even discussion of race as unnecessary and counterproductive. Powerful as it is, the insight that race is socially constructed does not magically inform us with strategies for overcoming race-class oppression.

The twist on the Ghanaian example only appears to be more mundane. As we walk in Kumasi, especially in neighborhoods we have not been in before, residents sometimes cheerfully shout, in English, "Hey, you are white!" This struck me as being a puzzling, as well as a spectacular, example of non sequitur until I realized that you almost never see whites walking more than a short distance there. The full thought was, "Hey, you are white and out walking around!" or "Hey, you are white and ought to have a car!" While the comment seemed purely "about color" or "about race," it was in fact about a behavior that made color worth commenting upon. Thus, while race is ideologically constructed, it is constructed from real, predictable, repeated patterns of life. Indeed, as Barbara Fields and Walter Rodney point out, it is this *connection* to reality that gives race such a powerful ideological appeal. Whites are not biologically programmed to have a car or motorbike, but in Ghana they seldom lack one, and this makes race seem very much to matter in a hot, hilly, dusty place where walking is work. To announce that what "really" predicts vehicle ownership are income, ties to multinational corporations, and roles in organized relief operations, missionary projects, or academic research would hardly dissolve the perceived connections of car and color. As Rodney's magnificent *History of Guyanese Working People* observes, perceptions of the world in terms of race have thrived because they have "seemed reasonably consistent with aspects of people's life experiences." Race is thus both unreal and a seeming reality. Its demystification cannot be accomplished by even an airtight intellectual case, but only by hard and immensely complicated cultural and political struggle.

Why Keep Talking about Race?

The stateside evidence that race is socially constructed, ideologically powerful, and fraught with complexity is more familiar but equally compelling. Electorally, as Thomas and Mary Edsall and others have shown, whiteness has become, to use Sivanandan's phrase, a "political color" that binds a disparate New Right coalition together and allows it to attract enough votes from fearful and embittered middle-class and working-class whites to rule. From the completion of mid-1960s civil right legislation through 1992, only one Democrat occupied the White House, and he after a particularly astute bow to the importance of "ethnic purity." From "benign neglect" to Willie Horton, even the lukewarm Democratic commitment to civil rights has left the party so vulnerable to suspicions of being "soft on race" that its leadership has engaged for eight years in a more-or-less open search for an unassailably white candidate in what has been called a southern strategy but is better understood as a suburban one.

Whiteness exercises such political force despite its thorough discrediting as a "cultural color," despite its having become the fair game of stand-up comics who reflect on the vacuity of "white culture" in a nation in which so much that is new, stirring, excellent, and genuinely popular—in music, fashion, oratory, dance, vernacular speech, sport, and increasingly in literature, film, and nonfiction writing—comes from African American, Asian American, and Latino communities. We face, in short, a mad and maddening situation in which the appeals of whiteness are at their most pitifully meager and the effectiveness of appeals to whiteness—from Howard Beach to Simi Valley to the ballot boxes—are at a terrible height. The great American writer Ralph Ellison saw it coming over a decade ago, and framed a question which goes to the heart of modern U.S. politics and culture with merciless precision:

> What, by the way, is one to make of a white youngster who, with a transistor radio, screaming a Stevie Wonder tune, glued to his ear, shouts racial epithets at black youngsters trying to swim at a public beach—and this in the name of the ethnic sanctity of what has been declared a neighborhood turf?

Unable to answer this question and understandably tired after a long period of racially based reactionary rule, there is every temptation for us to move from the insight that race is an ideological construct to the conclusion that it's high time to denounce it as both snare and delusion and to return to a populist politics of economic reform. Dwelling on race, or advocating "race-specific" remedies, is on this view suspected as counterproductive and even malicious. Thus Barbara Fields's staunchly materialist *New Left Review* article on the origins of U.S. racism ends with an astonishingly idealist castigation of a mother who asks her four-year-old if a playmate is 'black' and then laughs when the child answers that he is "brown." "The young woman's benevolent laughter was for the innocence of youth too soon corrupted," Fields writes, "but for all its benevolence, her laughter hastened the corruption." Fields argues that the woman, and radical intellectuals who emphasize race as a "tragic flaw" in the United States, give reality to race. She rather harshly suggests that in so doing they are like the Ku Klux Klan and the white murderers of the black teenager Yusef Hawkins. Others hold that we should refrain from the discussion of racial issues on the practical grounds that only economic issues can generate electoral success. The concrete proposals vary widely as to what should be emphasized instead of race. Fields proposes the interesting, but constitutionally fanciful, strategy of affirmative action based on class, while for William Julius Wilson and the many influential policy thinkers around the liberal journal *American Prospect*, the issues capable of disarming race are those in which the white middle class has a direct interest, especially jobs and health care.

Such strategies closely fit the chastened and dispirited mood of contemporary American liberalism, and they have some mass appeal among African American voters ready for anything but Reaganism (and albeit on low turnouts and with little alternative, therefore generally supportive of Bill Clinton's candidacy). Nonetheless, in my view initiatives avoiding discussion of race have little chance of success, even on their own limited terms. The absence of a liberal labor vote— both because so few workers are now organized and because a majority of those in white households containing a union member have voted for Reagan and Bush over the last three elections—makes prospects for an ongoing mildly progressive, class-based alliance inauspicious. Nor can Democrats be much more thorough at shutting up about racial justice than they already have been in recent campaigns. Clinton's reticence in offering comment on the Los Angeles rebellions is standard operating procedure (excepting the Jackson campaigns) regarding race for post-1972 Democratic presidential politics, not a new departure. The strategy of ignoring race has in that sense been well and truly tried.

For that matter, neither do the Republicans engage in much open discussion of race. They couch their appeals for a "white vote" in terms of welfare reform, neighborhood schools, toughness on crime, and "illegitimate" births. In the 1991 Mississippi governor's race, the right-wing Republican victor, Kirk Fordice, ended an antiwelfare campaign commercial with a still photograph of a black woman and her baby. He literally invited white Mississippians to vote against African American people, but did so without directly discussing race. In the wake of the Los Angeles rebellion of 1992, Bush's most vital soundbite ran, "For anyone who cares about our young people it is painful that in 1960 the percentage of births to unwed mothers was 5 percent—and now it is 27 percent." As the London *Observer*'s U.S. correspondent Andrew Stephen keenly observed, "To the millions of Americans who saw the all-important soundbite, what he was really saying was 'I'm talking about blacks, of course.'" Even the celebrated Willie Horton ad of the 1988 Bush campaign did not *say* anything about race. During the 1992 campaign Dan Quayle managed to play on hostilities toward black welfare mothers by talking about, of all things, white sitcom character Murphy Brown. Serious attention to race is already absent from U.S. politics, and it is the right that benefits.

But might the positive content of economic reform programs wean white voters away from race-based politics, opening the way for experience in campaigns that cross racial lines to nurture the insight that race ought not divide working people? Such a strategy has undergirded much of the white American Left's approach to race and class over the last century and more. Unions in particular have seemed such a promising venue for the gradual teaching of white workers that their real economic interests coincided with those of African Americans that endangering their organization by "premature" assaults on racism has been seen as running counter to the interests of not only class justice but also of racial equality.

To the extent that we argue that whiteness and various kinds of "white ethnicity" are reactions to alienation, an interesting modern case for this long-established strategy of overcoming white supremacy via an emphasis on class can be made. We may emphasize, as my *Wages of Whiteness* does, the role of powerlessness at work in opening people to settling for the fiction that they are "white workers." Or we may follow Frederic Jameson's "Reification and Utopia in Mass Culture" in stressing the ways alienation produced by bureaucratic structures and commercialized culture helps to undergird ersatz ethnicity among whites. In either case, it would seem that participation in authentic struggles against oppression and powerlessness could be a useful antidote to whiteness. When, for example, a "white rights" supporter of David Duke's 1991 gubernatorial bid in Louisiana stopped her litany of "blacks on welfare" myths ("They get new cars every year . . .") in an interview with *USA Today*, she added, "The state won't take care of me." Perhaps if there were a large, militant movement for decent health care, that woman might join it, press demands on the state, gain a sense of power, and, in the course of struggle alongside the black poor, question the myths she now recites.

It would be hard to imagine a successful assault on white supremacy that did not include millions of such small miracles, and that did not include a rallying around pressing class grievances. But far more problematic is the tendency to assume that a rediscovered emphasis on economic issues clarifies all, or even most, questions of political strategy where either race or class is concerned. The historical record of antiracist achievements of coalitions for economic reform is quite modest. From the National Labor Union through the populists to the CIO, whatever we wish might have been and whatever their other accomplishments, such coalitions did not dramatically deliver the goods where racial justice was concerned. Nor does the record show that common struggles necessarily "teach" common humanity lastingly. The Tom Watson wing of the populists spectacularly learned the lesson of black-white unity and more spectacularly forgot it. The experience of defeat—and there is no guarantee that class movements will win—particularly led to recrudescence of white supremacy. The dying convention of the National Labor Union respectfully entertained proposals by the southern racist intellectual Hinton Rowan Helper to forcibly remove blacks from the United States, while the Knights of Labor, so brilliantly egalitarian at its height, actually came in its declining days to approve a resolution to colonize African Americans in order to help "white labor." Why there are prospects for a better outcome in a new effort at economic-oriented reform that minimizes immediate emphasis on racial justice remains unclear, especially given that the substance of the tepid reforms on offer from neoliberals who spearhead the call for economic-based strategies is hardly the stuff great transformations of consciousness are made from.

Advocates of increasing the weight placed on economic reformist appeals and of continuing the silence surrounding race sometimes have internalized a kind of Marxism that wants to emphasize the objective reality of class relationships as against the ideology of race. I have no quarrel with that distinction, but in applying it we need to avoid imagining that workers objectively view the world through their class experience in one part of their brain and subjectively through the distorting filter of race in another. At the level of consciousness, class is anything but a faithful reflection of objective reality. Moreover, the subjective way in which white workers perceive and define class is thoroughly shaped in the United States by their whiteness. Two recent studies of contemporary New Jersey workers make this rather airy point concrete. In David Halle's excellent sociological study of chemical workers there, white male workers identify themselves as "working men" and as "middle class." They tend to see their white neighbors as being like them in class terms whether or not those neighbors are wage workers. They see black workers in jobs like theirs—workers more likely than the white neighbors to share AFL-CIO membership with the white chemical workers—as different in class terms, as "loafers" and "intruders." Even more striking is Katherine Newman's recent study of industrial decline, based on interviews with white former factory workers whose plant has closed in Elizabeth, New Jersey. Many of the workers process this stark class experience by arguing that the employer was forced to leave because it was impossible to turn profits while being forced to employ blacks and Hispanics. A movement that seeks to outflank a David Duke simply by popularizing the kind of unemployment and health care plans that would benefit the hard-hit whites who form a large part of his constituency runs head-on into the problem that many of the white poor, including not a few on relief, cast the welfare state as a scheme to benefit "those people." As an influential study quoted by the Edsalls puts it, for a key sector of the white electorate "virtually all progressive symbols and themes have been redefined in racial and pejorative terms." In such situations, one could as easily argue that attacking racism is a precondition for class-based reform as that class-based reform is a precondition for attacking racism.

Nearly half a century ago, C. L. R. James critiqued traditional left strategy on race and class by writing, "'Black and White, Unite and Fight' is unimpeachable in principle. . . . But it is often misleading and sometimes even offensive in the face of the infinitely varied, tumultuous, passionate, and often murderous reality of race relations in the United States." Many of those advocating single-minded emphasis on common economic grievances today might shy away from words like "Fight," from the mention of race in their slogans and even from slogans altogether. But we should still share James's unease with any political strategy that supposes that class grievances in the United States can be addressed without full attention to race.

The British theorist Terry Eagleton has held that gender and nation, like class, are socially constructed identities based on an alienation that "cancel[s] the particularity of an individual life into collective anonymity." But he has refused to follow "some contemporary poststructuralist theory" in concluding that we should therefore suppose that we can "go around" any of these identities rather than go "all the way through" them. He has argued practically that "because the truth remains that women are oppressed *as women*—that such categories, onto-logically empty though they may be, continue to exert an implacable force"—we must struggle over (and talk about) gender. We must pursue a political strategy "caught up in the very metaphysical categories it hopes finally to abolish." I would suggest that race is another such "ontologically empty" and "metaphys-ical" category that we must confront to abolish. Many leftists and liberals would perhaps grant the truth of at least parts of this critique of economism, but would still argue that, like it or not, "race-specific" politics have in practice simply been discredited as unworkable. In making a serious effort to locate "the left wing of the possible," they point to demographic realities and white voting patterns and emphasize the dangers of minorities "going it alone" by continuing to organize around particularistic grievances. Indeed the Edsalls and other recent writers who champion economistic strategies do so not out of a dismissal of the importance of white supremacy but—like the great early exemplar of such strategies, Bayard

Rustin—out of a very grim appreciation of racism's influence. In an important public exchange with Democratic North Carolina politician Harvey Gantt, the victim of Jesse Helms's race-baiting in a recent Senate election, the populist historian Lawrence Goodwyn argues for economic reform as the only viable Democratic strategy because he doesn't "see any other way to cope with the racism of the American electorate."

In opposing such economism, we must be humble enough to admit that it has triumphed as a strategy against reaction because existing alternatives to it have proven less than attractive. A liberalism based on halfhearted pursuit of affirmative action has not proven more popular than a liberalism based on halfhearted pursuit of job creation and health insurance. Attempts to combine and transcend the two approaches within a Rainbow Coalition have largely stalled. Initiatives to unite workers around revolutionary, rather than reformist, economic demands have had far less mass resonance than the appeals of a David Duke. In trying to stop a Duke, or a George Bush, opponents of reaction gravitate toward economic reformism almost by default. Supporting the pale populism of Eddie Edwards in Louisiana or Bill Clinton nationally is not so much the politics of lesser evil as one of last resort.

But as understandable as such "last resortism" is, it remains a dead end. The strategy generally fails, even on its own terms, by not keeping the Helmses, Bushes, and Reagans from victory (nor even keeping Duke from winning a majority of the "white vote"). More seriously, the caution and the fear of open discussion of race bred by constant attention to the immediate electorally "possible" blinds us to the real tensions within white supremacy. It leaves us unable to appreciate the ways in which a sharp questioning of whiteness within American culture opens the opportunity to win people to far more effective opposition to both race and class oppression. To take advantage of such possibilities requires that we not only continue to talk about race but that we pay attention to the most neglected aspects of race in America, the questions of why people think they are white and of whether they might quit thinking so.

Toward a Withering Away of Whiteness

When residents of the United States talk about race, they too often talk only about African Americans, Native Americans, Hispanic Americans, and Asian Americans. If whites come into the discussion, it is only because they have "attitudes" toward nonwhites. Whites are assumed not to "have race," though they might be racists. Many of the most critical advances of recent scholarship on the social construction of race have come precisely because writers have challenged the assumption that we only need to explain why people come to be considered black, Asian, Native American, or Hispanic and not attend to what Theodore Allen has marvelously termed the "invention of the white race." Coco Fusco sums up this central insight and its political import, writing, "Racial identities are not only Black, Latino, Asian, Native American and so on; they are also white. To ignore white ethnicity is to redouble its hegemony by naturalizing it."

To make its fullest possible contribution to the growth of a new society, activism that draws on ideas regarding the social construction of race must focus its political energies on exposing, demystifying, and demeaning the particular ideology of whiteness, rather than on calling into question the concept of race generally. In defending this position, three points deserve elaboration. The first is that, while neither whiteness nor blackness is a scientific (or natural) racial category, the former is infinitely more false, and precisely because of that falsity, more dangerous, than the latter. The second is that in attacking the notion that whiteness and blackness are "the same," we specifically undermine what has become, via the notion of "reverse racism," a major prop underpinning the popular refusal among whites to face both racism and themselves. The last is that whiteness is now a particularly brittle and fragile form of social identity and that it can be fought.

By far the most penetrating modern analysis of whiteness comes in the unlikely form of an essay of a mere two pages in a "lifestyle" magazine. Writing in *Essence* in 1984, James Baldwin reflected "On Being 'White' and Other Lies" and immediately put his finger on what sets whiteness apart as an American social phenomenon. "The crisis of leadership in the white community is remarkable—and terrifying—" Baldwin began, "because there is, in fact, no white community." It is not merely that whiteness is oppressive and false; it is that whiteness is *nothing but* oppressive and false. We speak of African American culture and community, and rightly so. Indeed the making of disparate African ethnic groups into an African American people, so lucidly described by Sterling Stuckey, is a genuine story of an American melting pot. In her passionate attacks on both the concept of an African American race and that of a white race, Barbara Fields characterizes African Americans as a "nation." Whites are clearly not that. There is an American culture, but it is thoroughly "mulatto," to borrow Albert Murray's fine description. If there is a southern culture, it is still more thoroughly mulatto than the broader American one. There are Irish American songs, Italian American neighborhoods, Slavic American traditions, German American villages, and so on. But such specific ethnic cultures always stand in danger of being swallowed by the lie of whiteness. Whiteness describes, from Little Big Horn to Simi Valley, not a culture but precisely the absence of culture. It is the empty and therefore terrifying attempt to build an identity based on what one isn't and on whom one can hold back.

Almost no Left initiatives have challenged white workers to critique, much less to abandon, whiteness. Baldwin's wonderful comment in the film *The Price of the Ticket*, that "As long as you think you're white, there's no hope for you," seems more poetic than political to radicals who have so long confined their struggles to encouraging whites to unite with blacks, and who have found it difficult to disarm racism, much less to think of abolishing whiteness. But a highly poetic politics is exactly what is required in a situation in which workers who identify themselves as white are *bound* to retreat from genuine class unity and meaningful antiracism. In a fascinating 1974 essay, outlining the preconditions for the emergence of united labor struggles, the great London-based theorist A. Sivanandan defied usual formulations of the relationship between race and class, writing that "in recovering its sense of oppression, both from technological alienation and [from] a white-oriented culture [the white working class must] arrive at a consciousness of racial oppression." On this view, the rejection of racial oppression by white workers must arise not just out of common participation in class, or even antiracist, struggles alongside blacks, but also out of a critique of the empty culture of whiteness itself. Rejection of whiteness is then part of a process that gives rise to both attacks on racism and to the very recovery of "sense of oppression" among white workers.

If it does not involve a critique of whiteness, the questioning of racism often proves shallow and limited. Indeed, at this horrifying juncture in race relations, most whites describe themselves as "not racists." Even David Duke packages white supremacy as a National Association for the Advancement of White People, allowing supporters to feel that, as one of them told *USA Today*, they are only doing the "same thing" as blacks in the NAACP. Even open Klan members now at times describe their organizations [as] "not racist." In St. Louis, young whites call blacks "nigger" on the "nonracist" ground that they are describing behavior, not genetics. "Black guys are nice and polite," they reason, "but niggers are pests." It is easy to regard such rationales as rank hypocrisy, especially in David Duke's mouth, but we should also face the fact that many whites genuinely feel absolved from being what they would call "bigots" or "racists." To most white students these terms imply being an "extremist," being "violent" or being "worse than average." Most students are sure that they are none of those.

The destructive term "reverse racism" grows out of this assurance among whites that they have transcended race. They are sure that they see the world based on merit, while multiculturalists, affirmative action officers, Native American fishermen, Black nationalists, and pointy-headed liberals "bring in race." An analysis that simply demystifies all conceptions of race without concentrating on critiquing whiteness runs the risk of reinforcing such widely and sincerely held notions.

The whole struggle against the concept of "reverse racism" is in fact terribly difficult when we fail to question whiteness and instead stay on the terrain of politics as usual. Conservatives creepily quote Martin Luther King, obscuring the fact that he himself was an advocate of affirmative action, as they hold that they are the true believers in raceless standards based on the "content of one's character." We try to argue from history to an audience not especially inclined toward the longer view. We hold that racism implies the systematic power to dominate and that since people of color lack such power, reverse racism is not a useful term. This perfectly valid point falls on deaf ears to the extent that the firmest believers in the reality of "reverse racism" are often precisely those whites most convinced of their own powerlessness. Our last despairing comments often begin with "But you refuse to see. . . ."

But those feeling victimized by "reverse racism" do see. They see in just the way, with just the blindnesses, that their assurance that they are "white" (but not racist) and have "white" interests demands that they see. In the Simi Valley trial they saw Rodney King, down and being kicked, but as one juror put it, somehow still in "control" of the situation and menacing the white police. When Bill Clinton signaled his whiteness by using his appearance before the Rainbow Coalition to attack the rapper Sister Souljah, he hoped to appeal to the way many whites see. Or perhaps he just sees that way. He railed against Sister Souljah's comment that it is unremarkable that black youth in South Central Los Angeles who attack and kill each other all year, would consider doing the same to whites for a week. Souljah's comment itself is not more than an exercise in introductory sociology, but Clinton offered a soundbite comparing Sister Souljah to David Duke. His demand that listeners imagine that the situation were reversed and that Duke made a statement like Souljah's was on one level absolutely perfect nonsense. What would the "reverse" be? Would Duke go to Simi Valley or Beverly Hills, and say that it is unremarkable that whites who attack each other all year would attack blacks for a week? The situation hasn't a reverse. Police do not single out whites for racial harassment and brutality. Hundreds of white youths are not killed in crack wars and gangbanging. Only whites could take Clinton's comment seriously. And they do.

But the Sister Souljah incident also ought to alert us to the fact that we need not just capitulate to whiteness. The Rainbow Coalition, before which Clinton spoke, mobilized tens of thousands of whites not only around its social democratic politics but around the idea that the fight against Reaganism should include people of color as central constituencies and as leaders. The Rainbow's most striking success in moving young white workers to act on the perception that the fighting style of the black freedom movement was more appropriate to their plight than anything in "white" politics—its mobilizing of Midwestern autoworkers in impressive 1988 rallies—did not, it is true, always translate into votes. The Rainbow's disorganization, lack of democracy, and timidity combined with the continuing power of race-thinking among whites to limit the extent to which white workers entered politics as nonwhites, but the possibility that they could do so within an organization agitating on both class and race issues was clearly present.

We may suspect, moreover, that many white young people strongly appreciate hip-hop artists like Sister Souljah far more than they do Bill Clinton. The tremendous popularity of hip-hop music and style among white youth has been written off as a fascination with violence and sexism among very young white suburban males; but the attraction is much broader than that. Rappers with varying messages appeal to male and female middle-class and working-class whites from grade school to adulthood. Unlike rock, which brought whites to African American music but quickly diluted the black influence and threw up white performers as the most celebrated stars, hip-hop is embraced by whites without any sharp tendency to expropriate it. In this it more nearly parallels white working-class attraction to soul music in the 1960s and 1970s (and still, see—by all means—*The Commitments*) and perhaps to reggae. Hip-hop offers white youth not only the spontaneity, experimentation, humor, danger, sexuality, physical movement, and rebellion absent from what passes as white culture but it also offers an explicit, often harsh, critique of whiteness.

Of course it would be ridiculous to claim that every white hip-hop fan is finding a way out of whiteness, let alone of racism. There will be no simple fix for the white problem in America and it is well to emphasize limits as well as possibilities. The "Guido" subculture in Italian American New York City, well described in the recent writings of Donald Tricarico, stands as an ambiguous example of both those possibilities and limits. Guidos have much adopted hip-hop and asserted a distinctive Italian American identity as against white American "wannabes." They refer to themselves as "Guineas," turning that anti-Italian, antiblack slur into a badge of honor. But the break with whiteness and racism on New York's streets is less than complete. As Tricarico nicely understates it, in many ways Guidos "resist identification with black youth" and "bite the hand that feeds them style."

Historically, the use of an (often distorted) image of African American life to express criticisms of "white culture," or longings for a different way of life, has hardly been an antidote to racism. The minstrel show expressed such longings beneath blackface while still holding African Americans in contempt in a perfect illustration of Herman Melville's wise observation that "envy and antipathy, passions irreconcilable in reason, nevertheless may spring conjoined . . . in one birth." In some ways the greater the longing has been, the greater the need to reassert whiteness and white supremacy. Nor, as Norman Mailer showed, largely unwittingly, in "The White Negro," has the use of African American culture to critique whiteness come without superficiality, fatuity, and paternalism. Loss of whiteness can have the beauty it does in a film like John Waters's *Hairspray* or the vapidity and arrogance it does in a film like *Soul Man*. And these extremes exist not just among, but within, individual whites. Finally, there is a sense in which whites cannot fully renounce whiteness even if they want to. The

Italian American heroine (in many ways, I think) of Spike Lee's *Jungle Fever* is as exemplary a race traitor as any seen on the big screen within memory: but when the police come, she is still white.

Even given all these problems, we cannot afford to ignore the political implications of the mass questioning of whiteness as a trend and a possibility in the United States. In a variety of settings, including even the Duke campaign, whites are confessing their confusion about whether it is really worth the effort to be white. We need to say that it is not worth it and that many of us do not want to do it. Initiatives against a Duke, or a Bush, should not only be class-oriented and antiracist, but also in a sense explicitly antiwhite, with a central focus on exposing how whiteness is used to make whites settle for hopelessness in politics and misery in everyday life. When a Clinton panders to whiteness, we should not let him off the hook on the grounds that his comments are only arguably "racist" as currently defined. Our opposition should focus on contrasting the bankruptcy of white politics with the possibilities of nonwhiteness. We should point out not just that whites and people of color often have common economic interests but that people of color currently act on those interests far more consistently—in politics, at the workplace, and increasingly in community-based environmental struggles—precisely because they are not burdened by whiteness. We should transform "reverse racism" from a curse to an injunction (Reverse racism!), campaigning for expanded affirmative action on the ground of both justice and the need to remove the privileges that tragically reproduce whiteness. Coalitions for economic reform need to be considered not only as vehicles for class mobilization and for the disarming of racism but also as places where whites learn that people of color currently make more close connections between class and community than whites do and therefore of course assume a central place in insurgent movements. If even MTV realizes that there is mass audience for the critique of whiteness, we cannot fail to attempt to rally, and to learn from, a constituency committed to its abolition.

❋ ❋ ❋

JUNE JORDAN
THE CASE FOR THE REAL MAJORITY (1982)

In the United States, race and class are fixed correlatives, despite occasional noise to the contrary. For black people, this correlation has meant the last and the least of available national resources, throughout our hated presence here. Right

Reprinted from *On Call: Political Essays*, by June Jordan. Used with permission of the June M. Jordan Literary Trust.

now, our national income represents a severely declining percentage of what our white counterparts enjoy.

This is known.

What begs for programmatic and rapid recognition is the equally important correlation between gender and class. Most of the American poor, white and black, are women.

What is not anywhere acknowledged, to date, is the specific composition of us, as a people. Most black Americans are black women. Most black women occupy the lowest paid, lowest status jobs in our society, when they can get a job. When they can't, they occupy the ranks of the most unemployed. (Bear in mind that, to be counted among the unemployed, you must actively seek work and not, as the media construct the fairy tale, whimsically evade really swell opportunities to make a living wage.) Most black children are raised by these same black women who receive the least-imaginable social and economic support even while they must endure the savage consequences of the most absurd theoretical censure by endlessly various male experts who, I have noticed, never offer to throw themselves in front of fast moving trains or trucks in order to stop the insanity of a killer system built upon the unpaid as well as the deliberately lowest paid labor of more than half of its citizens: the women.

If any of us hopes to survive, she or he must meet the extremity of the American female condition with immediate and political response. The thoroughly destructive and indefensible subjugation of the majority of Americans cannot continue except at the peril of the entire body politic. You might suppose this would be obvious to everyone talking about Freedom and Rights and Equality and Justice and the Spirit and the Future. But, apparently, this enormous and simple idea, the idea that the welfare of the majority will determine the welfare of the state, becomes an impossible concept to assimilate—once the majority has been identified as female.

In like manner, the penalties attached to black womanhood threaten all black people with ignominious extinction. Think about that. Think about "black people" without most of us caring for and about the rest of you. Think about "black people" without most of our children growing up able to eat and able to read what they need to take on the world, eye to eye.

Overall, white men run America. From nuclear armaments to the filth and jeopardy of New York City subways to the cruel mismanagement of health care, is there anything to boast about? Any safety and grace of a growing nature to claim? Is there any major and worldwide and man-made hazard to human life that cannot be traced to the willful activities of white men?

Overall, black men dominate black America. The leading cause of death for black men ages twenty-five to forty-four is murder by other black men! What is the leading cause of sorrow for black women? What is the leading cause of grief in the hearts of our children?

The huge and dire truth about white and black American women is trivial compared to what will happen to each of us if we refuse to transform this evil situation into a past reminder of a close call with collective death.

As Americans we live in danger for our lives. As black people we live in the valley of the shadow of death. I say look to the welfare of the majority—the women—if you would save yourself.

* * *

ALICE WALKER
THE RIGHT TO LIFE: WHAT CAN THE WHITE MAN . . . SAY TO THE BLACK WOMAN? (1989)

> What is of use in these words I offer in memory and recognition of our common mother. And to my daughter.

What can the white man say to the black woman?

For four hundred years he ruled over the black woman's womb.

Let us be clear. In the barracoons and along the slave-shipping coasts of Africa, for more than twenty generations, it was he who dashed our babies' brains out against the rocks.

What can the white man say to the black woman?

For four hundred years he determined which black woman's children would live or die.

Let it be remembered. It was he who placed our children on the auction block in cities all across the eastern half of what is now the United States, and listened to and watched them beg for their mothers' arms, before being sold to the highest bidder and dragged away.

What can the white man say to the black woman?

We remember that Fannie Lou Hamer, a poor sharecropper on a Mississippi plantation, was one of twenty-one children; and that on plantations across the South black women often had twelve, fifteen, twenty children. Like their enslaved

---

Reprinted with permission from the May 22, 1989, issue of the *Nation*.

mothers and grandmothers before them, these black women were sacrificed to the profit the white man could make from harnessing their bodies and their children's bodies to the cotton gin.

What can the white man say to the black woman?

We see him lined up on Saturday nights, century after century, to make the black mother, who must sell her body to feed her children, go down on her knees to him.
 Let us take note:
 He has not cared for a single one of the dark children in his midst, over hundreds of years.
 Where are the children of the Cherokee, my great-grandmother's people?
 Gone.
 Where are the children of the Blackfoot?
 Gone.
 Where are the children of the Lakota?
 Gone.
 Of the Cheyenne?
 Of the Chippewa?
 Of the Iroquois?
 Of the Sioux?
 Of the Mandinka?
 Of the Ibo?
 Of the Ashanti?
 Where are the children of the "Slave Coast" and Wounded Knee?
 We do not forget the forced sterilizations and forced starvations on the reservations, here as in South Africa. Nor do we forget the smallpox-infested blankets Indian children were given by the Great White Fathers of the U.S. government.

What has the white man to say to the black woman?

When we have children you do everything in your power to make them feel unwanted from the moment they are born. You send them to fight and kill other dark mothers' children around the world. You shove them onto public highways in the path of oncoming cars. You shove their heads through plate glass windows. You string them up and you string them out.

What has the white man to say to the black woman?

From the beginning, you have treated all dark children with absolute hatred.
 Thirty million African children died on the way to the Americas, where

nothing awaited them but endless toil and the crack of a bullwhip. They died of a lack of food, of lack of movement in the holds of ships. Of lack of friends and relatives. They died of depression, bewilderment, and fear.

What has the white man to say to the black woman?

Let us look around us: let us look at the world the white man has made for the black woman and her children.

It is a world in which the black woman is still forced to provide cheap labor, in the form of children, for the factories and on the assembly lines of the white man.

It is a world in which the white man dumps every foul, person-annulling drug he smuggles into creation.

It is a world where many of our babies die at birth, or later of malnutrition, and where many more grow up to live lives of such misery they are forced to choose death by their own hands.

What has the white man to say to the black woman, and to all women and children everywhere?

Let us consider the depletion of the ozone; let us consider homelessness and the nuclear peril; let us consider the destruction of the rain forests—in the name of the almighty hamburger. Let us consider the poisoned apples and the poisoned water and the poisoned air and the poisoned earth.

And that all of our children, because of the white man's assault on the planet, have a possibility of death by cancer in their almost immediate future.

What has the white, male lawgiver to say to any of us? To those of us who love life too much to willingly bring more children into a world saturated with death?

Abortion, for many women, is more than an experience of suffering beyond anything most men will ever know; it is an act of mercy, and an act of self-defense.

To make abortion illegal again is to sentence millions of women and children to miserable lives and even more miserable deaths.

Given his history, in relation to us, I think the white man should be ashamed to attempt to speak for the unborn children of the black woman. To force us to have children for him to ridicule, drug, and turn into killers and homeless wanderers is a testament to his hypocrisy.

What can the white man say to the black woman?

Only one thing that the black woman might hear.

Yes, indeed, the white man can say, Your children have the right to life.

Therefore I will call back from the dead those thirty million who were tossed overboard during the centuries of the slave trade. And the other millions who died in my cotton fields and hanging from my trees.

I will recall all those who died of broken hearts and broken spirits, under the insult of segregation.

I will raise up all the mothers who died exhausted after birthing twenty-one children to work sunup to sundown on my plantation. I will restore to full health all those who perished for lack of food, shelter, sunlight, and love; and from my inability to see them as human beings.

But I will go even further:

I will tell you, black woman, that I wish to be forgiven the sins I commit daily against you and your children. For I know that until I treat your children with love, I can never be trusted by my own. Nor can I respect myself.

And I will free your children from insultingly high infant mortality rates, short life spans, horrible housing, lack of food, rampant ill health. I will liberate them from the ghetto. I will open wide the doors of all the schools and hospitals and businesses of society to your children. I will look at your children and see not a threat but a joy.

I will remove myself as an obstacle in the path that your children, against all odds, are making toward the light. I will not assassinate them for dreaming dreams and offering new visions of how to live. I will cease trying to lead your children, for I can see I have never understood where I was going. I will agree to sit quietly for a century or so, and meditate on this.

This is what the white man can say to the black woman.

We are listening.

✳   ✳   ✳

RONALD TAKAKI
CREATING A COMMUNITY OF A LARGER MEMORY (1998)

> Of every hue and caste am I, of every rank and religion
> A farmer, mechanic, artist, gentleman, sailor, quaker,
> Prisoner, fancy-man, rowdy, lawyer, physician, priest.
> I resist any thing better than my own diversity.
> —Walt Whitman

In the twenty-first century, there will be no white majority in the United States. Ours will be a different "city upon a hill" than the one envisioned by John Winthrop. Ours will be a different "manifest destiny" than the one embraced by Thomas Jefferson and Frederick Jackson Turner. At the edge of this tremendous transformation is California, where within a few years whites will become a minority—just like blacks, Indians, Hispanics, and Asians. Across America by 2050, we will all be minorities.

As we approach this multicultural millennium, the "culture wars" over whether our diversity is leading to "the closing of the American mind" and "the disuniting of America" has stirred me to reflect on my own experiences. C. Wright Mills described the "sociological imagination" as the study of the intersection between history and biography. Throughout this book, individuals from the past to the present have shared stories that demonstrate the dynamic shuttles between self and society in the epic of multicultural America. For the conclusion of this history with "voices," I, too, have a story to tell—another of Whitman's "varied carols" of America.

When I was a teenager, I was not academically inclined. In fact, I was a surfer, but I was given an opportunity that led me to leave Hawaii and its beaches. During my senior year at Iolani High School, I took a course in religion from Dr. Shunji Nishi. I remember being impressed that he had a Ph.D. There were other Asian American doctors, but they were M.D.s. Here was a doctor of philosophy. I remember telling my mother about Dr. Nishi and asking her: "Mom, what's a Ph.D.?" And my mother, who only had an eighth-grade education, answered: "I don't know, but he must be very smart." I began to see Dr. Nishi as a role model, thinking that I, too, could someday have a Ph.D.

Dr. Nishi required all of his students to read *The Screwtape Letters*, by C. S. Lewis. These were letters sent by the chief devil, Screwtape, to his assistant, Wormwood, giving instructions on how to trick Christians into sin. For our weekly assignment, we had to read a letter and then write our own missive. We were to imagine ourselves as Screwtape and write essays that began: "Dear Wormwood." On my papers, Dr. Nishi wrote marginal comments like, "How do you know this is true?" "Interesting," and sometimes, "Insightful." In this way, a relationship developed between the two of us, through my letter-essays and his marginal comments.

During the second semester of my senior year, Dr. Nishi stopped me as I was walking across campus and said, "Ronald, I think you should go away to college." He told me about the College of Wooster, in Ohio, and asked if I would be interested in attending this fine school. I told him that I was unsure about going so far away, and that I had already been accepted to the University of Hawaii. Dr. Nishi said he would send Wooster a letter about me, and I quickly forgot about this conversation. Several weeks later, however, I received a letter from the dean of the College of Wooster, informing me that I had been accepted but then asking me to please fill out the application form. Looking back, I realize that this was an early version of affirmative action. I do not think the dean had even seen my transcript or SATs (which were not very high), but he probably thought I had potential and should be given a special opportunity. Perhaps he also hoped my presence at Wooster would help to diversify the student body culturally and thus enrich the educational experiences of all students.

When I arrived at Wooster, I noticed that there were only a handful of black and Asian students. Often my fellow white students would ask me: "How long have you been in this country?" "Where did you learn to speak English?" They did not see me as an "American." I did not look American and did not have an American name. They saw me as a foreigner. But my grandfather had sailed east to America in 1886, before the arrival of many European immigrant groups. Looking back at this experience, I realized that it was not the fault of the Wooster students that they did not see me as an American. After all, what had they learned in courses called "U.S. History" about Asian Americans?

After I graduated from Wooster in 1961, I entered the Ph.D. program in history at Berkeley. I was admitted on the basis of my academic record because affirmative action was not even a term yet. The Berkeley experience changed my life even further. Inspired by the moral vision of Martin Luther King, many Berkeley students had joined the civil rights movement. They, too, had "a dream" of an America that would live up to its high principle of equality. "Black and white together," they believed, "we shall overcome someday."

In 1964, they began holding civil rights rallies on the steps of Sproul Hall. They wanted to protest and bear witness against segregation and racial violence in Mississippi and Alabama; they also wanted to organize demonstrations against employment inequalities in the Bay Area. When the regents banned these rallies, the students rebelled in the Free Speech Movement [FSM], led by Mario Savio. The confrontation between the FSM and the regents culminated when the charismatic Savio told five thousand protesting students that the time had come when the institution had become so odious that we had to put our bodies in the wheels and gears of the machine and make it stop. Hundreds of them then marched into Sproul Hall, the university's administration building, and engaged in a massive sit-in. The police stormed the building, making arrests with clubs and handcuffs. Spontaneously, thousands of students went out on strike, and hundreds of teaching assistants including myself refused to meet with classes. The strike educated the faculty: it made them realize that they could not remain bystanders in this struggle. They had to stand with the students in affirming the view that the university had to protect freedom of speech and also had a responsibility to society. Facing student and faculty opposition, the regents were forced to designate Sproul Hall Plaza a free speech area.

This experience at Berkeley and my moral outrage at the murder of the three civil rights workers in Mississippi and the deaths of black children in the Birmingham bombings led me to focus my dissertation on the southern defense of slavery. I wanted to study the history of racism in America in order to understand William Faulkner's insight: the past is not even past. How do we free ourselves from our past, I wondered, if we do not even know this past? Prof. Charles Sellers was my thesis adviser. A civil rights activist scholar, he was the author of *The Southerner as American*. I also had the privilege of studying with several other leading scholars: Henry May, Kenneth Stampp, Leon Litwack, and Winthrop Jordan. Henry Nash Smith gave me training in literary criticism and an appreciation of literary texts as historical documents.

While I was writing my dissertation in 1965, Watts exploded. "The fire next time" had come to Los Angeles; riveted to their television screens for days, Americans across the country saw searing images—entire blocks engulfed in flames, snipers shooting at the police, chaotic looting, and angry crowds shouting, "Burn, baby, burn." "A riot," Martin Luther King observed, "is the language of the unheard." The message of Watts underlined the urgent need for universities to address the reality of the racial crisis.

Two years later, UCLA hired me to teach its first black history course. When I walked into class for the first time that fall, I found hundreds of eager and excited students packed into a large lecture room. They looked curiously at their professor, and I could feel them thinking, "Funny, he doesn't look black." Gradually, I earned their confidence in me as a teacher; I even became a faculty adviser to the Black Student Union. As I looked at my students in this class, I saw not only whites and blacks but also Asians and Mexicans. One of them approached me after class one day and said: "We're Chicanos, you know." That was the first time I had heard that nomenclature. "Now I do know," I replied.

This diversity inspired me to help initiate a new course: History 183, "Racial Attitudes in America: A Comparative Perspective"—a study of race reaching beyond the black-white binary to include also Native Americans, Mexicans, and Asians. For the first time in my life, I was studying the history of Asian Americans. As I developed and presented lectures for this course, I learned a valuable lesson: we need to rethink the very way we think about history. Turning away from approaches that were either Eurocentric or ethnic-group specific, I was pursuing a *comparative* study of our racial and ethnic diversity. In this revisioning of our past, I began to conceptualize a field of scholarship that would later become known as multicultural studies.

Meanwhile, I was swept into the student struggle for a more culturally diverse curriculum at UCLA. In 1970, I became the chairperson of the history department's ad hoc ethnic studies committee. At a meeting of the history faculty that spring, I presented our report: it urged the department to offer courses and make appointments in Asian American, Chicano, and Native American history. With hundreds of student supporters gathered outside of the meeting, the faculty reluctantly voted to accept what the students called the "Takaki recommendations."

That summer, after the students left campus, the history faculty rescinded their approval of the recommendations. Then the chairperson informed me that I would be given an "accelerated" review for tenure. This turned out to be the mechanism for firing me that fall. For months, students protested against this action, but were stymied and frustrated by the department's power to hide its decision behind the "confidentiality" of a "personnel matter."

During the political ferment of the previous spring semester, I knew I had been jeopardizing my career by campaigning for ethnic studies, but I thought my teaching and scholarship would be sufficiently strong for me to be granted tenure. My first book, *A Pro-Slavery Crusade: The Agitation to Reopen the African Slave Trade*, had been accepted for publication by the respected Free Press, and I had been awarded a fellowship from the National Endowment for the Humanities to complete a second book on nineteenth-century black novelists. Naively, I had believed I would be judged objectively on the basis of my merit as a teacher and scholar, and had underestimated the power and determination of my senior colleagues to remove me as a threat to the traditional curriculum. My dismissal was distressing, for I had a wife and three very young children to support. I was also worried that I would have no future as a scholar.

Fortunately, another path opened for me. The Ethnic Studies Department at Berkeley had been instituted in response to the 1969 Third World student strike, and they invited me to join this new program. The recommendation for my appointment was submitted to the administration and reviewed by university faculty committees. Coming to a very different decision than the one that had been reached at UCLA, Berkeley determined that my scholarship merited an appointment as an associate professor with tenure. In all likelihood, the decision was also based on an additional consideration—the awareness that Asian Americans were underrepresented in the social sciences and humanities and that my appointment would help to address this shortcoming. This occurred in 1972, after affirmative action had become a policy.

Seventeen years later, my work as a teacher and curriculum transformer at Berkeley reached a high point when the faculty approved a proposal for a multicultural graduation requirement—the "American Cultures Requirement." The impulse for this requirement had been initiated by the Berkeley students in 1987. That fall, a powerful transformation had occurred: minorities constituted 51 percent of the undergraduate student body. The America of the twenty-first century had arrived on our campus. Beginning in the early eighties, under Chancellor Ira Heyman's leadership, the university had committed itself to the pledge of "excellence and diversity." In terms of admissions, this meant affirmative action. Only qualified students would be admitted, but race would be an additional consideration.

This new diversity led to a rethinking of "excellence" in the curriculum. Under the leadership of the Associated Students of the University of California vice president Beth Bernstein and her assistant Mark Min, students began to discuss the idea of a required course for understanding America's racial diversity. The idea gathered support rapidly, and led to a student-sponsored symposium, "The Educated Californian of the Twenty-first Century." There were more than two thousand people in attendance, and out of this event came a proposal for a multicultural requirement. Student support was widespread: organizations of students of color as well as the fraternities and sororities enthusiastically endorsed the proposal. Students were asking the faculty to educate them about the reality of the peoples of the United States. Like the students of the FSM days, students expressed themselves through rallies and sit-ins.

Like the faculty of the time of the FSM, faculty again had to ask themselves: what is the mission of the university and what is its responsibility to society? The debate was intense and often acrimonious. Critics of the proposal castigated it as "political correctness," warning that the courses would constitute propaganda and indoctrination. Some of them also arrogantly reaffirmed the superiority of "Western civilization." On the other side, supporters reminded their colleagues that these courses would be taught by Berkeley faculty, teachers with Ph.D.s and appointments approved by faculty personnel committees. Noting that "civilizations," including "Western," have never been monolithic and pure, isolated from one another, they pointed out that American society is a vivid illustration of this crisscrossing of different cultures.

During the debate, most Berkeley faculty acted as intelligent and fair-minded people should. They listened to the arguments and evaluated the evidence. Individuals who had not previously thought about the issue now studied it. Many who had initially opposed the proposal began to rethink their views. Many of its supporters thought more carefully about the proposal and realized the need to include the study of European immigrant groups, especially from countries like Ireland, Italy, Poland, and Russia.

After a two-year debate, the Berkeley faculty voted affirmatively to establish a graduation requirement designed to broaden and deepen the understanding of racial and ethnic diversity in the United States. Its purpose was intellectual—to pursue a more inclusive and hence more accurate study of American society. The courses that fulfill this requirement would analyze *comparatively* different groups of Americans with roots reaching to Europe, Africa, Asia, and also North and South America. Students would examine our ethnic diversity as well as the ties that bind us as one people. The new requirement was implemented in 1991, and today, Berkeley offers more than 150 American Cultures courses taught by faculty in over twenty departments, from ethnic studies and history to music and literature and public health to business administration. Universities and colleges across the country have been seeking to emulate the "Berkeley model of multiculturalism."

Like the teachers at Berkeley and other schools, Americans in general have choices to make about how we define ourselves as Americans. These choices are not only intellectual but also social and political. Denying our multicultural past, we can fight our diversity by heeding jeremiads about the "disuniting of America" and by erecting borders that insulate "us" against "them," the "other." In erudite Eurocentric tomes, we can view our ethnic conflicts as "the clash of civilizations," and also denounce the study of our diversity as "the closing of the American mind." In nervous nativist backlashes against Asian and Latino immigrants, we can aggressively reaffirm Thomas Jefferson's vision of a homogeneous white America. We can cheer militant calls to take back "our" country, "our" culture, and "our" cities. In attacks on affirmative action, we can deny the reality that racial minorities still lack a level playing field in "the pursuit of happiness" through education and employment. We can cut welfare and even food stamps, punishing the poor for being poor, while we reduce taxes for the wealthy. We can accelerate America's expansion into the globalizing economy without concern or compassion for people victimized by the "disappearance" of work. We can vote for politicians who, like the aristocratic planters of seventeenth-century Virginia, unscrupulously exploit our economic anxieties and xenophobic paranoia for their own narrow political purposes. In short, we can resist our diversity and allow it to divide us and possibly even destroy us as a nation.

But as Americans we have a history that, if viewed in "a different mirror," can guide us toward an alternative future. Challenging the traditional master narrative of American history, this "democratic history" teaches us that "the blood of the whole world" flows through us. As Herman Melville observed, "we are not a narrow tribe." Though Americans represent a multiplicity of geographical origins, we can recognize our common membership in a "vast, surging, hopeful army of workers"—the "giddy multitude" of Bacon's Rebellion, which has become more multiethnic across the centuries. We can embrace Lincoln's vision of America as a nation "dedicated" to the "proposition" of equality—a principle conceived by founding fathers like Jefferson but consecrated by black as well as white Union soldiers in the bloody crucible of the Civil War. We can act affirmatively in carrying forward our nation's "unfinished work." With the end of the Cold War, we can shift resources from defense to a domestic Marshall Plan for the economic rebuilding of our cities, the reemployment of American workers, the creation of a national health care system, and the revitalization of our schools. We can still have "a dream." Ours can be a great refusal to allow this yearning for equality to be "deferred," and then "explode" or "dry up like a raisin in the sun." We can "let America be America," to use the poetic phrase of Langston Hughes. In the sharing of our varied stories, we can create a community of "a larger memory."

* * *

MANNING MARABLE
MULTICULTURAL DEMOCRACY:
THE EMERGING MAJORITY FOR JUSTICE AND PEACE (1991)

> We can no longer regard western Europe and North America as the world
> for which civilization exists; nor can we look upon European culture as the
> norm for all peoples. Henceforth the majority of the inhabitants of the
> earth, who happen for the most part to be colored, must be regarded as
> having the right and the capacity to share in human progress and to
> become copartners in that democracy which alone can ensure peace
> among men, by the abolition of poverty, the education of the masses, pro-
> tection from disease, and the scientific treatment of crime.... [So long as]
> the majority of men can be regarded mainly as sources of profit for Europe
> and North America... we are planning not peace but war, not democracy
> but the continued oligarchical control of civilization by the white race.
> —W. E. B. Du Bois, *Color and Democracy: Colonies and Peace*, 1945

Who is the emerging new majority for justice and peace in the United States? It
consists of 31 million African Americans, women, men, and children who have
experienced slavery, Jim Crow segregation, ghettoization, poverty, high rates of
unemployment, and police brutality. It includes the Latino population, which is
now projected to reach 35 million by the year 2000, more than double the 1980
census figure. Nearly two-thirds of the Latino population is Chicano. Like their
African American sisters and brothers, Latinos experience systemic racial and
class oppression. One-quarter of all Latino households are below the federal government's poverty line, compared to just 9 percent for whites. The average
annual family income for Chicano families is only $22,200; for Puerto Rican
households, $19,900 per year. Latinos and African Americans suffer double the
rate of unemployment, and triple the rate of homelessness experienced by whites.

Who is the emerging new majority in the United States? It is the Asian/Pacific
American population, doubling in size over the past decade to more than 6 million people. The images of affluence and the rhetoric of the so-called model
minorities mask the essential common ground linking Asian Americans to other
people of color. The brutal murder of Vincent Chin in Detroit and ethnic harassment of Asian people throughout the country, the efforts to undercut educational

---

Copyright © 1992 Manning Marable, professor of public affairs, political science, and history,
and director of the Center of Contemporary Black History at Columbia University.

opportunities and access for Asian Americans, and political maneuvers to divide and to compromise progressive political currents in Asian American communities, link these struggles to related issues for African Americans and Latinos.

The new emerging majority are our Arab American sisters and brothers, at least three and one-half million strong, who are subjected to political harassment, media abuse, and ethnic discrimination. The FBI surveillance, interviews, and intimidation aimed against Arab American leaders during the recent U.S. blitzkrieg of Iraq parallels the forced incarceration of thousands of Japanese Americans on the West Coast during World War II.

The new majority includes 2.2 million Native Americans who have been targeted for genocide by the U.S. government for more than two hundred years. The struggle of American Indians is simultaneously political, cultural, and spiritual; a struggle for national self-determination and sovereignty; the reclamation of the land; and the spiritual renewal of the strength and vision of a people.

And the new majority is connected inevitably with the hopes, dreams, and struggles of millions of poor and working-class women and men who are white—the homeless and unemployed, the small farmers and factory workers, the students surviving on student loans, and white women with children on Aid to Families with Dependent Children. We need to keep in mind constantly that 60 percent of all welfare recipients are white; that 62 percent of all people on food stamps are white; that more than two-thirds of Americans without medical insurance are white. Racial and national oppression is very real, but beneath this is an elitist dynamic of exploitation linked to the hegemony, power, and privileges of corporate capitalism over labor. There is no road for the oppressed challenging the power and the dynamics of racial oppression which does not also challenge and confront corporate capitalism.

What is the political future and prospects of this emerging majority? Before the end of this decade, the majority of California's total population will consist of people of color—Asian Americans, Latinos, Arab Americans, Native Americans, African Americans, and others. And not long after the midpoint of the next century, no later than 2056, we will live in a country in which whites will be a distinct "minority" of the total population, and people of color will be the numerical majority. The next half century will be a transition from a white majority society to a society which is far more pluralistic and diverse, where multilingualism is increasingly the norm, where different cultures, religions, and philosophies are a beautiful mosaic of human exchange and interaction. *That* is the emerging majority.

What is a progressive agenda for the newly emerging majority? We have to be committed to the completion of the civil rights agenda—legislation which protects civil liberties and human rights, which advocates expanded minority set-aside programs for the development of capital formation in our communities; the passage of the 1991 Civil Rights Act which reverses six discriminatory decisions of the U.S. Supreme Court. We won't have the basis for a just society until we realize the legislative agenda of Martin Luther King Jr.

But our responsibility is to go beyond the dream of Martin, seeking more than an integrated cup of coffee. People of color must radically redefine the nature of democracy. We must assert that democratic government is empty and meaningless without the values of social justice and multiculturalism. Multicultural political democracy means that this country was not built by one and only one group—western Europeans; that our country does not have only one language—English; only one religion—Christianity; only one economic philosophy—corporate capitalism. Multicultural democracy means that the leadership within our society should reflect the richness, colors, and diversity of our people. Multicultural democracy demands new types of power-sharing and social development for those who have been most oppressed. Multicultural democracy must mean the right of all oppressed national minorities to full self-determination, which may include territorial and geographical restructuring, if that is the desire of the oppressed nation. Native Americans cannot be denied their legitimate claims to sovereignty as oppressed nations and we must fight for their right to self-determination as a central principle of democracy.

Multicultural democracy must articulate a vision of society which is feminist, or "womanist," in the words of Alice Walker. The patterns of oppression and exploitation of women of color—including job discrimination based on gender, race, and class; rape and sexual abuse; forced sterilization; harassment and abuse within the criminal justice system; housing discrimination against single mothers with children; the absence of pay equity for comparable work; political under-representation; and legal disfranchisement—combine to perpetuate this subordinate status within society. No progressive struggles have ever been won for people of color, throughout history, without the courage, contributions, sacrifices, and leadership of women. No political agenda of emancipation is possible unless one begins with the central principle of empowerment and full liberation for all women of color, at every level of organization and society. Men of color must learn from the experiences and insights of sisters of color if they are to free themselves from their political, cultural, and ideological chains which reinforce our collective oppression.

Multicultural democracy for the emerging new majority of people of color must embrace the struggle against homophobia, the fear, hatred, discrimination, and oppression of lesbians and gay men. Homophobia is a form of social intolerance which has its most devastating impact upon people of color. By turning away from the concerns and political issues which motivate lesbian and gay activists in our communities, we construct vicious barriers between sisters and brothers, mothers and daughters, fathers and sons. We give comfort and support to the hate-filled homophobic politicians and evangelical Christian charlatans who attack lesbian and gay rights. We must recognize finally that any assault against the human dignity and personal freedoms of lesbians and gays inevitably undermines the basis for all progressive politics. When a lesbian of color is denied the right to keep her child, when a gay couple cannot adopt children, or when a lesbian is refused an apartment or job, all of us are violated, all of our rights are diminished. We must certainly build political coalitions and bridges between formations and organizations of all people of color and with specifically gay and lesbian activist groups. But we must also do much more to construct bridges of genuine support, dialogue and solidarity, challenging homophobic assumptions, homophobic policies and practices at all levels of society.

Multicultural democracy must include a powerful economic vision which is centered on the needs of human beings. Is it right for the government to spend billions for bailing out the fat cats who profited from the Savings and Loan crisis, while millions of jobless Americans stand in unemployment lines, desperate for work? Is it fair that billions are allocated for the Pentagon's permanent war economy, to obliterate the lives of millions of poor people, from Iraq to Panama, from Grenada to Vietnam, while 3 million Americans sleep in the streets, and 37 million Americans lack any type of medical coverage? Is it a democracy when you have the right to vote, but no right to a job? Is it a democracy when people of color have the freedom to starve, the freedom to live in housing without adequate heat, the freedom to attend substandard schools? Democracy without social justice, without human dignity, is no democracy at all.

The new majority for justice and peace must have an internationalist perspective. We must link our struggles domestically and locally with the battles for human rights and peace across the world. We are on the opposite side of the international barricades of Bush's "New World Order," which promises the "Same Old Disorder": disruption, political domination, and social destruction for the Third World, for working people, for the oppressed.

Multicultural democracy means taking a stand on behalf of all indigenous people, the Native Americans across the Americas, the Pacific islands, Australian, and across the world. It means expressing our political and moral solidarity with the masses of southern Africa, the battle against apartheid led by the African National Congress, the multiracial trade union movement, and all the women and men of South Africa who are fighting for democracy.

The emerging multicultural majority must support all struggles for self-determination, and especially the people of Palestine. Despite years of brutal repression, the closure of the universities, the deliberate destruction of homes, the Intifada continues, the hope of self-determination is not extinguished, and the dream of political freedom has not died. We must learn from the courage of the Palestinian people, and extend our support and solidarity. And with this same gesture of material and moral solidarity, we embrace the masses in Central

America, fighting U.S. corporate and imperialist hegemony. We find strength in the people of Cuba, standing nearly alone against the northern capitalist leviathan. The New World Order threatens the socialist revolution of Cuba, it threatens every oppressed nation and people in the Third World. Our response in pressuring the leviathan, challenging the system while inside "the belly of the beast," is our unique responsibility and our cause.

Unity between progressives of color is essential if multicultural democracy is to be achieved. This doesn't mean that we minimize the difficulties inherent in such a project, the differences of perspective which exist between groups. Unfortunately, the experience of oppression does not inoculate one from being intolerant toward others. There are white lesbians and gays who are racist, and people of color who are homophobic; there are Asian Americans who are hostile to Latinos, Latinos who are hostile to African Americans, and African Americans who are prejudiced against Asian Americans. We frequently speak different languages; we have different historical experiences, religions, political ideologies, and social values. But so long as these differences divide us into potentially antagonistic camps, the powers which dominate and exploit us collectively will continue to flourish. As long as we bicker over perceived grievances, maximizing our claims against each other, refusing to see the economic, political, cultural, and social common ground which can unite us, we will be victimized by capitalism, sexism, racism, national oppression, homophobia, and other systems of domination. The choice is ours.

No single group has *all* the answers. No single group is embodied with all the truth. But together, the collective path to human liberation, self-determination, and sovereignty will become clear.

Unity is a deliberate act of commitment, bridging the differences and emphasizing elements of common understanding. Unity must be constructed in a manner which establishes a sense of trust and shared experiences between various groups. No single group can determine all policies; no single constituency can dominate leadership; but each group must be respected and its perspectives recognized in this process.

How do we build political unity? We can begin by advocating activism which bridges differences across ethnic lines. Fighting for immigrant and refugee rights isn't a Chicano issue, or Asian American issue, but cuts across various groups and serves our collective interests. In February, when an investigation of border violence against undocumented workers occurred in the San Diego area, participating groups included the Japanese American Citizens League, the Break the Silences on Anti-Asian Violence Coalition, Los Angeles' Project on Assault Against Women, MAPA, SEIU, and UE trade unionists, and the San Francisco Black Fire Fighters' Union. Unity means building coalitions with a broad, progressive perspective.

We can construct unity by pooling our resources and energies around progressive projects designed to promote greater awareness and protest among the masses of people of color. This could mean joint mobilizations against the 1992 Columbian Quincentennial. Any "celebration" of the so-called conquest of the Americas and the Caribbean is a gross insult to the millions of Native Americans, Asians, and Africans who died in the expansion of capitalism, the transatlantic slave trade, and colonialism. We have the opportunity to denounce five hundred years of invasion, war, genocide, and racism, by holding teach-ins, demonstrations, and collective protest actions. We could initiate "Freedom Schools," liberation academies which identify young women and men with an interest in community-based struggles. A curriculum which teaches young people about their own protest leaders, which reinforces their identification with our collective cultures of resistance, will strengthen our political movements. The new majority must build progressive research institutes, bridging the distance between activists and community organizers of color, and progressive intellectuals who can provide the policies and theoretical tools useful in the empowerment of grassroots constituencies.

Progressives of color on college campuses must play a decisive role in the current debate on "multiculturalism" in higher education. Ideologues of the far Right—such as William Bennett, former secretary of education in the Reagan administration—are increasingly using higher education as the vehicle for pushing back communities of color. They've reduced student grants, attacked ethnic studies programs, undermined programs for the recruitment of working-class students and students of color, and criticized courses requiring a multicultural non-Western perspective for all students. This ideological offensive against diversity and ethnic pluralism in education is the counterpart to the racist vigilante violence and harassment against people of color which is proliferating in the streets and in our neighborhoods.

What is most revealing about the intellectual bankruptcy of these conservative critics of ethnic studies, open admissions policies, and multicultural diversity on campus is that their critique is silent on the actual power relationship between people of color and women, and the dominant, upper-class male elites who actually control American universities and colleges. People of color still represent small minorities of all university and college professors and administrators. The majority of white college campuses have no requirements for courses in ethnic or multicultural studies. The context for this debate occurs at a historical moment in which a conservative president vetoes a civil rights bill, the Supreme Court undermines affirmative action, and the economic and social conditions of African Americans, Latinos, and other people of color have deteriorated sharply. Therefore, to argue that people of color have the institutional means to intimidate thousands of white college teachers by demanding "political correctness," or that we have the authority to intimidate and to impose our multicultural imperatives on hapless white students, is at best grossly dishonest.

We must set the contours for the debate on multiculturalism in education, and recognize this as a central political task for the 1990s. We must assert that civilization, cultures, and language patterns from South and Central America, from the Native Americans, from Africa, the Caribbean, Asia, and the Pacific, have also profoundly influenced the pluralistic American experience, and the complex and contradictory identities of its people. Multiculturalism should approach each cultural tradition among people of color with an awareness of its own integrity, history, rituals, and continuity. We must recognize that the perspective of multiculturalism, the struggle to create a more democratic, pluralistic educational system in this country, is part of the struggle to empower people of color, to liberate our minds from the dependency of racist, sexist, and homophobic stereotypes. Such an education seeks not just to inform but to transform.

Finally, we must infuse our definition of politics with a common sense of ethics and spirituality which challenges the structures of oppression, power, and privilege within the dominant social order. Part of the strength of the black freedom movement historically was the merger of political objectives and ethical prerogatives. What was desired politically, the destruction of institutional racism, was simultaneously ethically and morally justified. This connection gave the rhetoric of Frederick Douglass and Sojourner Truth, W. E. B. Du Bois, Paul Robeson, and Fannie Lou Hamer, a moral grandeur and powerful vision which was simultaneously particular and universal. It spoke to the uplifting of the African American, but its humanistic imperative reached to others in a moral context.

Multicultural democracy must perceive itself in this grand tradition, as a critical project which transforms the larger society. It must place humanity at the center of politics. It is not sufficient that we assert what we are against; we must affirm what we are for. It is not sufficient that we declare what we want to overturn, but what we are seeking to build, in the sense of restoring humanity and humanistic values to a system which is materialistic, destructive to the environment, and oppressive. We need a vision which says that the people who actually produce society's wealth should control how it is used.

The moral poverty in contemporary American society is found, in part, in the vast chasm which separates the conditions of material well-being, affluence, power, and privilege of a small elite from the masses of others. The evil in our world is politically and socially engineered, and its products of poverty, homelessness, illiteracy, political subservience, race and gender domination. The old saying from the sixties—we are part of the solution or part of the problem—is simultaneously moral, cultural, economic, and political. We cannot be disinterested observers as the physical and spiritual beings of millions of people of color and the poor are collectively crushed.

Paul Robeson reminds us that we must "take a stand," if our endeavors are to have lasting meaning. The new emerging majority must project itself, not just as reforming the society at the edges in small ways, but project a program and vision of what should be and what must become reality. Can we dare to struggle, dare to build a new democracy, without poverty and homelessness; can we dare to uproot racism, sexism, homophobia, and all forms of social oppression? Can we dare to assert ourselves as an emerging multicultural democratic majority for peace, social justice, for real democracy? Let us dare to win.

❈ ❈ ❈

SALADIN MUHAMMAD
TWENTY YEARS OF BLACK WORKERS FOR JUSTICE (2001)

This year Black Workers For Justice [BWFJ] celebrates its twentieth anniversary. For two decades BWFJ has fought dozens of local battles in the South in defense of workers' rights and the black community. And for two decades, BWFJ has worked to win recognition for the central role of black workers in the struggle against the oppressive capitalist system we live under.

Black Workers For Justice was born in a struggle at a Kmart store in the city of Rocky Mount, North Carolina, in late 1981. Three black women workers were fired for challenging the racial discrimination by the local Kmart management. The fired workers first tried to gain support from established black civil rights organizations and church leaders who, while receptive, were cautious. They asked the workers to give details showing they had obeyed work rules—raising the bar for them to win support. Male chauvinism—constant questioning of the women's own perceptions—was clearly a factor.

The Kmart workers then turned to some black worker activists who had recently relocated to the area. Together they began to develop a black working-class perspective and organization. Their approach was that black women workers must take the initiative, present their own demands, and call on other community forces to join them in a united struggle. From its inception the new organization faced varying degrees of anticommunist suspicions and red-baiting but was not intimidated.

BWFJ was motivated by a political perspective that sought to build on the local Kmart struggle and spark a movement to organize black workers—in the U.S. South and nationally—into a conscious and leading political force. This perspective was influenced by a trend that went back to the League of Revolutionary Black Workers in the late 1960s with their slogan, "Black Workers Take the Lead." This trend had reemerged in the African liberation support movement of the mid-1970s, which viewed black workers as a leading force for black liberation and radical change. It led many black student activists to go into the factories, post offices, and other employment sectors to become part of and reattached to the working class.

Black workers were clearly seen as a key base by the new communist movement that grew out of the "New Left" during the 1970s. Yet some black liberation organizations which identified themselves as revolutionary nationalist, rather than as part of the New Left or the communist movement, also began to emphasize organizing black workers at the workplace as a primary base for their political organizational and ideological development.

The Main Task for Black Workers

This developing black workers trend had two main tendencies. One saw the main task of black workers as challenging, exposing, and isolating the black bourgeoisie for their collaboration with U.S. capitalism and imperialism. This tendency saw the African American liberation movement as an auxiliary to a revolutionary workers' movement that would be led exclusively by a multiracial and multinational communist party. This meant that the black working class, as the largest layer by far of the African American oppressed masses, would not have independence from the predominantly white U.S. working class. The effect of this would be to downplay or eliminate the right of African Americans to self-determination.

The formation of BWFJ was influenced by a second tendency. It saw the main task of black workers as organizing a conscious, radical, and independent mass base and leading pole within the African American liberation movement. It also saw the black workers' movement as an organized and active expression of the working-class demands and leadership of the African American liberation movement within the U.S. workers' movement, especially the trade union movement—thereby contributing to an antiracist and anti-imperialist radicalization of the U.S. working class.

BWFJ focused on making black workplace struggles key issues for the larger African American community in Rocky Mount and as far beyond as possible. Raising shop-floor issues in the church and bringing them to the community organizations and civil rights groups was and is standard practice for BWFJ members.

Voting Rights Struggles

In 1983 three members of BWFJ were part of a lawsuit against the town of Rocky Mount for violating black voting rights. Our acting as plaintiffs on the lawsuit was key in helping to shape the political identity of BWFJ as an indigenous worker organization in the black community. This countered the image of labor organizations as outside, impersonal forces—which is how the trade union movement, in particular, often appears to the black community.

The late Abner W. Berry, a founding member of BWFJ, veteran freedom fighter since the 1920s, and member of the U.S. Communist Party until the 1950s, was one of the main plaintiffs and strategists for BWFJ's participation in the suit. He saw it as an opportunity for BWFJ to offer leadership in a key battle in the African American struggle for self-determination. It would help to highlight the importance of organized black workers to the broader Rocky Mount and North Carolina black communities and could provide some community protection for the workplace organizing of BWFJ. With the trade union movement on the defensive after the Reagan administration's attack on the air traffic controllers union (PATCO) in 1980, the group's leaders felt that BWFJ would become isolated and defeated without the support of the broader black community.

Key BWFJ organizational components developed out of its participation in various struggles. The *Justice Speaks* newspaper began in 1981 as a regular leaflet during the Kmart struggle, and had, by 1983, become a newsletter connecting the various struggles and BWFJ committees that had developed. The annual Dr. Martin L. King Support for Labor banquet was initially a fundraiser for buses to the 1983 Dr. King national holiday demonstration held in Washington, D.C. Workers and activists from four main workplace and community struggles formed the initial core of the Fruit of Labor, BWFJ's cultural arm and singing group.

Relating to the Rainbow

The 1984 Jesse Jackson presidential campaign with its strong problack political power and pro-labor message, created a political climate that allowed BWFJ to more widely agitate, organize, and mobilize black workers at the workplace and in the communities. While uniting with the main issues and energy of the Jackson campaign, BWFJ decided not to form Rainbow Coalition chapters, fearing that Jackson might subordinate the Rainbow to the Democratic Party. BWFJ related to the Rainbow Coalition forces, forums, and program as a united front, maintaining independence to express disagreements where necessary. This independence allowed BWFJ to place emphasis on consolidating and developing key organizational components and political relationships in the course of Jackson's campaign.

In 1985 the first BWFJ Workers School was organized, drawing workplace and community leaders and activists from six North Carolina counties. African American history, labor history, the role and use of a workers' newspaper, the importance of black working-class culture, and the need for women's leadership were some of the main topics. Abner Berry and former SNCC leader Don Stone taught at this three-day Workers School.

Following the 1985 Workers School, the various BWFJ embryonic organizational components began to take off. *Justice Speaks* became a monthly newspaper within a year. A Women's Commission and a Trade Union Commission were formed. Annual Workers Schools were organized, and regular steering committee meetings were held. This allowed BWFJ to better focus on implementing its program and summing up the work.

The Women's Commission

The formation of the BWFJ Women's Commission in 1987 was an important development, not only for the group but for the general black workers trend, whose leadership had been largely black men. Instead of being just an internal commission that mainly reviewed and summed up work, it also became a semi-external, public women's organization, incorporating members beyond BWFJ's own ranks. The Women's Commission led the organizing work at the Rocky Mount Undergarment plant beginning in 1989.

The basic consolidation gave BWFJ confidence to forge links with other black worker activists and to help form the Black Workers Unity Movement (BWUM) in 1985. BWUM was an agitational, educational, and organizing network focused on regrouping and expanding the black workers trend and promoting a call for a national congress of black workers.

BWUM was limited in its geographic locations and in its concentrations in key industries and sectors. However, its impact showed itself at the Labor Notes Conferences beginning in 1986 and around the Labor Party Constitutional Convention in 1996. There, BWUM pushed for the creation of a black caucus, which led to the inclusion of key planks in the Labor Party Program. This experience exposed BWFJ to the rank-and-file trade union democracy movement and labor Left that was made up mainly of whites from areas outside of the South.

Labor Notes conferences helped BWFJ to make contacts that were vital for launching the Organize the South Campaign and undertaking Midwest and East Coast tours beginning in 1991. Key contacts, including leaders of *Labor Notes*, attended the 1989 BWFJ Workers School held in Rocky Mount and participated with organizers and workers from various workplace committees in shaping the direction of the Organize the South Campaign. Organizing around the tragic fire at Imperial Foods in Hamlet, North Carolina, which killed twenty-five workers and injured fifty-six due to fire exits' being chained shut by management, helped to draw attention to the Organize the South Campaign.

Union Organizing and International Ties

In 1994 BWFJ was key in helping to form the North Carolina Public Service Workers Organization of rank-and-file and labor support activists in public sector workplaces at eleven locations in seven counties. This laid the foundation for the eventual emergence in May 1997 of the North Carolina Public Service Workers Union–United Electrical Workers Local 150 as a statewide local with over 2,500 members to date.

In 1997 BWFJ's work to Organize the South expanded internationally through connections with the Transnational Information Exchange (TIE), an international workers' network organized in Europe and some Third World countries to foster labor solidarity and to empower workers to resist corporations' global production schemes.

BWUM, Labor Notes, and TIE forums enabled BWFJ to discuss and understand its work and strategic role within a larger national and international trade union, working-class, and pro-socialist context. This influenced major BWFJ decisions around strategic questions and created organizational pressures to function more as a cadre organization. There was a constant push within the leadership for a disciplined division of labor capable of maintaining and building on these relationships and for focusing sustained attention on these new alignments.

New Questions and Tasks

The membership growth within BWFJ itself has been far smaller than the numbers recruited into the workplace committees, unions, and community organizations and institutions that have been built by BWFJ. To build a black working-class presence and leadership in the African American liberation movement and in the broader workers' movement, we need a greater consolidation of BWFJ and a larger black workers' movement. Therefore, BWFJ must place a major emphasis on expanding throughout the U.S. South, training a wider layer of politically and ideologically committed cadre members, and working harder to develop a popular mass black workers' movement and culture—in its own right and in the form of BWFJ in particular.

There have been differences within BWFJ around questions of primary organizational focus, racial composition, and the political character and aims of the struggles. Some see BWFJ as mainly a statewide organization responding to spontaneous worker and black community struggles. Others see it as a conscious black working-class organization with a political program aimed at empowering, radicalizing, and mobilizing the working class and African American communities around short- and long-term needs and interests. We have united across these differences around a program that seeks to politicize immediate struggles and transform them into more conscious and wider challenges against the racist and sexist system of corporate rule.

The history of BWFJ has shaped its anticapitalist vision and program around questions of democracy, social and economic justice, human rights, women's equality, and international solidarity as fundamental pillars for a radical social transformation and a new society.

About Haymarket Books

Haymarket Books is a radical, independent, nonprofit book publisher based in Chicago.

Our mission is to publish books that contribute to struggles for social and economic justice. We strive to make our books a vibrant and organic part of social movements and the education and development of a critical, engaged, international Left.

We take inspiration and courage from our namesakes, the Haymarket martyrs, who gave their lives fighting for a better world. Their 1886 struggle for the eight-hour day—which gave us May Day, the international workers' holiday—reminds workers around the world that ordinary people can organize and struggle for their own liberation. These struggles continue today across the globe—struggles against oppression, exploitation, poverty, and war.

Since our founding in 2001, Haymarket Books has published more than five hundred titles. Radically independent, we seek to drive a wedge into the risk-averse world of corporate book publishing. Our authors include Noam Chomsky, Arundhati Roy, Rebecca Solnit, Angela Y. Davis, Howard Zinn, Amy Goodman, Wallace Shawn, Mike Davis, Winona LaDuke, Ilan Pappé, Richard Wolff, Dave Zirin, Keeanga-Yamahtta Taylor, Nick Turse, Dahr Jamail, David Barsamian, Elizabeth Laird, Amira Hass, Mark Steel, Avi Lewis, Naomi Klein, and Neil Davidson. We are also the trade publishers of the acclaimed Historical Materialism Book Series and of Dispatch Books.

Visit us online at www.haymarketbooks.org.